THE COLLECTED PAPERS
OF
ROGER MONEY-KYRLE

THE COLLECTED PAPERS OF ROGER MONEY-KYRLE

Edited by Donald Meltzer
with the assistance of Edna O'Shaughnessy

published for
The Harris Meltzer Trust
by
KARNAC

First published in 1978 by Clunie Press for The Roland Harris Educational Trust

This edition published in 2015 for The Harris Meltzer Trust
by Karnac Books Ltd, 118 Finchley Road, London NW3 5HT

Copyright © 2015 The Harris Meltzer Trust

The right of Roger E. Money-Kyrle to be identified as the author of this work has been asserted in accordance with §§ 77 and 78 of the Copyright Design and Patent Act 1988.

All rights reserved. No part of this publication may be reproduced, stored in a retrieval system, or transmitted, in any form or by any means, electronic, mechanical, photocopying, recording, or otherwise, without the prior written permission of the publisher.

British Library Cataloguing in Publication Data
A C.I.P. for this book is available from the British Library

ISBN 978 178220 292 9

Printed in Great Britain

www.harris-meltzer-trust.org.uk
www.karnacbooks.com

Contents

Table of Contents
Prefatory Note
Editor's Introduction
Author's Preface
Autobiographical Note
Acknowledgements

1	Belief and Representation (1927)	1
2	The Psycho-physical Apparatus (1928)	16
3	Morals and Super-men (1928)	28
4	Critical Abstract: Roheim's 'After the Death of the Primal Father' (1929)	38
5	The Remote Consequences of Psycho-analysis on Individual, Social and Instinctive Behaviour (1931)	57
6	A Psychologist's Utopia (1930)	82
7	A Pyscho-analytic Study of the Voices of Joan of Arc (1933)	109
8	A Psychological Analysis of the Causes of War (1934)	131
9	The Development of War (1937)	138
10	The Psychology of Propaganda (1941)	160
11	Towards a Common Aim: A Psycho-analytic Contribution to Ethics (1944)	176
12	Social Conflict and the Challenge to Psychology (1947)	198
13	Varieties of Group Formation (1948)	210
14	Some Aspects of State and Character in Germany (1951)	229
15	Towards a Rational Attitude to Crime (1953)	245
16	The Anthropological and Psycho-analytic Concept of the Norm (1955)	253
17	Psycho-analysis and Ethics (1955)	264
18	An Inconclusive Contribution to the Theory of the Death Instinct (1955)	285
19	Psycho-analysis and Philosophy (1956)	297
20	The World of the Unconscious and the World of Common Sense (1956)	318
21	Normal Counter-transference and Some of its Deviations (1956)	330
22	The Process of Psycho-analytical Inference (1960)	343
23	On Prejudice – a Psycho-analytical Approach (1960)	353
24	A Note on Migraine (1963)	361

25	Politics from the Point of View of Psycho-analysis (1964)	366
26	Megalomania (1965)	376
27	Review: W. R. Bion – 'Elements of Psycho-analysis' (1965)	389
28	Success and Failure in Mental Maturations (1965)	397
29	A Note on 'The Three Caskets' (1966)	407
30	British Schools of Psycho-analysis: Melanie Klein and Her Contribution to Psycho-analysis (1963)	408
31	Cognitive Development (1968)	416
32	On the Fear of Insanity (1969)	434
33	The Aim of Psycho-analysis (1971)	442
34	Reviews: Meltzer *et al.* – 'Explorations in Autism' (1976)	450
	Ginsberg *et al.* – 'Introduction to the Work of Bion' (1976)	451
35	On Being a Psycho-analyst (1977)	457
	Chronological List of the Published Writings of Roger Money-Kyrle	466
	Reviews	468
	Index	470

Prefatory Note

This book is for Mr R. E. Money-Kyrle on the occasion of his eightieth birthday.

It is the first time that his papers have been collected in one volume. He and his readers now have the opportunity of a long view, from 1927 to 1978, of his writings; the evolution of his thought in these fifty and more years is fascinating. Mr Money-Kyrle belongs to the English tradition of the first quarter of the twentieth century, a time of wide horizons, and his project is correspondingly ample – an attempt to understand man and the world man makes for himself. He uses the knowledge of psycho-analysis to illumine areas in biology, anthropology, politics, ethics and history, in addition to making contributions to clinical and theoretical psycho-analysis itself.

In his books *The Meaning of Sacrifice*, *The Development of the Sexual Impulse*, *Aspasia*, *Superstition and Society*, *Psycho-analysis and Politics* and *Man's Picture of his World*, the reader will find a full exploration of several subjects first approached in these shorter writings. However, some papers – in particular his important later ones on psycho-analysis: 'Cognitive Development', 'Fear of Insanity' and 'The Aims of Psycho-analysis' – still wait for him to expound more fully. I very much hope that Mr Money-Kyrle will write for his public another book.

EDNA O'SHAUGHNESSY

Editor's Introduction

'I think both criticisms exaggerate an element of truth which each side has gradually become more able to admit' (*Psychoanalysis and Philosophy*). This type of statement recurs throughout the work of Roger Money-Kyrle and perhaps expresses better than any more lengthy statement could do the essential quality of the man and his contribution to psycho-analysis and modern thought. 'Criticisms exaggerate', 'element of truth', 'gradually', 'able to admit' – let us examine a moment the credo that is contained in these few words.

'Criticisms exaggerate' – from his earliest philosophical paper on one can see that Mr Money-Kyrle was convinced that judgment about the world, and about ourselves and our fellow men, is adversely affected by our hostility. The wish to find fault, as an expression of envy in particular, but driven also by submission to our persecutors, blinds us to the virtues of our enemies and the faults of our allies. The papers of the war and post-war period are deeply concerned to understand the phenomena of Nazism and Appeasement alike.

'Element of truth' – such envy and hatred induce the projection of hated parts of the self out into the world, obscuring our capacity for observation of the external world and depriving us of the conflict which drives our inquiry into the internal world. The papers on ethics, a rational attitude towards crime and his attempt to establish a concept of 'normal' character (in the 'medical' and 'ideal' sense, not the statistical) focus uncompromisingly on the love for and search for truth.

'Gradually' – but only bits of the truth can be found as science, guided by the models of the world and its problems adumbrated in speculative philosophy, probes the external and psychology the internal world. Only this piecemeal revelation of the truth can liberate men from the more primitive models which affect their judgments and guide their actions.

'Able to admit' – but the rectification of this model of the world involves men in a transformation of their values, for while the truth may liberate them from persecutory anxieties, it imposes upon them love for the worlds, both inner and outer, and consequent guilt for the damage caused by their greed and destructive envy.

This seems to me to be the essence of Money-Kyrle's wisdom and, like Socrates who knew how little he knew, no man is wiser than he. The pleasure of working closely with him these last ten years has brought a little of this wisdom to my work, for where I learned psycho-analytic theory and technique from others, I learned the meaning of psycho-analysis as a thing in-the-world from him. I believe now that modesty, patience, kindness and forbearance to judge are more important ingredients of an analyst's contribution to the psycho-analytical process than theories.

DONALD MELTZER

Author's Preface

That this collection of papers, essays and reviews appears at all I owe to two friends and colleagues, Dr Donald Meltzer and Mrs Edna O'Shaughnessy, who not only assisted at every stage of its preparation but also found me a publisher. And when I remember that they are both full-time working analysts with no spare time at all, I am staggered by their generosity and can find no adequate words to thank them. My debt to my wife and my three analysts can be deduced from my 'Autobiographical Note'.

In deciding near the end of one's life whether to republish what one has written in it, two questions may confront one: will the work increase one's reputation? and will younger people be able to benefit from it? I suspect the first question has to do with that craze for immortality which has bedevilled our species ever since it learned to talk, to remember and to think, and reached its climax a few thousand years ago in the deification of kings, etc. And if so, the motive behind it is rather hollow.

But the second question: 'will younger people be able to benefit from it?' is a very serious one. I do not know the answer. In reading through the papers, the earlier ones in various degrees of obsolescence or just boring, and fluctuating from idealist philosophy to an almost behaviourist position, to ethics and to pure analysis, do seem to represent an oscillating series which perhaps tends to converge to some distant limit. In other words, I like to think that these works are a series of approximations towards some distant truth. If so, there may be some who would like to read it, and better still, to carry on the work.

I am also grateful to Mrs Barbara Forryan for an outstandingly competent Index and to Lord Horder, who has published two of my former books and generously corrected the proofs of this one.

Autobiographical Note

I was born on 31 January 1898, three weeks prematurely – not as planned in London but in a cottage or small house on my maternal grandfather's place in Hertfordshire, the fourth and youngest child of Major Audley Money-Kyrle and his wife Florence Cecilia Bosanquet, daughter of Horace Smith-Bosanquet and his wife Cecilia (*née* Bosanquet) of Broxbournebury, Herts. I had two sisters, nine and six years older than myself (who believed it to be their duty to teach me to be polite to women) and one brother about four years older, who died shortly before I was born. He was born crippled (spina bifida), but I was always told how good and beautiful he was (which photographs prove to have been true). He was also very brave and always in pain, poor little boy. I expect I was at least unconsciously envious of him and probably believed that I had magically brought about his death. I was said to have been a difficult baby, but all the pictures of me from about three or four onwards show a plump and robust little boy who seemed to have a very good opinion of himself.

My parents were devoted to each other and the love and kindness I received from them made the later discovery of my Oedipus complex a very lengthy process.

Owing to the death of his elder brother, my father had inherited two places from his father, Homme House, Gloucestershire and Whetham, Wiltshire – only to find the larger one, Homme, fairly heavily encumbered. So he let it and waited for the lease of Whetham (which had been let for the most of my grandfather's life) to fall in. This happened in 1900 when I was two, and Whetham has been my home, if only for weekends, almost ever since.

Partly because I had been ill just before going to a private school at ten, I was well below the average educational level when I got there, and I soon gave up trying to catch up. Nor did I do so at Eton – except in science, when I shocked my house master by winning the school prize for physics. My father had died suddenly while I was still at my private school, and my mother, who was a recognized beauty still in her forties, remained a widow, either refusing all offers or making it clear that none would be acceptable.

In the summer of 1916 I left Eton and joined the Royal Flying Corps; and during an engine course at Oxford first saw my future wife skating (in the old English style) round an orange with several dons on the frozen, flooded meadows, and thought her very beautiful. In the summer of 1917 I was posted to no. 1 squadron at Beilleure and six weeks later was shot down – possibly by the future General Göring, at this time one of the three deputy flight-leaders in the Richthofen Circus. About a year later I was back in France with 94 Squadron, but the war ended just before we went into action.

I then put in three applications: for a forestry course; to go to Russia in a squadron, Major Hazel, my old flight commander in no. 1 squadron, had been promised; and for priority demobilization as a student. Hazel's squadron was cancelled and the priority demobilization came through before the forestry course. So I left France in February 1919 and after several days in a cattle truck which could not make up its mind whether to take us to le Havre or Cherbourg, I arrived in England.

About five days later I was an undergraduate at Trinity College, Cambridge, in the middle of a term and of a year, sharing rooms with Francis Magoun – later professor of English at Harvard University – who had also been in no. 1 squadron (disguised as an Englishman). I had supposed that my 'Physics Prize' was proof of my ability to take a Tripos Degree at Cambridge. However, I soon found out I was as far behind Tripos standard as I had been behind the expected standard at my private school and again gave up hope. Moreover, as I discovered long afterwards, I unconsciously believed I had been responsible for a fatal accident just before the end of the war – and as this probably linked with my guilt to the brother who died before I was born, I became overtly neurotic, shunning my fellows as if I had the mark of Cain, which unconsciously I must have felt I had.

It was about then that I also discovered that, instead of a comfortable income from two properties, I had a negative income of about £400 a year. I then sold Homme, for which I think the older tenants never forgave me.

It was then that I first heard of psycho-analysis (from E. F. Collingwood, a remarkable man who may have profited from analysis and who much later became a lecturer in mathematics at Trinity). I saw a psychotherapist recommended by him, and – although I went back later to take a 'Special in Economics' (which Collingwood also took, as neither of us dared face the Tripos) – I went down and started an analysis with Ernest Jones. This I camouflaged by going into a bank.

Eighteen months later, hearing from Gaillard Lapsley, my Trinity tutor, that I must keep two more terms and at once take the first part of the 'Special in Economics', if I wanted a degree at all, I left the bank and also Ernest Jones, who, after my two terms at Trinity, kindly arranged for me to continue my analysis with Freud in Vienna, where I hoped to repair my tarnished academic reputation. Meanwhile, and on an exploratory visit to Vienna in the Easter vacation, I again met my future wife and three weeks later married on an egrotat (3 days' leave) from Trinity. I then finished the term and got my B.A.

At that time, as the exchange was enormously in England's favour, we settled very comfortably in Vienna; and as my wife was sociable and popular (although she made no conscious effort to be either) we were soon on very friendly terms with Professor Moritz Schlick, a brilliant and delightful man, with whose help I eventually got my Ph.D. I remember I had suggested calling my dissertation 'Wirklichkeitslehre (Theory of Reality)', but he most tactfully suggested 'Beiträge für Wirklichkeitslehre' (Contribution to Theory of Reality). I kept my contact with Freud quite secret until the end when I discovered that Schlick, too, was most interested in Freud's work, but had also kept his interest secret! In Vienna we also met Frank Ramsay, the mathematician, Lionel Penrose, later Professor of Genetics at London University, Adrian Bishop, a brilliant if somewhat erratic person who became headmaster of a Turkish school, and L. B., later Professor Sir Lewis, Namier – all also being secretly analysed. Our eldest son was born in Vienna and my mother and younger (unmarried) sister came out to be with us for this event. At the same time my wife also wrote her thesis for a B.Sc. in anthropology

('Anglo-Saxon Magic') for Oxford. She chose this degree because it had a blue hood to its gown, she always claimed.

After getting my Ph.D. we returned to England. I had hoped perhaps to acquire a D.Sc., but as I was told I was not eligible to try for one, I took another Ph.D. at University College, London with the assistance of Professor Flugel. The dissertation was 'The Meaning of Sacrifice', my first psycho-analytical work, for which I was elected a Fellow of the Royal Anthropological Institute, and about the same time, with Ernest Jones's approval, I was elected an associate member of the British Psycho-Analytical Institute under the condition that I should not attempt to practise.

So for the next few years we, and an increasing family (in all four sons, and now eleven grandchildren), lived at Whetham. I was put on the managing bodies of one or two small schools, co-opted as a member of the Educational Committee of the Wiltshire County Council, and appointed by them a member of the Council of Bristol University. I owed these appointments to Keith Innes, late Fellow of Trinity, who was Director of Education for Wiltshire. I was made a J.P. and eventually 'pricked' as High Sheriff.

This was the end of such activities, for which I felt I had no vocation (possibly because I was only a second son). In, I think, 1936 we had a serious motor accident (my wife cracked her skull and I broke my thigh); and while in hospital John Rickman visited me and persuaded me to try to have a Training Analysis with Mrs Klein. This I started before the Second World War. However, at the beginning of the war I was called up, and after various postings was sent to the Staff college for three months, and then to Air Ministry, at which I stayed in the same job and same rank for four years.

This, however, enabled me to continue my analysis, and, as I had not been posted away, as soon as I had learned my job and could do it in half the usual time, I wrote a paper for which the Society voted me a full member.

At this time I made one perhaps serious mistake. At John Rickman's suggestion, and thinking he would not advise me against Melanie Klein's wish, I joined the Control Commission after the war, and went to Germany for about six months and broke my analysis. It is true that Melanie Klein took me back

AUTOBIOGRAPHICAL NOTE

afterwards but with reduced sessions and only for a few months, so I had probably deprived myself of a normal termination.

We moved to London and from then on I have worked as a practising psycho-analyst – sometimes a worrying but always an enthralling occupation – and have also written five books and several papers over a fairly long period of time.

Everyone has their troubles, which are nearly always partly self-made, and certain events have troubled the serenity of our lives. But this is as much as I am prepared to divulge of my autobiography. What I have written is, as far as I remember, true; but of course it is not all the truth.

Whetham
Calne, Wilts.
21 August 1977

Acknowledgements

We wish to thank Lord Horder and Miss Morag Harris for their generous assistance in the preparation and proofing of the text and Mrs Barbara Forryan for the preparation of the index.

THE EDITORS

I

Belief and Representation[1]

> Galileo and the Inquisition are only in error in the single affirmation in which they both agreed, namely that absolute position is a physical fact — the sun for Galileo and the earth for the Inquisition.
>
> A. N. Whitehead, *The Principles of Natural Knowledge*, p. 31

INTRODUCTION

The thesis that will be advanced in this paper is that what have been considered rival beliefs are often in reality rival representations of the same belief. It may be said of one representation not that it is truer but that it is more convenient than the other. In particular it will be argued that the differences between the main conceptions of the world, theistic, mechanistic, and idealistic, are at least in part differences of this type, that is that they differ more in convenience than in truth.

1. BELIEF AND REPRESENTATION

Belief

It is usually assumed that at least we know what we *mean* when we assert that anything exists, but that we can doubt the

---

[1] Dieser Aufsatz sucht den richtigen Gedanken, daß in der Philosophie bloße Differenzen der Darstellung oft fälschlich für Differenzen der dargestellten Überzeugungen gehalten werden, auf den Gegensatz einiger Weltbilder anzuwenden und zu zeigen, daß sie innerhalb weiter Grenzen nur verschiedene Ausdrucksweisen für einen und denselben Glauben sind. Es liege ihnen eine gemeinsame Wahrheit zugrunde, die der Verfasser in der Weise der Immanenzphilosophie formuliert. Die dergestalt für den Positivismus ins Feld geführten Argumente sind nicht prinzipiell neu, aber in so frischer und persönlich-origineller Weise vorgetragen, daß sicher mancher Leser Anregung und Vergnügen daran finden wird. Ich glaubte deshalb die kleine Arbeit meines Schülers für die Publikation empfehlen zu sollen.　　　　　　　　　　　　　　　　　　　　　　　M. Schlick.

Symposion, Heft 4, 1927.

truth of this assertion. It is these assumptions that I propose to question. Propositions are often said to be true if there *is* a fact which corresponds to them and false if there is not. They are supposed to assert the *existence* of this fact. Thus if I say, 'The tree exists' or 'the electrons exist' or 'other people's minds, or God exists', I am supposed to be making statements which are *capable* of truth or falsehood, and are true or false according as to whether there *are* or *are not* corresponding entities. If I consider what I mean by these assertions, I find myself increasingly bewildered as to what I do believe when I make them. I shall start then with a theory of belief which does seem to me intelligible, and which is applicable to conditional propositions. From this point of departure I shall return to consider what, if anything, is meant by the existential type.

When we believe anything, we have *firstly* a certain *complex of ideas* in our minds characterized by a peculiar feeling of conviction (James, *Principles of Psychology*, ch. 21); *secondly* a certain *disposition* to be surprised should sensations corresponding to certain of these ideas occur without those corresponding to the rest. Thus, when I believe that the table is in the next room, my consciousness contains an image of the room with the table inside it, together with the feeling that characterizes this ideal complex as 'anerkannt' and not merely as 'vorgestellt'. I possess at the same time a *disposition* to be surprised should the sensation of the room occur without including that of the table.

If ab is the ideal complex, $A\bar{B}$[1] (or $\bar{A}B$) is a combination of sensations that would evoke surprise. The state of affairs AB which would *not* cause surprise may be called the object of the belief whose content is ab. The content may be said to represent or illustrate the belief. A belief is not unambiguously determined by its object (or by its content), for AB is the object either of the belief that $A\bar{B}$ is impossible or that $\bar{A}B$ is impossible (of $A > B$[2] or $B > A$). Thus the sensa complex 'the falling of the tree at two o'clock' is the object either of 'When it is two I shall see it fall' or of 'If I see it fall it will be two o'clock'. The latter statement does not imply the former.

Assertions that appear to attribute to anything an indepen-

[1] Read: 'A and not B' or 'A without B'.
[2] Read: 'A implies B'.

dent existence in an independent world are often found to attribute to it merely a position in our world conception, and this is a system of ideas whose order is the same as the order of sensations we believe possible. Apparent differences of opinion as to what exists in this sense are not differences of belief at all, but differences in the representation of belief. It is this kind of difference that will occupy us here, and when we have investigated it we shall perhaps see more clearly what room for genuine disagreement still remains, and whether there is any other meaning of existential propositions not reducible to the conditional form.

Analogous representation. It is only seldom that the content resembles the object of a belief in anything beyond its general structure. Relations that are complex and obscure are represented by those that are simple and familiar. We express our beliefs about electrical phenomena in terms and pictures that are appropriate to hydrodynamics, about our minds in terms appropriate to our bodies, and about the uttermost foundations of the world in pictures derived from our everyday environment.

Neither the pressure nor quantity of electricity passing through a wire is a matter of experience. But if the reading on the volt and ampere meter is correlated with the pressure and quantity of water, the glowing wire with the heat generated by friction in a narrow pipe, the structural similarity becomes exact. The negative plates are said, then, to contain a fluid under pressure, and the wires the same fluid in motion, not because anything possessing the imminent properties of a fluid has been or will ever be observed, but because such language completes the analogy. This kind of picture is an economy of thought. If I want to know what will happen when I charge a battery, I have only to remember the familiar effects which may be produced by water under pressure and what electrical phenomena are correlated with these. If I am told by an empirical mechanic that a bad contact is a short circuit and will cause the battery to run down, I have only to remember the hydrodynamic analogy to see that he is talking nonsense, whereas without it such problems would entail an intolerable strain on the memory.

Again the obscure and complex changes in our feelings are most easily remembered, studied or anticipated, with the assistance of some simple picture. As we read of Egos, Super-Egos, Ids and Censors we people our brains with conflicting manikins. Next time we expel half-formed and unpleasant thoughts from consciousness we recognize our feeling, which had hitherto passed unnoticed, as the activity of the censor. The word or concrete picture is the pin on which the obscure and fleeting may be fixed and carefully examined.

Multiple representation. If representation can be analogous it can also be multiple, for there can be many analogies to one object of belief. Of two analogies that convey the same belief, one cannot be truer but only more convenient than the other. This suggests that when we dispute about what the world really is, we may be disputing about how we shall represent what combinations of sensa we consider possible and what impossible, and not about what these combinations are. That is we may disagree not in our opinions but in how we represent them.

Literal representation. There is sometimes, however, room for genuine disagreement. If I believe that electricity really is a fluid, my hydrodynamic picture represents two beliefs; it is correlated, not only with the observed phenomena, but also with that which I believe to be concomitant with this, the behaviour of certain particles. That is, I believe that parallel with the observation of the makro-phenomena, certain instruments not yet invented would disclose mikro-phenomena literally resembling the hydrodynamic picture. I do not as a matter of fact believe this, so that for me the fluid theory is an analogy, a correlated picture, and nothing more, though an analogy that is extremely close.

When, therefore, we assert that the electrons exist, we mean firstly that they are constituents of our representation of the world. This representation conveys certain beliefs about the readings we expect to observe on our volt and ampere meters. But it may, if taken literally, convey the further conditional proposition that under certain circumstances we expect to see the entities we have called electrons.

Existential propositions. Are then all existential propositions exhaustively analysable into conditional statements about what we consider possible and what impossible combinations of experience?

There is of course the sense in which anyone perceiving a sensum may assert that it exists. It may also be said of sensa which we are going to have, that they will exist (or of sensa that we have had, that they have existed). I may believe that the sensa complex 'the falling of the tree' *would* happen at two if I were there to see it. I believe further that it *will* happen, if my being there is itself something that *would* happen under conditions that are themselves conditioned mediately or immediately by my present experience. If anything is conditioned by a train of conditions conditioned by the present, we say it will happen unconditionally, or that it will exist. Common sense, on the other hand, regards the falling of the tree as an event that will exist whether I shall be there or not, and is as justified in its definition as the idealist is in his. The realist attempts to convert the idealist from the error of his ways by reciting grounds for inferring that the tree, in his language, will fall. He does not prove more than that, in idealist language, he would see it fall, if he were there, a conclusion with which the idealist is in complete accord.

That half-circle of continuous green we call a distant tree, is seen on a close inspection to be composed of a multitude of leaves; and we speak of the sensa complex that is the multitude of leaves as being always there waiting to be seen, as being the real tree of which the half-circle of continuous green is but the appearance. It is permanently there in the sense that its memory image is a constituent of our world conception. The analogy of the tree suggests that a closer inspection of all that is continuous may disclose an atomic structure. A close inspection of what can only be divided in certain ways shows the divisions before their separation, and we are led to suppose that whenever we find such divisibility the parts must have existed separately, that is that a previous examination would have disclosed them. Now substances can only be joined or separated in fixed proportions, so that we suppose that their structure must be atomic. This means, firstly, that our picture of the world is atomic, secondly, that the behaviour of substances is exactly analogous to that of things which a close inspection invariably shows to be composed of parts. It does not mean that the atomic structure exists independently of us, in any other sense than that in which the sensation of the multitude of leaves exists independently of us. To mean more would seem to mean that a sensation can exist without existing. But in fact the assertion that the world is atomic implies less than the assertion that the tree is composed of leaves. For the leaves in our commonsense picture of the world may become sensations, whereas the atom images never can.

When, therefore, I predicate existence of my table, of the electrons, of the soul[1] or of other people's minds, I seem to attribute to them firstly a position in a certain system of ideas, which is called respectively the material world, the scientific world, the animistic world or the pluralistic world of mind. If I deny their existence in this sense, I merely mean that I do not use this system of ideas in which they have a place to convey my beliefs about the possible combinations of experience. In the second place conditional propositions may be implied by these assertions. 'My table exists' means also: 'If I see my room, I shall also see my table'. 'The electrons exist' may mean: 'Under certain circumstances I should see them.' This I do not believe, so that the electrons exist for me only in the first sense. They are parts of the indispensable furniture of my thought, and nothing more. I do not believe in the soul in either sense. It is not an indispensable constituent of my thought, nor do I expect to see it. 'A's mind exists' does not seem to mean anything in the conditional sense. Any attempt so to interpret it begs the question. It is not helpful to say that having some part of A's consciousness is the condition of having a consciousness. Thus, the proposition: 'If I saw A's face in the mirror instead of mine I should have A's consciousness', presupposes that I have at least part of A's consciousness, his face in the mirror, already. Further, introspection has failed to disclose to me any meaning of my belief that other people's minds exist, except that which attributes to them a place in my conception of the world. I find that if I go on to say that I believe this system of ideas to correspond to some permanent reality beyond, I have

[1] I.e. in the metaphysical sense.

BELIEF AND REPRESENTATION

merely invented another system of ideas which I call the real world as opposed to the one I call my conception of it. This is what logicians do when they want to say that a proposition is true if there is a fact which corresponds to it, and false if there is not.[1]

There seem then, only two senses in which the existence of anything, other than a present sensa complex, may be affirmed: one which affirms that it has a place in some system of ideas, and one that asserts that it will under certain conditions, that is together with certain other experience, be experienced. Since we can represent our beliefs by means of different illustrations, a disagreement in the first sense, if it does not involve a disagreement in the second also, is a question not of belief but of convenience.

Most systems of philosophy contain parts which are supposed to transcend our capacity for experiencing them. To assert the existence of such things can have no meaning in the second sense, for they are by definition excluded from conditional propositions that state under what circumstances they would become experiences. Other people's minds and scientific objects are of this type. Systems that contain such entities may, however, be useful, if the possibilities of experience can be made to depend more simply upon them than upon each other. To assert the existence, on the other hand, of anything not supposed to be transcendent has a meaning in both senses. 'The ash-tree in the garden exists' means not only, 'It is a constituent of that system of ideas I call the material world', but also, 'When I see the garden I shall see the tree'. If I mean by 'the ash-tree' the atoms that compose it, my assertion has only the one meaning, 'It is a constituent of the system of ideas I call the external world'.

It is supposed that existential propositions have some sense more ultimate than this. If I am right they have not, and all philosophical discussion as to the real nature of the world is idle in so far as it affects neither our beliefs, nor the economic representation of these beliefs. Our tendency to feel that propositions that assert the existence of the electrons or of other people's minds really do mean something more ultimate, seems

[1] I am not sure that I now (1977) agree with this. See Postscript.

7

to be due to a confusion between thinking and believing, between representation and belief. It is true that I think of the electrons and other people's minds as being there; but my expectations are not altered by this. My expectations as to the possible combinations of experience may be the same whether I represent matter as being unanalysable sensa combinations and other people as senseless automata, or whether I adopt a more usual view. If further it is agreed that believing anything about the world is more than just thinking of it as constructed in this manner, it is difficult to see what this 'more' can be if it is not having a disposition to be surprised, should sensations corresponding to this picture occur differently arranged.

II. DEVELOPMENT OF OUR REPRESENTATION OF THE WORLD

Starting from a certain theory of belief we have distinguished between a belief and the mental picture we use to represent it. We have seen that representation may be analogous and therefore multiple; that is that the same beliefs can be represented in various ways. We have seen further that that part of the import of existential propositions, which cannot be reduced to the conditional form, concerns representation rather than belief.

Since representations differ in convenience, it remains to discuss how far preference for a particular type is rational and how far irrational and to select that type which seems most satisfactory. In order to do this we will discuss how, out of the materials given in consciousness, we have built our varied conceptions of the world. This will give us at the same time an opportunity to illustrate the conclusions to which we have already come.

The Perceptual Field

In the terminology of Hume consciousness may be divided into impressions and ideas, or, what is the same thing, into sensations and images. These differ from one another in distinctness and in other characteristics enumerated by him. Ideas are reproductions of impressions, and impressions are patterns of colour, sounds, tactual sensa and the like. The visual field contains a varying background, and a more or less permanent foreground, which, in ordinary language, is the sensation of that part of ourselves that we see. The perceptual field is the visual field supplemented by certain images. Visual contact between part of the self (that is the permanent foreground of our field of view) and any of those relatively stable colour complexes we call sense objects is invariably accompanied by a sensation of hardness. Further, contact between two objects of the environment is visually similar to contact between the hand and one of these; it evokes therefore the image which is the copy of the tactual sensa that would have accompanied this. Finally any visual object, even when not in contact with anything, excites the idea of hardness. That is, we feel emphatically what happens to other objects as though it had happened to ourselves. And even when nothing is happening to them, we see them only together with the image of that feeling of solidity which varies, but never completely disappears, with the violence of the events in which our own body is seen to play a part. Or still more shortly – tactual images are evoked by visual sense objects and the sense world becomes a world of substance.

The External World of Common Sense

What is called the external world of common sense is an ideal construction resembling an amplified perceptual field. It is composed of reproductions of perceptual fields pieced together in the order in which they originally occurred. Any part of it can come into being when and as we chose, with or without that foreground which we call ourselves. In this sense, unlike the perceptual field, it exists independently of us, independent alike of our movement and our presence. Any particular field of view corresponds to some part of the external world; it is the original of which this part is the ideal copy; and as sensations vary, lighting up now that part of the ideal extension of our environment, we say that we are moving in the external world from place to place.

Since the order of sensations we believe possible is the same as the order of corresponding images in this ideal construction, it forms the representation of those beliefs which enable us to find our way about. The representation is direct and non-symbolic.

The External World of Speculation

Just as the external world of common sense is the ideal *extension* of our perceptual field, so are the worlds of speculation ideal *refinements* of the external world of common sense. There are three main types of such representation: the anthropomorphic, the mechanistic and the mathematical.

These world conceptions are not only built of memories pieced together in the exact order in which the original sensations actually occurred. They contain parts which never have nor could be seen. As long as different forms of such systems are taken literally the beliefs which they represented are different. If, however, the unseen entities which they contain are admitted to be transcendent, beyond the possibility of experience; if the catalogue of those situations which would not cause surprise is the same, the beliefs must be the same, although their representations may be widely different.

The anthropomorphic. There is probably a stage in our lives when wishes are thought to be all-powerful. The important difference between image and sensation lies in that the former is, whereas the latter is not, directly subservient to desires; and the recognition of this distinction is a late and precarious acquirement. The child's desires are represented as fulfilled, and only experience which he most reluctantly accepts, teaches this difference between impression and idea (Freud, *Totem und Tabu*, 2. Aufl., ch. 3, especially p. 112). Later this omnipotence is attributed to others, to our parents and superparents, who are supposed to exercise it solely with reference to our own desires, either to thwart them if we feel guilty, or to assist them (that is to thwart those of others on whom we have succeeded in projecting our sins) if we do not.

We shall tend therefore to attribute everything that happens to the action of some creator, whose purposes are in accordance with our needs, and a theistic picture may remain our main mode of representation even after it has lost all literal meaning. If we are teleologists we may not think as concretely as this, but we shall use words that will betray that some such picture once was there.

The mechanistic. If, on the other hand, we are of a less pious disposition, we shall, once we have discovered that we are not ourselves all-powerful, be careful to contend against the demoralizing suspicion that our parents or superparents possess this property. We shall in fact repudiate with anger and perhaps even with a little fear the teleological conception of the world. We shall remember that contact between two of those relatively stable colour complexes we call objects (Mach, *Die Analyse der Empfindungen*, 9. Aufl., p. 2) was found to be the necessary antecedent to their motion. We shall remember that when parts of ourselves have entered into any of these encounters a sense of hardness and effort has been experienced, and we shall think of this hardness whenever we see contact of any kind. We shall in short prefer a simple mechanistic picture of behaviour with which to correlate all observed uniformities.

It has been found that this system is less satisfactory than was at first supposed. The grosser physical changes of liquids that boiled or froze could be accounted for along these lines, that is, they could be correlated with a simple mechanistic picture; but action at a distance remained unexplained. There have been numberless mechanistic systems invented to account for gravitation, so great was our reluctance to draw our pictures from anything except what is most familiar. It was thought that no explanation that was not mechanistic could be ultimate, and it was the goal of physicists to reduce all movement to movement through contact. It was thought that this sort of action needed no explanation, that it had an *a priori* necessity denied to other uniformities, and all this simply because it was familiar. Logically it is not unthinkable that the billiard ball might turn green, or disappear or do anything rather than depart in the direction and at the speed in which it always does depart.

That particles should attract or repel each other is a form of behaviour to which there is no close parallel in experience. It is found, however, that a system that accepts this sort of activity as ultimate can be correlated with the combinations of sensa complexes we believe possible more closely than the strictly mechanistic picture. This might with sufficient ingenuity be saved, but the aether 'squirts' or 'vortices' would make it cumbersome. These forms of representation would be equally true, in that the possible combinations of sensation could be calculated from either. But the one would be more convenient than the other, as the astronomy that describes the movements of the planets as elliptical is more convenient, though not more true, than that which describes them as composed of cycles and epicycles *ad infinitum*.

The mathematical. The first sort of mechanism admits only action through contact; the second admits attractions and repulsions that are irreducible, but still restricts us unnecessarily to familiar pictures, in which permanent substances play a part.

Our belief that the table is in the next room, that is, that it can be experienced in and only in the room, is represented by an image of the table in the room. But this image is a complex of many qualities that we would do well to simplify. We say that the real table is a complex of atomic events, and reduce the qualities of our picture to hardness, shape and motion. We can convey our belief that the sensa complex we call the table will be, and will only be, experienced together with the sensa complex we call the room, by a picture containing certain clusters of atoms corresponding to the table and others corresponding to the room. But we can go still further; we can replace the pictured four directions in space-time[1] by four series of real numbers, a point by an ordered set of numbers, or co-ordinates, one selected from each series, and the presence or proximity of matter by another set, called potentials. We thus have a purely arithmetical construction, freed from all irrational restrictions, with which to correlate the possibilities of experience. If anything is observed and we desire to foresee the sequel, we have only to remember what complexes of numbers are correlated with it, to calculate what complexes come next in the time order, and finally to remember what sensations are correlated with these. It is simpler and more accurate to calculate the dependence of one sensa complex on another through, rather than without, the mediation of such systems, because their laws are purely quantitative and far simpler than those holding directly between phenomena.

It is a peculiarity of the scientific picture of the world, that the number of its distinct qualities decreases as it is refined.

---

[1] These cannot of course be visualized all at once.

The sense table is hard and coloured; the scientific table is at first composed of particles that are hard and energetic, but which possess no colour, and later of a colony of places where the measurement of the angles of triangles gives strange results.

The Place of Mind in Nature

The dualistic view. It has for a long time been known that consciousness is dependent upon the brain, that is, that our states of mind are dependent upon that part of the extended and refined edition of our field of view we call our brains. Further, as has been pointed out, we suffer under an almost irresistible compulsion to represent interdependence of any kind by mechanistic or anthropomorphic pictures. Our common conception of the dependence of mind on matter is a blend of both these types.

The soul was once to us what the demon that animates the train is to the savage now, the man within the man that worked him. We no longer, like Descartes or the savage, expect to see the soul as the result of a surgical operation, and if we believe that the soul is extramental our belief in it, like our belief in the electrons, does not amount to much. As long as we are agreed on the sort of behaviour we expect of our neighbours or of chemical and electrical phenomena, it is a matter of personal convenience whether our picture of the world contains souls or electrons, or not. Only if we take our picture literally and expect souls to be revealed by surgical operations, or electrons by microscopes do we believe anything different from those whose conceptions of the world do not contain these entities.

Now the anthropomorphic picture of the soul within the brain gives us an opportunity of representing consciousness as mechanistically dependent upon the external world. The soul takes photographs through the eyes, and whenever it has taken a photograph, it hastens to look up those that came next after it before, so that it can repeat them if they are pleasing and avoid them if they are not. This picture, perhaps not so definitely expressed, underlies the whole of our psychological vocabulary when we talk of thinker, thought, and thing thought of, or use any of the expressions that represent this trio.

The external world is still often thought of as literally outside consciousness (Avenarius, *Der menschliche Weltbegriff, II.*

Abschnitt, und Bemerkungen zum Begriff des Gegenstandes der Psychologie, 2. a, b), as the landscape is literally outside the camera that contains the picture. We are apt, therefore, to regard our field of view as belonging to the outer or inner world, according as to whether we are considering our own minds or those of other people. We shall either expect to find their consciousnesses inside their brains, or to wonder how, since the external world is outside consciousness, we can know anything about it. For, on the one hand, it would seem that we must at least know its structure since we use it to explain sensation. We say, for instance, that this patch of green is caused by a disturbance in the aether modified and reflected by the atoms of the grass, which has set up a chemical process in the retina and brain. On the other hand, since all thought is but the rearrangement of sensation and sensation is eternally inside, we can know nothing of the outside world.

The difficulty involves a genuine false belief, but departs when we remember that the external and internal worlds are built largely of the same material, and that the picture that represents them like photograph and landscape as causally interdependent and spatially separated is convenient though it has no literal meaning. Modern realists do not, of course, think as naively as this, but their thought is largely verbal and is the survival of some such picture.

The idealist view. The scientific world is the field of view filled out by memory and refined in imagination until it has no resemblance with the complex of varying sensations from which it was derived. The present field of view resembles a bit of the world of common sense; this in turn corresponds with the scientific world, but does not resemble it except in structure. The present field of view is therefore correlated with a part of the scientific world, the part of which it is said to be the sensation. Thus the sense table is correlated with the atoms that compose it. But since the behaviour of the atoms that compose the brain is dependent upon that of those that compose the table, the sense table is also correlated with the behaviour of the atoms of the brain (Schlick, *Erkenntnislehre*, 2. Aufl., §32). By using this correlation, the calculation of everything that has been or will be experienced will probably be most economically effected. Instead, when we want to foresee the future, of proceeding from the present sense occurrence to the atomic events that are said to compose it, to their sequels, and back to the sense occurrence which they compose, we shall make the journey from the present to the future sensa-complex via the corresponding atomic events said to be happening in our brains.

What we call the external world is, then, a purely mathematical construction (ibid. §32) which helps us to summarize the possible combinations of sensation. This construction is the monistic universe of physics; correlated with those parts of it that are called brains is the pluralistic universe of mind. Minds are composed of image and sensation, of that which is and that which is not directly subservient to desires. Sensation corresponds to the part of the world of physics which is the refined edition of this sensation. But it, and not only it, but the mind as a whole, is also correlated with the part of the world of physics that is the refined edition of the sensation of the brain. The former correlation is used in the construction of physics, the latter will be used in its future application. Minds are dependent upon their own past, and upon other Minds; the world of physics was invented to express, and therefore to calculate, this interdependence as easily as possible.

Such a conception of the place of mind in nature does not tempt us to think of the external world as literally outside consciousness (ibid. §33); and it enables us to avoid many problems which ought never to have occurred. At the same time the mathematical conception of the external world which it involves permits us, free from irrational regard for habitual modes of thought, to select that form of representation which is most convenient.

Postscript [*1977*]

I would now suppose that our notion of a permanent world, including both material and psychic objects, is achieved by projective identification both of our sense of touch into material objects and of parts of our own psyche into creatures felt to resemble ourselves. But I do not know if this really affects the argument in the paper.

2

The Psycho-physical Apparatus*¹

An Introduction to a Physical Interpretation of Psycho-analytic Theory

The psycho-analytic doctrine is divided into two parts which should never be confused; into facts, and into the pictures that represent them. Freud himself has been careful to make this distinction and has repeatedly affirmed that his pictures are not to be mistaken for existences. If, however, we take as pictures something which does exist, and which has an independent correlation with the facts that it is to represent, certain advantages are won. Thus, if we know that there is a correlation between neural and psychic processes, the former, which are more easily visualized, may be used to represent the latter. Such a representation has the advantage over purely fantastic analogy in that it is less likely to deceive, and more likely to suggest undiscovered uniformities. Brain physiology is itself the object of a science. Two sciences known to be correlated advance twice as quickly after the correlation has been observed. Knowledge of both is pooled. Each illustrates points in the other that hitherto remained obscure. Advance in one is immediately transferable to the other. Thus, two geometries that had been studied independently doubled their rate of progress after the discovery that the points of one were correlates of the straight lines of the other.

It is the purpose of this paper to outline the sort of correlation between behaviourism and psychology which I believe will be some day established.

* B. J. Med. Psych., vol. VIII, 1928.
¹ [1977 – This paper is almost purely behaviouristic but I leave it in because Frank Ramsay liked it.]

THE PSYCHO-PHYSICAL APPARATUS

1. THE PHYSICAL APPARATUS

The nervous system is subject to stimuli external to itself. These may be either external to the organism, such as an injury, or internal to the organism, such as the periodic urges of hunger or of sex. It continues to react until these stimuli are *removed*. But not only does it remove stimuli; it *avoids* them. The presence of avoidance mechanisms seems especially to distinguish the organism from other machines. Hence some psychologists have supposed that the nervous system is more than a machine. It is not, however, impossible to imagine a mechanism that learns to remove and to avoid stimuli. The nervous system seems to be such an apparatus, presumably because this characteristic is of survival value.

(a) Removal

For reasons probably connected with the properties of the synapse the reactions that have in the past most often followed a given stimulus tend to recur without trial and error, on the repetition of the stimulus. It has been pointed out that the appropriate reaction, that is, the reaction that removes the stimulus, must occur once on every occurrence of the stimulus. Until it occurs the stimulus remains. Hence, since there is no such necessity for other reactions to recur, it is probable that the appropriate response will occur most often, and that in consequence the disposition to this response will in time become greater than the disposition to other, inappropriate, responses.[1] This is perhaps not a complete account of the learning of removal mechanisms, but further investigation along these, or similar, lines will probably discover a purely mechanical, yet adequate, theory of the facts. For economy of words I will call a reaction that removes a stimulus a *removal*.

The appropriateness of a removal depends not only on the stimulus, but also on the environment, that is, on other initially indifferent stimulus patterns. The reaction of eating is only appropriate to hunger in the presence of food. I will call such a necessary condition to the adequacy of a removal a *means*. A

---

[1] The learning of appropriate responses is of course further speeded up by the inhibition of those inappropriate reactions that lead to increased tension. Inhibition and avoidance will be considered later.

17

removal in the absence of a means I will call an *inadequate removal*. The adequate response to a stimulus in the absence of a means is to seek the means. This too is learnt, by ourselves or our ancestors, through trial and error. A reaction that seeks a means I will call a *seeking*.

What we consciously imagine that we seek are always means, not ends. The object of a wish is not complacency; it is definitely exciting; it is something that stimulates. It is a beef steak, not fullness; a lady, not sexual satiation. The end, unlike the means, is a situation without stimulus, without urge, a state of equilibrium. We cannot, *ex hypothesi*, imagine such a state. To do so would be to form an image without content.

(b) Avoidance

Another fundamental property of the nervous apparatus is that the usual antecedent, or concomitant, of a stimulus sets off the reaction appropriate to the stimulus. A part of a spatio-temporal stimulus pattern sets off the reaction formerly evoked by the whole. This is probably also due to the properties of the synapse. Energy from the antecedent stimulus, originally of small importance, is drained off along the track opened by the subsequent excitation so that a path of low resistance, or reaction disposition, is formed. In future the usual concomitant stimulus alone evokes the reaction. Thus the presence of food, that is of a means, evokes the reaction appropriate to hunger, and the burnt child dreads the flame. The sight of the flame, formerly the concomitant of the burn, evokes the removal mechanism before the burn occurs. The burn is thus avoided. Such a removal mechanism which is set off before its original evoking stimulus I will call an *avoidance*. Its evoking stimulus I will call a *threat*.

Sometimes an avoidance is in opposition to some other impulse which is then *inhibited*. Thus, if a child tended to grasp bright objects, the avoidance that would develop after a burn inhibits the grasping response. The same stimulus pattern, the bright object, evokes first the seeking and then the avoidance. The energy of the seeking is diverted to avoidance.

Just as a removal is inadequate if it occurs in the absence of a means, an avoidance is *irrelevant* if its evoking threat is an accidental, rather than an invariable, antecedent of the stimulus that is avoided. Thus, if the burnt child avoids bright but cool objects, his reaction is irrelevant. The evoking stimulus of an irrelevant avoidance may be called a *false threat*.

An irrelevant avoidance that avoids a means is not only irrelevant, it is *pernicious*. Thus if a cool bright object is a means to the removal of some want and is avoided, its avoidance is pernicious. Perhaps the whole theory of neurosis could be built up from the theory of pernicious avoidance.

II. THE PHYSICAL APPARATUS

It is a working theory of most psychologists to assume that there is a one–one correlation between nervous and mental processes. I believe that this theory is correct, but its detailed application is difficult.

I have used the word correlation to avoid the word 'parallelism' and its associations with a certain solution of the psychophysical problem. Some philosophers avoid the problem by asserting that consciousness *is* neural activity seen from within instead of from without. Taken literally this attitude seems a manifest absurdity; for the neural event correlated with the awareness of green is surely different from the green as a constituent of consciousness. But the verbal identification is at least as legitimate as that in the statement that green *is* an electromagnetic disturbance of such and such a wave length, or, that heat *is* kinetic energy. Here we use the same word for a conscious presentation and for that part of the so-called external world which we correlate with it. The convention, if it is realized to be such, is a convenient economy of language.

But the linguistic equation of neural with psychic events is even more justified than that of a colour with its wave length. For, since the colour can be either image or sensation, the wave length, unlike the neural process, is only the usual, not the invariable, concomitant. Further, the neural process, like the external world of which it is a part, is for the physiologist a 'possible percept', something that might be seen in a microscope, and, for the physicist a 'concept', a singularity in world geometry; for neither a 'Ding an sich'. If we must have a metaphysical reality that the observed neural process represents, this can only be the correlated psychic process. Hence, if we mean by 'neural process' what the metaphysician means, a 'Ding an sich', the neural process *is* a psychological event. If, however, we mean what the physiologist or the physicist means, a possible percept or a concept, the neural process *represents* the psychological event. After this explanation I shall sometimes use the same word indifferently for a neural process and for the correlated psychological event.

Let us now consider to what neural processes *conscious* processes correspond. If consciousness contained only sensations, we might at first suppose that it is the correlate of receptor stimuli. But we possess images as well as sensations and it is evident that these do not bear any simple relation to external stimuli. Closer investigation discloses that sensations too do not correspond so closely to these stimuli as we might at first suppose; for, when we are inattentive, stimuli occur without the sensations that usually accompany them. Thus sensations can fail to occur with, and images can occur without, the stimulation of the corresponding receptor patterns. We must, then, conclude that consciousness is correlated, not with the stimulus of receptors, but with the stimulus of neural patterns that are more central. The study of lesions suggests that it is correlated with cortical events.

The nervous discharge may be divided into sections which we may speak of respectively as peripheral or central tension patterns. We know that the same (or a similar) central pattern may be evoked by a part only of the peripheral pattern that formerly evoked it. We may suppose that conscious events are correlated with central patterns; and that such an event is a sensation or an image according as it is evoked, or reproduced, by the whole, or a part, of the original peripheral pattern. A 'pure' sensation is a valid and useful concept; but only approximations to it are found.

We shall now see how far the nervous apparatus can be made to picture or reflect some of the psychological concepts of the Freudian school. As a first hypothesis I will assume that there is a nervous apparatus within the nervous apparatus, and that this inner system behaves to the stimuli of the outer system as this mechanism behaves to the stimuli of its own peripheral receptors: that is, the inner system learns to *remove* or to *avoid*

THE PSYCHO-PHYSICAL APPARATUS

highly charged stimuli from the outer system. I will further assume that consciousness is correlated with tension patterns in the inner system. Freud, though he has been careful not to commit himself to physiological analogies, seems often to have had some such picture in mind.

Since we assume that psychic processes must always be correlated with nervous processes, we must suppose that there are psychic events corresponding to tensions in the outer, as well as in the inner, system. These, since they are by hypothesis not conscious, may be said to be unconscious. Similarly we might suppose a hierarchy of vaguely differentiated systems from the receptor to the effector end of the nervous apparatus, each with its separate consciousness dissociated from the rest.

For the moment we shall stick to two systems, one behind the other, the tension patterns of which correspond respectively to conscious and unconscious thoughts. We can speak of the patterns of either system as stimulated or quiescent. To complete the psycho-physical parallel we may speak of the corresponding ideas as *charged* or *uncharged*. A charged idea corresponding to a tension pattern in the inner system is actual and conscious; a charged idea corresponding to a tension pattern in the outer system is actual and unconscious. An uncharged idea belonging to either system is not actual, but potential; it corresponds to a neural disposition; it does not exist except as a convenient object of thought.

Let us next try to discover whether certain psychological mechanisms disclosed by psycho-analysis can be correlated with the nervous mechanisms that we have postulated. A parallel between hallucinatory gratification and inadequate avoidance, and between neurotic repression and irrelevant and pernicious avoidance at once suggests itself. It may be that these parallels will prove superficial, but they seem to deserve investigation.

(a) *Hallucination*

We have assumed that the inner nervous apparatus behaves to the stimuli of the outer system as this latter behaves to the stimuli of its own receptors, that is, to the periodic inner needs of the organism and to the injuries of the external world. The nervous system as a whole learns to remove high tension stimuli, but removal mechanisms are only appropriate in the presence of certain other, initially indifferent, stimuli, or means. Inadequate removal, however, sometimes occurs, especially in the learning period, or when the adequate response is inhibited by a threat. The hungry child sucks in the absence of the nipple. Such inadequate reactions seem to correspond to Freud's Pleasure Principle. According to him, the hungry child remembers the last occasion on which it was fed and is satisfied – at least for a time.

The same mechanism occurs in dreams in which the desired condition is hallucinatorily produced, and, in a modified form, in the wish that anticipates its object. A wish, for Freud, is the memory of a situation that satisfied a want; it is distinguished from the hallucination in that the wish is no longer mistaken for reality. More precisely, a wish is an hallucination that has failed to bring satisfaction. The hallucination seems really to satisfy the want. But in the wish the unpleasure of the want in part remains. Between the hallucination and the wish there is a continuous series. Broadly speaking, the more vividly we wish the less we strive. Some people are content to dream; others act. Those who act do not waste much time in wishing.

Thus an hallucination, and to some extent a wish, resembles an inadequate removal. Like other faults in evolution they may both have acquired a secondary function that is useful. In inadequate removal the organism reacts as if the means were present. Psychologically the means is ideally reproduced. Physiologically the same neural tension pattern is reproduced in the central system as if the external means were present. Whatever the external pattern, the same internal pattern gives the same conscious state. Hence the ideal presentation of the absent means. In the hallucination the neural reaction is identical with the reaction to the reality; in the wish it is a weakened copy, producing an implicit play of muscle tone. In both tension seems to be reduced, but more in the hallucination than in the wish.

We have seen that a means, rather than an end, is the content of a wish or an hallucination. The wish or the hallucination may occur either because the adequate response to the absence of a means, the seeking of the means, has not yet been discovered, or because the seeking has been inhibited.

If the adequate response is inhibited, for reasons that may be rational or pernicious, the inadequate response and its attendant wish, or hallucination, may provide the only possible outlet for energy. But the source of energy is not, in general, so easily avoided, so that the unpleasure of the wish persists.

Where, however, the source of energy is not a real want, but a false threat, the hallucination may completely remove it. As if two falsehoods make a truth, we hallucinate a heaven to escape the fear of death, which is irrelevantly avoided as a weaning, or castration. Similarly, the hallucinatory gratification of the hungry infant, of which Freud speaks, may remove a false threat of hunger, the temporary absence of the mother, rather than the real want.

But to real stimuli the appropriate response is to seek means, rather than to react as if they were already present. The neural mechanism is predisposed to seek those it has already found on past occasions. Thus its hedonic flight from tension is bounded by its experience. This perhaps explains Freud's observation that repetition is more fundamental than the search for pleasure. He finds a tendency to return to past states of equilibrium; to return from the man to the child; from the child to the embryo; and from the embryo to lifeless matter. But old means sometimes become threats, so that what was once sought is avoided. It is this direct avoidance of old means that diverts the search for the Nirvana into ever more circuitous routes.

New means are found to take the place of old by trial and error. But such experiments are not only explicit. In fantasy we discover new satisfactions which we can afterwards actually create. Thus the wish that may have been originally a useless by-product of evolution, an inadequate response, has acquired a highly useful function.

(b) *Repression*

If the wish and the hallucination correspond to inadequate removal in the central apparatus, we are tempted to suppose that repression must correspond to avoidance. We learn from Freud that unpleasant ideas that are repressed can exist in the unconscious. These may never have reached consciousness, or they may have been forgotten. In searching for the neural parallel we are tempted to suppose that repression is for the central apparatus what avoidance is for the total system. A difficulty at once arises. The total nervous apparatus avoids stimuli by so reacting that the receptors are prevented from coming in contact with the source of stimulus. But, it would seem, that the internal system cannot escape the peripheral system in the same way that the peripheral system escapes the external world. If tension is piled up in the outer system, nothing in our scheme suggests a method by which the central system can withdraw to safety and, as it were, widen the synaptic boundary. The external system can actually reduce the tension in its receptors. The central system cannot do so directly. It can at most determine in which direction the energy will flow.

Freud speaks of a counter-charge (*Gegenbesetzung*) that repels a thought from consciousness. What can be the physiological version of this picture? Freud would perhaps reply that his conception is admittedly analogical and animistic, that he required a concrete picture to fix and represent the important processes that he had discovered, and that he chose it from the current events of the day. Thus ideas are repressed by other ideas mobilized like armies to repel invasion; or a 'censor' is established to prevent their publication. Let us see if we can give a neural interpretation to these pictures.

Seeking seems to be inhibited by the substitution of avoidances. Somewhere in the series of situations arising from a train of seeking responses a threat occurs. This evokes the avoidance into which some of the energy of the seeking is drained. The rest is drained into what is called symbolic expression. Physiologically, the censor may be defined as the collection of avoidances that inhibit the seeking of certain sexual means. It inhibits by draining, into its own avoidances, energy that would otherwise flow into seekings. Thus the energy is not so much blocked in one path, or set of paths, as enticed into another.[1] The neural disturbance in the other path must then be the physiological correlate of Freud's counter-charged idea. Let us see what sort of threats are important for repression.

---

[1] It is true that the avoidance may 'interfere' with the seeking by bombarding it with impulses of a frequency that reduces it to complete fatigue. But it would seem that the impulse must first short-circuit from the seeking to the avoidance, before the avoidance can block the seeking.

THE PSYCHO-PHYSICAL APPARATUS

We have seen that the nervous apparatus learns to react to a threat as to the original high tension stimulus, and that in this way the latter is avoided. Similarly to the threat of a threat there is a reaction that avoids the threat. Psycho-analytically one of the most important threats is the absence of a means, or the threat of the absence of a means. The absence of a means at first evokes an inadequate response, the removal that would be adequate only in the presence of the means. Next the adequate response to the absence of the means is learnt, that is, the means is sought. Finally the absence of the means acts as a threat and sets off the seeking mechanism before a real want has developed. Thus the child at first sucks when it is hungry, whether the mother is there or not. Next it substitutes for, or adds to, this response the response of crying. Finally, it cries when it is left alone, whether it is hungry or not. We know from analysis that the threat of the absence of a means is one of the most powerful agents of repression. The child is again and again prevented from finding, or remembering, the means for the satisfaction of its developing sexual needs by the threats of weaning, or of castration. If it behaves indecently the mother will be annoyed, her loss will be threatened, or like the breasts, the faeces, and the toys, that he has already lost, his most precious possession, his penis, will be taken from him.

In these examples the means, or provisional end, of one urge is the threat of another. The seeking response to the need is inhibited. Energy accumulates at the receptor end of the apparatus from which there is no escape. Generally the threat is false, and the avoidance consequently pernicious. The little boy's mother would not really leave him, nor would his father really castrate him, even if he did admit his precocious cravings.

When seeking is in this way inhibited, two opposite results may follow. Other means are sought, and these may be either progressive or retrogressive; they may lead to responses more adequate to the child's maturer self, or to more infantile regressions. The conflict at the anal phase may compel advance to the genital or return to the oral stage of development. It is at present difficult, in a given case, to foresee which result will be determined. Another result of such inhibition is that the act gives place to the wish, the inadequate response, the incipient reaction in the absence of the means. This momentarily reduces tension, but is, in general, unable to remove the source of stimulus.

But we have not explained how the wish itself can be repressed; nor what happens to it then. Whether it is blocked, or drained off elsewhere. Whether it remains as a disposition, or an unconscious reality. Nor how it returns in a symbolic form.

Our picture of the nervous system suggests that the energy of the wish is drained[1] into the path that inhibits its expression. Since the urge, the means to which the wish anticipates, remains unsatisfied, the organism remains in a state of tension felt as unpleasure or as anxiety. But the path of the wish and its fulfilment is undisturbed. The energy is drained off elsewhere in less satisfying discharge. It is the displacement of this energy that turns us from contented hogs to discontented philosophers, and is responsible for all the neuroses, as well as for all the 'higher values' we possess. It provides the barrier to the direct road to Nirvana and to death. Other values, cultural or neurotic, may be found. But such values are hedonic second bests. It would be interesting to speculate how much of life we owe to rational, how much to irrational, avoidance.

So far we have interpreted the censor as a collection of avoidances which drain energy into hedonically inferior paths, and the counter-charged idea as the correlate of an avoidance. But what of the concept of the Unconscious? Is it a term given to all the wishes and reactions we should display were we not inhibited? Or do these wishes still exist in dissociated corners of the mind? These seem questions that can be determined by physiology alone. The unconscious is by definition inaccessible. We cannot find it to see if it is actual or potential. Even when we succeed in destroying irrelevant inhibitions, we do not know whether what we now find existed previously in an actual or a potential state. Even the presence of symbolic expression does not prove that the symbolized is more than a disposition – an inhibited tendency from which the energy is drained away. But if we could take sections of the nervous apparatus, we might observe the alteration of the tension patterns during the development of some inhibition. If the tension patterns in the outer sections remained unaltered,

---

[1] Perhaps the word 'drained' is a convenient, but inaccurate, description of a process by which path A first stimulates, and is then interfered with by, path B.

while only the inner sections, which we correlate with consciousness, were distorted, we should suppose that psychic processes corresponding to these outer sections existed, and composed the Freudian unconscious.

One last question remains. How does the repressed return in symbolic form? The energy is not all diverted into those reactions that inhibit the repressed activity. Nor, in general, is the energy reduced; for the reaction is inhibited that could remove its source. It flows, partly into the avoidance reaction, partly into associated paths. With these latter are correlated the symbolic, or symptomatic, expression of the wish. The resemblance between symbolized and symbol is often patent to everyone except the employer of the symbol. If a similarity were recognized, the symbol would have to evoke the path of the thought symbolized, and this is *ex hypothesi* impossible. Thus the frigid virgin is not reminded of her repudiated function by the snake that in her dream crawled into a hole.

CONCLUSION

In this paper I have tried to construct a plausible neural apparatus, the physiological processes of which could be correlated with the psychological processes discovered by the Freudian school. I am aware that the attempt has not been altogether satisfactory, but I am convinced that something on these lines is possible, and will one day be achieved. Such an event would be of great benefit both to physiology and to psychology: for, once the details of the parallelism have been worked out, any advance in one science will be immediately applicable to the other. But the temptation to twist psychoanalytical facts to fit physiological theories must be resisted. Our views on nervous mechanism are speculative; our knowledge of psychology is based on facts.

3

Morals and Super-men*

Some Ethical Problems from the Psycho-analytical Standpoint

1977 Introductory Note – Only dead sciences fail to develop. But in a vital science, such as psycho-analysis, the theoretical substructure tends to develop fairly rapidly. The following paper, written in 1928, was based on theories which have largely been modified or replaced since then. I would have written it quite differently today, but have left it in for the benefit of those who might be interested in comparing it with the different way I have tried to deal with similar subjects in later papers – and in particular after the Second War by which time I had had an analysis with Mrs Klein.

Moreover, if the title seems pretentious now, the notion that such a mythical being as a 'perfectly analysed man' could exist and be free from 'inhibitions', the notion that he might also be free from morals could then have seemed well worth investigating.

INTRODUCTION

Religion has been defined as: 'un ensemble de scrupules qui font obstacle au libre exercice de nos facultés.'[1] But definitions that are epigrammatically expressed seldom cover more than half the common connotation of the concepts to which they are applied. And this is no exception; for the totality of a man's inhibitions does not, as a rule, exhaust his religion. I suggest, however, that such a description is adequate to delineate the scope of morals.

It may be objected that there are inhibitions that are not moral and morals that are not inhibitions, and that the proposed definition neither is covered by, nor covers, the common

---

* *B. J. Med. Psych.*, vol. VIII, 1928.
[1] Solomon Reinach, *Orpheus*, p. 4.

meaning of the word. But I think that these objections are less weighty than they seem.

Conscious inhibitions are clearly moral. But a man may be unable to do something of which his conscious morality approves. Such inhibitions he would not at first regard as moral; but psycho-analysis would show that they are due to an infantile morality that had become unconscious. Thus all inhibitions are, in a wide sense, moral.

Again, most morals are clearly inhibitions. But there are 'shalts' as well as 'shalt nots' in the ten commandments. Actions determined by such precepts do not appear to be inhibitions. But if they are the free expression of altruistic inclinations they are not moral.[1] And if they are not free they are based on inhibitions. Thus all morals, in a narrow sense, are inhibitions.[2]

I will therefore define morals as the totality of human inhibitions. Other definitions could be given, but this one seems to accord with the original meaning of the word – with a meaning that still requires a name.

There have been free-thinkers, perhaps in all the great civilizations of the world, who have seen clearly that many religious inhibitions are based on ignorance and superstition. And there have been sophists, since the time of early Greece, who have generalized this observation and have assumed that the rational man would be free from all internal restraints.

Such a conclusion has profoundly disturbed the minds of other thinkers, and since the days of Socrates there have always arisen philosophers to combat it, and to seek a rational foundation for morality. Sometimes these anti-sophists are merely shocked because their own irrational inhibitions are threatened. But often they are moved by the consideration that without restraints civilization would be impossible. Some, while seeing that such restraints are necessary, have believed them irrational and have taught that rulers in their own interest should promote the ignorance and superstition of the masses. Even Plato believed that the workers of his republic could only

[1] In the first meaning of this word.
[2] [I would now (1977) think that there are two types of morals, one based on persecutory anxiety derived from a fear of projected hate, and one on depressive anxiety derived from consciousness of the injury one has done in phantasy or fact to people and causes which one loves.]

be reconciled with their lot by myths invented for the purpose by the guardians. And such a concession is the thin end of the wedge that leads to the view of Thrasymachus that the *Republic* was written to discredit. In the same principle Dostojewski's Grand Inquisitor saw the foundations of the Roman Church. But this solution did not satisfy Dostojewski; for in *Crime and Punishment* he created a character who, although free from superstition, failed to free himself from morals.

Today the same problem presents itself in a new form. Psycho-analysis removes inhibitions. What would a completely analysed individual be like? Would a society of such individuals be stable? Would it be pleasant?

TYPES OF INHIBITION

Inhibitions may be either conscious or unconscious, and conscious inhibitions may be either based on fear or accepted by the ego.

Conscious inhibitions based on fear are again of two kinds; for the fear may be rational or irrational. Thus, if a man refrains from stealing because he does not want to go to prison, his inhibition is conscious and rational. But if he refrains from stealing because he does not want to go to hell, his inhibition is conscious and irrational.

Conscious irrational inhibitions depend upon ignorance and superstition. But conscious rational inhibitions based on fear are an insufficient protection for society. Therefore those who believe that all inhibitions are based on conscious fears do not desire to educate the masses.

But there are also conscious inhibitions accepted by the ego. A child may at first refrain from stealing because stealing is detested by someone he loves; and because he fears to lose this love. But since he tends to imitate those he loves[1] he will adopt this disapproval and will hate stealing of his own accord. Such inhibitions are accepted by the ego; they are not based on fear, but on the imitation of a hero.

The hero may be a real person or a fiction; but belief in his existence does not affect his imitation. Many Christians no

[1] For reasons that are still obscure.

longer believe in Christ; but they love him and try to follow his example. George Moore's St Paul remained a Christian even after he discovered that the Christ he worshipped existed only in the hearts of men.

Thus conscious inhibitions accepted by the ego are not based on ignorance, but on imitation. They cannot be destroyed by argument. But they can be destroyed by a new love. If a boy finds a new hero, he will acquire new scruples and will lose the old.[1]

Many inhibitions are unconscious. They were perhaps conscious to the child, but they have been forgotten. I suppose that they include both rational and irrational inhibitions based on fear, and inhibitions accepted by the ego. That part of the ego that contains such unconscious inhibitions is called the super-ego.

The moral prohibitions of the super-ego are formed like those of the ego. They are the prohibitions of an infantile ego that has become unconscious. They were originally the supposed commands of parents and nurses which have been adopted or introjected.

Since the super-ego is unconscious, its morality is automatic and without adaptability. Unlike conscious morality based on fear it is independent of ignorance and immune to reason. Unlike conscious morality accepted by the ego it is independent of present affections. It is unchanged by a change of allegiance.

But by analysis the super-ego can be made conscious, and then it is amenable to the same influences as the ego. Those inhibitions that are based on rational fears will remain. Those that are based on irrational fears will be removed by knowledge. And those that have been introjected may be lost if the old allegiance is incompatible with the new. Thus the man whose ignorance both of nature and of himself had been removed would lose all inhibitions based on irrational fears and outgrown loves. He would retain only that morality that was founded on rational fears and on the imitation of those persons he still consciously admired. Would a society of such individuals survive or perish?

[1] Therefore one should display the morals one desires others to possess.

THE NEUROTIC AND THE PERVERT

When a psycho-analyst speaks of a normal individual he does not mean an average person, but a person whose inhibitions have been as far as possible removed. Thus, the normal man is really the super-man. It is this deity whose morals we wish to determine. We may commence by fixing the characters that he does not possess; but which are conspicuous in his rival claimants to the earth – the neurotic and the pervert.

Both neurosis and perversion are due to unconscious inhibitions. That the super-ego is responsible for neurosis is fairly clear; but it is not obvious that a perversion can be due to an excess of inhibition. A perversion, however, results from fixations at primitive stages of development; and such fixations result from an inhibition of the stage that would otherwise have been reached.

Psycho-analysts divide sexual development into three stages – the oral, the anal, and the genital – which are again subdivided. The normal individual alone has reached the final stage. Both the pervert and the neurotic are fixed at a more primitive level.

The pervert differs from the neurotic in that some of his pre-genital sexuality is expressed almost in its original form. His eroticism is oral or anal rather than genital. His affections may be expressed sadistically or masochistically rather than as love. But the neurotic is repressed at the pre-genital as well as at the genital level. He must therefore disguise his sexuality as painful symptoms before he can relieve it.

Distinct from, but similar to, the pervert or the neurotic is the individual with the pervert or neurotic character. He has no gross abnormalities or symptoms; but his character is composed of near derivatives of these. Like the pervert and the neurotic his sexuality has not reached the final genital stage. It is partially inhibited at this level. Like the pervert and the neurotic his sexuality is fixed, at least partially, at the oral or the anal, or at most an early form of the genital, stage. But unlike the pervert he is not conscious of his fixation; and unlike the neurotic he does not express it in symptoms distressing to himself. Instead he expresses it in character traits that are distressing to others, or useless to himself.

Corresponding to the neurotic and the pervert, pre-genital

characters fall roughly into two types – the incompetent and criminal. The repressions of the criminal will only permit him to function anti-socially. Those of the incompetent prevent him from functioning at all. Neither are fully capable of developed love, nor of the social derivatives of this impulse.

The characteristics of neurotic and incompetent, or of pervert and criminal, can be classified according to the fixations that can occur. There are sucking oral types who prey upon their fellows or expect to be breast fed by the state. There are biting oral types who are sadistically avaricious, or who, reacting against such tendencies in themselves, are over-ready to discover it in others. There are productive anal types well suited to a capitalist society and repressed productives who regard wealth as vile. There are retentive anal types who are ungenerous, or who, reacting against their unconscious inclinations, are excessively conscientious, systematic and precise. And lastly, there are the phallic types of the first genital phase whose genital eroticism is developed, but who are still narcissistic and inadequately capable of a full object love.

THE NORMAL

The normal individual is so rare that his traits are less easy to describe. He will not be as arrogant as Nietzsche's super-man; for a limitless contempt of others is incompatible with a developed object love. Nor will he be a medieval Christ; for the meek have repressed the masculine component in this love. He will not be a Shavian ancient, a dementia praecox in the restitution phase, clear-headed but emotionless, capable of apprehending only the form of experience without its content.

Merejskowski's emperor Julian came nearer the concept of the normal when he dreamed of the Hellenic gods, not as they had been, but as they would become. After the neurotic Christendom of the dark ages had passed away Greek art would be rediscovered, and man would perfect the work that he had so long laid aside. The asceticism that refused to wash lest it should be led into temptation, or to think lest it should be excited to revolt, could not last for ever. Joy, beauty, and learning would return. They would even be disembarrassed from the last impurities of folly.

Perhaps Mr Wells envisages a similar ideal when he pictures a race of nude philosophers who punctuate their contemplations with free and amorous adventures.[1]

Psycho-analytic theory provides a definite base for such speculations. The normal man will be without genital inhibitions, he will enjoy an adequate sex life. He will not be fixed at a pre-genital level. He will not be unduly narcissistic. He will be capable of full object love.

The man who is capable of object love will have outgrown former stages. He will have outgrown his egotism, his ungenerosity, his dirtiness, his covetousness, and his parasitism.[2] But such characteristics of early stages of libidinal development he will not have repressed; he will have exchanged them for qualities that give him greater pleasure. Thus he will not possess the typical reactions that arise when early stages are repressed rather than outgrown. He will not be meek, nor gushing, nor fastidious, nor aggressively self-denying or independent. He will be neither pervert, nor neurotic.

But the normal man will retain some inhibitions – those based on rational fears and on the introjection of persons he still consciously admires. Since he will have outgrown his narcissism, those founded on personal fears will be unimportant.[3] But he will retain unweakened those based on introjections that he consciously approves. I believe that such restraints, acting upon normal individuals, would be sufficient to protect a culture which had already been evolved, and to secure those sublimations necessary to its further growth.

Therefore a society of normal individuals would probably be stable, and would almost certainly be pleasant. None would menace unduly the interests of his neighbours, and each would be able to protect his own. Laws would be unnecessary to curb the criminal or bolster the incompetent. And if there was a government at all, it would not greatly matter from which section of the community it was selected; since there would be

---

[1] [I would now (1977) question the word 'free' because I think a well-analysed (or 'normal') person would try not to torment his or her stable partner with suspicions of his or her promiscuity.]

[2] Corresponding respectively to the narcissistic, the second and first anal, and second and first oral stages.

[3] For, as Freud has shown, men can be physically afraid only when they love themselves.

no perverts to exploit, nor neurotics to mismanage, the public affairs. Is such a society likely to arrive; or is it a Utopian dream?

EDUCATION

The normal individual, as here defined, is rare today. The usual types are pervert or neurotic, criminal or incompetent. But, if the theory of psycho-analysis is correct, the normal could be produced by breeding and education.

It is recognized that the factor of inheritance helps to condition the development of abnormalities. But it is at present impossible to isolate this factor. A blue-eyed child possesses this character because he has inherited it from his parents; not because he has been brought up in the shadow of their example. But if a child resembles his parents in their neuroses, or in their perversions, we do not know how far he has inherited, and how far he has caught, these defects.[1] That is, we do not know how to apportion the responsibility for psychical abnormalities between inheritance and environment. The inherited disposition may be so strong that almost any environment would bring it out, or so weak that only exceptional circumstances could do so. The strength of the original disposition we cannot measure; but by analysis we can discover the events that developed it. Similarly, in studying the conditions of normality we must for the present neglect the eugenic factor and concentrate on the factor of education.

Education in the full sense of the word conveys knowledge of two kinds – knowledge of the world and knowledge of the self.[2] And corresponding to these two types of knowledge are two types of education – enlightenment and psycho-analysis. Enlightenment removes only those inhibitions that are based on conscious ignorance and superstition. But psycho-analysis eliminates those that are unconscious and whose very existence has only recently been discovered.

The genital inhibitions that distinguish the pervert from the normal are unconscious; so are the additional pre-genital inhibitions that distinguish the neurotic from the pervert.

---
[1] Except in cases where the abnormality is due to gross physical defects.
[2] Roughly speaking, knowledge of sensations and knowledge of ideas.

Therefore enlightenment alone cannot make a neurotic into a pervert or a pervert into a normal.

But inhibitions based on fears which are both conscious and irrational can be removed by enlightenment. If a man is already otherwise normal, enlightenment will not release antisocial impulses; for such impulses will have been outgrown. If he is already incompetent or neurotic it will not cure him, nor will it make him pervert; though it may make him more neurotic by removing the hope of a Paradise in which what he has missed in this life will be enjoyed in the next. If, however, he is already criminal or pervert, and restrained only by the fear of hell, enlightenment will make him a menace to his fellows. Therefore, those philosophers who have feared to educate the masses had grounds for their misgivings; for by education they understood enlightenment alone.

Before Freud it was possible to remove only those inhibitions that were founded upon ignorance and superstition; not those that were unconscious. But psycho-analysis can eliminate repression and convert the neurotic and the pervert into the normal. And, if the conclusions of this paper are correct, the normal is an asset and cannot be a menace to society. Therefore the world has nothing to fear and much to hope from analysis. Can it justify this hope?

It must be admitted that psycho-analysis is tedious and costly; that it requires a high degree of intelligence both in the doctor and in his patient; and that even when these conditions are fulfilled it does not always produce super-men. Nor is it very effective with the pure pervert who has no strong incentive to alter his condition. But the pervert is generally also a neurotic, and analysis does cure neurosis. And even when the cure is incomplete, it starts a development that continues of its own accord. Thus analysis, even under present conditions, will raise the efficiency of many and create some super-men.

But there is no reason why analysis should always be confined to the re-education of those who have already gone astray. A start has been made with the analysis of children, and with the study of ways of preventing the development of those inhibitions that would otherwise distort the normal growth. If these problems are solved, all problems of sociology and ethics will solve themselves, and a society of super-men will rule the earth.[1]

Thus, while enlightenment alone is dangerous, analysis alone is beneficial, and the combination of the two is even better. Will enlightenment destroy society before analysis has had time to save it?

[1] [This is overoptimistic, but without some overoptimism at the beginning, one might not pursue one's chosen work to the end. Whether this was true of Freud and Melanie Klein I do not know. But they were both overoptimistic at the beginning.]

4
Critical Abstract*

Abstract of Dr Giza Roheim's paper, 'After the Death of the Primal Father' (read at the Berlin Congress of 1922 and published in the ninth volume of *Imago*).

It is difficult for two reasons to do justice to Dr Roheim's paper in a short abstract. Firstly, because the value of his investigation consists as much in its wealth of material and incidental suggestions as in its positive conclusions. And secondly, because the topics with which it deals are not always separated in a way which makes them easy to summarize. I shall, however, try to present his main conclusions, and some of his evidence for them, as clearly as I can; though I know that I shall run the risks both of missing some important parts of his argument and of misinterpreting others.

Dr Roheim's arguments are mainly of two types, arguments from the present to the past, or from a later to an earlier date, and arguments from the past to the present, or from an earlier to a later date. I will try to treat these separately and will label them respectively *Reconstructions* and *Applications*.

Thus I have divided my abstract into two parts, each of which is again subdivided, as follows:

I. *Reconstructions* (a) of the primal crime of parricide from the Egyptian story of Osiris, and (b) of the events which followed this primal crime from primitive funeral rites.

II. *Applications* of the reconstruction of primal parricide and the reactions to it to solve certain psychological and anthropological problems, such as: (a) the origin of melancholia and mania and of funeral rites; (b) the origin of obsessional neurosis and of the medicine man; (c) the origin of birth ceremonies; (d) the origin of anxiety hysteria and paranoia.

* *B. J. Med. Psych.*, vol. IX, 1929.

I. RECONSTRUCTIONS

(a) *Reconstruction of the Primal Crime of Parricide from the Egyptian Story of Osiris*

Osiris, the son of the Sky-goddess Nut and of the Earth-god Sebk, had intercourse with his sister Isis while they were still within their mother's womb. He became the ruler of Egypt, and went through the land, reforming the wild customs and introducing agriculture and civilization. And in his absence his brother Set ruled in his stead. But on his return Set, with seventy-two accomplices and the Aethiopian queen Aso, conspired against him. At a feast they persuaded Osiris to lie down in a chest and when he had done this they closed the lid with nails and threw it in the sea (83).[1]

The chest was found by Isis, but she put it aside to visit her son Horus in the swamps of Buto. In the meantime Set, while hunting a wild boar, came across the body of Osiris, tore it in fourteen pieces and scattered them abroad. Then Isis sought the pieces, and found them all except the phallus which had been eaten by the fishes. So she made a wooden phallus instead and conceived from Osiris Horus who became the avenger of his father. In the battle, Horus lost his sight because Set threw dirt in his eye. But Set was defeated and lost his testicles. After the victory Horus became ruler of Egypt, like his father (83-4).

It is well known that one of the most fundamental means to the distortion of the first version of a myth is to duplicate, or multiply, the actors, so that each is represented in the later version by several persons. Now there are Pyramid texts which reveal no opposition between Horus and Set, which regard them as twins, or as one god with two heads. If, therefore, for the moment we eliminate Horus the avenger from the story we arrive at the following version. Horus (or Set) with the help of Isis killed his father the wild boar Osiris, dismembered, castrated and ate him (84). And this reconstruction is confirmed by a remark of Plutarch that the crocodile, which was sacred to Set, is the most disreputable of all animals, for he kills his father and has intercourse with his mother (85).

Now the fate of Osiris was only the repetition of the fate of

---

[1] Numbers refer to pages in *Imago*, vol. IX.

his own father; for, according to one account, he not only had intercourse with his sister Isis (who was a duplicate of his mother Nut) while they were still in the womb, but also castrated his father Sebk. Thus Osiris was a composite figure of a whole series of fathers who had been killed by the hand of their sons. Against him Horus and Set, and their accomplices, formed a unity. After his death this unity divided, and the hostile brothers, Horus the avenger and the principle of Good and Set the murderer and the Spirit of Evil, fought until Horus won and became the ruler of Egypt like his father (85).

Thus Roheim finds in the legend of Osiris a further record of that series of primal crimes with which Freud has made us familiar in his *Totem und Tabu*.

(b) *Reconstruction of the Events which Followed the Primal Crime from Primitive Funeral Rites*

To the Egyptians the slain Osiris was the prototype of all the dead, and everyone became Osiris after his death. Thus the legend of Osiris was repeated in the funeral ritual. If, therefore, funeral rites in general were modelled ultimately on a primal crime of parricide, it should be possible by studying such rites to reconstruct the state of the primal horde *after* the death of the father (85).

There are many customs among primitive or semi-civilized peoples in which a death is followed by a battle of the survivors. This battle may be either ceremonial, like the Olympic games in honour of the dead, or more serious, as in South Australia, where it is fanned by mutual accusations of murder (88). When a man of the Unmatjera or Kaitish tribe dies, his hair is given to one of his stepsons. The recipient of this gift must then set himself at the head of an expedition and challenge one of the other stepsons to a duel. After sufficient wounds have been given and received the combatants embrace and the first stepson gives the hair to the second, who in turn must challenge a third. And this process continues until all the stepsons have fought (88–9).

If we project these events into the primal horde we obtain a glimpse of the relations which must have followed the death of the leader. The stepsons were the husbands, or future husbands, of the dead man's daughters. Originally they were the brothers of the primal horde. After their crime their organization broke up and the former friends became foes (89). There was a state of *bellum omnium contra omnes* which lasted until a new leader succeeded either in killing his brothers, or in forcing them back into the group (87).

The reconstruction of this state of war within the leaderless brother horde is confirmed from other sources. Thus Atkinson observed that the young males of Ungulata (Huftieren) combine together (against the Leader) and then continue fighting among themselves until the old condition of females with one male leader, and a brother horde, is again established. The same battle is recorded in the Maori myth, which corresponds to the Greek story of Kronos, Uranos and Gaia, in which the separation of Sky and Earth was followed by a war of the brothers who had united against their father (88).

II. APPLICATIONS

The second and longest part into which I have divided Roheim's paper is concerned with *applications*, that is, with arguments from the past to the present or from an earlier to a later date.

It will perhaps facilitate a just appreciation of this part of his argument if I at once state the fundamental principle that seems to underlie it. This principle, which is sometimes explicit and sometimes implicit, is that individuals inherit not only the innate neural *structure* and corresponding mental *tendencies* of their ancestors, but some of the acquired neural *modifications* and corresponding mental *experiences* as well (88). From this it follows that the explanation of the symptoms of individuals in terms of their infantile experience is not complete and that it must be supplemented by an account of the experiences of their ancestors (86). It is in this ancestral experience that Roheim specializes, and from it he explains both abnormalities in the individual and customs in the race.

(a) *The Origin of Melancholia, Mania, and Funeral Rites*

Funeral rites. Primitive peoples regularly inflict serious wounds upon themselves after the death of their relations. And Preuss, as long ago as 1896, attributed these customs to an evil conscience and a desire for self-punishment (85). Now in many rites the original hostility to the dead is manifest. The corpse is beaten, stuck through with an arrow, mutilated or bound, or the ghost is driven away. Thus, the wounds which the mourners inflict upon themselves clearly result from aggressive impulses which have been turned in upon the self. And this result is confirmed by our knowledge that no neurotic has an impulse to suicide who has not formerly had an impulse to murder (86).

But, argues Roheim, the primitive mourner's aggressive impulses need not necessarily have been directed against his dead relation. And even if he possessed no such impulses he would abreact in the funeral rites an inherited sense of guilt. He is haunted by the ghost of countless slain fathers whose death he caused, and must atone for in his own body (86). Thus Roheim derives the unconscious destructive impulses and their inversion (together with the sense of guilt that this produces) from events which accompanied a series of primal crimes. He works out the details of this development as follows.

Destructive impulses are inverted because of inhibitions, and we may suppose that these inhibitions were originally external (87). The first inversion of such impulses, and the first division of the ego, is to be found in the war of the primal brothers which followed the murder of their father. Each fought to overthrow those with whom he had been united against the father; each behaved as the father had behaved before him; and each became, as it were involuntarily, the avenger of his father. Each broke out of the mass and became an individual, a personality who stood out against the mass, like the father before him. There was a further physical basis for this identification; for the sons had killed the father, eaten him, clothed themselves in his skin, and won his shin bone, his hair or his head as a trophy (89).

But this identification was not complete. Part of the personality remained a revolutionary. And for this part the battles which followed the death of the father were but new editions of the first great slaughter (89).

Now that part of the ego which was formed by the introection of the father came in its turn to inhibit what the father had formerly prevented. But the other part remained the mass-ego of the brother horde, and so were built the foundations of those two parts of the self, which are known respectively as the ego-ideal and the actual ego (90). Thus the identification of the brothers with the father resulted in the splitting off of a part of the self. And their external conflict was the cause of that inner division, which lives on in us in the conflict of actual-ego and ego-ideal (91-2).

The war of the primal brothers is, therefore, also the ultimate cause of the turning inwards of destructive impulses in the funeral customs of primitive peoples.

Melancholia. In the same reaction to the series of primal parricidal crimes Roheim seeks the origin of melancholia. There is a similarity between the mourning of savages and the sorrow of the civilized. Both include self-reproaches and tendencies to self-punishment. In melancholy there is, further, sleeplessness, disinclination for food, and a remarkable decline in the self-preservative instinct. Exactly in the same way the primitive mourner tortures, punishes and symbolically kills himself (92).

The self-reproaches of the melancholic originate from a critical factor within the ego; the conflict is between the two chief directions within the self. But originally these self-reproaches were reproaches directed against another person, who has become identified with a part of the ego. In the same way the self-punishments of primitive mourners were originally aggressive tendencies directed against the dead, that is, the father (92-3). Thus melancholia, like mourning customs, results from the inversion of destructive impulses. (But there is a complication which I may mention in passing. For, while the original hostility was directed from the ego to the father, the self-reproaches are directed from the introjected father to the ego. I can only suggest that the destructive impulse must have been projected on to the father before he was introjected.)

Roheim next seeks a common origin for the regression of libido in melancholia and certain other elements in primitive mourning customs. 'Of the three factors in melancholia, loss of the object, ambivalence and regression of libido into the ego, the first two recur in the obsessional neurotic's self-reproaches after a death (Freud)' (93). And these Roheim has already rediscovered in primitive mourning rites. It remains for him to rediscover the third – that is, the narcissistic regression of libido – and to trace it to its primal source (93).

This libidinal regression in melancholia is expressed especially in *refusal of nourishment* and in obstinate *silence* (93). So that we should expect to find that primitive mourning customs include equivalent taboos. In Australia the widow and the avenger, after they have eaten some of the dead man, may not speak; or, as an alternative, the eating of red-blooded animals may be tabooed. In Melanesia the abstinence after a death is attributed to the belief that the dead may have turned into food. And if the tabooed food is the same as that which at other times is eaten in a feast, it follows that the feast is itself a repetition of the sin of anthropophagy (93).

Roheim, at this point, feels that he is on the trail of the answer to the question: What is the real sin of the melancholic? or: In what situation were those mechanisms first developed which still operate in melancholia? After the death of the primal father, both the group organization and the psychic unity of the brothers collapsed. Outside raged the war of the rivals; inside the conflict between ego-ideal, which represented the father, and the old actual-ego. The sons had eaten the father; they continually desired to repeat their act; but something within them had become the father and inhibited the repetition of their sin (93-4).

That tabooed food is really identified with the primal father is confirmed by the Maori belief that such food is inhabited by a divine being. Thus the prohibition of anthropophagy spreads gradually to other foods, until there develops that increasing refusal of nourishment which is so characteristic of melancholia. The totemic taboos of food may be derived from the same source as the fasting of the mourner, or regarded as a permanent mourning taboo (94).

The melancholic refuses nourishment and punishes himself in every way, because he has committed the great sin of killing and eating his father. Through this act he has introjected the father as ego-ideal and reproduced internally, as the conflict of ego-ideal and actual-ego, the old conflict of father with son and brother with brother.

(Thus, it is clear that for Roheim a causal relation subsists between melancholia and mourning rites on the one hand and the reaction of the brother horde to parricide on the other. He would not agree that melancholia and mourning rites were due merely to the inversion of the destructive impulses of the civilized or primitive child *before they were expressed in action.* For him this inversion was acquired as the result of the acts of primal men and has been inherited, in a greater or lesser degree, by their descendants.)

Mania. The next part of Roheim's argument is concerned with an explanation of the periodicity of melancholia and mania. For, as he says, when we have found melancholia, mania cannot be far off (94).

Since there is so much similarity between mourning and melancholia, and since melancholia is followed by a phase of mania, one might expect that a period of mourning would be succeeded by a phase of triumph. And this expectation, though unjustified by the behaviour of the normal civilized man, is fulfilled by that of the savage. Among primitive people the period of mourning is frequently terminated by an orgy, a feast or a warlike expedition (94–5).

In Timor, at the end of the mourning period, great numbers of animals are slaughtered to satisfy the immense appetites of these people. They devour the meat half raw and drink only the strongest arrak. Under the influence of the alcohol the women spring up and begin to dance and to beat drums. At first they move slowly; then ever faster and with more noise. Meanwhile, the men, fascinated by the excitement, dress themselves in their battle array, and join the dance. The frenzy grows ever greater, until the dancers collapse exhausted. Thus here also, as in the psychoneurosis, mania follows melancholia (95–6).

In Australia the mourning period is ended either when the bones of the deceased have been ceremoniously collected and broken, or when his death has been revenged by the execution of the supposed murderer; that is, of the man whom the medicine men cite as the cause of the death. In Africa an animal may be offered instead of a man. But, in all these cases, the murder, which every death is to the unconscious, must be repeated; either on the corpse itself, as where its bones are broken, or on a substitute (95). Thus, just as the melancholic, who attacks himself, becomes the maniac, who attacks others, so the primitive mourner, who wounds himself, becomes the avenger, who wounds others (96).

Now we know from Roheim's previous argument that the avenger identifies himself, or part of himself, with the man he mourns. It is therefore especially interesting to learn that after he has avenged the death, and repeated the crime of which he unconsciously felt guilty, he identifies himself with the new victim. The Warramunga, after they have avenged a death, make a cigar-shaped model of the avenger out of the hair of his victim. This model is called a *tana*, and, as it plays a great rôle in the marriage ceremonies of these tribes, it must be a penis symbol. The kidney fat of the victim, which Wundt had already recognized as a sexual symbol, is also appropriated. And in these and other ways the avenger appropriates the powers and potency of his victim, and identifies himself with him (96).

But the second victim, who is introjected by the avenger, is already a double of the first. If, for instance, the bones of the first victim are burnt, his murderer, in virtue of their mystic unity, will surely die (96-7). Or again, the skulls, brought back after the head-hunting expedition which terminates the mourning period in Nias, become guardian spirits and are kept with the skulls of true ancestors (97). Thus the second victim is a double of the first and the vengeance is a repetition of the crime of which the avenger feels himself guilty.

But at the same time the act of vengeance frees the avenger from the anger of the ghost of the first victim. In Nias, when a king dies, a great number of heads must be procured. The head hunters, when they have done this, go to the grave of the king, and the eldest son makes his offering to the dead with the following words: 'Free from reproach is the man, free from sin is your son, you have received your share, your honour, your reward.' Then he goes home and the priest prays to the ghost of the dead: 'Do not be angry any longer with our children, you have been paid in full, do not be angry any longer with our sons, you have received your glory and your honour.' Thus the enemy falls as a substitute for the son, who would himself suffer from the anger of the dead if he did not find another victim (97).

The connection between the last three stages of Roheim's

argument will perhaps become clearer if I try to summarize them as follows. In virtue of three identifications – that of the first victim with his murderer, and those of the avenger with both – the act of vengeance is at once a repetition of the murder and a suicidal atonement for it. Roheim, however, hardly stops to record this valuable anthropological result; but applies it immediately to the psychological problem of the origin of mania. Since the triumph that follows the primitive mourning is a repetition of the crime, mania is also a repetition. But it is not an immediate repetition of the primal crime which caused the first mourning; it is a repetition of a repetition of this crime. And for this reason, mania still follows melancholia, and does not precede it (98).

Rutting period. Thus Roheim reduces melancholia and mania respectively to the primal brothers' mourning for their father, and to the fresh crime that terminated this mourning. But in the periodicity of the psychoneurosis he sees a relic of the two seasons into which the life of our pre-human ancestors was divided. These two seasons I will call in English the rutting season and the eating season (Periode der reinen Nahrungsaufnahme). Only in the rutting season could the aim-inhibited sexual impulses break out in their old form. Only in the rutting season could the brothers acquire the courage to attack the father. The behaviour of a maniac is not unlike that of an animal in the rutting season. And, if mania is a repetition of the rutting period, the overflowing of object-cathexis would be explained. Then melancholia would correspond to the pure eating period, in which libido is withdrawn from objects and concentrated in the ego. But it would correspond not to a normal but to a disturbed eating period. For eating is disturbed by guilt, by the division of the ego. The melancholic does not eat because he has eaten the primal father (98–9).

(Before passing on to the next topic of Roheim's paper, it may be relevant to observe that the part of the argument which refers to the periodicity of melancholia and mania, does not necessarily involve Lamarckian assumptions. For the periodicity of rutting and eating, which Roheim rediscovers in the manic-depressive, may have been acquired by variation and selection alone.)

(b) *The Origin of Obsessional Neurosis and of the Medicine Man*
The Australian shaman, in his initiation, is supposed to be torn in pieces by ghosts and put together again in a supernatural form. And the ghosts that do this are ancestral spirits; that is, representatives of the father imago. Thus the initiation is the reversal of the story of the killing of the primal father. It symbolizes, by the mechanism of reversal, the sons killing, eating and introjecting the father, and thereby winning a superinfantile or supernatural power (100).

But certain features of the initiation remain unexplained. The Australian shaman is especially characterized by two appliances, his magical quartz crystal and his magical bones. If we can show these to be objectivations of human impulses, we shall have solved the problem of the Australian medicine man, and probably also found the origin of the spirit of medicine and of science in general (100).

The quartz crystal must be in some way connected with the intestines, and be some kind of stuff into which the flesh of the devoured father has been changed. For the spirits disembowel the future medicine man and equip him instead with brand new intestines and with a quartz crystal which he keeps in them or in his stomach. Some of the Australian tribes say that the quartz crystal is the excrement of the Sky-god. It is, therefore, an excrement symbol, and we may guess that it represents the excrement of the eaten father, or his flesh which has become excrement. And in confirmation of this supposition we find in West Australia that the magical stuff *boglia* is acquired at the death of the father; and that the only source of it is the human body, especially the anus. Thus we can understand why the quartz crystal is the source of the shaman's power (101).

This crystal can be used for making people ill as well as for curing them. And it is probable that the evil purpose was the older, and that medicine is a reaction formation against black magic (102). This supposition receives some confirmation from its ability to explain a custom among the Kobéua. The doctors of these people are paid by gifts of many kinds. But there is one notable exception. They are never paid in arrows. Now the arrow is one of the special weapons of the evil magician. So that to give the doctor arrows would be a tactless allusion to his less reputable past (103).

So far Roheim has reached two conclusions: that the medicine man makes use of excrement symbols, and that he is derived from the black magician. The next step is to show that the magician is also fixed at the anal level. And this is not difficult; for his method of killing people is to burn their excrement (103). Thus in the black magician we find a stage between the anal-sadistic perversion and the obsessional neurosis. A displacement of the direct anal-sadistic activities has already taken place; for the act of killing is performed only on the excrement and in the hallucinatory wish fulfilment. But these tendencies have not yet been fully repressed. This repression occurs when the black magician becomes the medicine man who heals instead of killing. Thus the origin of medical science, like the origin of the obsessional neurosis, is to be found in the repression of the anal-sadistic impulses. The first obsessional neurotic was at the same time the first doctor (103).

This connection between the medicine man, and the obsessional neurotic is well illustrated by a clinical case reported by Brill. The patient is fifty-nine years old, and suffers from obsessional neurosis. He is obsessed by fears that someone will be killed. In his childhood he had exhibited anal erotic tendencies, and a remarkable inclination to cruelty. He soon learnt to shoot, and went about killing small animals and birds. At puberty he became suddenly sympathetic. And one day, after shooting a squirrel, he suffered from qualms of conscience. After this, he found it difficult to shoot. When the patient was eighteen a serious obsessional neurosis developed. He suffered, among other things, from constipation, which no medicine could help, until one day he invented the following cure. He took a reel of thread on which was a picture of a child and rolled it until he saw the picture, which he then stuck with a nail. This game had the desired effect. Later he modified it by drawing on a piece of paper a picture, which he imagined to be a girl, and throwing his pen at it. Or, when he was in the country, he took his gun and fired a few shots in the air, imagining that he was shooting Indians. The parallel between shooting and defecation is here clear. Not being able to shoot, and the repression of sadism, was expressed in the inability to defecate. This patient repeated exactly the rites of the primitive magician, who also sticks nails into pictures, either as a love charm or to secure vengeance. Once the patient, while playing with pens and nails, developed the obsessional fear that a nail had fallen out of the window and had been swallowed by a child. This thought caused him the greatest anxiety. One step further, and he would have developed the compulsion to take needles out of children, in order to save them from the death that he wished to cause (103–5). In the same way, the medicine man shoots some substance that causes illness, such as the quartz crystal, into his patients, and then sucks it out again (103).

The chief characteristic of the obsessional neurosis, the feeling of compulsion, is found in the primitive medicine man in two forms. First there is the original form. The medicine man believes that he is compelled by the invincible power of the spirits to act against his will. Every day he observes a complicated ritual, which must at all costs be performed. Freud once called the obsessional neurosis the taboo-disease, and the medicine man is more than his fellows surrounded with taboos. But in the primitive medicine man the sense of compulsion is also found in a projected form. He believes in the compulsive power of his ritual, which is the projection of that compulsion of which he is himself the victim. Now Ferenczi has explained the infantile sense of omnipotence as the projection of the anal urge which cannot be withstood. And in fact the medicine man materializes his power in an excrement symbol, the quartz crystal. Therefore his magical formulae, like his habit of collecting the most varied and useless objects in his medicine bag, is again the result of his anal fixations.

Another characteristic of the obsessional neurotic is his compulsive questioning. This is derived both from his ambivalence and his libidinal cathexis of thought, and is well suited to account for the origin of medicine, and of science in general (105–6).

Oral factors. Roheim next turns to the oral erotic factors in primitive medicine which he has not yet explained. It will be remembered that Abraham has designated the first phase of libidinal development as the oral or cannibalistic phase (107). And, since the medicine man, or shaman, not only incorporates his ego-ideal by eating his father, but also heals by sucking, we must suppose that he is fixed at this level (107). The oral activities of cannibalism and sucking are still more evident in the evil magician. He is regularly described as a blood-sucker and man-eater. In Central Africa the magician can turn himself into a hyena or a leopard or some other animal which eats corpses, and magic and cannibalism are denoted by the same word. Similarly, in the Betoya language the same word is used for witch doctor and jaguar. Among the Ba Tonga the black magician inherits his power from his mother; it is absorbed with his mother's milk. And later he kills others by sucking their blood (107-8).

After further illuminating examples, Roheim continues his comparison between the black magician and the medicine man. The magician steals excrement to burn. The medicine man can cause illness, but he also heals it; he shoots excrement symbols into the body and sucks them out again. As the life-saving activities of the medicine man are the reversal of the life-giving activity of the mother, so are the corresponding physical processes partially reversed. The child sucks milk from his mother and returns it in the form of excrement. The medicine man shoots excrement symbols into his victim, and sucks out, not milk, but these same excrement symbols. In the evil magician we find unsublimated sadistic impulses. In the medicine man we find the same impulses; but owing to his identification with his patient, they are in an inhibited, that is, a sublimated form. The evil magician allows blood to flow from the veins of his victim, or he sucks it out, until he dies. The medicine man does the same thing to his patient. He bleeds him, or sucks blood or other substances from the wound, or licks the injured spot. But instead of entirely eating up his patient, as he had begun to do, he heals him (109-10).

So far Roheim has illustrated the oral and anal elements in the magician and the reaction formations against these fixations in the medicine man and the obsessional neurotic. It remains for him to reduce medicine and the obsessional neurosis to the primal crime. Only those brothers, he says, who were strong enough secured a piece of the father to eat. And in these, repression commenced through the oral and anal counter cathexis of the corpse. These formed the first club, and their repressed impulses gave rise to secret rites. Among them there were dispositional differences. Some were more fixed in those impulses which are connected with the taking of nourishment, that is, they were fixed in the oral and anal erotic stages of development. These remained permanently fixed on the counter cathexis. They did not cease to eat the dead father and to identify themselves with his rotting corpse; though the rest had overcome this stage at the end of the mourning period. The father whom they had eaten was the repression within them. He was that which divided them, which inhibited them in the execution of their genital Oedipus desires, and compelled regression to the pre-genital stage. Through the further repression of this stage the science of medicine was developed in the past, just as the obsessional neurosis is developed in the present (112).

(c) The Origin of Birth Ceremonies

The Arunta, in order to multiply kangaroos, bleed themselves over the rock grave of their common ancestor. Hence, since blood letting is a coitus symbol and the grave is a symbol of the vagina, the ancestral father must have acquired a female character. And it is probable that he acquired this character when the brothers, by eating him, revived the oral erotic pleasure of sucking at the breast (113).

This same displacement of libido seems to underlie the rebirth ceremonies in rites of initiation and consecration. The primal brothers ate the slain father. But the initiates are supposed to be eaten by a male being and reborn by him. Thus not only is the original story reversed, but the original object has become the mother as well as the father.

Roheim also says that the initiates identify themselves with the father instead of the mother, and thereby fulfil the purpose of the rite, which is to release the youths from the influence of the women and attach them instead to the male society (113–14).

Thus I take Roheim to mean that the initiation rite symbolizes three things; eating and being eaten by the father, and being reborn by him. By eating the father, the initiates identify themselves with him, and him with the mother from whom they received their milk. And these two identifications, of the sons with the father and of the father with the mother, combine to determine the reversal of the fantasy of eating the father. For the sons have indirectly become the mother who was in their infancy eaten by them, and the father has become the mother who conceives by eating human flesh.

There are many rites in which a rebirth from the father, who is at the same time the mother, is represented. Among the Basuto the candidate for purification is dragged through a hole in a slaughtered animal. When Peleus captured the town of Iolcos, he killed the king and queen and marched his army into the city between the pieces of their bodies. Now this queen was supposed to be in love with Peleus, and in her disappointment to have persuaded her husband to try and kill him. Thus the story, like the legend of Potiphar's wife, is a distortion of the Oedipus motive, in which the marching of the army between the pieces of the king and queen must symbolize incestuous coitus and rebirth (114–15).

The purificatory value of such rites seems to be explained as follows. In the primal horde the brothers expiated their deed through eating their sire and converting him from the hated father to the loved mother. They ate the father as in infancy they drank their mother's milk, and perhaps they also crawled through his body in order to free themselves from the sin of incest by repeating it in a new form (115).

(d) The Origin of Anxiety Hysteria and Paranoia

In the pre-human period of our history there were no inhibitions. But there were two barriers to protect the ego from the limitless pretensions of the libido. Firstly there was the periodicity of the rutting and non-rutting seasons. And secondly there was the resistance of the father. When, through an improvement in the food supply, humanity lost the non-rutting period, the ego had to find some new way of protecting itself against an excess of genital libido. This was especially necessary after the death of the father, and was accomplished by eating and introjecting him as the ego-ideal which barred the way to the mother.

But at the same time the corpse gained libido which was transferred from the mother's breasts. So that the hated father became the beloved dead. Since, however, this love could not be satisfied it was converted into fear [*sic*]. The guilty murderers, says Roheim, feared to be eaten by those animals that fed on corpses like themselves. And behind this fear was the wish to be sexually assaulted by the father (116–17). (But the trend of Roheim's argument seems to imply that these animals were first feared for another reason – because they awoke the son's unconscious oral desires to feed upon the corpse.)

The same mechanism explains the wolf phobia in the history of an infantile neurosis published by Freud. And, in general, the infantile anxiety hysteria is an attempt of the ego to avoid the pretensions of an earlier love. But in the history of the human race, this necessity to control the limitless pretensions of the libido can only have arisen after that separation of genital and ego impulses, which is so characteristic of animals, had come to an end. And from this it follows that animal phobias are repetitions of philogenetic totemism, not merely in their unconscious content, but also in their libido economy (i.e., in their conversion into fear of libido which cannot be employed) (116–17).

This conversion of homosexuality into fear is also the mechanism in paranoia. The paranoiac feels himself hemmed by the supernatural emanations of certain people who are obviously father substitutes. And Roheim seeks the key to these delusions of persecution in the homo-erotic impulses of the brother horde. After the death of the father, the brothers became rivals and each saw in the others reproductions of the conquered father. Each had eaten the father, and the fear of him recurred as fear of the brothers. By killing and eating their father they had also had symbolic intercourse with him (117). And perhaps I shall not misinterpret Roheim's meaning if I finish the argument which he breaks off as follows. The fear of the brothers for each other, and the origin of paranoia, was the conscious reaction of their unconscious desire to repeat with each other the intercourse which they had enjoyed symbolically by eating their father.

SUMMARY

The main points of Roheim's paper may perhaps be summarized as follows.

The story and the funeral rites of Osiris, especially when compared with similar myths and customs, record a series of primal crimes followed by brother wars.

These primal events left engrams in the race which account both for primitive customs and neurotic symptoms.

When the primal father was eaten he was introjected and became the ego-ideal, whose conflict with the actual-ego lives on in the self-punishments of the primitive mourner and in the self-reproaches of the melancholic. These internal conflicts are repetitions both of the primal revolution and of the brother war.

The war of the brothers gave place to a war with strangers, and for this reason primitive mourning rites are followed by expeditions of revenge, and melancholia is followed by mania. The periodicity of melancholia and mania is also a survival of the periodicity of the non-rutting and the rutting periods.

The ego-ideal, that is, the introjected primal father, inhibited genital impulses and thereby caused oral and anal regressions. Those individuals in whom such regressions were permanent became magicians, obsessional neurotics, or doctors. All three are alike in their oral and anal fixations; but differ in the degree of repression and sublimation of these pre-genital impulses.

By eating the primal father, the brothers identified him with the mother whose milk they had once drunk. Hence the initiate's ceremonial repetition of the primal crime was distorted to symbolize, not only parricide, but also coitus and rebirth.

The corpse of the primal father, by acquiring a maternal character in addition to its own, became the object of both active and passive homosexual desires. Because these desires could not be fulfilled they were projected and gave rise to totemism, anxiety hysteria and paranoia.

APPRECIATION AND CRITICISM

Every psycho-analyst will admit the probability of Roheim's vivid reconstruction of the lives of primal sons; and will appreciate his rediscovery of similar psychic mechanisms both in the customs of savages and in the symptoms of neurotics.

But there may be some who will doubt whether the explanation of this similarity requires that Lamarckian theory which

Roheim obviously accepts. To such critics the presence of identical mechanisms in primal lives, primitive rites and neurotic symptoms, would seem to be due to similar dispositions to incest and parricide – dispositions which have been acquired by variation and selection, and which are expressed in the acts of primal man and in the wishes of the primitive or cultured child. But to suppose further that such similarities result from an inherited experience would seem to the Darwinian critic to involve a most dangerous biological assumption which is required only to belittle the importance of the experience of the individual child.

However, the value of Roheim's paper consists perhaps more in his discoveries of parallels than in his Lamarckian explanations of them. And this value is unaffected by the issue of the dispute between rival evolutionists.

In conclusion, I must repeat my hope that in making an abstract of this paper I have neither omitted nor misinterpreted anything that is vital. I have given Roheim's paper, like the body of Osiris, after it has been dismembered and reunited. I hope it will not, like Osiris, have been robbed of anything of prime importance.

5

The Remote Consequences of Psycho-analysis on Individual, Social and Instinctive Behaviour*[1]

In this paper I have made use of a rather behaviouristic interpretation of psychological mechanisms which I am elaborating elsewhere,[2] but which must be briefly recapitulated here.[3]

The organism, as I understand it, is so constructed that it must react to the *primary* stimuli of *injuries* and *needs* until they are *removed*. It also reacts to the *secondary* stimuli of *threats* as if they were primary and so *avoids* real injuries and needs; and its removal and avoidance reactions often involve as preliminary reactions the *seeking* of *means*.

The terms used in this paragraph more or less explain themselves; but, since they will be employed throughout the subsequent discussion, it is perhaps desirable to illustrate them by examples. Two primary types of stimuli were distinguished and called *injuries* and *needs*. A cut or a burn is an injury; hunger

---

* *B. J. Med. Psych.*, vol. XI, 1931.
[1] This paper was read before the medical section of the British Psychological Society on 27 May 1931. My thanks are due to all those with whom I have discussed it either before, at, or after the meeting.
[2] In my forthcoming book, *The Development of Sexual Impulses*. This paper is largely taken from the last chapter, and appears here by the kind permission of Messrs Kegan Paul. I have no doubt that a correlation between behaviouristic and psychological mechanisms will be eventually established and that, in particular, it will some day be possible to give an account of the effect of psycho-analysis in behaviouristic terms. But I am not yet sure how far the attempt to do so which is presupposed by this paper has been successful. Some of the psycho-analysts have told me that they find their science unrecognizable in my behaviouristic garb. How far this is due to the use of different language to express the same facts, and how far it is due to defects in my theory, I am not at present able to judge.
[3] [Although I still (1977) think it might be possible to express psycho-analytic truths in behaviouristic terms, I now believe that the desire to do so may be a defence against full acceptance of psycho-analytic discovery, not merely in theory, but as something one has become familiar with as a conscious part of oneself.]

or sexuality a need. Two types of secondary stimuli were also introduced, *threats* and *means*. The visual impression of a candle is a threat to the burnt child. The visual impression of a beef steak is a means to a hungry man. So much for stimuli. Among reactions three main types were distinguished, *removals*, *avoidances* and *seekings*. Withdrawing the hand is the removal reaction to the primary injury of a burn. Withholding the hand is the avoidance reaction to the threat of the candle flame. Eating is the removal reaction to the primary need of hunger. Hunting game may be a seeking reaction which is a necessary preliminary to this removal.

Now the organism sometimes makes mistakes which may be called *inappropriate reactions*. These seem to be principally of two kinds. The organism may avoid something which irrelevantly resembles a real threat, or it may seek something which inadequately resembles a real means. If a burnt child avoids electric light bulbs he is avoiding something which irrelevantly resembles a candle and his reaction may be called an *irrelevant avoidance*. The stimulus to an irrelevant avoidance may be called a *false threat*. If a hungry infant seeks his thumb he is seeking something which inadequately resembles the nipple, and (apart from the secondary erotic satisfaction of his act) his reaction may be called an *inadequate seeking*.[1]

I believe, though I have not worked it out in sufficient detail, that what the process of re-education known as psychoanalysis really does is to eliminate, or recondition, irrelevant avoidances and inadequate seekings. The primary aim of psycho-analysis, in opposition to the avowed aim of all other therapeutic methods, is not to cure but to make conscious. The cure is a secondary result, and its mechanism has, I think, always been rather a mystery. This mystery, however, disappears if we regard neuroses as made up of irrelevant avoidances and inadequate seekings. The process of analysis compels the patient to recognize these for what they are, and he in consequence naturally discards them.

[1] Dr C. P. Blacker, in the discussion of this paper, pointed out that even false threats may produce a real stimulus. For example, an irrelevant fear may cause the secretion of adrenalin just as much as a real fear. In such cases the reaction which avoids or removes the false threat is adequate to the adrenalin stimulus even if it is irrelevant in the sense that it is part of a train of reactions evoked by a situation which irrelevantly resembles a real threat.

REMOTE CONSEQUENCES OF PSYCHO-ANALYSIS

Apart altogether from psycho-analysis, there appears to have been throughout evolution a definite, though fluctuating, growth in self-knowledge, that is, in consciousness of motives. But psycho-analysis has very greatly accelerated this process. It seems, therefore, possible that we are on the threshold of a rational age, in which our species will become increasingly conscious of their motives, and increasingly able to distinguish adequate from inadequate seekings and relevant from irrelevant avoidances. But, lest I should be accused of a too light-hearted optimism, I will add that I am speaking of geological rather than of historical periods of time.

If such a process of enlightenment is really taking place it becomes interesting to speculate concerning its theoretical limits. What types of inappropriate reaction are likely to be eliminated by the kind of self-knowledge which analysis is giving its patients and, to some extent, to the world at large? Are any of the sublimations, and even instincts, we most value strictly speaking inappropriate reactions? Are they endangered? Should we be worse or better off without them?

A. INDIVIDUAL CONSEQUENCES

If the symptoms, sublimations and perversions of the individual were carefully considered it would probably be found that they were all inappropriate reactions to the situations which first evoked them, but that some had acquired a secondary relevance or adequacy. Indeed the presence of a secondary real value may perhaps be used as a criterion to distinguish the sublimation from the symptom and to a lesser extent from the perversion.[1] Further, it seems to be the presence of this secondary real value which protects the sublimation from the destructive effect of a theoretically complete analysis.[2]

---

[1] In some cases, of course, a symptom has a rather spurious secondary value. It may, for instance, be the means of securing a pension. But I will neglect such complications in the interests of simplicity.

[2] I am not satisfied that the presence of a secondary adequacy or relevance is the only criterion which separates those inadequate and irrelevant reactions which are not destroyed by self-knowledge from those that are. Probably a better criterion could be given in hedonic terms. But I do not yet know what is the physiological correlate of pleasure. It is almost certainly not diminution of stimulus.

(1) *Negative Symptoms*

Irrelevant avoidances with no secondary relevance seem to make up the reaction formations in the neuroses. Thus the phobias and the compulsions are characteristic neurotic avoidances. A phobia of snakes, for example, is an irrelevant avoidance of a particular phallic symbol. Such avoidances are superimposed upon seekings. It is not quite so obvious that the compulsions are irrelevant avoidances because they are rather more complicated. But although they may be fused with inadequate seekings their foundation is a reaction formation, or an avoidance. Thus in a case quoted by Freud a young girl could not sleep without a lengthy ceremonial to prevent the possibility of her bolster touching the end of her bed. The contact between these objects symbolized to her the union of her parents which in her ceremonial she symbolically and therefore irrelevantly prevented.[1]

Irrelevant avoidances of this nature may be called negative symptoms. They have no secondary relevance and they tend to disappear when they are understood.

(2) *Negative Sublimations*

Irrelevant avoidances that have a secondary relevance form one type of sublimation. Thus the statesman who devotes his life to the protection of his country against a remote danger may owe his energy to a symbolic or irrelevant resemblance between the idea of foreign aggression and the unconscious fear of castration. But if the danger happens to be real this type of anxious patriotism has a secondary relevance and is a sublimation rather than a neurotic symptom.

Irrelevant avoidances of this kind might be called negative sublimations. They have acquired a secondary relevance and may in consequence survive the exposure of their first motive.

[1] A case reported by Reik (Endphasen des religiösen und des zwangsneurotischen Glaubens, *Imago*, XVI, 26) well illustrates the fusion of an inadequate seeking with an irrelevant avoidance. A neurotic young woman suffered from the obsessional fear lest she might have left the tap on in the bathroom and from the compulsion to go there several hundred times each day to make quite sure. The analysis recalled a scene with her bridegroom, in which she had feared that he might have an ejaculation. Her compulsive action, in which she had to turn the tap on in order to see that it was properly turned off, symbolized at once her desire to secure this event and her reaction against this desire.

(3) *Positive Symptoms*

Inadequate removals and seekings without secondary adequacy make up the positive side of the neuroses. They may be best illustrated in hysterical symptoms. Thus an hysteric, in situations in which the normal man would have an erection, may develop a deep blush or a swelling of the foot or react in some equally inadequate manner. Such reactions do not merely have no secondary adequacy, but they are usually acutely painful. They are inadequate not merely because the adequate reaction does not happen to have been discovered, but because it is actively inhibited. To cause their disappearance it is not sufficient to disclose their inadequacy, which is usually obvious enough. It is also necessary to discover the irrelevance of the inhibition. But analysis can and does secure both these discoveries. Such symptoms have no secondary relevance and tend to disappear when they are fully understood.

(4) *Positive Sublimations*

Inadequate seekings with a secondary adequacy make up what we may term the positive sublimations. Thus the statesman who devotes his energies to the conquest of another country may owe his motive to an unconscious desire to conquer a woman. But aggressive imperialism, if it is successful, may have a secondary adequacy as a reaction to a real economic need. It might therefore survive the loss of its original motive.

(5) *Perversions*

Lastly, we may distinguish a type of removal or seeking which is semi-adequate, and I think that the perversions should be included in this class. A perversion is a regression to an earlier level of development. It may be adequate to infantile needs, but it is not wholly adequate to the adult needs into which these earlier ones have developed. Thus the sexual impulse is partly developed from and includes the oral, anal and urethral needs of infancy. But if the genital reaction is inhibited the sexual needs of the adult cannot be satisfied. The perversion, however, which is a regression to an earlier reaction that may have been adequate to the pre-genital needs of the infant, is still a partial satisfaction. Therefore the perversion, unlike the neurotic symptom, does not leave the despondence of complete futility, and it is in consequence more difficult to cure. If the inhibitions of the genital response are understood, the perversion will be largely replaced by a more adequate response. But when it involves no serious inconvenience it may survive as a part of the preliminaries of the adequate genital reaction.[1]

(6) *The Elimination of Inappropriate Reactions*

The fundamental effect of self-knowledge is, we have argued, the elimination of inadequate or irrelevant reactions. The neuroses, which are wholly irrational in this sense, will therefore tend to disappear. The perversions, which are partly inadequate, will tend to be replaced by more adequate impulses; while the sublimations, which possess a secondary adequacy or relevance, will be likely to survive the loss of the motives which originally produced them.

But we may inquire whether in a society of completely enlightened individuals sublimations ever could arise. It would seem at first sight that if children discovered, or were taught, the real means to all their needs immediately these first occurred, and were never deceived by false threats, they might be deprived of those errors which would later be so useful. But it is inconceivable that such a condition could occur; for children must teach themselves by trial and error, and they acquire the mistakes which develop into sublimations before they can understand enough to learn from others. False threats of castration in particular, and of aphanisis in general, inhibit the discovery of adequate seekings so that a great variety of inadequate substitutes are quickly developed. If, however, psychology ever began to endanger the sublimations of the child, the adult, who had learnt their secondary value, would be likely to postpone such a destructive education.

B. SOCIAL CONSEQUENCES

We will now turn to consider the possible social consequences of increased self-knowledge. To the psycho-analyst the great

[1] [I would now (1977) define a perversion in a stricter way to describe a sado-masochistic defence – ultimately against mourning (see D. Meltzer, *Sexual States of Mind*).]

mass movements of society are collective neuroses or collective sublimations. We have seen that the effect of that deepening of self-knowledge, which psychology will bring, will tend to eliminate neuroses in the individual. We have now to inquire which of the social manifestations have no secondary relevance or adequacy. These, since they are comparable to the negative and positive symptoms of the individual, seem doomed to ultimate extinction. The process may be slow, and it may not be continuous, but it will be sure. There may be dark ages in the future as in the past. But from time to time there will be waves of enlightenment which will surpass all their predecessors, and there are no sands of irrationality which will not be eventually submerged.

We shall attempt here to separate the rational from the irrational in religion, morality and politics, and therefore to predict their fate.

(1) *Social Consequences – Religious*

Religion is made up of avoidances as well as of seekings, and the negative side is almost certainly the older. Thus when Freud speaks of an obsessional neurosis as a private religion he is thinking chiefly of the negative and more archaic side of religion, for the obsessional neurosis is composed chiefly of avoidances.

(a) *Negative religion.* Negative religion may be again roughly subdivided into two kinds, according to whether what is avoided is the threat of punishment for rebellion against God, or whether it is the impulse to rebellion itself.

We know that when the Oedipus complex is repressed the hostile tendencies are often projected and inverted against the self and feared as a threat of punishment. It is this threat from the inverted hostile impulses of the self which is feared in the first type of negative religion. The religious melancholics who suffer from it are tortured by constant fear of Hell fire or of the wrath of God. Their attempts at propitiation by self-punishment provide some outlet for their inverted aggressiveness, and where the sexual impulse is also inverted the penance may give a masochistic satisfaction.

The first step in the understanding of a pathological fear of the wrath of God exposes this fear as an irrelevant avoidance of an inverted aggressive impulse. The next step exposes this inverted impulse as inadequate because it is directed against the self instead of against the external object which originally provoked it. Thus at a certain phase in the process of enlightenment the fear of God may be replaced by a more primary hate of Him, which may alternate or co-exist with an even stronger love.

The second type of negative religion which we defined as the fear of rebelling against God, rather than as the fear of the wrath of God, occurs when the aggressive impulses are repressed without being inverted against the self. Just as the obsessional neurotic devotes his energies to the avoidance of any action which resembles, however remotely, the execution of his unconscious hostile wishes, so the negatively religious man of the second type is always over-anxious lest he should do anything hostile to his God. His religion is a mass of ceremonials and taboos. He must pray in a certain manner in order to prevent the intrusion of blasphemous thoughts. He must fast on certain occasions, like the savage whose totem is taboo, to repress his theophagic inclinations. And he must undertake no enterprise on the Sabbath lest he should repeat the dismemberment of his totem god which once occurred on this day. Analysis would convince him that his elaborate rites avoid the symbol rather than the reality of revolt and that they are therefore irrelevant. Thus he also would pass into a stage in which his irrelevant obsessional avoidances of revolt against God were replaced by a conscious ambivalence.

If such an individual's understanding of his own motives terminated with the realization that he hated God, he would remain ambivalent, and might alternate between militant atheism and passionate belief. But the avoidance of revolt determined by the more powerful love would be at least relevantly directed against a conscious hostility rather than irrelevantly against mere symbols.

If, however, his self-understanding continued to deepen he would soon realize that God was a symbol for his father, who would then become the object of his conscious ambivalence. In other words, he would realize that his hate of God was inadequate because it was directed against the wrong object.

The last and final stage of the analysis would be to show that this hate is in itself inadequate.

There was nothing psychologically inadequate or irrelevant about the original construction of the Oedipus complex, except in so far as the incestuous impulses which started the whole process were partly founded not on real needs but on false threats of needs. But what is inadequate and irrelevant is the survival of hate long after the time at which it might have been really appropriate. The basis of the Oedipus complex of the adult, which is the persistence of incestuous impulses, is perhaps not even wholly inadequate.

The persistent unconscious seeking of the mother seems to be made up of two parts, one adequate and one irrelevant. In so far as she is sought as a means to the removal of real oral and genital needs she is sought adequately. But in so far as the motive for this seeking is loneliness, that is, a false threat of hunger and aphanisis, the seeking is an irrelevant avoidance of a false threat, i.e., it is due to a neurotic anxiety. Therefore one element in the continued seeking of the mother who was known in the first months of infancy is not so much the seeking of an object which inadequately resembles a real means, as the seeking of an object that no longer exists. Analysis cannot prevent us from seeking the impossible. But, what is more important, it can convince us that our fathers are no longer the real impediments to our desires and that to hate them is to hate inadequately. Freud seems to believe that this hate is indestructible and is a permanent danger to society,[1] but we may perhaps adopt the more optimistic view that it is preserved by an unconscious misunderstanding of the causes of frustration and that it can be analysed away.

(b) *Positive religion.* We may turn now to positive religion. Positive religion is not made up of avoidances but of seekings. The dominant note is not the fear of the wrath of God or fear of revolting against Him, but an intense desire for an ever more intimate union with Him. For the psycho-analyst it is not hard to understand the development of these impulses. The demands of the child are insatiable and doomed to disappointment. All

---

[1] Das Unbehagen in der Kultur.

his life he dimly remembers the mother of his first months who seemed to fulfil all his needs and all his life he seeks her. She is the ideal woman whom he will some day meet and who will make him happy, and unless he realizes that this dream is an impossibility his marriages are likely to be numerous and of short duration.

Paradoxically as it may sound, one of the first mother substitutes to which the child partially transfers his intense affection is his father. At this age he makes little distinction between the sexes, and when his mother ceases to satisfy him completely he readily expects what he misses from that other member of his family whom he sees more rarely and who in consequence has less opportunity to disappoint him.[1]

The father is therefore not only the main impediment to the realization of the incestuous impulses but also the object to which they are first most likely to be transferred. As the impediment to the realization of incestuous impulses towards the mother, the father becomes an object of hate. But the love which is transferred to him represses this hate. In the inverted Oedipus complex even the rest of the love which is not transferred to the father is projected upon him and inverted to the self, so that the child not only loves his father as he loved his mother, but desires to be loved by him.

Just as the mother disappoints the first incestuous desires, so too the father disappoints them in their inverted form. But the child, once he has formed this concept, never forgets it and seeks it in his idea of God.

We have next to inquire how far the seeking of God in positive religion is inadequate, and to what extent it is likely to survive the spread of a knowledge of psychology.

If a personal God in the form of an all loving and all powerful father really existed He would undoubtedly satisfy some of the deepest yearnings of present humanity. He would be an adequate substitute for almost every human loss, and the certainty that this was so would remove almost every human fear. He would thus comfort the afflicted and calm the anxious. Unfortunately, however, the belief that such a being exists does not appear to

[1] [It would now (1977) seem that this *conscious* lack of discrimination between the sexes is a defence against an innate preconception of the true distinction, which remains unconscious.]

be empirical, but seems to be founded upon desire alone. Thus we must conclude that positive religion can fulfil no real needs.

But how, then, are we to account for the fact that religion has comforted and still does comfort millions of individuals who without it would find life not only empty but intolerable? We have seen that although inadequate seekings cannot fulfil real needs they may nevertheless remove false threats. Religion, therefore, since it combines an apparent adequacy with a real inadequacy, is perhaps of this nature, and is a relief only to a neurotic anxiety.

The adult requires different means to satisfy his needs from those of the child, yet the absence of means which were necessary to the child may still operate as false threats. The absence of the mother was once a threat of hunger and pregenital deprivation. The absence of the father was once a threat of his death for which the child's unconscious had so often longed. The belief in the existence of the God who is a symbol of the mother and the father in one person removes the old threat of the loss of the mother and at the same time reassures the unconscious that it is no murderer. Certain individuals cannot tolerate the loss of either of these supports. If they were to lose the ideal of God as the perfect mother their anxiety would be insupportable; if they were to lose the ideal of God as the father, they would introject Him and their unconscious hate would invert against themselves. Thus the idea of God is required as an object both of love and of hate. But this anxious love and this hate are both largely inappropriate impulses; for the mother is no longer necessary[1] and the father is no longer an impediment to a vital desire. The completely normal individual in the course of his development would, I think, learn the irrelevance of some of his infantile anxieties, seek his real needs no longer in his mother but in some object more adequate to them in their adult form, would be reconciled with his father and introject him as a conscious part of his ego without danger. Such an individual would have few false threats which could only be removed by some fictitious means. The real deprivations and anxieties of this life would

---

[1] i.e., the fear of being without her is due to a false threat.

thus become not too heavy for him to bear, and he could dispense with his belief in God if the absence of evidence in His existence convinced him that such belief was no longer rational. Therefore, I think that the great edifice of religion, both in its positive and in its negative form, is doomed to fall before the slow but inevitable widening of self-consciousness which modern psychology will bring. Religion may be an exquisite illusion, but it is built on superfluous fears and hates. It thus involves anxiety, which is unnecessary for its devotees, and intolerance, which is tiresome for their opponents. We may regret the passing of much that was beautiful in the childhood of our culture, but we shall admit that the gain is greater than the loss.

(2) *Social Consequences – Moral*

After considering the possible fate of religion it is natural that we should next inquire about the future of morality. Morality is supposed to consist of both precepts and prohibitions. But the prohibitions are not only older but also more fundamental, for precepts when analysed are seen to be only the converse of prohibitions. Thus the taboo 'n'insulte pas tes parents de peur de mourir (aussitôt)' is, as Reinach has pointed out, the origin of the precept 'honore tes parents afin que tu vives longtemps.'[1] Even the man who devotes his life to some great altruistic cause would probably admit, if he were honest, that his motives were partly the fear of the reproaches of his conscience if he failed to pull his weight in some way in society. And in so far as his motives are not negative, but are due solely to altruistic love of his fellows, they are not the result of precepts and are therefore not moral.[2] This is of course ultimately a matter of definition, but it would seem best in the interests of clarity to agree that morals are made up of prohibitions, and that purely positive impulses, in so far as they are not merely the converse of prohibitions, are not moral, however altruistic they may be.

[1] Reinach, *Cultes, Mythes et Religions*, 1905, 1, 5–6.
[2] [At the time I wrote this passage, I believed that the sole source of morality was the super-ego. I now (1977) believe there is a second and slightly later source which begins to form in the depressive position, discovered by M.K. and expresses itself in acts of reparation which are probably closely linked with the precepts (rather than the prohibitions) of morality.]

REMOTE CONSEQUENCES OF PSYCHO-ANALYSIS

We may therefore apply Reinach's definitions of religion to morality and define it as 'un ensemble de scrupules qui font obstacle au libre exercice de nos facultés'.[1] Morality is thus akin to negative religion. In negative religion a jealous God is believed to avenge all transgressions against His commands. In morals this God is replaced by the conscience, or, to give it its modern and more comprehensive name, by the super-ego. Formerly morals were inseparable from negative religion; the conscience was the voice of God. But the agnostic who refuses to accept the objective existence of God still has a conscience which is really the disembodied voice of God. Thus morality is a modern form of negative religion.

But, whereas God is recognized by analysts as a projection of the father, the super-ego is supposed to be an introjection of him. There is, however, a great difference between introjecting the father into the ego and introjecting him as a super-ego; the former strengthens the personality while the latter weakens it. The super-ego is distinct from the ego, and it differs from God only in that it is a disembodied edition of Him. Probably because the super-ego is not objectified but disembodied it is regarded not as a projection but as an introjection. Since, however, it is distinct from the ego it is still in a sense a projection. It is probably not introjected into the ego because it is needed as an external, if nebulous, object of homosexual love.

In the unconscious the old incestuous impulses of childhood still from time to time strive towards their old object. They then awaken the old sexual rivalry and aggressiveness which is perhaps an innate accompaniment of the sexual impulse. This aggressiveness, or hate, is directed first towards the Imago who is the symbol of the father who once suppressed them. But the Imago is also loved, so that the hate is repressed, projected and inverted against the self and felt as guilt. This lasts until the unconscious incestuous impulses are also inverted, and the whole cycle ends in some form of masochistic penance.

In negative religion this penance is more or less recognized for what it is, but in the unconscious and automatic morality, which has so largely replaced religion, it may be some form of

[1] *Orpheus*, p. 4.

neurotic suffering, or some misfortune which the subject does not even recognize as self-inflicted. Thus the case of a stockbroker has been recorded who periodically suffered heavy financial losses owing to temporary misjudgments which were really the result of his own inverted hate.

The same process of repression and inversion may follow, not only the periodic return of direct substitutes for the old incestuous impulses, but also their remotest sublimations. The inhibited impulses seek ever more inadequate substitutes for their original means, and each in turn may be followed by the same process of repression and inversion. Where the substitutes are still anti-social the Imago has thus been a far more efficient guardian of society than the law. But where they are no longer anti-social and have secondary real value, both to the individual and society, the function of the Imago has been to produce useless and crippling neuroses.

Having formed some idea of the inhibitions of the Imago, we have now to inquire how far these are irrelevant and therefore unlikely to survive. And, if they are mainly psychologically irrelevant, whether the society of the future is likely to relapse into the destructive anarchy characteristic of the family life of primeval man.

We may suppose that society will pass through the same stages of enlightenment as the individual in analysis. The first stage will expose the irrelevant similarity between the inhibited sublimations and the incestuous impulses they symbolize. With this insight the neurotic inhibition of sublimations will decrease.

Many of the more direct sexual substitutes would be next freed. The impotent would become potent, the frigid more sensual and the prude less chaste. But, since the freed sexual impulses would still be only partially adequate substitutes for the original incestuous impulses, they would be unlikely to bring complete satisfaction. Discontented monogamists might become insatiably promiscuous in pursuit of an impossible goal.

Still further enlightenment would begin to disclose the partial inadequacy of the incestuous impulses themselves; for they unconsciously outlive the period in which they could really remove needs. They would also be shown to be irrelevant in so far as the threats which they seemed to remove were always or have subseqently become false.¹ With this insight into their partial inadequacy and irrelevance, the sexual activities, which had been already freed from the inhibitions of the Imago, would become simpler and more satisfying, and, although there might be less chastity than before, there would also be less useless promiscuity.

After the realization of the partial inadequacy and irrelevance of the unconscious incestuous impulses, and the recognition of the Imago as a projection of the father, he would be seen to be no longer a rival and he would be no longer hated. At the same time he would be less loved, for the love which was originally transferred to him from the mother would find a more adequate substitute in a real woman. Since he would be no longer hated he could be introjected without danger to the ego. Since he would be less loved he could be more easily given up as an object. Thus introjection into the ego would probably be his fate. The ego would be strengthened at the expense of the super-ego.²

With the final introjection of the Imago, less as a super-ego than as a part of the ego, the individual would become more the arbiter of his own morality. This morality could then be consciously modified; but the basis of it would still be the standards of his Imago, that is, of his father and the series of father substitutes under whose influence he spent his early years. He would no longer be oppressed by this image; he would become like it. The normal man does in fact, without

---

[1] I again allude to that part of the child's dependence upon its mother which is due to false threats of hunger, castration and aphanisis.

[2] What, as far as I can make out, seems to be the orthodox view of what happens in analysis is roughly as follows. The super-ego is largely (but not wholly) projected upon the analyst who becomes the father Imago. As long as the positive transference lasts the patient cannot dispense with the analyst: as long as the negative transference lasts he cannot introject the analyst without hating himself. But when both the positive and negative transference have been analysed (that is, in my terminology, when a good deal of the transference has been shown to be inadequate and irrelevant) the patient can give up the analyst, i.e. the father Imago. The Id, however, must have some substitute for what it is about to abandon. The ego therefore copies or introjects his idea of the analyst (which corresponds largely to his idea of his own father) and so becomes himself the substitute for his Id's affection. By this means the ego seems to be strengthened at the expense of the super-ego. This is, of course, not the whole story; but, as far as it goes, it seems to be a correct description of the facts.

analysis, approximate to this position. But in the past those who have come up to this standard of normality have been few and far between, whereas in the future the moral individualist may be the rule.

Will the result be anarchy and the destruction of society? The basis of an individualist morality (i.e., an ego-morality as opposed to a super-ego-morality) is transitive; it is inherited, not as an innate possession, but as a form of property. Its survival in the future depends upon the present. It requires the continuity of family tradition. Thus there is no reason why conscious morality should not survive the most complete enlightenment. But will this be a sufficient safeguard for society? Although the unconscious and automatic basis of present morality will be largely lost, it will be less necessary. For the same process which proves it to be irrelevant discloses at the same time the psychological inadequacy of most of the antisocial impulses it was its function to repress.

It is unconscious hate bred of the real or imagined deprivations of humanity which is the real danger to society. These deprivations are partly self-inflicted and partly inflicted by society. That is, they result partly from our own irrelevant inhibitions and partly from the prohibitions of others. They are also partly not real deprivations at all, but false threats of these which have survived from infancy. With an increase in self-knowledge all these sources of real or imagined frustration will tend to dry up. There should be less unconscious hate, and less conscious discontent.

(3) *Social Consequences – Political*

We may also expect that greater self-consciousness will produce changes in our political life. Just as morals have become the modern equivalent of negative religion, so political idealism seems destined to fill the place in men's lives once occupied by positive religion. In positive religion the perfect parents and the perfect home, which we dimly remember from our first infancy, are sought in a world of illusion beyond the grave. In political idealism we seek to create the perfect government and the perfect state in this world, or to become ourselves the perfect race.

In political idealism, if we are not deluded, we do not ourselves expect to enjoy the utopia of our dreams. We do not, however, renounce them altogether but project them upon future generations. Political idealism is therefore more altruistic than religion.

But both are founded on the same unrenouncable desires, and both are in consequence almost equally unable to entertain the thought of the non-existence or impossibility of their ideals. Just as the religious man wilfully ignores the absence of all evidence for the existence of what he so much desires, so the political idealist will generally refuse to see the difficulties in the way of the realization of his utopia. Both also display the same intolerance and the same aggressiveness against those who differ from their views. Political idealism, however, seems to be somewhat nearer to reality than religion. It is not quite so irresponsibly certain of its results. It at least makes a pretence of testing the feasibility of the measures it proposes. And this tendency to scientific doubt and self-criticism seems to be increasing. Therefore political idealism may perhaps yet learn to test not only the feasibility but also the desirability of the new world before it has destroyed the old.

What a man desires for his class, his country or his race, is a projection of what he desires for himself. If he could himself realize this desire he would not be so likely to project it. If he has repressed it severely he may project it upon others without himself wishing it for them. But if it is less severely repressed, or if it is not repressed at all, but merely under present conditions impossible, he is likely not only to project it upon others but also to desire it for them. In this way a man transfers his ambitions to his children or builds ideals of what he wants society to become or to avoid, and, if his capacity for altruistic projection is great, work towards such distant aims may become the main preoccupation of his life.

But if a man is mistaken in what he thinks he wants or fears for himself, he is also likely to be mistaken in what he thinks he wants or fears for that projection of himself which is the world at large. Psychology, we have seen, helps the individual to discover what he really wants and what he need not avoid. Inadequate and irrelevant political ideals do no great harm to the individual who holds them, but they may be disastrous to his contemporaries and his successors. Therefore a psychology capable of eliminating such mistakes has a value to society at large.

Different objects may be equally adequate means to the same need, so that if the same situation evokes different desires in different people it does not necessarily follow that one desire must be less rational than the other. Similarly two political ideals may differ without either being necessarily mistaken. Therefore we must not expect of psychology that it will eliminate all political conflict, but only that by exposing the irrelevance of many political ideals it will greatly diminish it.

Pryns Hopkins has pointed out that a man's politics are mainly determined by his Oedipus complex.[1] Perhaps it would be more correct to say that they are determined partly by this complex and partly by his social position. A man may have either a positive or a negative Oedipus complex and he may have either a high or a low social position. The combinations of these two sets of factors give four typical kinds of politics, two reactionary and two progressive.

Those who have positive Oedipus complexes, if they are plutocrats, tend to identify the masses with their fathers and become reactionary, but if they are proletarians they tend to identify the rich with their fathers and as automatically become progressive. On those who have negative Oedipus complexes the accident of social status has the opposite effect. If they are plutocrats they tend to identify the masses with the father, to whom they wish to surrender, and become masochistic revolutionaries, and if they are proletarians, who see an image of their fathers in the rich, they may become masochistic reactionaries. Although there are numerous individual complications and exceptions, this scheme seems to be a fairly general rule. Often the Oedipean reaction is disowned and projected upon others, so that a politician may deceive himself, and his constituents, into the belief that he is disinterested, when he has merely projected the conscious part of his indignation upon the class with whom he identifies himself.

Thus the politics of the majority of people, who feel strongly about such things, are probably expressions or projections of their own particular brand of Oedipus complex. Since the

[1] Pryns Hopkins, *Fathers or Sons*

desires of this complex in the adult are largely inadequate or irrelevant, his political ideals, in so far as they have no secondary value, are also largely inadequate or irrelevant. They are therefore likely to be demotivated when he acquires a completer knowledge of himself.

Must we therefore conclude that a spread of knowledge of psychology will destroy all political ideals, and leave humanity profoundly apathetic about its future? No: for there are individual desires which are adequate and rational, and among these there are many which we cannot ourselves fulfil and which it is easier to project upon others than to renounce utterly. Some of our ambitions may be inadequate, some of our sorrows and our fears may be irrelevant, but, when all this is allowed for, there must be many things which the most enlightened among us would still want and which we cannot have. A higher standard of comfort, more opportunity to choose our own work, greater physical strength and beauty and intellectual power – these are things which we may legitimately desire for our descendants if we cannot obtain them for ourselves. But less conscious and less rational motives are apt to lurk behind even these altruistic aspirations.

Consider, for instance, the demand for comfort. It is difficult to fix the standard of comfort which we really require, but it is certainly much more modest than we imagine that we want. Any psycho-analyst would agree that a large part of the demand for luxury owes its existence to a neurotic inability to find satisfaction in the simpler instinctual pleasures of life. And this conclusion is confirmed by the well-known fact that luxury is disappointing and that the more it is provided the more it is desired. The desire for luxury is therefore largely an inadequate seeking of something which it symbolizes or inadequately resembles. Moreover, it seems to be one of the prime evils of social and economic life. For it gives rise both to uncharitable greed in those who vainly hope to satisfy it, and to excessive envy in those who do not have this hope. Purely political or economic changes are unlikely to abolish these dangerous emotions. But a more perfect understanding of our real needs would almost certainly devaluate the idea of luxury and thereby provide a more secure and peaceful economic future. If the irrational demand for excessive luxury were reduced, the economic problem of securing a reasonable degree of comfort for everyone should be easy to solve.

I should like, before concluding this section, to give one example of a sociological aspiration which seems to me to be free from the reproach of psychological inadequacy or irrelevance. The projected desire for physical and mental progress is rarer than the projected desire for comfort or freedom. But it is the fundamental motive of eugenists, and this type of political idealism is likely to become more common.

There are three stages in the development of the eugenic ideal. Firstly, there is the desire to rediscover as objects of love those imaginarily perfect beings which we knew in our first infancy. This desire gives rise to the fantasies of romance and the longings of positive religion. Next there is the tendency to give up this ideal as an object and to attempt to introject it. In this stage we wish to be our ideals rather than to find them. The third and last stage involves the partial renunciation as impracticable of this desire for personal perfection and its projection upon our descendants, with whom we identify ourselves. Those who reach this stage are likely to become eugenists and active propagandists for racial improvement.

The ideal parents, which we all unconsciously still seek, would satisfy us if they could be found. Therefore, that part of the desire for them which is based on real needs rather than false threats is rational, even if it cannot be fulfilled. The eugenic ideal is further removed from the original desire than its more direct expression in positive religion, but it is at least more likely to be fulfilled.

C. BIOLOGICAL CONSEQUENCES

In the last two sections we have considered some of the individual and social consequences of an increase in self-knowledge. In this we shall attempt to foresee what effect, if any, this knowledge could have on evolution. We have already raised the problem of whether psychology could endanger the sublimations of the individual. We may now inquire whether it could weaken the instincts of the race.

The reactions which natural selection tends to evolve are those which best secure the survival of the species. But the modifications in these reactions which memory tends to fix, or intelligence to produce, are those which most economically remove or avoid injuries and needs. No doubt the reaction which most economically removes or avoids a given need or injury is often also the reaction which most effectively secures the survival of the race. But this is not necessarily so. It thus seems theoretically possible for an intelligent generation to substitute for its instincts other reactions which are more efficient at removing and avoiding primary stimuli, but which have a negative survival value to the species.[1]

I will take two examples. The sexual need is determined ultimately by the periodic accumulation of certain chemical substances. When these are excreted the need is temporarily removed. The direct excretion of these substances by masturbation does not, however, satisfy in the same way as the more complicated method which our instincts prescribe. For masturbation does not satisfy the desire for an intimate union with some person who is loved. And this desire, which Moll has called the impulse of contrectation, appears to be the only adequate removal reaction to that curious and disquieting sense of personal incompleteness which from time to time afflicts every member of the species. Now it is quite possible to argue that this sense of personal incompleteness is not a genuine need at all but a false threat analogous to a neurotic anxiety. In the child a longing for the mother is first evoked by hunger, and then by loneliness which is perhaps ultimately

[1] I have assumed throughout this discussion, as a fundamental principle, that the individual must necessarily select the most economic route to the removal of injuries and needs *that he has discovered*. In so far as we can identify pain with intensity of stimulus, this principle might be called the principle of negative hedonism. Observation, however, suggests that at least the human organism sometimes deliberately delays a final removal to some needs (e.g. nutritional, anal, urethral and sexual) in order to prolong or increase *pleasure*. What are we to make of this tendency? Can it be reduced to a special form of negative hedonism – perhaps to the avoidance of false threats? Or must we postulate a 'positive hedonism' by which the individual seeks certain kinds of stimuli – not merely as means to the removal of more primary stimuli or of false threats – but also on their own account? I cannot imagine what physiological mechanism can be correlated with such a positive hedonistic tendency. But if it existed if would doubtless protect instincts against the possibly destructive effects of the negative hedonism which we have so far alone considered. It might, however, involve new dangers of its own of an opposite type. For there is no more guarantee that the train of reactions which involves most pleasure must be in the interests of the race than there is that the train which involves least pain has this attribute.

only the threat of hunger. But in the adult loneliness is no longer a real danger. Therefore, the longing for the mother symbol, which still persists, would appear to be an irrelevant avoidance of a threat which has lost reality. In mammals, at least, the contrectative impulse appears to be largely derived from this oral impulse of the child for its mother, which has survived its original purpose and been adapted by evolution to serve a racial end. If so, it would seem theoretically possible that intelligence might weaken or destroy this part of the sexual impulse. Such a modification might economize stimuli in the individual; but it would naturally be lethal to the species.[1]

The second example concerns the instinct of self-preservation. Removal reactions are determined by needs. They continue until the need ceases, so that their aim may be said to be the removal of needs. From the point of view of evolution the best removal is that which most promotes the survival of the species. But from the individual's point of view it would seem to be the reaction that most quickly removes the need which is the best. Now the quickest and most final method by which an individual can remove his needs is to put his head in a gas oven, or to adopt some other equally painless method of self-extermination. He does not do so, partly because he thinks in terms of seekings rather than of removals, and partly because of the instinct of self-preservation. The impulse of self-preservation is ultimately the impulse to avoid the pain of injuries. And although death is painless it is to most of us a false threat of pain. But even those who are convinced that there is no pain in death do not often kill themselves. However great their need they remain

---

[1] Impulses which remove needs might be divided into those that are 'ingestive' (e.g. nutritional impulses) and those that are 'excretive' (e.g. anal and urethral impulses). Ingestive impulses necessarily involve the seeking of means, whereas excretive impulses could presumably be satisfied without the aid of external objects. The fact that the sexual impulse, which (at least in the male) is excretive, requires an object seems to me a real problem. I have suggested that in mammals the fusion of a sexual with outgrown nutritional impulses may contribute to secure that preliminary seeking which is indispensable for the continuance of the race. There must, of course, be other factors (i.e. those operative in premammals), but the possibility remains that they, like the nutritional component, may be, strictly speaking, irrelevant from the point of view of the individual – traps set by evolution to prevent the individual from removing his needs otherwise than in the interests of the race.

obsessed by the image of the means which evolution has determined that they shall seek in order to remove it, and do not take the short cut which their intelligence suggests.

The danger that self-knowledge will destroy instincts is of course remote. But it is just possible that the individualists of the future may be not only too lazy to propagate their species, but that they may even discover that the lethal chamber is an easier and more permanent means to the removal of their needs than the circuitous method of sowing, reaping, harvesting, and eating and love-making which they now employ. If this should ever come to pass the universe will be clear for the growth of some species of ant or termite whose instincts are less sullied by intelligence.

If man could become truly capable of seeking only the shortest route to the removal of his needs and injuries, his unpleasures and his pains, it seems to me inevitable that he would ultimately learn to seek only his painless extinction. But he is unlikely ever to discover the shortest route to his complete and utter satiation. Certain false threats and irrelevant fears will remain with him as an entailed estate, which he may recognize intellectually but not emotionally, and which will prevent him from escaping from his needs except by the circuitous routes which serve not his purpose but the continuation of the race. For this reason I do not think that instincts have anything to fear from the growth of self-knowledge.[1]

If the instinct of self-preservation remains strong in the individual it is natural that he will reconcile his inevitable extinction by transferring this desire to the race. It will become for him a matter of grave concern to provide a new refuge for his species in another planet when the earth has become cold and uninhabitable, or in another solar system when the sun itself has shared a similar fate, and even to foresee some hope of immortality in spite of the second law of thermodynamics which seems to doom the entire universe to destruction. The

[1] Professor Simons pointed out in the discussion, that Schopenhauer believed that certain 'dynamic illusions' were essential to the survival of the race. Miss Searl wrote that I had neglected 'the dynamic force of life itself'. Possibly this 'force' can be identified with the hedonic principle which, in the note at the beginning of this section, I now suggest may be required to qualify the 'entropy' principle. If pain can be correlated with stimulus, pleasure cannot be correlated with reduction of stimulus.

first two cataclysms could probably be avoided with sufficient mechanical ingenuity, so that the racial altruist who has projected his fear of death upon his species would wish for a social system that promoted a knowledge of pure physics and its applications, and would deplore all tendencies to play after our past labours in communistic garden cities, and so to waste the few billion years of grace which precedes the destruction of the earth.[1]

Such a method of escaping from the doom of the earth involves a modification of our environment; it is an alloplastic adaptation. But if we are to escape a final and still remoter destruction our adaptations must be also autoplastic; they must involve a modification of ourselves. So far we have developed from the amoeba by means of variations which we have not influenced and selections which we have not controlled. But the time is coming when we may be able surgically to influence the chromosomes and promote any type we choose, and already we could purposefully select spontaneous variations if we were agreed upon what variations to select, and upon the method of selecting them. Therefore it is becoming important to decide the direction in which we want to influence evolution.

It is, of course, impossible for us to imagine that it would be pleasant to be organisms entirely unlike ourselves. Our amoeboid ancestors would probably have agreed that their simple aquatic life was preferable to our more troubled existence. And similarly it is difficult to imagine ourselves with pleasure as the bodiless cerebrums which we may some day become. The preferences of the amoeba were of no importance, for they did not control evolution. With us, however, the case is different, for we can control our future. If we prefer to remain unchanged, or to degenerate into less intelligent and more appetitive types, we could do so. But if we wish to live for ever we must continue to adapt ourselves to our environment as well as our environment to ourselves, and we must further foresee and anticipate the adaptations which one day will be necessary.

If we self-consciously follow out some such racial ambition

---

[1] Haldane, in an interesting story of the end of the world, imagines the sidereal colonists who escaped from the earth, to have been dominated by this kind of racial altruism.

as I have suggested, it seems possible that the destiny of man will be a solitary exception to the general degradation of inanimate matter. While the rest of the universe is breaking up into simpler and ever simpler particles, man may conceivably continue that process of increasing complication which the organic world, as an infinitesimal exception to the inorganic, has already pursued for so long; and he may end as a single gigantic brain which operates throughout the ages without the least dissipation of its remaining energy. Since the rest of the universe would have disappeared, this brain would have no necessity for organs of locomotion or perception; since it would conserve its own energy, it would take no nourishment; and since it would be immortal, it would not need to reproduce itself. Its correlated mental activities would be unthinkable to us. But though it would have no external perceptions and no desires which it could not immediately from itself fulfil, it could still narcissistically enjoy an acute awareness of itself. It would be like the Spinozistic God, pure Being, engaged eternally in the contemplation of its own perfection. But the human philosopher may legitimately wonder whether this or race extinction is the more preferable goal.

6

A Psychologist's Utopia[1]

INTRODUCTION

A society may be said to be *secure* when its members are protected from each other and *free* when their natural desires are not inhibited. An Utopia may be defined as a society which is both secure and free. Most societies are neither secure nor free; for the inhibitions which are intended to protect them are a cause of discontent.

Many have attempted to construct utopias. Theologians, politicians, lawyers and economists have made proposals. But their efforts have not been rewarded with success. A psychologist may perhaps be permitted to try his hand, even though he has been warned by the greatest master of his science that the problem is insoluble.[2]

I. THE DEMON OF CIVILIZATION

The offensive weapons of the males of many species appear to have been first evolved as an aid to the sexual instinct before they were adapted for the pursuit of game or for self-defence. (They were, perhaps, used to master the resistance of the female even before they were adapted for sexual combats.[3]) We may suppose that instincts fall into the same order of precedence and importance as the structures which they use. Thus, aggression in the mastery and defence of a mate is probably the most fundamental kind of aggressiveness there is. Indeed, this view is confirmed by the intimate association which still

[1] This paper was originally read before the University College Psychological Society, 10 December 1930. My thanks are due to this Society and especially to Dr Flügel for many valuable suggestions.
[2] Freud, *Das Unbehagen in der Kultur*.
[3] Messe-Doflain, *Tierbau v. Tierleben*, quoted by Roheim, *Animism, Magic and the Divine King*, 250.

A PSYCHOLOGIST'S UTOPIA

subsists between sex and aggression in all species. The carnivor may attack its prey and the herbivore may fight in self-defence; but the most ferocious battles are between rivals for a mate.

The review of these biological facts suggests two conclusions: firstly, that aggressiveness in general is an innate response to frustration, especially sexual frustration; secondly, that the peculiar aggressiveness of man is more often due to sexual frustration than it seems. We may consider these conclusions in turn.

The view that aggression is simply a reaction to frustration would seem self-evident if it had not been denied by Freud. If he is right in supposing that it is an independent impulse, which can exist apart from frustration, the hope of an utopia is indeed remote. There is, therefore, a strong non-intellectual motive for disagreeing with him. But although the most offensive of Freud's theories have usually been found to be correct, I am in this case still unconvinced.

Having agreed to treat aggression as a response to frustration – especially sexual frustration – we may return to enquire whether the aggressiveness of man is also mainly a reaction to unsatisfied sexual desires.

The duel, that ancient institution which was so recently abolished, was generally a sexual combat. But, with the exception of the siege of Troy, and the attack of the Romans upon the Sabines, our wars and revolutions appear at first sight to have been political or economic rather than erotic. Possibly, however, an investigation of the Unconscious may convince us that not only the periodic eruptions of society, but also the slumbering discontent which characterizes the intervals between them, possess a sexual motive.

No part of the discoveries of psycho-analysis has evoked such wide-spread incredulity and disgust as the Oedipus complex. It is now generally admitted that such a complex does exist in a large number of neurotics. But it will be a long time before its ubiquity, and the depth of its social ramifications, will be fully realized outside the restricted circle of practising analysts and their successful patients. Probably it can never be quite understood by those who have not been analysed. Therefore the thesis that the Oedipus complex is the core of that slumbering aggression and discontent, which is a constant danger to society, is certain to evoke more opposition than assent. Nevertheless, I am convinced that this thesis is correct, and I will try to summarize it as plausibly as I can.

The most conscious expression of the Oedipus complex was perhaps written by Stendhal in his autobiographical book, *Vie de Henri Brulard*.[1] He remembered that he was in love with his mother at the age of six, that his love was in essence that of a grown-up person, that he wished to cover her with kisses when she had no clothes on, that he hated and was jealous of his father, and that this jealousy endured years after his mother's death.

It is rare for a child of six to be still conscious of such feelings, and yet rarer for him to remember them when he is a man. But the experience of psycho-analysis has shown beyond doubt that these feelings are almost, if not quite, universal at an earlier age, and that they survive, or recur, in the unconscious.

An individual may either never find a substitute for his mother, or he may unconsciously return to his first love when some substitute has proved unsatisfactory. In the first case his unconscious state is said to result from a *fixation*, in the second from a *regression*. These distinctions will be important in the subsequent discussion. Where there is a fixation at, or a regression to, an inhibited incestuous desire that aggressive rivalry which was first awakened by the father is also present. It is this pair of unconscious incestuous and parricidal impulses which compose the Oedipus complex. The subject of such a complex may be conscious of his emotions, but he is not conscious of their objects. He is, therefore, the prey of an indefinite and unattached love and hate, which may become temporally directed to any symbol. Sometimes the hate may be inverted against the subject himself. He then becomes a neurotic who is dangerous to himself, and useless to his fellows. But more often the indefinite desire and aggression combine into a vague discontent.

It is the Oedipus complex behind this discontent which is the demon of civilization. In times of peace it is an impediment to real content. And periodically, it explodes in the social upheavals of war and revolution. In the intervals of quiet, the

[1] The full passage is quoted by Havelock Ellis, *Psychology of Sex*, vii. 24–5.

discontent is dissipated in various directions, so that no single party is strong enough to break through the restrictions of its fellows. The different causes cancel out each other. But a discontent which is only attached to symbols is readily transferable and highly infectious. Thus an epidemic is always liable to sweep through society and to unite a whole people in a common desire and a common hate. Then there is a war or revolution and a cause is won. But afterwards the people are disillusioned and split into rival factions which render each other comparatively harmless, until a new doctrine arises to unite them in a fresh discontent.

II. THE ERUPTIONS OF THE DEVIL

(1) *War and Revolution*

When we realize the intensity of the unconscious incestuous and parricidal desires of the civilized individual today, it is not hard to reconstruct what must have been the life of primeval man. In many species, including man, the sucking impulse of the young is later adapted to courtship and reappears as the erotic lick or bite or kiss. In man the long period of infancy is likely to overlap the dawning of the true sexual impulse. Among primitive people this period may last several years. Therefore, among primitive people it is especially likely that the first object of the ripening sexual impulse should be the same as that which satisfies its oral component. The frustration by the father of this desire must inevitably awaken that aggressiveness which was especially evolved to deal with impediments to an erotic aim. We may suppose that there was once a time when repression was insufficient permanently to check such impulses, and when sons actually fought their father for the possession of their mother and their sisters.

Mythology is saturated with dim records of this period, or at least with open expression of the fierce desires which are now so sternly repressed. The most ancient gods habitually disregarded the incestuous and parricidal taboos of their people. We may therefore, with Freud, suppose that primeval society was composed of families each ruled by a father who jealously kept all the women for himself, and that the first revolutions sought incest by means of parricide.

I have elsewhere suggested[1] that the internal stability of the family was the result of war. In war the desire for the mother could be transferred to the women of the hostile group, and also to a disputed hunting territory, for the earth is a well-known symbol of the mother. Then the hate of the father would be diverted to the hostile warriors and the family would be for a time united. Gradually such war would become an institution. The father only would be endogamous. The sons would agree to acquire their wives by capture, and would accept their father as a leader in their battles. In the most primitive tribes today everyone, including the leaders, are exogamous, and, although they now generally acquire their wives by barter, we may suppose that they once did so by capture. But a relic of the still earlier period survives in the mythology. For the totem or deified ancestor is incestuous and free from the endogamic taboo.

Thus war, which is a peculiarity of the human species, was at first an alternative to revolution. The problem of securing internal stability without it is perhaps still unsolved. The rulers of a discontented people still preach an offensive or defensive imperialism in the hope of diverting the aggression from themselves. A nation is nearly always discontented when it is neither afraid of nor jealous of a rival.

It will be objected that our present wars and revolutions are economic, and that they have no resemblance to the upheavals of primeval man. But our fundamental impulses are still the same, even if their expression is more sublimated. It was no verbal analogy to say in the last war that the French were fighting for their mother land. The word 'la Patrie' evoked a sentiment which came straight from the unconscious.[2] The most successful propaganda was couched in sexual language. The cry that Germany had violated the neutrality of Belgium produced in this country a martial ardour which no passivist government could have withstood. We were next told that the German soldiery were raping the women of the invaded territory. We accepted such statements without investigation and our fury doubled. Economic motives may perhaps appeal

[1] *The Meaning of Sacrifice.*
[2] Dumas wrote of this cry: 'C'est une mère à l'agonie qui criait: "A moi mes enfants".' *La Comtesse de Charny,* v. 194.

to statesmen; but, unless there is actual starvation, no people can be made to fight who are not fired by some catchword which has a deep symbolic meaning.

The sexual motives behind war would perhaps become still clearer if we could examine the private fantasies of those who take part in it. These fantasies are usually kept secret, and it is in consequence difficult to record them. But they are known to be very common. I think they consist generally of two parts: an heroic deed and an erotic reward. Perhaps the young soldier, before he has become disillusioned by the sordid facts of war, dreams that his valour is watched by some lady, or that he rescues a damsel in distress. Such fantasies may remain as war's consolation after they have ceased to be its motive.

Modern revolutions, like modern wars, with all their complications, are really of the same form as their primeval prototype. Historians may discuss their motives, but the motives which they propose are seldom fundamental. Novelists are often more profound. Thus, of two of Dumas's revolutionaries, one, the youthful Gilbert, was in love with an aristocrat, and the other, Ange Pittou, was in love with the mistress of an aristocrat. In both cases their politics were first determined by these frustrated emotions. It is, indeed, possible to read a symbolic Oedipus legend into the story of these two characters. The rival of Gilbert was the king, that is, a father-symbol. His later royalism was only the atonement for his former crime. The rival of Ange Pittou, on the other hand, was the brother of the lover of the queen. A queen is a well-known mother-symbol, and the two brothers may perhaps be regarded as duplicates of each other. The Oedipus motive behind revolution is still more evident in Schiller's drama, *Don Carlos*. For here it is the prince's passion for his step-mother which determines his revolt against his father.[1]

I do not suggest that every revolutionary is influenced by conscious erotic motives of this kind. In most cases the symbolism is probably more subtle and could only be unravelled by an individual analysis.[2] But in discussing more closely the socialist movement of today we shall find reasons to believe that the two motives of revolution, namely, a desire for a new

---

[1] Rank, *Das Inzest-Motiv*. [2] See Prynse Hopkins, *Fathers or Sons?*

world and a hatred of those who seem to bar the gate, are derivatives of the two motives in the Oedipus complex.

We have tried to trace the fundamental motives of war and revolution to the same source. If the social upheavals of the past were carefully reviewed, it would probably be found, in each case, that the apparent cause was a symbol which mobilized the Oedipus complexes of the people. Thus the psycho-analytical anthropologist would be able to construct a philosophy of history. In it mankind, like the house of Atreus, is pursued by a series of fatal calamities which each repeat, on an ever-grander scale, the rutting battles of the primeval herd.

(2) *Religion and Socialism*

From time to time there arise in the world men of peace who have sought to free their fellows from the perpetual circle of internal and external strife to which they are at present bound. These are the great religious and social teachers who have dreamed of a better world either in this life or beyond the grave. But, though they have looked forward to a time of perpetual peace, they have generally preached one last crusade which should be as it were a war to end war. Sometimes, indeed, this last battle was to be entirely spiritual. But the disciples have descended to a more material arena. Christ would have wept at the sight of the blood which was shed in his name, and Rousseau would have been deeply shocked by the revolution of those who were fired by his doctrine. But perhaps they both foresaw that violence would be the necessary concomitant of even the sublimest cause. Thus there is an aggressive side to every vision of utopia. We may suspect that these two aspects are derivatives of the two motives in the Oedipus complex.

Religion and socialism are the two most conspicuous examples of movements which aim at the realization of a better world. We may study them first as consolations and secondly as outlets for aggression.

(2a) *Religion and Socialism as consolations.* Psycho-analysis has thrown some light on the fundamental and unconscious motives which have led men to seek so passionately for a golden age in this world or in the world to come. The infant at the breast, and still more, the foetus in the womb, knows neither anxiety nor pain. All his needs are stilled as soon as they arise, and he has not yet suffered or learnt to dread some deprivation. Soon, however, he experiences disappointment and learns to fear. The external world is discovered and apprehended as a hostile place, and even the mother, who once seemed to be the most perfect part of the child himself, is found to be a distinct and disappointing individual.

As he grows older, the normal child learns to tolerate his world with all its imperfections. He becomes capable of accepting unpleasant truths. He finds tolerable substitutes for what he has lost. But there are many who never find such substitutes, and still more who return in unconscious fantasy to their first haven when some substitute has proved imperfect. These unconscious fantasies are represented in consciousness by a cherished illusion which modifies the present or distorts the future. The psychotic denies the whole world of fact and substitutes for it a world of his own creation. Perhaps no one is entirely free from similar, though slighter delusions. But we are each incapable of discovering our own and we defend it with a passion which is immune from reason.

The great systems of religion are examples of such delusions. They posit the protecting womb and perfect mother which the child once knew and which the believer symbolically hallucinates, because the child which has survived in his unconscious is not strong enough to tolerate their permanent loss. These features are clearly evident in early religion. The grave and the abode of the dead were once conscious models of the womb, and the Egyptian king imagined that he would be suckled hereafter by a goddess. In the later patriarchal religions these elements are obscured. But the Christian heaven appears to be both anthropologically and psychologically a derivative of the womb[1] and the God who creates and protects his children 'even as a hen gathereth her chickens under her wing' (Matt. 23: 37) has suppressed his consort only because he has usurped her functions.

Socialism is a doctrine which seems likely to overthrow religion and take its place.[2] But psychologically both movements are of the same nature. Man has grown tired of waiting

---

[1] See Rank, *Das Trauma der Geburt*. [2] See Le Bon, *Psychologie de Socialisme*.

passively for the second coming, and he has lost faith in a world beyond the grave. 'Heaven in our own time' has become his battle cry. Socialism is thus the consolation which has to a large extent taken the place of an imagined future life in which all will be well. For hundreds of years, men, especially the weak, the oppressed and the unhappy, have endured this life only because they imagined it to be but the threshold of a better life to come. Science has weakened, where it has not destroyed, this belief, and probably it will never again be held with its former intensity – at least, so long as the present culture lasts. But the same forces which destroyed religious belief suggested a substitute. The discovery of evolution, which proved us to be animal rather than divine in origin, suggested that we might at least become more splendid animals. This consolation may have been sufficient for eugenists who could enjoy by proxy the excellences of the coming super-man. But the ordinary mortal could not so easily project himself into his remote descendents. He needed in his own life some promise of better things. The doctrine of evolution was applied to institutions rather than to species and man imagined that he could rediscover a perfect haven in a society of his own creation.

(2b) *Religion and Socialism as outlets for aggression.* The vision of socialism is, as we have seen, an opium dream which deadens the pains and soothes the deprivations of real life. But it also satisfies a more sinister and less obvious demand. In this it is again the successor of religion.

Freud believes that the destructive impulses of man are as fundamental and as insatiable as those of sex; but that they are even more concealed. Just as libido may lurk behind an ascetic desire to rescue the fallen (I know of one man whose homosexual desires were aroused by the contacts he made in a passionate attempt to rescue others from this tendency), so may aggression be satisfied in a fanatic hatred of cruelty in others. Thus psycho-analysts have sometimes observed an unusual degree of unconscious sadism in those who join societies for the prevention of cruelty to animals or children. They may even find an outlet for this sadism in inflicting penalties upon those who do not meet their standards. In like manner the most idealistic socialists can see nothing but callousness and cruelty in the society they wish to overthrow. The most honest among them admit that they desire to make their chosen enemies suffer.

Whether Freud is right in regarding aggression as a fundamental and independent impulse, or whether it is only a reaction to the frustration of other impulses, it is certainly present in far greater quantity than a cursory observation of the behaviour of the civilized man would lead us to suppose. Psycho-analysis has shown that the unconscious of the most peaceful individual is often saturated with hate. And the actions of the most cultured nations in the last war should leave no doubt that this hate may become manifest. After the war the peace neurosis was even more common than the war neurosis. Those who became neurotic because their aggressive impulses, which for five years had been given full play, had to be suddenly repressed, were more numerous than those who collapsed because they could not tolerate the physical dangers that they ran.

Religion is supposed to be founded upon love. Yet the psycho-analytical anthropologist is beginning to understand that hate is an equally necessary constituent. Religious people – though there are some honourable exceptions – are seldom either charitable or tolerant. I have heard a saintly cleric sigh for the power of the Inquisition for one day. But to understand these anomalies and to discover similar contradictions in the humanitarian socialist, it will be necessary to say something about the foundations of religion.

The origin of religion is probably to be found in the sacrificial rites which have occurred in some form among every people. Following the lead of Freud (*Totem und Taboo*) and others of his school (e.g., Reik, *Probleme der Religionspsychologie*) I have attempted in another place (*The Meaning of Sacrifice*) to show that sacrifice is essentially at once a symbolic act of parricide and a self-punishment for this deed. Sacrifice is therefore an expression of the Oedipus complex of primitive man. In later forms the intention of parricide is hidden behind other motives, such as the desire for communion with the deity, the wish to present him with a gift or to do him homage. The expiatory motive is generally also clear. But in the earliest sacrifices the victim was a father-god, and although the latter offering was a scarcely recognizable descendant of its more august forebear, probably it still symbolized the father to the unconscious.

Thus, if this view is correct, the central rite of religious worship was a cathartic outlet for an immense amount of unconscious aggression. This aggression appeared partly in a direct and partly in an inverted form. And, since its object was also loved, it was eroticized as sadism or masochism. The distinction between these two is, however, not always clear; for the worshipper tends to identify himself with his victim so that his sadism is partly masochism by proxy.

The religious group is bound together by ties of love to a common leader, who is himself the divine successor of the patriarch of the primeval family.[1] But the attitude to the leader is not pure love. It is ambivalent, a blend of love and hate. Normally the hate is repressed, but from time to time it breaks through in the act of sacrifice. The sacrifice is thus a periodic revolution which deposes an old god, who is, however, at once reincarnated in the person of a successor.

We may ask what happens to the hate in the stable periods between two acts of deicide. It may be inverted against the self and expressed as melancholy and the sense of sin. But it is also liable to be turned outwards towards other groups; for the group is essentially hostile to all those whom it does not include. Perhaps for this reason the religions in which the original virility of sacrifice has least survived are the most intolerant. For this reason also, the idea of a universal religion is probably self-contradictory; for a condition to the stability of the group is that there should be an object to attract the hate which would otherwise disrupt it.

Some may object that religion is no longer aggressive to those who do not share it. But this is only because religion has itself decayed. Christianity, like Islam in the days of its strength, was aggressive; it came to bring not peace but a sword. Some of the non-conformist sects, in which religion is still a force, still detest those of a different persuasion with a persistence worthy of the Holy Inquisition.

Revolution occupies a similar position in socialism to sacrifice in religion. They are both symbolic parricides, which

---

[1] See Freud, *Massenpsiphologie und Ichanalyse*.

A PSYCHOLOGIST'S UTOPIA

open the way to salvation, that is, to the mother. In religion a god is immolated, in socialism a ruling class is to be destroyed. The results of this procedure is heaven or utopia.

There have been many types of ruling class which have attracted the collective envy of the people. But whether they have been aristocracies of privilege or plutocracies of wealth they have all possessed, or seemed to possess, something which has excited that aggression, which was once directed to the leader of the herd in the period of rut. Indeed, it would not be surprising if statistics showed that revolts still occur most frequently in spring and autumn.

(2c) *The delusion of Religion and Socialism.* Those who devote their lives to the conquest of the promised land of religion or socialism are dominated by two beliefs: the belief that their ideals are realizable and the belief that they would be satisfying when found. I shall suggest to the religious that the first of his axioms is unfounded and to the socialist that the second of his assumptions is definitely false.

The reality of the Christian heaven can only be verified beyond the grave. But there is nothing, except the wish, to lead anyone to suppose that it exists. If, however, there were such a place, it would no doubt fulfil the desires of those who want to live there.

A socialist utopia, on the other hand, in which every industry was publicly owned, and in which every citizen was rewarded in proportion to his service to his fellows, is more likely to be realized than enjoyed. There are three types of inequality in the world at present: that due to innate physical and mental characters, that due to the industry and thrift of individuals, and that due to the posthumous benevolence of deceased relations. Of these, the first cannot be easily abolished by legislation, the second would probably be a necessary incentive in any state. Only the third would be eliminated by any practical socialist. There would be difficulties, but they could perhaps be overcome. There might be a tendency to leave unendowed the artist or scientist whose work was in advance of his time, and who at present subsists either on his own fortune or on that of the few who appreciate his importance. But a sufficiently enlightened administration might deal effectually with such cases.

Thus the goal of socialism is theoretically realizable. But the road to it is difficult and dangerous. The practical problem of the socialist is to take over the control of capital without destroying it or driving it away. And this problem, at least in our country, has not yet been solved. It is made difficult for the capitalist to fulfil his functions and little is done to secure their fulfilment by anybody else. The capitalist, therefore, tends to employ his resources elsewhere and so to diminish the wages fund, or to leave the country altogether and to deprive the exchequer of his taxes, or to spend upon himself his wealth while it is still his. In all these three ways wealth is either wholly lost to the community or diverted from a productive to an unproductive source. But what makes the situation still more alarming is that a great part of that which is successfully taken from the capitalist is not used in productive state enterprise, but is withdrawn from industry altogether and spent as current revenue. A ruthless persistence in this policy might indeed secure equality, but at an enormous price. The socialist party may eventually elaborate a less costly programme of transformation. But until they do, only those who set an enormous value on their ultimate goal can rationally support them.

Undeniably, there is much which is artistically pleasing in a socialist utopia. It has a simple and complete structure which seems to contrast favourably with the ragged and fortuitous nature of its competitor. But would its inhabitants be really much happier than those who live in our present, imperfect world? The chief claim of socialism is not that it is more efficient, nor more likely to raise the standard of the masses, but that it is more just. The masses are told, and they have come to believe, that they have a grievance. Those who have earned much sometimes receive little, and some who have not worked at all inherit the luxuries which the industry of others supplies. It is this type of inequality which the socialist abhors and which he would like to abolish.

Now, it is interesting to observe that this kind of inequality was not always regarded as unjust. Until recently it was accepted as natural that a man should leave his possessions undiminished to his son; and because it seemed natural it was no grievance. There are always some whose Oedipus complex is peculiarly unstable and who are conscious of great envy without being conscious of its cause. They have, therefore, attached this envy to the nearest symbol and have become indignant at the disproportion between merit and reward. They have preached their indignation and awakened dormant feelings of a like nature in those who listen to their words. Such discontent, since it feeds on unconscious impulses which slumber but never die, is infectious and has spread quickly throughout the world. Thus socialism is a remedy to cure a symptom which it has itself produced.

The great revolutions of the past have been caused by the same unconscious forces operating with other symbols. Often they have been directed against one man, a ruler who was unfortunate enough to become the symbol only of the unpleasant side of the father. An epidemic of hate, which had little relation to the real character of the king, swept him from his place. More recently, however, it has been a class which has evoked this hate.

A class which is the object of a revolution must have some character which renders it an apt symbol of the unpleasant side of the father. It must possess something of which the masses are deprived. In the French revolution, this was not wealth, but privilege. A rich bourgeois was a citizen and a brother, but a poor aristocrat was not. The world has now swept away the inequalities before the law which the French revolution was promoted to destroy. But if a French revolutionary could return today he would be surprised to find the same discontent.

At present the disproportion between merit and reward is the apparent cause of envy, and idealists have devised a system which would eliminate this grievance. But we may predict that if they are successful the old envy will reappear in a new form. Privilege and the disproportion between merit and reward are not the only inequalities. We may expect that, if inequality due to inheritance is swept away, that due to individual merit will be the next candidate for the post of symbol for the unconscious hate of the Oedipus complex.

There are, indeed, symptoms that such a transference has already begun to take place. The unions endeavour to insist upon a flat rate of pay and object to the introduction of piece rates. And there is some evidence that in Russia the ruling intelligentsia have inherited the unpopularity as well as the power of their Tzarist predecessors.

Finally, when all artificial inequalities are removed, there remain those natural inequalities which cannot be so easily destroyed. But possibly the objection to eugenics, which is evident among many of those who embrace the socialist creed, is an indication that legislation may some day be introduced to prevent the birth of those who might be more healthy, more beautiful, or more intelligent than their fellows.

III. AN UNTRIED REVOLUTION

If the argument of the last sections is correct the real cause of unrest is neither legal, economic nor physical. It is psychological and a derivative of the Oedipus complex. Therefore it cannot be cured by the lawyer who removes privilege, nor by the economist who adjusts rewards to merits, or equalizes them altogether, nor even by the breeder who seeks uniformity before quality in his stock. Each of these may, perhaps, remove a symptom, but they cannot touch the real disease. They may provide some alleviation, and their work should not be altogether despised. But only the psychologist can determine whether the malady is curable, and, if so, prescribe a cure.

Freud, in his latest book, *Das Unbehagen in der Kultur*, seems to think that there is no remedy. For him aggression is indestructible, and will always appear in the Oedipus complex and in the manifold situations which symbolize it. If, however, aggression is not an independent impulse but a reaction to frustration, we may hope that once the real nature of the frustration has been discovered it may be removed. The result would be a peace nearly as sublime as, and far less dull than, that which even the pious only hope to find in heaven.

The psychologist, who admits that he dreams of an utopia and preaches a crusade, must be prepared to see turned against himself the same weapons which he has forged against his adversary. He must at once admit that his longing for a better world is a symbolic expression of his unconscious longing to return to the mother of his first infancy, and that his hostility to those who stand in his way is derived from that aggression which was first awakened by his father. But the psychologist is at least aware of the nature of his malady. And for this reason he is more likely to cure it than the economist, who can only detect a single symptom.

The psychologist, once he has recognized the origin of unrest in the Oedipus complex, will next enquire why in some persons the legacy of this complex is more persistent than in others. The answer has already been given by Freud. Inhibitions produce fixations at, or regressions to, a state of mind which would otherwise have been outgrown.

Now these inhibitions are of two kinds: repressions and suppressions. While repressions are unconscious and automatic, suppressions are due to the conscious morals or conventions which the individual derives from the society of which he forms a unit.

The repressions are much the most severe, and the fundamental deprivations of this life are due to them rather than to suppressions. Moreover, once they have been acquired, they cannot be destroyed except by the long and costly process of analysis. Must we, therefore, conclude that the only cure for the unrest of the world, which the psychologist can offer, is to psycho-analyse its members? Such a recommendation would be entirely futile; for it is obviously impossible to carry out.

If, however, we investigate the process by which repressions are built up, we shall find that although their collective cure is impracticable, their collective prevention might be more easily obtained. A repression is an introjected suppression. The child is compelled to refrain from certain acts by persons whom he loves. Later, when he is withdrawn from or outgrows the influence of these persons, his own moral character is found to have absorbed a part of theirs. This process is termed introjection by the psycho-analytic writers who have described it. By it the unconscious conscience, or super-ego, is formed. Thus repression presupposes a previous suppression.

The suppressions of an individual can be eliminated by educating his environment rather than by analysing himself; and this is an operation that, unlike analysis, can be performed *en masse*. Therefore, pernicious repressions, since they are ultimately dependent upon suppressions, can be prevented more easily than they can be cured.

The problem of the sociological psychologist is now clear. He must determine what inhibitions are responsible for those regressions and fixations that produce unrest. And he must invent a society in which these inhibitions would not arise. Thus, like the economist, he may seek to prevent an internal malady by modifying the environment. But, unlike the economist, he will attack the ethical rather than the economic structure of society.

I believe that incestuous fixations and regressions are due less to the primary repression of the Oedipus complex than to those secondary repressions which prevent an erotic transference to adequate substitutes for the first love object of the child. If I am right, it is therefore less the incest taboo than the secondary sexual conventions of society which are ultimately at fault.

We are here approaching the most difficult part of this investigation. It is easy to assert vaguely that the sexual conventions of society should be changed. But it is extremely difficult to recommend the precise changes that should be made. Nevertheless, we shall attempt to foresee, as best we may, the consequences of the progressive elimination of our taboos on adultery, fornication and precocity.

(1) *Adultery*

Let us suppose that while the other sexual taboos remain in force that against adultery collapses. Society no longer condemns the unfaithful nor condones the jealous. It admits that the individual's post-marital erotic life is his own affair, and denies to the husband or wife a prescriptive rite to the unwilling affections of his partner. In certain classes in France and elsewhere, the first of these conditions is already realized. But, with a singular inconsistency, the same neighbours who are so indulgent to the unfaithful are equally tolerant to the vengeance of the deserted. The satisfaction of both conditions by a transference of disapproval from adultery to jealousy has, so far as I know, only been attempted by a few isolated intellectuals. And, since these are often of emotional instability, it is difficult to generalize from the success or failure of their experiments. It is necessary to foresee the consequences of such a shift in the conventional standards in an average society.

It is not, of course, possible to abolish jealousy by social disapproval. But the jealous could at least be made to feel that their sentiment was a peculiarly egoistic form of greed, which should be controlled if it has not been outgrown.[1]

The civilized individual is highly differentiated and requires a rare combination of physical, mental and emotional qualities from the partner who will fulfil his needs. Under the present system the partners are not even supposed to be acquainted with each other's physical qualities before they are united. This restriction More remedied in his Utopia. But the mental and emotional qualities are far more difficult to foresee. The husband may discover that the attentive fiancée has become the wife who is indifferent to or jealous of his life's ambition. Or the wife may find that the art which is everything to her is meaningless to her husband. Lastly the emotional qualities of a person include those erotic nuances which are so vital to the permanence of a union based on sex, and which are not correctly discovered in the fiancée by the lover who hallucinates only according to his desires. For these reasons, the probability of that ill-controlled lottery called marriage proving a success is very slight. A few may pick a winner, but these have generally made a surreptitious examination of the tickets.

When we remember the probabilities against an idyllic match, we need no longer wonder that so many should either deceive or detest their legal partners. I do not know whether statistics of infidelity have ever been collected. But a circular for this purpose directed to all those who had been married ten years or more is hardly likely to receive honest replies. If, however, they were honest, I believe that two-thirds of the men and perhaps one-fifth of the women would state that they had at least once deceived their spouses. The consequences of such deception are perhaps not so serious as those of an unwilling fidelity. Nevertheless, they are obviously injurious. Even a marriage which is not completely monogamous may yet have great value; for good companionship and united cooperation may be associated with some promiscuity. But if the promiscuity has to be concealed, the companionship

[1] 'Love and jealousy are both instinctive emotions, but religion has decreed that jealousy is a virtuous emotion, to which the community ought to lend support, while love is at best excusable'. Bertrand Russell, *Marriage and Morals*, p. 17.

suffers together with the honesty which is one of its first conditions.

Many individuals who value honesty with their friends above every consideration, are sometimes faithful for no other reason than that to be otherwise would necessarily involve deceit. A man may be more dependent upon his wife than upon any other woman, and yet desire madly sometimes to sleep with someone else. But, if he knows that his wife's pride, fostered by the approval of her friends, is greater than her love, he has the alternatives of being dishonestly unfaithful and deceiving her, of being honestly unfaithful and losing her, or of suppressing his desires. If he chooses this last alternative his wife becomes an object which frustrates life's intensest urge. Such an object inevitably awakens that slumbering ferocity which is the explosive evolved by nature to obliterate all obstacles to a sexual goal. This situation sometimes leads to murder. But more often repression is sufficient to convert it into that mixture of irritability and depression falsely attributed to a disorder of the stomach.

Such a surly puritan is, however, more likely to be aware of the cause of his distemper than his chaste and irritable wife. She also doubtless suffers from the results of some incompatibility of temperament, though her greater inhibitions render her wholly unconscious of the true origin of her malady. An analysis of her dreams, however, would reveal an intimate association between those days which were especially aggravating and those nights in which her unconscious fantasy dallied with some lover. Havelock Ellis[1] is struck by the frequency with which even the most devoted wife dreams of a love affair with someone who is not her husband. Havelock Ellis denies the importance of such dreams; but they disclose a general, though inhibited, inclination to infidelity which, where there is any serious incompatibility of temperament, cannot fail to provide a constant source of irritation and a cause of regression to the Oedipus complex.

There is little doubt that if the relation between husbands and wives were less possessive and more companionate, there would not only be less irritability, but also less promiscuity in

---

[1] *Studies in the Psychology of Sex*, vol. VII.

the world. If they were good companions who could sympathize with each other's emotional excursions, they would not only be better tempered but also more satisfying to each other. For, firstly, the incompatibility of temperament would have decreased and, secondly, the element of restraint, which turns the best palace into a prison, would have been removed. There is a classical story of a man who had always lived in his native town, without the least desire to leave it, until he was forbidden to do so. Then he was, for the first time, possessed by a desire to travel, which compelled him to break the decree and suffer the penalty for his disobedience.

An alteration of the present social attitude towards adultery would not, of course, be a panacea for all our social troubles. There are many neurotic individuals whose incestuous fixations render them incapable of satisfaction with any real person. These, no doubt, would become more promiscuous. But at least the consequences of their discontent would tend to be limited to the relatively small circle of their lovers and would afflict less the greater number who now suffer from the manifold activities into which they at present sublimate their insatiable aggression. There are, however, a majority, in whom the Oedipus complex is less the result of fixation than of regression, who have only been prevented by the present system from permanently transferring their affection to a compatible and satisfying mate. For these there would be a greater probability of a full life and therefore for contented citizenship.

Perhaps the Austrians were not overwhelmed by Bolshevism because they were, more than other people, intuitively aware of the real cause of their social discontent. An acquaintance of mine, who was in Vienna during the post-war revolution, seeing a great procession coming up the street, hastened to take refuge. To his surprise and amusement, he soon read upon the banners no demand for the instantaneous execution of all capitalists, but the more fundamental desire for easier divorce.

(2) *Fornication*

In the last section we tried to anticipate the consequences of a modification in the existing taboo of adultery while the other sexual taboos remained in force. But clearly a great part of the desire for adultery would of itself cease if the taboo on fornication were also weakened. The main cause of unhappiness in marriage is an incompatibility of temperament which previous experience would have discovered and avoided. At present this experience is theoretically denied and marriage is scarcely better than a lottery. The removal of the taboo on adultery would do something to remedy the consequences of an unfortunate choice; but the abolition of that on pre-marital incontinence would decrease the probability of its ever being made. Among the Trobrianders, according to Malinowski[1] each individual, after many shorter unions with other members of his tribe, usually finds a satisfying permanent mate. For us, since we are more highly specialized and therefore less easily content, the number of trials might be greater (the percentage of adequate mates is smaller), but they are also more required.

Not only would an increase in pre-marital intercourse increase the probability of discovering really compatible mates, it would also provide an invaluable preparation for the more serious union of marriage. Among primitive peoples the puberty ceremonies of the youths and maidens usually terminate in some practical instruction in the mysteries of sex. But with us, there is no school of love provided by the Minister of Education. In fact, all practical instruction in this art is theoretically denied. Most men, indeed, acquire a knowledge of its grosser principles. But usually only at the hands of some commercial artist who is herself incapable of the spontaneity necessary to the finer technique. The young Frenchman is far better educated in these matters than the young Briton or American, and perhaps for this reason he is a much better husband. The average unmarried woman of all civilized countries is, however, still a virgin. Many remain in consequence so clumsy in the art of love that they quickly lose their legal partners in reality, even if they retain them in appearance. They are thus likely to become those innocent parties in divorce who, as Havelock Ellis has pointed out, are nearly always guilty.

It is well known that the present taboo on pre-marital incontinence is a relic of the time when a woman was the chattel

---

[1] *The Sexual Life of Savages.*

of her father or her husband. This system now finds few avowed apologists. But the unconscious jealousy of fathers, as well as of husbands, is perhaps still concealed behind the argument that promiscuity of any kind must lead to the birth of children without two parents to protect them. The question whether it is desirable for children to have fathers is more uncertain than it seems. But I will assume uninvestigated the conventional conclusion. It is not true, however, that promiscuity necessarily leads to such children. Even among the Trobrianders the birth of illegitimates is very rare, and with our knowledge of contraception (and perhaps with abortion permitted) it should be of negligible frequency.

Many other objections will, of course, be made. It will be said, for instance, that a woman's virginity is her most valuable possession which she should wish to keep sacred for the one man she will really love. But this is no argument against the proposals of this section. The suggestion is not to compel persons to be incontinent who do not wish it, but only to remove the prejudice against those who do. If anyone is anxious to wait until she can stake everything on a single lottery, she can still do so. In a few cases such a sacrifice of earlier pleasures may bring a real reward. In the rest easier divorce would remove the irrevocability from a mistaken choice.

(3) *Precocity*

We come now to the subject of precocity, by which I understand sexual indulgence before the age of puberty. Thus, while in the section on adultery we discussed promiscuity after marriage, and in that on fornication incontinence between puberty and marriage, in this we shall consider the abolition of taboos on pre-pubertal sexual activities.

There is, perhaps, no normal form of sex expression which is so tabooed as precocity. The adulterer may be fined for alienation of affection, the fornicator may be excluded from select society, but the precocious child, who might have been thought to be less responsible for his actions, may be summarily expelled from his school for an act which he never knew was regarded as a crime. One might suppose that such actions, which are thus condemned with a sentence which may wreck a life, must be the monstrous abnormalities of a degenerate heredity. But we learn from zoology, anthropology and psychology that nothing is more normal than the occurrence of sexual play from infancy to adolescence. Zoologists have observed this play in young apes and monkeys, who, in imitating their elders, gradually perfect those instincts which will be necessary to them when they are full grown.[1] Indeed, it may be plausibly argued that such precocity, like all play, is necessary for this purpose. Malinowski has recorded similar behaviour among the young Trobrianders[2] which has apparently the most beneficial results. Finally, psycho-analysts have discovered that like caricatures of the adult, sexual impulses occur regularly in our own children, but that they are repressed in the latency period from about the age of five till puberty.

Let us examine more closely this phenomenon of a latency period, for in it the character of our civilization is formed. Psycho-analysts have long ago observed that it is peculiar to man, and we may note that the Oedipus complex is also confined to this species. Further, Malinowski has stated that a latency period does not occur among the Trobrianders, and also that among this same people he can detect no trace of the Oedipus complex. Ernest Jones has denied this last observation, but it seems probable that incestuous fixations are less prevalent among these savages.

We may suggest the following explanations to reconcile these two opposing views. We may agree with Ernest Jones that the Oedipus complex is inevitable in the human child. His long period of infancy must determine that the same object which first satisfied his hunger should also be the first object of his dawning sexual love – a love which includes a strong oral element. The father's jealousy must inhibit the free expression of this love, and evoke aggressive impulses towards himself. But only where an alternative expression of these erotic feelings is equally suppressed should we expect to find serious fixations at the infantile incestuous stage. Among the Trobrianders, who indulge unrestricted in sexual play from a very early age, apparently no impediment is placed in the way of such alterna-

---

[1] Zuckermann, 'The Social Behaviour of Apes and Monkeys', a paper read to the Psycho-Analytical Society, February 1903. Marias, 'Baboons, Hypnosis and Insanity', *Psyche*, October 1926.
[2] *The Sexual Life of Savages.*

A PSYCHOLOGIST'S UTOPIA

tive expression. Probably for this reason the latency period is absent and the Oedipus fixations less pronounced.

In earlier sections we have traced the slumbering discontent of our civilization to unsatisfied fixations at, or regressions to, infantile incestuous desires. We have seen that the probability of regression would be reduced by discarding some of our taboos on adultery and fornication, but that fixations could not be cured in this way.[1] We now see that the fixations could also be reduced if the taboo on precocity were abandoned, so that the child would be free to transfer his dawning sexual impulses to a more suitable object than his mother.

It may be objected that repression, however injurious to some individuals, is essential to the formation of that morality which has made civilization possible. But probably the formation of a super-ego which would insure the respect of the father, and of the generation which symbolized him, would be secured by the repression of the Oedipus complex alone. The further repression of all alternative outlets to the infantile incestuous desires is more likely to impede than to facilitate this work. For repression which undertakes too much is liable to break down.

We have left one sole taboo untouched as a sufficient protection to society. But the systematic investigator should ruthlessly enquire whether this taboo is really necessary. If the child were allowed full play for his incestuous impulses there would be no repression, no transference to the father of inhibited impulses and no introjection of paternal prohibitions at the natural termination of this transference.[2] It is difficult to imagine that an individual brought up in this way could ever display the self-restraint necessary for any co-operation with others. Therefore one taboo is perhaps necessary to culture; but the collapse of most of the rest could hardly fail to facilitate its task.

If precocity were less suppressed there would be less incestuous

---

[1] The repression of incest, of precocity and of adult extra-marital relations may be called respectively, primary, secondary and tertiary repressions. It is possible that the decay of tertiary repressions alone might produce a conversion of invested into direct aggression, which would increase the instability of society. Only from the decay of secondary repressions can we expect any great reduction of fixation, frustration and aggression.

[2] Unless, as some psycho-analysts think, the superego is now innate.

fixation. If there were less fixation there would also be less regression; for those who have been the last to transfer their love are the first to return to its original object. If there were less fixation and regression there would be less motive for unconscious hate. And if there were less unconscious hate, there would be less conscious discontent, and less danger of those collective eruptions of aggression which periodically afflict society.

(3) *The Ethical Revolution*

A progressive attack upon the post- and pre-marital and pre-pubertal taboos is an untried revolution. Its consequences cannot therefore be foreseen with certainty. But I have argued that it is much more likely to be beneficial than the political, legal or economic revolutions of the past or present. For it is the only revolution which can hope to reach the unconscious causes of discontent. Thus I believe that a state in which there was less sexual inhibition would not only be freer but also more secure.[1]

It should be as easy to mobilize the present discontent of society against our sexual taboos as it has been to unite it against our economic system. Since we must have some outlet for our aggression let us be sure that it is well directed.

SUMMARY

(1) Aggressiveness is not an independent impulse, but is a reaction to frustration – especially sexual frustration.[2]

(2) In the Oedipus complex frustrated sexual desires and the inhibitions which frustrate them are both unconscious.

(3) The aggressiveness, which is a reaction to the frustration of the Oedipus complex, may be inverted and manifest itself as neurosis, or remain direct and manifest itself as free discontent.

---

[1] Possibly such a state would also have less sublimations. There is, perhaps, a conflict between the interests of one generation and another. Part of our artistic and scientific legacy to posterity may be a by-product of our own neurosis and discontent.

[2] This proposition is fundamental to my thesis. But we must wait for further psycho-analytic research to disprove or confirm it.

(4) The social discontent, which has always been a danger to society, is a manifestation of the Oedipus complexes of its members. It cannot be removed by purely economic means.

(5) Everyone has had an Oedipus complex, but whereas some individuals remain fixed in it or regress to it, others outgrow it and transfer their incestuous desires to more satisfactory objects.

(6) A decrease of sexual taboos would increase the probability of such transference and decrease the probability of such fixation and regression.

(7) A decrease in the number and intensity of Oedipus fixations and regressions would involve a decrease of frustration and consequently of aggression. There would therefore, be less inverted aggression, that is, neurosis, and less direct free aggression, that is, social discontent.

This paper may perhaps be aptly terminated by a single quotation from Bertrand Russell.[1] 'If the world remains filled with malevolence and hate, the more scientific it becomes, the more horrible it will be. To diminish the virulence of these passions is, therefore, an essential of human progress. To a very large extent their existence has been brought about by a wrong sexual ethic and a bad sexual education. For the future of civilization a new and better sexual ethic is indispensable. It is this fact that makes the reform of sexual morality one of the vital needs of our time.'

Postscript (1977)

If I were to write this paper today, I would have done it differently. I think I was theoretically aware that the basic conflict between capitalism and socialism is intra-psychic. I was probably much less aware, intuitively, of this fact and could not recognize my picture of the socialist as a split-off envious, constructively impotent and very angry part of myself. Moreover, I think that this part of me claimed, on the basis of a deal of projective identification with my mother, that I understood her much better than my father. But this knowledge, analogous to that of the engineer and the physical scientist, was totally different from another sort oriented more to the psyche of real people, which my father had in abundance. It is also probably true that in this field, though constructively impotent,

[1] *Marriage and Morals*, p. 211.

I felt I had a real amount of destructive potency against my parents and older siblings.

Beyond this point familiarity with the intra-psychic parallel is unlikely to help us very much. The trade unions are no longer impotent and this perhaps has relieved their basic grievance; and it remains to be seen whether they will use their new power destructively or refrain from doing so. They may also find new ways of using it constructively.

So much for the general modification I would now make in the paper. But my specific argument that a reduction in sexual restriction would decrease our social discontent would also appear to be in need of modification. For while the sexual restrictions have been modified, social discontent expressed as a sense of social injustice has probably increased. In part, I think unconscious envy is much less decreased than I formerly believed. But, as I said earlier, the social classes whose position most inclined them to envy are no longer impotent and it remains to be seen how they will use their present powers.

One last point. While at the time of writing this paper I made no distinction between jealousy and envy, I now realize, on the basis of Mrs Klein's book, *Envy and Gratitude*, that while jealousy is based on disappointment in love, envy springs from hate, desires only to destroy, and, from a common sense point of view, is much the worst emotion. As to jealousy, it is so normal and indestructible – though it can be reduced if the delusional element in it is abolished – that I now think there is much to be said for monogamous marriages, in which each side refrains from torturing his or her partner with justified suspicion that he or she, when out of sight, is in the arms of a rival. And with regard to envy, so far as the demand for social justice is partly based on unconscious envy, it is debased by the vile odour of hypocrisy.

7
A Psycho-analytic Study of the Voices of Joan of Arc*

The psycho-analytical enthusiast, who is not a practising physician, may turn to history for patients on whom to try his hand. But, whereas the practising analyst has the free associations of the living patient before him, the psycho-analytical historian must be content with dead records, which, by comparison, may seem hopelessly inadequate. Often they may be misleading, and sometimes positively false. Moreover, he cannot question them further, to confirm or to correct his views. At best, therefore, he can only hope to depict a personality which is psychologically coherent and consistent with the most plausible tradition. He cannot even guarantee that his portrait is the only one which satisfies these two conditions. But he may comfort himself with the reflection that, though his difficulties are greater than those of the practising physician, his responsibilities are less; and that his mistakes are unlikely to do harm.

The most reliable data for an analysis of Joan of Arc are to be found in her answers to the judges at her trial.[1] But, since these alone are scarcely sufficient, they must be supplemented from the traditional representations of her character. These fall mainly into three groups. The first, which depicted her as a sorceress, has been revived in a modern form by Professor Margaret Murray, to whom Joan was the incarnate goddess of a pagan cult – a rustic survival from neolithic times. The second tradition depicts her as the epitome of all abstract chivalrous and Christian virtues. This view began during her life and received official sanction at the Trial of Rehabilitation. It still remains the chief inspiration of the more sentimental

---
* *B. J. Med. Psych.*, vol. XIII, 1933.
[1] *The Trial of Jeanne d'Arc*, translated by W. P. Barrett.

biographers. The third tradition is the product of a rational age. To Anatole France, Joan was a bemused hysteric, who happened to be a useful mascot to the army in a superstitious age. But, even to M. France, she was no ordinary hysteric. Indeed, to me, her image by this iconoclast seems more superb, because more real, than that painted by her declared adorers. My own view of Joan approximates to that of M. France – except that I credit her with more intelligence and with a more heroic end.

We all know the main elements of her history. Her life was dominated by her Voices, and was the consistent expression of their commands. Emanating from apparitions of St Michael, St Margaret, and St Catherine, they told her to drive the English from the land, and to crown the Dauphin king. With great difficulty, she visited him at Chinon, and was then, by his order, examined by the ecclesiastics of Poitiers, who declared that she seemed to come from God rather than from the Devil. Next, she was sent with an army to Orleans, where her confidence and reputation so terrified her enemies and encouraged her friends that she was able to relieve the siege. After some months of victories and a few checks, the Burgundians captured her at Compiègne and handed her over to the English. Finally, she was tried as a witch and heretic by French theologians of the Anglican party, and after recantation and relapse, she was burnt at Rouen. She was still under twenty when she died.

Since the interests of the chronicler are different from those of the psychologist, the records are most scanty where they are most important. Jeanne was born on 6 January 1412, or thereabouts, during the Twelfth Night celebrations of the peasants of Domrémy. Her father was the most important farmer in the village; her mother was very pious; and she had two brothers and a sister, Catherine, who died young. As a child, Jeanne looked after the grazing animals, as peasants' children do today. She also played and danced with her companions, and hung garlands on a fairy tree. This is nearly all that is recorded of her early childhood. Yet somewhere within this period, probably in infancy, we must place the origin of those visions which caused her to be worshipped as a saint, and burnt as a scion of the Devil.

PSYCHOLOGICAL STUDY OF VOICES OF JOAN OF ARC

The visions themselves seem to have begun, when we might expect them, at the age of puberty[1] – at the time when those early sexual impulses, which are regularly repressed by the Oedipus complex, are re-animated in the unconscious by the imperative demands of endocrine development. One summer noon, as Jeanne was in her father's garden, she saw a light and heard a voice from the direction of the church which said, 'I come from God to help you to be good. Jeannette, be good and God will help you.'[2]

Jeanne was very frightened; but she said nothing either to her parents or to the curé. Later, she heard the voice again: 'Jeannette, be good.' The third time she heard it she knew that it came from St Michael.[3]

One day he said, 'St Catherine and St Margaret will come to guide and help you in what you have to do. You will believe them. And what they will say will come to pass by the commandment of our Lord.'[4] This promise caused her great joy; for she knew all about these saints and loved them well.

About this time we may infer that another change was occurring in the life of Jeanne. She played less with her companions and sometimes neglected her father's herds. She had always been pious; but now 'she confessed often and communicated with an extraordinary fervour. She went to mass every day. She could be found at all hours in church, sometimes prostrated on the stone, sometimes with her hands joined and her eyes turned to Our Lord or Our Lady.'[5]

Gradually the visions became more frequent and more distinct. Soon, she not only heard, but also saw, touched and even smelt the sweet fragrance of her saints. And they for their part became more definite in their demands.

'You must go to France,' said St Catherine and St Margaret.[6]

---

[1] At the age of thirteen. *The Trial*, p. 54.

[2] Anatole France, *Vie de Jeanne d'Arc*. The sense, but not the words of this and the following quotations from M. France accords with Jeanne's answers at her trial. See *The Trial*, pp. 54–5, 123, 177–8.

[3] *The Trial*, pp. 55, 122. Her replies were not always consistent. She also said she heard the voice many times before she knew it came from St Michael.

[4] Cf. *The Trial*, p. 122.

[5] *Vie de Jeanne d'Arc*, I. 55. Cf. Jules Quicherat, *Procès de condemnation et de réhabilitation*, II; *The Trial*, p. 65.

[6] Cf. *The Trial*, p. 55.

'Daughter of God,[1] you must take the Dauphin to Reims, that he may be consecrated with the holy oil', said St Michael. The apparitions also told her to crown the Dauphin king,[2] and in all things they gave her great comfort and promised aid.

In a few months the Voices were prophesying her wounds,[3] and then her capture.[4] She had done nothing in the world except by God's command, she told her judges at the trial.[5] Only when she tried to escape from prison by leaping from the tower of Beaurevoir, she disobeyed them; for they had told her not to escape.[6]

Anatole France has done nearly all that pre-Freudian psychology can do to explain these mysteries on a naturalistic basis. He has investigated the legends of St Michael, St Margaret, St Catherine and of St Remi, the patron of her village, who anointed his emperor with a sacred oil. He has argued that they must have been familiar to Jeanne, and that her own tasks were largely modelled upon the stories of these saints. Yet all such stories cannot have played a larger part in the construction of Jeanne s visions than that played by the residual experiences of the previous day in the construction of a dream. To recognize such current associations is not to understand the dream, for they are only reproduced because of their aptness to express thoughts and wishes which remain unconscious. If the residues are different the manifest dream is different; but the unconscious desires remain the same. Similarly, if Jeanne had been familiar with different saints, her life task might have been different; but the unconscious thoughts which underlay it would have been the same.

The attention of psycho-analysts, of recent years, has been increasingly directed towards the superego, that obscure force within us which is not yet wholly understood. It was first recognized, under the name of the censor, as a resistance against dream analysis, that is, as a force which prevents patients from becoming conscious of their repressed desires.

---

[1] Jeanne told her judges that the Voices often used this appellation. *The Trial*, p. 102.

[2] She confessed that she was the angel from God who brought the crown, *The Trial*, p. 334.

[3] Ibid. p. 74.   [4] Ibid. p. 95.   [5] Ibid. p. 70.   [6] Ibid. p. 91.

Soon, however, the concept was generalized to include all inhibitions against the free expressions of natural instincts. Next, the criticism that the terms censor and superego were anthropomorphic and reminiscent of the mythological psychology of a bygone age, was invalidated by the discovery that the entity denoted by these terms was indeed a person – namely, the introjected image of the patient's first concept of his parents. The discovery of other functions of the superego was not long in following. It was found to include commands as well as inhibitions, and to be the force which compels certain individuals to devote their lives to obsessional work rather than to play, and prevents them from finding any happiness except in the fulfilment of some task. Then, for some years, analysts concentrated on the sadistic qualities of the superego. They found that it was the force which compels certain persons not only to perform a duty, but also to become martyrs to a cause. And lastly, Freud has suggested that it may also provide comfort to those who surrender to its will.[1]

Some of the manifestations of the superego have always been familiar. Unlike ourselves, our Victorian fathers were each provided with a mighty conscience, which they thought to be the voice of God and generally obeyed. But it has remained for our present age to recognize the true origin of this voice, to understand its commands, and to see that they are not always in accord with the sentimental humanitarianism of our time. The Inquisitor, no less than the liberator of slaves, followed the dictates of his conscious conscience and his unconscious superego.

Three clear and distinct elements may be distinguished in Jeanne's Voices; they told her to be good; they promised her aid; and they commanded her to perform a task. And we may add that they foretold and drove her to her doom. Now these three elements and the fourth which is less clear, are the four characteristics of the superego. Jeanne's saints, then, were projections of her superego; and, since they were exceptionally well defined, we may hope by studying them to discover something not only about Jeanne but also about superegos in general.

---

[1] Freud, 'Humour', *Internat. J. of Psycho-Analysis*, IX, part i.

PROHIBITIONS

Jeanne had always been a pious and obedient child; yet her Voices told her to be good. She was herself aware of a deep if vague guilt, or she would not have confessed so often. Probably it was this sense of guilt which destroyed her normal life and took all the pleasure from her games. But what can have been the hidden temptation which weighed upon her mind? Clearly, she did not know herself; for she confessed often, which means that the recitation of her trivial conscious misdemeanours brought her no permanent relief. Psycho-analysts are familiar with such conditions, and they know that when a religious patient is unable to remove a sense of sin by innumerable confessions, this sin is to be found in their old friend the Oedipus complex. Some of Freud's critics used to think the Oedipus complex was peculiar to the Victorian generation, or at least to patriarchal societies. Its ubiquitousness, however, even among matriarchal peoples, has now been proved by the recent work of Roheim.[1] We shall, therefore, be guilty of no rash assumption if we suppose that Jeanne, like all other children, was afflicted by this complex. In her, indeed, it must have been peculiarly strong.

Children with purely positive Oedipus complexes direct their main love towards the parent of the opposite sex, and introject the parent of the same sex,[2] who is the sexual rival and chief source of inhibition, to form the basis of their superegos. In children with purely negative Oedipus complexes these dispositions are reversed. But pure complexes are convenient fictions, and actual individuals lie somewhere between these two extremes. Both parents are loved, both are rivals, and both contribute to the superego – though in varying degrees. Jeanne, as we shall see later, showed clear traces of such a mixed complex. But, for the moment, we need only notice that her saints – the projections of her superego – were of both sexes.

The primary function of the superego is to repress the incestuous desires of infancy; but if it is abnormally severe, it may also inhibit all later sexual impulses. Jeanne's saints were

[1] *Internat. J. of Psycho-Analysis*, XIII, parts i, ii.
[2] [Or projectively identify with him or her.]

PSYCHOLOGICAL STUDY OF VOICES OF JOAN OF ARC

of this nature. When she reached the age of puberty they told her to be good, and by this they meant 'be pure'. Such at least was the meaning which Jeanne herself attributed to their command, for she vowed, in their presence, to retain her virginity for ever.[1] And we are told that she was in fact so pure that she excited no carnal lusts even in the soldiers with whom she camped. Moreover, she was intolerant of impurity in others. She drove off the loose women who followed the army, and is even said to have broken her sword upon the back of one of them. The reactions of her own soldiery to these proceedings are not recorded. Her enemies, however, persisted in calling her a harlot – an accusation which always made her weep.

COMMANDS

Jeanne's Voices did not only tell her to be good; they imposed a task. They commanded her, like St Remi, the patron of her village, to anoint her Dauphin with a sacred oil and to crown him king. She was also told to relieve the siege of Orleans and to chase the English from the realm.

Psycho-therapeutists, of all schools, are familiar with such life tasks. Jung, for instance, having noticed that mental health has some correlation with their successful accomplishment, and neurosis with a failure to fulfil them, encourages his patients to perform their duties. Freudians, on the other hand, confine themselves strictly to analysis, and renounce the rôle of mentors. For, apart from the difficulty of giving moral advice in the absence of all absolute ethical criteria, such forbearance is rewarded by a deeper insight into the unconscious motives and structure of the superego.

The superego is not content that the ego should sin no more; it demands that restitution should be made for past sins which cannot be undone. Moreover, it makes no distinction between thought and deed. If the child has wished to separate its parents, to take something from, or to destroy, one or both of them, its superego treats it as if this wish had been accomplished. 'You must make restitution,' says the superego. 'Unite what you have separated. Give back what you have

[1] *The Trial*, p. 101.

taken. Recreate what you have destroyed.'[1] An analysis of a 'life task' will show that it is a symbolic satisfaction of some such demand. Thus, the eclectic philosopher who devotes his life to the reconciliation of incompatible beliefs, may be trying to undo the sin of Atlas, who separated his parents Earth and Sky; the author of a magnum opus may be restoring to his mother the child he once wished to steal; the builder of a spire may be giving back to God the phallus which he wished to take from his father[2]; and the metaphysician, to whom the universe is animate, may be recreating, on a grander scale, the parent whom he once wished to destroy. Yet all the time the forbidden wishes of the past live on in the unconscious (i.e., the Id), so that the same task which symbolizes the restitution may also symbolize the repetition of the crime.[3]

The task of Jeanne was to anoint and crown the Dauphin, and to drive the English from the land. Princes and kings are well-known symbols of brothers and fathers. Therefore, it seems likely that one of the unconscious motives of Jeanne's task was to restore to her own brother or father something which she had once wished to take from them.

Adler has familiarized the world with the masculine protest of women. He has pointed out that most small girls wish to be boys, and that some women are never reconciled with their sex. Unlike Freud, however, he has refrained from a literal interpretation of his own results. It is easier to say, with Adler, that most girls wish to be boys, than, with Freud, that they wish to have a penis. And, for this reason, the Adlerian doctrine has been generally accepted. Yet all deep analyses show clearly that the Adlerian 'masculine protest' is only the semi-conscious expression of the Freudian 'penis envy'. Those who have not been analysed cannot expect to have any direct insight into the truth of Freud's conclusions, but it is perhaps possible to

---

[1] [I would now suppose that reparation is not primarily a superego function but is first developed in the ego during the 'depressive position' – though it may later be taken over by the superego.]

[2] A small boy of four, I know, often pretends to steal his father's nose. He also has an imaginary pet lion called 'Nose', who behaves in a thoroughly aggressive and phallic manner.

[3] Thus the feudal clansman often combines undying loyalty to his own chief with undying hatred of the leader of a hostile clan. Since both are father symbols, his martial ardour satisfies two opposite desires, namely, the wish to save and the wish to kill the father.

show that they are plausible. Most animals are bisexual. Hen birds, cows, bitches and female apes often attempt to mount their companions, so that there is nothing strange in the occurrence of similar masculine impulses in women. And, if we once accept the presence of the impulse, we naturally expect to find a desire for the organ which alone can satisfy it fully. The real problem is not to explain the existence of the desire; but to account for its repression.

That Jeanne's complex personality contained strong masculine elements is surely evident from her life.[1] She wore men's clothes, was skilled in horsemanship and war, and delighted in her good sword of St Catherine of Fierbois. Moreover, her chief sorrow in leaving her native village of Domremy was her parting from her little friend Hauviette, with whom she sometimes shared a bed. We may be certain that this relationship was pure and unsullied by any conscious carnal lusts; but the unconscious impulses behind such youthful infatuations are now well known. We may assume, therefore, without rashness, that Jeanne, like many other little girls, passed in infancy through a strong homosexual phase. She must have suffered from Adler's masculine protest; and this must have been the conscious expression of an unconscious penis envy. In short, she had once been jealous of her father or her brothers and desired to possess the weapons of their sex. A high degree of hereditary homosexuality, or the fact that the mother and sisters happen to be more lovable than the father and the brothers may cause such desires to be unusually developed. The intensity of Jeanne's masculine protest was probably due to both these factors; for, there is some evidence of hereditary masculinity in the report that she was without menses, and this may have been strengthened by the contrast between a gentle mother and a father who told her brothers that either he or they must drown her if she followed the soldiers to the war.

Jeanne, however, was pious and must have soon repressed her negative Oedipus complex and the penis envy which it involved. Perhaps at the age of puberty her feminine nature began to assert itself more strongly, so that at this time the unconscious

---

[1] Her judges were clearly struck by her masculinity, for they asked her 'if she had wanted to be a man . . .,' *The Trial*, p. 64. 'In all things', they wrote, 'she behaves more like a man than a woman', *The Trial*, p. 158.

conflict became unbearable, and the guilt more strong. At any rate, it was then that her Voices began to tell her to be good and to impose a task upon her. Part of this task was to crown the Dauphin king.

Anthropologists, no less than psycho-analysts, are familiar with the symbols of royalty and power. All early kings magically secured the fertility of their land, and the sceptres, whips and crowns with which they were invested were phallic emblems intended to help them in this task. To the unconscious, the regalia of authority have always had this meaning; the crown which Jeanne was told to give her Dauphin can have been no exception to this rule.

At Rouen, Jeanne's courage and intellectual superiority to her judges make her answers rank, with those of Socrates, among the supreme defences of history. Yet there was one exception to the clarity and accuracy of her replies. When asked what was the sign she had given to the Dauphin she at first refused to tell; and then, when pressed to answer, she said that it was a crown, fashioned by no earthly hands and brought by an angel from heaven. In the end, she seems to have confessed that she was herself the angel. This answer has perplexed apologists, like Andrew Lang, who devotes much space to the argument that the story was an allegory which Jeanne invented in order to conceal the real nature of the sign. She may indeed have wished to keep some secret; but her choice of this particular fantasy for the purpose is not without significance. It was the dramatized fulfilment of the main task of restitution which her Voices had imposed upon her, and which she had in fact fulfilled.

We are now in a position to collect the threads of this long argument. One conclusion, fantastic as it may seem, is forced upon us. Jeanne, in her infancy, had a negative Oedipus complex. Like many little girls she coveted the phallus of her brothers or her father; but repressed this desire and reacted against it with guilt. Therefore her superego imposed upon her the task of restoring what she had wished to take. This task she symbolically fulfilled; for she it was alone who caused her Dauphin to be crowned. All analysts must have had patients with almost identical ideas. Thus the life of Jeanne, so far as we have considered it at present, only differs from those of many other perplexed neurotics, in that it was played out upon a grander stage.

With this conclusion, however, the last word about Jeanne's task has not been said. The fulfilment of such duties is seldom consistent, and analysts are accustomed to find, by the side of all atonements, a symbolic repetition of the crime.

Subsidiary only to Jeanne's wish to restore the crown to the Dauphin, was the wish to chase the English ravagers from the 'doux pays de France'. It is sometimes said that Jeanne created the idea of France – an idea which has been the basis of the subsequent nationalism of the fiery people of that land. At least her own feeling for the 'Isle de France' seems to have been similar to that of later romanticists for 'la patrie'. The symbolism of this concept is very clear; for, French patriots themselves, in times of war, have compared their country to a mother violated by an alien foe. It is therefore easy for Freudian psychologists to see in such language a repetition of the son's fury at the idea of his mother's submission to his father. Thus the fantasy of rescuing the Mother Land from a foreign enemy is a common derivative of the male positive Oedipus complex. And its occurrence in Jeanne is further evidence of an inversion of the normal feminine reaction to her parents. But its chief interest here lies in its association with the task of restitution. The bad qualities of her first idea of her father must have been projected upon the English, and the good qualities upon God, St Michael and the Dauphin. According to a legend, of doubtful authenticity but consistent with the psychology of Jeanne, she persuaded the Dauphin to make over to her the realm which she had reconquered. She then formally presented it to God, and gave it back, in trust, to the King. Although probably exaggerated, this story may contain the germs of truth. In it, she symbolically twice takes the mother from the father, and twice gives her back to him. In most life tasks, similar repetitions of the crime and the atonement can be detected.

COMFORT AND AID

When Jeanne's Voices told her to be good and to restore the crown to the Dauphin, they were behaving in the well-known manner of all superegos. But when they comforted her and promised her aid,[1] they seem to illustrate a less familiar aspect of these mysterious beings. For, with the exception of Freud's paper on Humour, there has been little suggestion that superegos can be kind as well as stern. Since those who are not in conflict with their conscience feel no need for mental treatment, evidence for the benevolence of superegos is unlikely to be conspicuous within the psychiatrist's consulting room. The anthropology of religion, however, can perhaps help to fill the gap.

In the age of faith and superstition, the superego was objectified as God. Even the gods of primitive people helped in battle and did not confine their activities solely to the punishment of breakers of taboo. When Christianity was in its bloom, men lived with a vivid sense of the proximity of a God, who could love and lead them to eternal bliss, or hate and damn them to Purgatory and Hell; and their peace of mind depended upon which of these two attitudes they believed Him to have adopted towards themselves.

There are many records of men who have passed from a conviction that they were surely damned to a certainty that they were saved, and such conversions are still common among evangelicals today. A similar transformation from misery to bliss can be seen in any nursery. A child is disobedient. It tries to hold out against the domination of its parent. But, in time, the sense of loneliness and lack of love is too strong for it to bear. It cries, says it's sorry, is forgiven, and feels that everything has come right again. In religious conversion, therefore, something must occur which is analogous to the repentance and forgiveness of the disobedient child; and this suggests that, like the parent, the superego is capable of loving those who surrender to its will. We find, indeed, that to most Christians, repentance and good resolutions are the conditions of the sense of conversion and relief from sin. A slight variant of this creed states that faith is the necessary and sufficient condition; but, since doubt is really only the symptom of an unconscious revolt, these two theologies amount to much the same.

The Augustine view that salvation depends solely upon the caprice of God is more difficult to understand. It is of course a

[1] She spoke frequently of their great comfort, both at the beginning of her career, and during the long months of her imprisonment and trial. See *The Trial*.

logical deduction from the axiom of divine omnipotence; but even logical deductions are seldom accepted, unless they can be made to correspond with some unconscious wish. Perhaps the doctrine was developed by those who were so convinced of the inevitability of sin (that is, of their unconscious hatred of their father) that they despaired of deserving forgiveness, and could hope for salvation only from a being who could love some of them, at least,[1] in spite of all their hate. That is, they could hope for salvation only from a masochistic God. Now Christ loved them in spite of the fact that they were guilty of his death. He allowed them, as it were, to love him sadistically (i.e., in the only way possible to their ambivalent unconsciouses); and, in return, they were prepared to love him masochistically themselves, and to seek martyrdom in his name. In this way they developed a symmetrical sado-masochistic relation to their superegos, which appears to have been satisfactory to all parties concerned.

Thus all forms of religious conversion represent a reconciliation between the super-ego and the ego, which repeats the reconciliation between the parent and the rebellious child. Before it, everything is misery, depression, and a deep sense of personal incompleteness; after it, everything is joy and confidence in the sense of being loved. In a successful analysis, a similar change occurs; but here it is less due to the surrender of the ego to the superego, than to the discovery that most of the causes of conflict belong to infancy and have no rational justification in the present.[2]

It is time to return to the saints of Jeanne. She said that they at first filled her with perplexity and doubt. What were they, she asked, and how could she fulfil their extraordinary commands. Now this doubt, like all religious doubt, seems to be the expression of unconscious revolt. At first, we may suppose, Jeanne's unconscious rebelled against her superego; and therefore, like all sinners and neurotics, she felt sad, weak, and

[1] Why, having got so far, did these theologians not imagine that everyone was saved? Presumably, because they could not give up the sadistic pleasure of imagining their rivals in hell.

[2] [I would now (1977) think that the reconciliation comes about because the persecuting part of the superego has been deprived of its projected sadism which has been reintrojected into the ego, and that this in turn allows the ego to become aware of and mourn its own sadism to its good internal objects, which are then felt to forgive it.]

miserably insufficient for her task. She was like the disobedient child, whose world is all awry, because it is conscious of a lack of love. Soon, however, she seems to have submitted to her Voices; and then her inferiority and doubt gave place to confidence and joy. Like the child who has been forgiven, she felt that nothing in the world could cause her fear, since she was loved once more. In like manner, all those who are sustained by a complete sense of their ability to accomplish a just cause, owe their amazing confidence to the sense of being the beloved object of their superegos. They are the chosen people; and they are as fearless as children who are secure in the certainty of parental love. Moreover, Jeanne's superego contained both parents; she was supported by St Margaret and St Catherine, no less than by St Michael and God.

THE SADISM OF THE VOICES

The superego may bring support to those who surrender to its will; but it is also hard. The Christian God may comfort the afflicted; but His gifts not infrequently include the martyr's crown. That He should reserve a place of torment for those who resist Him, is comprehensible to the conscious human will; but that He should also persecute the submissive, is more difficult to understand.

The superego is the introjection of the child's first image of its parent, and this image is already distorted by the projection of its repressed desires. Infantile sexuality is highly sadistic, so that the parental image, and the superego which is formed from it, is more cruel than any real parent is ever likely to be. Moreover, the superego is almost unalterable, so long as it remains unconscious. For this reason, submission to it does not greatly change its character, but only makes its sadism easier to bear. Indeed the surrender is a masochistic surrender. The tormented ego reinterprets the sadism of the superego as a kind of love, which satisfies, at least in imagination, the feminine component of the sexual impulse. This is the only erotic gratification which a severe superego allows.

Both Jeanne's female saints were martyrs, and one was also the chosen bride of Christ. St Margaret had said to the Roman governor that, since Jesus had died for her, she for her part desired to die for him. She was then tied to a post and whipped, and her flesh was torn with iron hooks. Finally, after resisting the seductions of the devil, who appeared to her both in the form of a fearful dragon and of a kindly man, she was beheaded. Her soul escaped to Heaven in the form of a dove.[1]

St Catherine was a pagan king's daughter, of great beauty, intelligence and charm who, at first, refused all her lovers on the ground that they were not good enough for her. But when the infant Jesus offered to marry her, if she would be baptized, she became a Christian, and henceforth refused to sacrifice to idols. Meanwhile, the emperor, becoming aware of her beauty and no doubt being irritated by her surrender to a rival, sent fifty philosophers to argue with her and convince her of the folly of her ways. But she converted them all, as well as the commander of the army, and the empress, whom she crowned with a mystic crown. Persuasion having failed, the emperor turned to threats in order to bend her to his will. But she again refused to sacrifice to idols, saying that she preferred to offer her flesh and blood to Jesus Christ, her lover, her teacher and her spouse. As the result of this behaviour, she was condemned; but the instruments of torture being miraculously broken, the sentence was less easy to execute than to pronounce. Eventually, however, the exasperated emperor succeeded in cutting off her head. At the moment of her death, a voice was heard from heaven saying: 'Come, my beloved wife; the door of heaven is open.'[2]

There is little doubt that these legends were known to Jeanne, and that they affected her profoundly, because of their appeal to something in her own unconscious. We have argued that, in infancy, she was jealous of her father and wished to take his place. In other words, her original impulses were masculine and homosexual. For this reason, she refused all earthly lovers, and her superego was built mainly in the image of her father. But, at the same time, her normal impulses made her love her father, or the superego in his image; and as these impulses became stronger, the conflict became more fierce. Since her superego contained the projection of her own infantile aggressive desires, it was sadistic, and a feminine

[1] Anatole France, *Vie de Jeanne d'Arc*, I, 37–8.   [2] *Ib.* I, 40–7.

surrender was hard. Moreover, submission involved a psychical castration, the surrender of her masculine desires. Decapitation is a common symbol of castration and both Jeanne's female saints had been beheaded before entering into eternal bliss. To her unconscious, their ecstatic martyrdom must have represented a mystic union with the father – a feminine and masochistic surrender to a sadistic superego like her own.

Most women can discard their masculine aspirations, if the hope of children is strong enough to compensate them for their loss. And Jeanne may have been no exception to this rule. Her judges accused her of having boasted to de Baudricourt that, after accomplishing her task, she would have three sons, a pope, an emperor and a king. Upon hearing this, de Baudricourt is said to have offered to give her one of them. To which she answered: 'No, gentle Robert, no, this is not the time; the Holy Spirit will find a way!'[1] If this story is true, Jeanne may have thought that, like St Catherine, she would be a holy bride. But, at the same time, she may have thought that, like her saints, she would first have to endure some trial. She would last but a year, or a little more, she told her friends. Perhaps she knew that before receiving her reward, her Voices, like the God of her two favourite saints, would claim something terrible which she would have to give.

Already at the beginning of her career Jeanne's sweet and kindly Voices began to show faint signs of their kinship with the Furies of the Greek tragedian. There was no escape from their insistent demands, nor from the perils which obedience inevitably implied. They forced her many times to risk her life; first at the hands of her father, who threatened to drown her if she left her home; then in the numerous engagements into which she rushed with such gallantry and fire. They forced her to risk injuries and insults which to her were worse than death. Robert de Baudricourt at first wished to keep her as a harlot for his troops, and then, finding that she was unsuited for this rôle, he advised that she should be well beaten and sent home. Perhaps, like the Arabian physician who recommended this treatment for a Spanish duchess, he felt that it might be an apt cure for her frigidity.[2]

---

[1] *The Trial*, p. 151. [2] Havelock Ellis, *Psychology of Sex*, III, 130.

PSYCHOLOGICAL STUDY OF VOICES OF JOAN OF ARC

When her Voices said that she would be wounded she took care that their prophecies were fulfilled. Since they also prophesied her capture, they may have been responsible for some unusual rashness during the fatal sortie from Compiègne. But only towards the end of her life did their intentions become quite clear. At this time she seems to have rebelled against them. They told her not to attempt to die, or to escape by leaping from the tower of Beaurevoir; yet she leapt, and thus almost escaped the more gruesome death to come. For a time, she seems to have been able to conceal from herself the fate which they prophesied for her. They told her that she would be delivered through great victory; or they said, 'Take all things peacefully: heed not thine affliction (*martire*). Thence shalt thou come at last into the kingdom of Paradise.'[1] At first she thought that they promised an earthly succour; but, in the end, she realized that they were only offering a martyr's crown. Once more, indeed, she rebelled against them; for, when she was condemned and no succour came, she believed for a moment that they had deceived her. It was then that she recanted and was reprieved. A few days later, however, she again submitted to her Voices. She knew at last that, all along, they had destined her body to be burned. After an agony of remorse her confidence returned, and declaring that her saints were indeed from God, she went to meet her fate. Quietly she suffered the executioner to chain her to the stake, and even when the fire began to creep about her flesh she was still steadfast and resigned.[2] Perhaps some ecstasy of work accomplished and of sin atoned may have sustained her during the long minutes of intolerable pain – until at last she cried aloud to Jesus, and died.

THE HALLUCINATORY INTENSITY OF THE VOICES

To say that Jeanne's Voices came from her superego is to make only a small contribution to the problem of her life. For we all have superegos, yet few of us are able to perform such tasks as hers. Many other characteristics of her Voices remain to be

---

[1] Andrew Lang, *The Maid of France*, 269; *The Trial*, p. 155.
[2] Opinions differ as to whether she was resigned or in a state of collapse. I prefer to believe the more heroic version.

explained. Of these, the most interesting is perhaps the hallucinatory intensity with which they spoke.

In the fifteenth century, everyone believed in saints and demons, so that even normal people must have been inclined to interpret the monitions of their consciences as objective realities outside themselves. But Jeanne's Voices seem to have possessed a vividness which far surpassed the experiences of more ordinary folk. Socrates, also, heard voices, which gave him wise advice, and to the same mysterious category all mediumistic phenomena belong. Therefore, the problem of the vividness of Jeanne's Voices has a general importance apart from its historic interest.

Among dreams, there are some which are distinguished by the peculiar sense of reality which they invoke, and when an analyst is confronted by one of these, he suspects that it is related to a traumatic experience of infancy. Thus, Freud's most famous patient,[1] when he was four and a half years old, dreamed that, as he lay awake at night, the window opened slowly and disclosed a tree on which were several wolves looking fixedly at him. He then really awoke in great terror, and could only be comforted with difficulty – so real had the vision seemed. The full analysis of this dream took five years; but in the end it was interpreted completely and the neurosis disappeared.

In early infancy the patient had seen something which was the first cause of all his later troubles. During an attack of fever, he was sleeping in his parents' room, when he awoke and opened his eyes to see them in the act of coitus. At first he forgot the incident, which seemed to leave no impression upon his mind. But in later childhood, when his Oedipus complex was at its bloom, he saw two sheep dogs behaving in the same way. This reawakened the dormant memory and evoked the dream. In sleep, his unconscious reproduced the old scene once more, which this time excited the most intense castration fear; for, in so far as he was masculine, he became the rival of his father, and in so far as he was feminine, he realized that he must lose his penis in order to be loved. But the memory itself remained unconscious. The manifest dream contained

---

[1] Freud, 'From the History of an Infantile Neurosis', *Collected Papers*, vol. III.

only the associated ideas. The opening of the window stood for the opening of his eyes; and what he saw was not his parents, but the associated wolves. Moreover, they were not engaged in coitus, but were looking fixedly at him, as he had looked when he saw his parents two and a half years before. But though the recollection remained unconscious, the anxiety which it evoked took a concrete form and produced his first neurotic symptom – a phobia of wolves.

If those dreams, which are peculiarly vivid, are due to some such traumatic experience of the remote past, it seems possible that day dreams of hallucinatory intensity may have a similar cause. Jeanne used to fall into a trance and see visions of St Michael, St Margaret and St Catherine. Clearly, these visions were partly founded upon actual pictures or statues of these saints, which she had seen and admired. But why should these statues or pictures have been so important that they returned to her in visions throughout her life? The wolves of Freud's patient haunted his dreams only because they reminded his unconscious of a traumatic event. The analogy suggests that the pictures or statues of Jeanne's saints may have returned in visions, because they reminded her unconscious also of some experience which obsessed it.

It may seem gratuitous to suggest that in her infancy Jeanne had some experience analogous to that of Freud's patient. Nevertheless, I will assume this as an hypothesis, in order to see how far it is capable of explaining the facts. Perhaps the early experience at first seemed to be forgotten. But an image or picture of St Michael, seen in later childhood, would be well suited to revive the unconscious memory; for, he was usually represented as a mounted knight, transfixing the demon with his lance.[1] This picture, and the memory with which it was associated, would then excite her unconscious jealousy, and intensify her Oedipus complex. Like Freud's patient, she would both fear to be loved by her father, and hate him because she wished to take his place. But, whereas Freud's patient developed a phobia of wolves, Jeanne submitted to St Michael. Though she kept up her masculine attitude to the

---

[1] *Vie de Jeanne d'Arc*, I, 34. Jeanne consistently refused to describe St Michael in detail. But she said he had wings, and appeared 'in the guise of a most upright man', *The Trial*, pp. 84, 124.

outside world, she was feminine and masochistic to her superego. Only for her execution, which her unconscious must have treated as a kind of marriage, was she resigned to female dress.

If to Jeanne's unconscious St Michael was the virile father, who were St Margaret and St Catherine? Her dead sister was called Catherine, and this fact may have influenced her to select a saint of the same name. But what perhaps impressed her most were their images – there was one of St Margaret in her native church[1] – with their golden crowns.[2] We have already mentioned the importance of crowns to Jeanne, and have argued that her wish to crown the Dauphin was a reaction to the guilt of an unconscious penis envy. But here these royal emblems occur in a rather different context. We may again turn to the case histories of neurotics for some parallel which may help explain this feature.

The condition known as fetishism is fairly common and has been much discussed by the psycho-analytic school. The typical fetishist is a man obsessed by some attribute of the lady of his choice – for example, her corsets or some other feature of her dress. Thus the hero of Masoch's novel *Venus im Pelz* was especially attracted by this lady's furs and by her whip. Freud has collected much evidence to show that such conditions are due to the shock of an early discovery. The small boy at first quite naturally supposes that everyone possesses those sexual organs which are so important to himself. Like the famous 'wolf-man', however, he may wake up one night, and see his nurse or mother in a position which enables him to discover that his first belief was false. For a time, this discovery may seem to be forgotten; but, later, when his castration anxiety is stimulated by the Oedipus complex, he may see something which reminds him of it. He may then react to the fatal memory with horror, and his unconscious may be obsessed, for ever, with the desire to prove it false. In later life, the fur-coated Venus reminds him of the pubic hairs he once saw, instead of the more substantial object he expected. But this Venus is equipped also with the phallic emblem of the whip, so that he is reassured and can love her without horror. To a similar

---

[1] Honiteaux, *Jeanne d'Arc*, p. 6.
[2] Jeanne told her judges that the heads of St Margaret and St Catherine were 'crowned in a rich and precious fashion with beautiful crowns', *The Trial*, p. 68.

phallic symbolism, many of the great goddesses of antiquity owed their power and charm. Diana was a huntress with a bow, and the Minoan female deity was always associated with snakes.

At first sight it might seem fantastic to suppose that a similar fetishism can occur in girls, for they might be expected to believe that their mothers are built in the image of themselves. Small girls, however, when they first discover that their older brothers are provided with male organs, are apt to still their penis envy with the belief that the difference is only due to age, and that the clitoris is destined to grow to the same size as its phallic homologue. But such a belief is shattered by the discovery that the mother is herself without this organ. For this reason, the discovery of the real nature of the adult female organs may be traumatic in girls as well as boys; and they also may become obsessed with the desire to prove this knowledge false.

Analogy with such cases suggests that Jeanne was of this type, and that her wish to grow a penis was once nearly shattered by the discovery that the mother was without this all-important organ. The picture or statues of St Margaret and St Catherine with their phallic crowns, might then become obsessions, because they symbolically denied the truth, and enabled her to cling to the unconscious belief that she too would some day possess a similar crown. Moreover, the legends of these saints would tend to confirm and elaborate the unconscious fantasy suggested by their statues. For, though both were beheaded, both received the martyr's crown, and thus symbolically regained what in their feminine surrender they were compelled to lose.

Thus a single event, analogous with the experience of the 'wolf-man', in the early life of Jeanne, may have determined the form of her Oedipus complex, and caused her to see visions of St Michael with his lance and of St Margaret and St Catherine with their crowns.[1] These saints, since they were symbols of her parents, spoke with the voice of her complex superego, and commanded her to make restitution for her

[1] I do not wish, however, to suggest that the assumption of a 'primal scene' in the early life of Jeanne is more than a guess – a guess which may give one explanation of the vividness of her apparitions, but which obviously cannot be confirmed.

jealous and envious desires. Without the element of past reality behind them, they might have been mere fantasies lacking the vividness of true hallucinations. Without this vividness, they would hardly have inspired that faith and supreme confidence which enabled her to perform their stupendous tasks.[1]

[1] This paper was in the press before the appearance of Dr Ernest Jones's paper on 'The Phallic Phase' (*International Journal of Psycho-analysis*, January 1933). If Dr Jones's argument is correct, Jeanne's masculine phase, which I have assumed to be primary, must have been already secondary to a still earlier feminine phase; and her hypothetical discovery of the anatomical difference between the sexes must have been a rediscovery of an instinctive knowledge which had been repressed. Otherwise the argument would remain unchanged.

8
A Psychological Analysis of the Causes of War*

Many different theories of the origin of war have been suggested. Quite possibly they may all be true. Each of them may help to explain some wars; some of them may help to explain all wars.

We can divide these theories into two main types: those which deal with what medical science would call *precipitating* causes and those which deal with predisposing or *constitutional* causes. Take, for instance, the analogy of a cold. Here exposure to infection, or to the weather, are precipitating causes. But these alone would not be enough to produce a cold without some constitutional disposition – a weak chest, enlarged tonsils, or whatever it may be.

So it is, I believe, with the social disease of war. Many things, sometimes quite opposite things, may be precipitating causes: such as political assassinations, or having an army so big that it annoys your neighbours or so small that they are tempted to ignore you. These may be compared with going out in the rain or forgetting an overcoat. There remains, however, the constitutional disposition. People who dislike pacifism often say that it is human nature to fight and that human nature can't be changed. How far is this true?

UNCONSCIOUS AGGRESSION

The psycho-analytical school of psychology, founded by Freud, has recently made some important discoveries about the destructive impulses in man. And Dr Edward Glover, in particular, has applied them to a study of the causes of war. That man in a state of nature is an aggressive animal was always fairly obvious. It was also clear that the civilized man could return to savagery much too easily for his own or other

* *The Listener*, 7 November 1934.

people's safety. But what was not known was that the destructive impulses, which break out in war, are always present in our unconscious minds. We know nothing about them because they are repressed [or split-off]; but they are there and ready to break out.

If this is admitted, we begin to understand one of the reasons why wars so often happen, even when everyone seems to be trying to prevent them. We are like people who go about without knowing that their pockets are full of dynamite. The more we realize this, the more likely we shall be to take all possible precautions.

Apart from some sublimated outlets, in work or sport, the destructive impulse of the average civilized man is, as I have said, normally repressed [or split-off]. He is unconscious of it. But it is always liable to manifest itself in various ways. In the first place, it may be *inverted*, that is, turned inwards against himself. When this happens, he will feel inhibited and depressed. Most ordinary fits of depression are in fact caused in this way. If the inverted aggressiveness is very intense, as in melancholia, he may even kill himself. In the second place, his unconscious aggression may be *projected*, that is, disowned and attributed to someone else instead. He doesn't know that he wants to injure other people; but he thinks that other people want to injure him. He gives way to unjustified feelings of suspicion. He becomes 'sensitive' and 'touchy' about quite imaginary slights. In extreme cases, such suspicions are recognized as pathological as in the delusions of persecution met with in a type of insanity called paranoia. Lastly, the unconscious aggression may break out in a direct form, and the peaceable citizen may become aware of a desire to kill. But before this can happen his normal conscience must be modified; he must believe that he has a righteous cause. This change occurs in the homicidal maniac who believes that his crime is not only just but an actual duty. A rather similar change occurs in quite normal people during war.

The study of cases of melancholia, paranoia, and homicidal mania helps us to recognize psychological mechanisms which are present, to some slight extent, in all of us. These mechanisms may not greatly influence us as individuals; but they sometimes have a great influence on us as members of a state.

PSYCHOLOGICAL ANALYSIS OF THE CAUSES OF WAR

NATIONAL PARANOIA

The psychology of a state can become like a caricature of the psychology of the individuals that compose it, in which the most dangerous and irresponsible traits are accentuated and the saner and more cautious ones obliterated altogether. For long periods a nation may be sane, peaceable, and contented. Then there comes a change and it develops all the symptoms of some well-known insanity. In particular, it may become paranoiac, that is, suffer from delusions of persecution.

The individual madman is irrationally suspicious because he projects his unconscious aggressiveness upon his neighbours. The normal citizen is too sane to do this. But he, too, has a load of unconscious aggressiveness; and there is little to prevent him from projecting it upon strangers – especially upon those abstract personifications of strangers called foreign powers. It is even a positive relief to him to find some distant object for his latent indignation; and the Press, of course, is under a strong temptation to cater for this demand. Quite trivial 'incidents' are given an undue prominence as news, and these excite an exaggerated suspicion of some foreign power. And, since suspicion readily begets suspicion, the foreign power soon becomes suspicious in its turn. A stable country feels uneasy at the growth of some vital and progressive neighbour and begins to seek security in treaties and in an increase in arms. This immediately excites the suspicions of its neighbour, who develops a kind of claustrophobia, a feeling of being encircled and shut in. Thus the two nations, or groups of nations, come to regard each other with a mutual and very dangerous distrust. Like two paranoiacs, each takes defensive measures which confirm the other's fears.

I do not believe that any modern nation has started a war unless the bulk of its citizens believe in the justice of their cause. The repressed aggression is there, of course; but the civilized conscience must be satisfied before allowing it to break out. The suspicion itself provides the fiction of a righteous cause. Like the individual paranoiac who becomes homicidal, the paranoiac nation may start a war which it honestly believes is necessary for its self-defence. What was originally an unjustified suspicion helps to create the very catastrophe it wishes to avoid. Thus fear, as Dr Inge has said, is really the main cause of war.

WAR FEVER

Once war has broken out the last vestiges of sanity disappear. The tendency to suspicion is stimulated by propaganda. Soon each party imputes the most atrocious and unlikely crimes to its enemies, so that each commits real outrages in revenge.

The individual seems to lose his individuality; he becomes submerged in the group. His private conscience, which forbids manslaughter, is exchanged for a group conscience, which commands it. The peaceable citizen suddenly discovers that he has developed a desire to kill and, at the same time as a sort of compensation, he finds that he is also ready to be killed for his country. He feels elated; the emergence of these impulses from the unconscious is a positive relief. This, I think, is why war fever spreads so quickly.

Prolonged wars of course produce many neuroses – the so-called cases of shell shock. But there are also peace neuroses, due to the damming up of aggression, which are cured by war. The individual doesn't feel altogether comfortable so long as his destructive impulses are repressed. As I have said, they often turn against himself, frustrating him and producing a sense of inferiority and a feeling of depression. But in war time, with what appears a righteous cause, the aggression can find an external object.

Moreover, war provides opportunities for self-sacrifice, as well as for direct aggression. Most of us, although in this rational age we may not admit it, have an inner need for self-sacrifice. The world owes most of its progress to this impulse; and that this can be so easily utilized in war is one of the tragedies of human nature. As a friend of mine, who is not a psychologist but a diplomat, said some years ago: a nation's latent masochism is quite as dangerous as its latent sadism – a paradox which is explained in detail in Dr Glover's book.[1]

---

[1] *War Sadism and Pacifism*, by Dr Edward Glover. Allen and Unwin, 3s. 6d. [The friend mentioned was Arthur Yenchen, who had been at the British Embassy in Berlin in 1932 and was subsequently shot down after the war had begun on his way to Madrid where he was Minister.]

PSYCHOLOGICAL ANALYSIS OF THE CAUSES OF WAR

Thus war releases immense quantities of normally unconscious aggression in many forms. The resulting mania does not subside until all the countries involved are utterly exhausted.

Let me recapitulate what seem to be the chief constitutional causes of war. Firstly, there is the existence of unconscious destructive impulses. Secondly, there is the tendency for these destructive impulses to be projected. It is this which produces what I have called national paranoia. It gives rise to national delusions of persecution. It makes nations over-suspicious of their neighbours. Thirdly, there is the danger that these suspicions will end by provoking an excuse for the outbreak of the destructive impulses, which might otherwise have remained repressed.

REDUCING INTERNATIONAL FRICTION

If this analysis is right, what ought we to do? Another great war, as we are often told, would very likely shatter our civilization altogether. At best, those of us who were unfortunate enough to survive it would have only lived to suffer the loss of many of the people we cared for most. The prospect is appalling.

Sir Norman Angell suggests an international police force. But the nations are unlikely to pool their forces *before* they have learnt to trust each other. In the meantime, if our armaments increase the suspicions of our possible enemies, should we scrap them at once? If your neighbour is already mad, to go about armed may make him more likely to attack you; but you cannot be sure that he will not do so if you disarm. Perhaps it is best to compromise, as we do in this country; to take some precautions while trying to make them as little provocative as possible.[1]

More generally, if we appreciate the psychological forces at work, if we realize how easy it is to stir up insane fear and hatred between nations, and how difficult it is to calm them afterwards, we shall try more than ever to avoid all forms of provocation. Here the responsibility of the Press is very heavy.

---

[1] As far as I remember we had voted large sums for rearmament by then but it was not until 1940, when I was with the Air Ministry that I began to suspect that not much had been spent before the war.

If peace is to be preserved, undue prominence must not be given to the kind of foreign news that excites our indignation – even though this is just the kind of news we enjoy reading most. Institutions like the League of Nations and the various Foreign Offices exist partly to reduce the inevitable friction between nations. I should be the last to underestimate the value of their work; without it war might be continuous instead of merely periodic. But as long as the constitutional causes of war remain, it seems almost too much to hope that we shall be vigilant enough to avoid all the precipitating causes. There is the ever present danger that the nations may go mad again as they have so often done before.

GROUND FOR ULTIMATE HOPE

There is, however, one ground for ultimate hope. War is irrational, not so much because it seldom pays as because of the group hatreds that make it grow out of what is originally unjustified fear. For exactly the same reason, the unconscious destructive impulses, which cause the fear and the hatred, are themselves irrational – at least to a very great extent. To explain this point would be extremely difficult – because I should have to talk about psychological discoveries, by Mrs Klein and others, which are so recent that they are not yet fully worked out. One thing is, however, fairly clear. The paranoiac mechanism of projection has been found to operate in children during the first and psychologically most important years of their lives. The young child projects some of its destructive impulses upon its surroundings. It fills its world with imaginary dangers. It becomes terrified of imaginary lions or wolves. To cope with these dangers, it develops a further aggressiveness, which is again repressed and projected. In this way a vicious circle is set up which produces an accumulation of unconscious aggressiveness – an accumulation to which, as I believe, not only war but also many of our other social troubles are ultimately due. This overgrowth of aggressiveness may be inevitable, in the sense that we may be unable to do very much to prevent children from developing it. But it is not incurable; because it is not rational. In the last analysis it is founded on a whole system of infantile delusions; therefore it can be reduced to reasonable and even useful proportions, if this system of delusions can be destroyed.

To do so is the aim of psycho-analysis. Psycho-analysis tries to make the individual neurotic saner, and therefore happier in himself and less of a nuisance to his friends. It is the youngest of the sciences and its future is still unknown. But we may at least hope that the insanity of nations, like the insanity of individuals, will steadily, if slowly, fade away under the growing light of knowledge.[1]

[1] At this period I overestimated, as did Melanie Klein herself, the social benefits likely to be achieved by psycho-analysis, particularly child analysis.

Footnote to article – Considering that the friend mentioned on p. 134, note 1 had taken me to hear Hitler speak in 1932 just before he became Chancellor and that we were both convinced from that moment that Hitler could be stopped only by force, I find the rather mild note I struck in this broadcast rather difficult to understand. I did not say that in my view Hitler had already passed the point of no recall. And whether this was from a fear of making things worse, or some lingering uncertainty about Hitler's motive or just from fear of becoming unpopular at home when, except for Churchill and his supporters, everyone seemed all for peace, I do not know.

9
The Development of War*[1]
A Psychological Approach

I. MOTIVES OF WAR

According to Bacon, we should collect our facts before we start to theorize. But facts are so numerous that the pure Baconian would never get beyond the collecting stage. In practice we all start with a theory and look for facts to fit it, and are sufficiently scientific if we are prepared to modify the theory every time they fail to do so. In other words, we proceed by a series of approximations.

(1) *Conscious Motives*

As far as conscious motives of war are concerned, many theories have been suggested. In the first place, it has been attributed to necessity and the struggle for existence, that is, to the pressure of the population upon the food supply. And those who hold this view usually accept it as the common lot of animals as well as men. But among rabbits, over-population brings starvation and disease, not war – and biologically this may be more beneficial to the species. Even the higher carnivores do not, so far as I know, prey upon their own species when food is short. Man, of course, does fight for food and land to grow it in; but he fights quite as often for other causes, or for no sound cause at all. Indeed, I imagine it would be true to say that primitive man fights most readily when all his economic needs are satisfied. The season of plenty is the time of war. Mars was a god of spring as well as battle – and significantly enough of marriage too.

* *B. J. Med. Psych.*, vol. XVI, 1937.
[1] Read before a Meeting of the Oxford University Anthropological Society on 5 March 1936.

An alternative theory attributes war to ambition, either of rulers or of private companies or of whole nations. This certainly covers a large range of wars, that is, if ambition is defined to include far more than rational self-interest. Territory, markets, and simple pillage have been objects of war; but so have heads or other trophies, and sacrificial victims.

According to yet another theory, the desire for vengeance is the commonest cause of war – especially among primitive peoples, who believe that the dead persecute their living kinsmen until their death has been avenged. Among civilized peoples, the revenge motive often reappears, in a moralized form, as a sense of righteous indignation.

Lastly, war has been attributed to fear, since nations become aggressive when they expect to be attacked.

Each of these theories, then, contains a partial truth; so that man fights for a great variety of motives. In other words, he has a warlike disposition that is very easily inflamed. Until recently, this disposition would have been dismissed as an evolved character – since natural selection often favours the most ferocious species, and sexual selection the most aggressive males. But with the growth of psychology, and especially of psycho-analysis, we have ceased to take the evolution of our impulses so much for granted, and have begun to study the way in which they are actually developed in the individual.

(2) *Unconscious Motives*

According to psycho-analytic theory, conscious motives are influenced, both in form and degree, by unconscious motives, which have been developed in infancy and childhood. Like everything else in science, psycho-analysis is not static. Its account of these unconscious motives is not quite the same today as it was a few years ago – or as it probably will be a few years hence. But having an empirical basis, its past conclusions have been modified and extended, not scrapped.

(a) *The sexual theory.* If in the very early days of psycho-analysis, Freud or one of his followers had been asked to explain war, he would have said that it was the outbreak of all that civilization normally repressed, that is, of all that normally exists only in the unconscious.[1] In particular, since at this time he was mainly preoccupied with sex, he would probably have argued that most offensive weapons are phallic symbols, and that in dreams stabbing or shooting an enemy often symbolizes a sexual assault. And from this he might have concluded that an outbreak of war was, to some extent at least, an outbreak of perversion sanctioned by the state.

(b) *The Oedipean theory*. If an analyst had been asked the same question a few years later, he would have explained war in terms of the Oedipus complex, as this was originally formulated by Freud.[2] The male child wishes to monopolize his mother, and tends, at least unconsciously, to hate and fear his father as his most important rival. Since, however, he also loves his father, his three feelings – unconscious hate and fear, and conscious love – towards the same person form an intolerable conflict. From this conflict the boy escapes by a partial inversion. That is, to some extent he exchanges his masculine attitude towards his mother for a feminine attitude towards his father. He becomes a good son.

Interestingly enough, a rather similar reversal of attitude from masculine to feminine occurs in the young baboon when he unsuccessfully challenges some older male.[3] But in the boy the partial inversion towards the father is more sublimated and leaves a more permanent impression. He repeats it in his relation to elder boys or masters at school, and later to his chief, his commanding officer, or his king. It is, therefore, among other things, the basis of that loyalty which cements the human group. And loyalty, with the cooperation it makes possible, is one of the main factors that distinguish human warfare from the promiscuous fighting of the ape.

But to return to the Oedipus complex: the repressed hate does not simply disappear. It lives on in the unconscious and is evoked towards other types of father symbol. Thus two types of father symbol affect the boy throughout his life: one evokes

---

[1] Cf. Freud, 'Thoughts for the times on War and Death' (1915). *Collected Papers*, IV.

[2] Cf. E. Jones, 'War and Individual Psychology', *The Sociological Review*, July 1915. Also Money-Kyrle, *Aspasia*, 1932.

[3] Zuckerman, *Social Life of Monkeys and Apes*, 1933.

his loyalty, the other his hate. As a child he may develop an animal phobia to put beside his admiration of his father; at school some boys or masters he will hero-worship, others he will detest as bullies. And as a man, his loyalty to his own chief, or to his own group as a personified ideal, will be balanced by his detestation of some other leader, or some other group. And for this reason he will be pre-disposed to war.

There seems even to be a positive correlation between the amount of veneration for one's own leader or country and the amount of hatred directed against one's enemies. The extent to which a Napoleon, a Mussolini or a Hitler is deified is a measure of the militant ardour of his people. Indeed, up to a point at least, the process of dichotomy seems to increase with civilization: among Central Australians, according to Roheim,[1] gods and devils do not yet differ very greatly from each other. The magic of one's own chief may be bad as well as good.

A further result of the splitting of the father image into two figures is that the gods of one people are the devils of another. This is true not only of Central Australians and Ancient Semites, but also of civilized nations. A Napoleon, a Mussolini, or a Hitler may be a god in his own country, but these same three names have a diabolic ring in the ears of many of their neighbours.

Where the two symbols into which the infantile ambivalence has split the original father image are both members of the same community, the result is a tendency to civil rather than to foreign war – or at least to intolerance in politics. Gladstone and Disraeli were almost god and devil to their respective partisans. There is of course a certain inverse relation between war and revolution: an increase in the probability of one decreases the probability of the other – a fact well understood by dictators who raise war scares whenever they are in danger of becoming unpopular at home.

(*c*) *The paranoiac theory.* Such, broadly speaking, is the psychoanalytic theory as it might have been outlined a few years ago. If an analyst were asked the same question today, he would not, I think, repudiate this answer, but would concentrate on

[1] *Riddle of the Sphinx*, 1934, p. 129.

deeper factors he had formerly neglected[1] – factors that are being exposed by child analysis and especially by the work of Mrs Klein. He would point out that aggression begins earlier and has a more complicated history than that given in the Oedipean account. The most important events in this history begin while the child is still at its mother's breasts, when sucking develops into biting. This stage is apparently accompanied by phantasies of eating up or biting into the mother to acquire or to destroy certain mysterious substances or objects which are believed to be inside.

It is not surprising that the infant should regard his mother as the depository of all good and nourishing substances, nor that his first biting impulses should be directed against her. But the fact that he also regards her as full of all kinds of dangerous and evil objects requires an explanation, which, as I understand it, is roughly as follows. The infant does not start life with ready made concepts of other people. At first his world consists of 'part objects' – breasts, hands, faces, etc., that attract his attention because they are associated with the satisfaction or thwarting of his needs. Moreover, he attributes his own feelings to these objects. His attitude towards them is 'animatistic', if I may borrow the word from Dr Marett. He feels them to be alive, but not possessed by spirits. In so far as he loves them, he feels that they are themselves benevolent; but in so far as he is aggressive towards them, he feels them to be malignant. In particular, he wishes – if one may use the word 'wish' at this stage – to eat parts of his mother, and therefore attributes similar cannibalistic impulses to these parts. In psycho-analytic language, he projects his oral-sadism upon them.

This whole process is complicated by another mechanism – that of introjection. Perhaps because of a confusion between thought and deed, the child comes to believe that he has, as it were, swallowed all these good and bad objects. He then feels full of *mana*, of magic power for good or evil. But in so far as the introjected objects are malignant, he feels them as dangerous both to himself and to the things he most loves; and to escape this new anxiety he projects them again. This is the

[1] Cf. E. Glover, *War, Sadism and Pacifism*, 1933.

THE DEVELOPMENT OF WAR

vicious spiral of projection and introjection – a spiral because the hate and fear is intensified with every repetition of the process.

If this part of the theory sounds fantastic and incomprehensible, we should remember that it forms a sector of the psycho-analytic front line, which is not yet tidied up. But the analogy between the mind of the infant, as drawn by child analysts, and that of the primitive medicine man, as described by anthropologists, will be close enough, I hope, to show that something is being discovered of great importance to both sciences.

The next stage of development also has its anthropological parallels: the passage from infancy to childhood involves the progress from animatism to animism. The infant's world contains only its mother and itself, not as integrated personalities, but as a conglomerate of animatistic part objects. The child's world begins to assume a more familiar shape; but it is not yet materialistic. It is no longer composed of dangerous and helpful substances or objects; but it is haunted by good and evil spirits. The child, whose infantile unconscious still wants to eat its parents, is afraid of being eaten by a witch, or perhaps by a tiger under the bed or in the shadow by the wall. He is still projecting his cannibalism; but this now forms evil personalities rather than malignant objects.

As in the infancy period, projection and introjection succeed each other. The child tends to introject the fairies and witches he has created. Now, for reasons I do not fully understand, an introjected evil spirit can have a variety of effects: the child may fear it as dangerous, or he may accept it. If it is dangerous, it may threaten himself *or* others. In so far as it threatens himself, it gives rise to a feeling of depression or hypochondria, and may then be said to form part – the threatening and inhibiting as opposed to the comforting part – of his superego. In so far as it threatens others, he will be afraid of his magic power for evil. But in so far as he accepts it, it will give him a rather manic sense of strength. He may then be said to identify himself with it.

This manic process in the child seems to be the prototype of war psychology in the adult. By identifying himself with his evil spirits, the child re-acquires in an offensive-defensive against his imaginary dangers the aggression he originally projected to create them. The European child, though according to Roheim[1] not the Central Australian child, does this in his games. I remember a small boy of two developing a very real terror of an imaginary lion, which haunted a certain tree stump of peculiar shape, and was, I have no doubt, the embodiment of his own projected aggression. At first he was much too terrified to go near it; but after a time he began to say that he himself was a lion, and then felt quite brave enough to go and roar at the other lion in the tree stump. In other words, he reintrojected, and identified himself with, the frightfulness he had projected. Most children master their terrors in their play by this mechanism. It replaces timidity by aggression. But just as the timidity was itself irrational, so is the aggression greater than is often justified by the real dangers of the external world.

Every child goes through a phase in which he projects his own aggression in this way, and peoples his world with imaginary dangers – although the extent to which he does so depends upon his innate aggression and the degree to which it has been evoked. So far as he does not outgrow this phase, or reverts to it in later life, he suffers from delusions of persecution and is classed as a paranoiac. And so far as he defends himself against his imaginary dangers by identifying himself with them and incorporating their strength, he may be described as manic.

The difference between the normal and the abnormal is a matter of degree. The normal individual does not suspect his foreign neighbours without cause; but if they threaten him he may exaggerate the danger, and adopt a rather manic defence. Moreover, this attitude may be intensified by the example of his friends, and especially of his political leaders, who are father figures and therefore the keepers of his conscience. In periods of discontent, an abnormal individual – the fiery demagogue, who still roars at tree stumps because these still contain imaginary lions – may be chosen leader, because he points out a scapegoat for the people's latent suspicions. Even if no bite were behind the roar, he awakens paranoiac and manic responses both in his followers and in those he verbally attacks; and so makes real what was once an imaginary danger.

[1] *Riddle of the Sphinx*, 1934, p. 157.

THE DEVELOPMENT OF WAR

This might be called the 'paranoiac' theory of war. At first sight it seems very different from the 'sexual' or 'Oedipean' theories; but actually the three psycho-analytic theories go some way to complete each other. Even the sexual theory was right as far as it went, though it did not go very far. The paranoiac theory gives the early stages neglected by the Oedipean. Not the father, but the mother, or rather part of her, is the first object of aggression.[1] The hated father, with which the ontogenetic account began in the classical Oedipus theory, is now seen to be not so much a real person as a projection of the child's own impulses towards his mother.

Lastly, the paranoiac theory explains the irrationality and the instability of most of this aggression. As far as one could see from the Oedipean theory, the hate was a perfectly rational result of the child's jealousy. But according to the paranoiac theory, this jealousy is already paranoid. Here is a very important difference. Man's fundamental nature may not be so aggressive after all: what is innate may be only a small fraction of the end result of the paranoid defensive process of projection and introjection. If so, man's remoter prospects of peace become much brighter; for there is no reason why education should not reduce the intensity, or at least remove the dangerous effects, of the psychotic phase through which every child seems to pass.

II. THE DEVELOPMENT OF WAR

Not only do the three psycho-analytic theories of man's warlike disposition supplement each other; they also supplement rather than supersede the evolutionary theories. By combining them all, therefore, we ought to get the latest stage in a series of approximations to the truth. No doubt many further stages remain to be worked out; but it should at least be possible to give some tentative account of the origin and development of war.

(1) *The Origin of Aggression*

One unsolved problem which is impossible to shirk occurs at the very outset: the fundamental nature of aggression is still

[1] At a very early stage, aggression seems to be directed against a composite figure of the two parents, and has as its aim their separation.

obscure. Three views seem possible. Aggression may be an independent instinct, it may be a reaction to frustration, or it may be a quality of specific instincts.

(a) *Independent instinct.* According to Freud, aggression, both when it is turned inwards towards the self or outwards against an external enemy, is an expression of the death instinct, or Thanatos, which with Eros form, he thinks, the two fundamental impulses of life. I have never felt very satisfied with this view, because it seems to confuse a perfectly definite impulse of aggression with a rather vague principle of what might be called 'biological elasticity'.[1]

(b) *Reaction to frustration.* The view that aggression is simply a response to frustration always seemed more plausible to me. But this is not entirely satisfactory either. Some kinds of frustration seem to be more tolerable than others. Moreover, the males of many species are said to be aggressive in the rutting season even when they are not frustrated.

(c) *Quality of specific instincts.* According to the third view, aggression is a quality of specific instincts. Or, more precisely, it originated as a quality of one instinct, with which it is still most closely connected, and has been later adapted, both phylogenetically and ontogenetically, to the service of other instincts or impulses as well.

If so, there are two obvious possibilities: its origin may have been nutritional or sexual. The oral aggression of infants, which far exceeds the functional requirements of sucking, recurs not only in the foreplay of the sexual act, but, in dreams and perversions, as a substitute for it. Does sex here borrow its aggressive component from nutrition, or is the infant's oral aggression already sexual in character? This is the sort of psycho-analytic problem that phylogenetic studies might be able to decide. But so far biology can tell us far less about the evolution of

---

[1] Organisms, whenever they are stimulated either from within or without, continue to react until by so doing the stimulus ceases. They may thus be said – if one may use the expression in a purely behaviouristic sense – to 'seek' a maximum quiescence. This has been called the 'Nirvana Principle'. But Freud goes further and believes that organisms have an inner tendency to return to the condition from which they have been disturbed – ultimately to death. This is what he calls the 'Death Instinct'.

THE DEVELOPMENT OF WAR

instincts than about the evolution of the organs that the instincts use. To some extent, of course, the evolution of the impulse can be inferred from that of the organ; so that it would be interesting to trace the evolution of the various offensive organs with which many species are equipped. In most cases such organs seem to have belonged primarily to the male sex; and in some cases, although I am doubtful on this point, they are said to have been originally organs for mastering the female before they became general weapons of offence.[1] If so, a type of aggression first specialized as part of the masculine response to the female may have been adapted to sexual rivalry, transmitted by cross inheritance to the female, and so have been used by both sexes to add to the supply already in the service of the nutritional and other impulses, such as, in the female, the defence of the young.[2]

This is admittedly a speculation. But whatever its origin, aggression does seem to be most closely associated with the masculine sex impulse; and with a sex hormone – since the bull is more aggressive than the ox. Moreover, among the higher animals at least, its most ruthless expression is to be found in the rutting battles of rival males. Indeed, with very few exceptions, sexual rivalry is the only motive for fighting between members of the same species. And from this one may perhaps infer that at some period in our own prehistory man attacked man only when he desired to take his wife.

(2) *The Origin of War*

Among the higher animals there is no parallel to human war. War consists in fighting, between members of the same species, *in cooperation*. And in the rutting battles of animals only the first two items in this definition are fulfilled.

The ape is man's nearest relation; and we are apt to assume, perhaps with insufficient right, that his sociology is not far removed from the direct line of human culture. Here at all events the similarities and differences are especially interesting. The baboon, so far as I gather from Dr Zuckerman's account,[3]

---

[1] Hesse-Doflein, *Tierbau und Tierleben*. Quoted by Roheim, *Animism, Magic and the Divine King*.
[2] Natural selection has doubtless developed further what was originally evolved by sexual selection. [3] Zuckerman, *Social Life of Monkeys and Apes*.

has no war in the sense that one group attacks another. Fighting, which nearly always seems to have a sexual motive, is all against all. There is also no revolution: the males, so far as they combine at all, combine against whichever of their number happens to be in difficulties, and not necessarily against the leader, as in Freud's hypothetical Primal Horde. In short, there is no true cooperation either *under*, or *against* a leader.

What is sometimes called cooperation does not go beyond the stage at which feeling and action are contagious. The thrill of battle may be as contagious in the baboon horde as in the human group; but to the ape there is *no call to take a given side*. All he knows is that a scrap is on, which he does not want to miss, so he attacks the nearest animal within his reach. The same feelings may overwhelm the man who finds himself at the edge of a free fight outside a pub. But the man is capable of fighting *under a leader, with one group against another*; the ape apparently is not.

Nevertheless, in the ape horde one of the Freudian conditions of cooperation is already present. The young bachelors, who have been unable to secure wives, often attach themselves to an older male. Moreover, their reaction to defeat, after an unsuccessful challenge, is often feminine: they sometimes present themselves like females and are ridden by their victors.[1] Without this homosexual component, or this capacity for inversion, animals like baboons, whose rutting season lasts all the year, might be unable to tolerate more than one male in each group. But the baboon has few inhibitions; and probably for this reason, the erotic tie is not sublimated into the sustained loyalty characteristic of the human group.

There is thus a wide gap between animal aggression and human war. Unlike animals, man fights his own species for other than directly sexual aims. And unlike animals, he cooperates with his own group against another group of the same species. To attribute this to a vague gregariousness is merely to name what has to be explained.

Perhaps it would be easier to explain why man fights against other groups, if we first ask why he does not fight against the members of his own. The answer is that there is a

[1] Zuckerman. Paper read to the Psycho-Analytical Society. See also *Social Life of Monkeys and Apes*.

THE DEVELOPMENT OF WAR

taboo on the slaying of kinsmen, which is not an instinct but a cultural acquisition. The sexual battles of even the highest animals take place within the group; the ape is incestuous and fratricidal. Man may neither marry his kinswoman nor kill his kinsman. Therefore, if he can forgo neither love nor hate, he must be exogamous, and, if I may coin the word, 'exoctonous'[1] or 'extrahomicidal'.

This cultural theory takes us a good deal further than any evolutionary theory of aggression; but it leaves several points obscure. How are the taboos on endogamy and the murder of kinsmen (endoctony) developed? And why, if the homicidal impulse is inhibited in one direction, does it break out in another?

Human culture, like human structure, must have developed by almost imperceptible degrees from that of our animal progenitors; what sudden spurts there may have been cannot have been large. But the missing links in the cultural chain are far more difficult to fill than those in morphology. Freud, following Darwin and Atkinson, outlined a psychology for what is known, rather vaguely, as the Primal Horde. To some extent, the Freudian outline has been filled in by the speculations of his followers, especially Reik and Roheim. But in spite of such efforts, the dark ages of prehistory, when man was developing his conscience, his sublimations, his neuroses and his perversions, remain tantalizingly obscure.

Of one fact, however, we may be fairly certain: namely, that Primal Man – I will not try to define this term – had an infancy period far longer than that of the highest ape. And probably this infancy period was bought at the expense of a certain disharmony in sexual development. In childhood, like our own children, he passed through a period in which he was at once too precocious and too retarded.[2] If we may assume this much, we may, I think, infer that he had his parental complex more or less as we know it today. This complex is not identical in different individuals, and no doubt differs in different cultures, and was rudimentary, shall we say, in Eolithic times. But if it existed at all, it involved far more than

---

[1] From κτείνω, to kill.
[2] Roheim, *The Riddle of the Sphinx*, p. 246. See also J. R. Marett, *Race, Sex and Evolution*, p. 242.

a temporary inversion towards the father, or leading male, as in the ape horde. It involved the development, by projection and introjection, of a kind of spiritual parent, or multiplicity of parents – ghosts, gods, devils, Imagos, superegos, call them what you will – whose influence outlived the period of infancy and survived the real parents' absence or even death. Moreover, then as now, there was probably some tendency for ambivalence to split these spirits into two types, good and bad, loved and hated; and to identify the good with one's own leader, whose magic was consequently on the whole beneficent, or with one's own group, and the bad ones with strangers, who became thereby enemies full of evil magic.

This dichotomy may not have been as distinct as it is now. The divine and devilish may not have become clearly separated from each other. Nevertheless, identification with a parental ghost, or superego, to give it its psycho-analytic name, must have given a greater security to the leader, or group of leaders, than they can have enjoyed in the animal period when the strength of their arms was unsupported by any *mana* or superstitious awe. The inversion towards them must have been more sublimated and more prolonged. Within their own clan, their wives and lives must have been comparatively safe. In other words, incest and parricide – or perhaps I should say endogamy and the murder of kinsmen – must have been, at least to some extent, taboo.

Now such taboos or inhibitions leave a fund of sexual and aggressive impulses unsatisfied. These would tend to find outlets in various ways: in hunting, in the conquest of environment, in magic, and in rudimentary war. Since wives were probably difficult to get at home, wife-raiding may have been one of the earliest sources of conflict between group and group. Whether or not the ritual of marriage by capture is a cultural survival of such raids is a matter for anthropologists to determine; but the ritual is at least evidence of a tendency that is likely to have been once realized with less restraint. What I wish to stress, however, are the unconscious rather than the conscious motives. Given a fund of repressed aggressiveness that could seldom be satisfied within the group, and a tendency to identify strangers with devils and evil magicians, intergroup battles might have been precipitated by many causes.

Since the enemy or stranger was probably identified with the hateful aspects of the clansmen's own Imagos, killing him would be an act of special significance. If he was also eaten, this would be less because his flesh was good than because one thereby mastered him completely and absorbed his mysterious power.

The psychology of the leader who led these early raids was probably different from that of his followers. They projected the good aspects of their Imagos upon him, and so made him a good sorcerer or god. He on the other hand probably introjected his Imago, and perhaps even identified himself with it. That is, he had the sense of being possessed by a god, or perhaps even of being himself a god. He may have acquired this manic disposition from his predecessor by some ritual of incorporation, or he may have been naturally of a manic type. In any case, his own delusions, and those of his followers about him, fortified each other and so maintained the solidarity of the group.

But if, as I suggested, the Imago was not yet very clearly split into its good and bad aspects, the solidarity of the group is likely to have been none too secure. Revolts against the father or the leader, much as Freud describes them in *Totem and Taboo*, may have been common. The fundamental difference between man at this epoch and animals is, however, clear: in virtue of his parental complex, man could combine *under* a leader, or *against* a leader; he could be *loyal* or *disloyal*. And if an old leader were deposed, a new one would soon take his place, if he were not, as is more probable, already as the leader of revolt. Perhaps the fate of each leader in turn, as Freud suggests, may have been similar to that of the Divine King of later times: as his strength weakened, he too may have been eaten by his followers, who thereby both satisfied their unconscious hate and participated in his magic strength.

(3) *War in Primitive Communities*

In passing from primal to primitive man as he is today, we pass from the field of speculation to that of ascertainable facts. And here, I must confess, I tread with greater diffidence. Some anthropologists, for instance, Sir James Frazer,[1] speak of war

[1] *Man, God and Immortality.*

as endemic among primitive tribes. Others exhort us to admire the peaceful savage. Such discrepancies are certainly confusing, and not easy to resolve, since the European authorities, with scant regard for science, have usually abolished primitive warfare before anthropologists have had time to study it.

Some primitive peoples seem never to have fought at all. Of those who do, or rather did, the ostensible motives have been very numerous. To the wife-raiding, which I suggested as possibly the original form, must be added the pot-hunting of cannibals, head and other trophy hunting, the blood feud, the attack on or defence of land, pillage and perhaps some other miscellaneous motives, such as the search for sacrificial victims. Some of these seem rational enough; others, such as head-hunting, do not.

But perhaps the most striking feature is that a sexual motive – which in animals is almost the sole cause of fights within the species, and is likely, on this and other grounds, to have been one of the earliest motives in human war – seems to have become relatively unimportant. Indeed, wife-raiding, except in myths[1] or as a branch of slave-raiding, seems to exist only as a ritual.

Admittedly, then, the similarity between primitive warfare and the supposed wife-raiding of Primal Man is not very close. There are, however, some grounds for thinking that, to the unconscious at least, the enemy is equated with a sexual rival. The desire to capture trophies is an almost universal feature of war. And in primitive war, the trophy is often a phallus, or at least a phallic symbol. Testicles are still, I believe, collected by some of the Somali tribes[2]; and other desired trophies, such as heads, teeth, ears or noses, are, to the Freudian at least, unmistakably phallic symbols. With these objects the slain foe's dangerous power in love or war passes to the victor. Moreover, the capture of a trophy, or the killing of a man, is often a necessary preliminary to marriage.[3]

---

[1] E.g. the *Iliad*.

[2] The men of Mowab, New Guinea, after slaying a great warrior, wear his penis in order to increase their strength. *Hastings Encl. Rel. & Eth.*

[3] Where a woman victim does as well, the original custom may have been debased. Or, in view of an unconscious identification between murder and rape, the murder of a woman may seem as apt a test of manhood as the murder of a symbolic rival.

Not only may the enemy unconsciously symbolize a rival; the act of killing him sometimes seems to be unconsciously equivalent to a sexual assault. In dreams, at all events – if you will accept the testimony of psycho-analysis – killing often symbolizes copulation, and the two are identified in a primitive war charm quoted by Roheim.[1] A comparison between death magic and love magic, or between war dances and erotic dances, might perhaps reveal similarities tending to confirm this view.

But if the psycho-analytic theory has any truth, war is far more than a distorted version of animal fights between rival males. It is, as we have seen, an end-product of a psychotic process. Unlike animals, man is haunted by the good and evil spirits into which his ambivalence has split his first concept of his parents. So far as he has introjected this concept, these good and evil spirits are felt to be inside him. If he further identifies himself with them, he is in a state of mania or exaltation – benevolent exaltation in so far as the spirits are good, malevolent exaltation in so far as they are evil – he feels that he *is* a god or a devil. More usually, however, introjection does not include identification: he merely feels he is *possessed* by a god or by a devil. In so far as he is possessed by devils, and is not, like the medicine man, in league with them, he is depressed, melancholic, hypochondriacal or suicidal. Now the primitive savage, from all accounts, suffers as much from these troubles as the most civilized neurotic, with this difference – that the savage in believing himself bewitched comes much nearer to the truth. By projecting his devils into stones or trees, into the wind, the rain storm or the angry sea, or by identifying them with strangers or sorcerers, he can exchange his melancholy for an apparently external danger. To the neurotic individual, though perhaps not to the society that contains him, this is a psychological gain. The external dangers can be dealt with more easily; the storm devils can be propitiated or driven off, and the strangers can be killed. Indeed, the killing of them is, I believe, often an obsessional or ritual act, which, on account of its magical attack on his unconscious bogeys, saves the savage from his neurotic fears.

[1] *Animism, Magic and the Divine King*, 1930, p. 20.

If the savage is a cannibal and eats his victims, he converts an imaginary danger into an equally imaginary source of internal strength: he absorbs their magic power. But this psychological advantage may have a double edge. In so far as his identification with the warriors he has eaten is incomplete, the internal power may be felt as dangerous to himself as well as to his enemies. In other words, the cannibal passes into a state in which the introjective mechanisms again predominate. Then perhaps he resorts to ceremonies of purification to get rid of the dangerous power he has absorbed. But if he does so, and projects his devils once more into the external world, he may soon feel compelled to go and kill and eat another stranger. The psychological process is therefore likely to be cyclical: a depressive phase of introjection passing into a paranoiac phase of projection, and this in turn into a manic phase of identification, after which the cycle starts again. My argument is based only on the analogy of what is found in civilized neurotics and psychotics; how far it holds of actual cannibals only field work can decide.

In head and other trophy hunting, the underlying mechanisms are probably similar to those in cannibalism. To eat a thing is to possess it in the most elementary way; and psychologically the desire to own seems to be a derivative of the desires to eat. The child tries to eat its toys, and in the unconscious the sense of ownership and the sense of having eaten something often seem to be equivalent. Thus we might expect the head-hunter to introject the magical powers of his victim when he wins the trophy almost as well as if he had eaten him outright.[1] If he does not keep the trophy, but gives it to his chief or god, this is probably because it is too dangerous for ordinary mortals to possess, and must belong to those strong enough to resist its magic powers. Although it may be too dangerous for the common man, it is at least a source of strength to the community of which he forms a part.

The same kind of mechanisms seem to underlie another, and, according to Frazer, the commonest cause of primitive warfare, namely, the blood feud. According to the savage, death is always due to murder, either natural or supernatural;

---

[1] The possession of the trophy gives magical power. See Haddon, *Head-Hunters*.

THE DEVELOPMENT OF WAR

and if the dead are not avenged, they take vengeance on their own kin. Therefore a dead man's kinsmen look for a sorcerer to kill. This may be explained, I think, by assuming that their own consciences are never clear. Their own evil magic, their own internal devils, may have done the deed. So to escape their self-reproaches, and the vengeance of their deceased relation, they project their internal devils upon a strange sorcerer instead. This motive becomes almost conscious in the story of Kwoiam, one of the cult heroes in the Torres Straits, who exacted blood vengeance for the death of his mother, whom he himself had killed.[1]

The other motives for primitive warfare, the defence of or attack on land, pillage, slave-raiding, etc., seem rational enough. But I believe there is always some admixture of the irrational motives I have described – though, of course, the rational and the irrational may be combined in very different proportions.[2]

How far the unconscious mechanisms vary in different cultures, and whether or not they inevitably lead to war, are difficult questions. Some primitive peoples are said to be entirely peaceful. Perhaps they are innately less aggressive; or perhaps their educational system stimulates aggression less. But the possibility remains that they are less warlike only because they are more depressed, that is, because more of their aggression is turned inwards. The pacific Septchacs (of India) are said to commit suicide if they are insulted.[3] From their own point of view, this is hardly preferable to war.

(4) *War in Semi-civilized and Civilized Communities*

The passage from primitive to semi-civilized or civilized war is accompanied by further changes. The motive is progressively desexualized, rationalized and moralized. The method is more highly organized: killing has ceased altogether to be a private matter, and belongs only to the state; it is less frequent, but on a larger scale and more prolonged.

In the first place, the conscious sexual motive has completely

---

[1] Haddon, *Head-Hunters*, p. 143.
[2] The Malays and the Iban combined for piratical forays, the Malays for plunder and the Iban for skulls. Haddon, *Head-Hunters*, p. 326.
[3] Dr Marett – Private communication.

disappeared – except for occasional outbursts when an army storms a town. But a faint echo of the more archaic cause of rivalry seems to linger in the idealism of soldiers, who often feel they are fighting, not only for their king, but also in some way for their wives and daughters, and for their country, that is, to protect their mother land from an invasion, which is metaphorically described as rape. Moreover, the enemy is usually most hated because he is accused of committing atrocities on women. In reality, rape, at least by civilized armies, is probably rare. But the whole symbolism of invading, attacking or killing, may have this meaning in the unconscious. Each side accuses the other of acts which they have themselves repressed, and only symbolically enjoyed.

In the second place, the other motives seem to have become more rational. Trophy-hunting and blood vengeance give place to the search for colonies or markets. That the more primitive motive of trophy-hunting[1] may still be present is, however, proved by the case of a man, quoted by Dr Glover,[2] who used to creep about in no man's land to draw the teeth from as many dead bodies as he could find. And as to the alleged disappearance of the blood feud, it should be sufficient to remember that the Great War started with the murder of an Archduke. Even the rational motives are less rational than they seem. The civilized man's desire for power, prestige and possessions far exceeds his reasonable desires for necessities and comforts. This, as Roheim says, is a real puzzle to the comparatively contented Duau Islanders. A rather paranoid anxiety is, I believe, again the underlying motive. To the Faust-like European, the world presents a perpetual challenge: he cannot stand still, but must conquer perpetually, or sink into depression. This drive takes many forms; when it is imperialistic, the usual result is war.

Lastly, war has become moralized with civilization. Modern nations take great pains to convince themselves of the justice of their cause. But this is only a development of a process that is very old. Departed spirits commanded their kinsmen to avenge their death; and in historic times, if the gods did not always

---

[1] Some of the importance once attached to teeth, testicles or hands, has been transferred to such emblems as the flag.
[2] *War, Sadism and Pacifism*.

order war, their consent must be at least obtained. If the auspices were unfavourable, it was postponed. The ancient Jews, from whom we have derived so many of our ethical ideals, massacred their enemies at the command of Jahveh. Mohammedans, Catholics and Protestants offer familiar examples of religious wars; and for a time it seemed that Russia intended to propagate her new faith with the sword. In the Great War, Germany felt it her duty to spread her culture; and not long ago our own talk of the White Man's Burden justified acts that we should now condemn; for the present generation, in England at least, feels that fighting is only justified in self-defence, or to defend the principle of Collective Security. But the moral element was always there, and has merely changed its form. In the beginning, the war chief was identified with the superego, and was therefore the keeper of the conscience. Later this rôle was partly taken over by the ghost of slain relations, then by gods, then by the idea of the State, personified as a father or a mother, and finally by an abstract ideal.

That such changes, by themselves, have much effect on the frequency of war seems rather doubtful. Even if war was felt everywhere to be justified only in self-defence, it might still continue. For nations are paranoiac about each other, each seeing in the defensive measures of its neighbours a sure confirmation of its fears. And once a nation has persuaded itself that it will be attacked, it feels justified in choosing the opportunity that suits it best.

III. SUMMARY

To sum up what seem to me the main features in the development of war: the higher animals are aggressive for a variety of reasons, but seldom attack their own species except for motives of sexual jealousy. They do not cooperate either under or against a leader. Man differs from animals in that he has a conscience; that is, he forms an ideal of his parents, which survives the period of childhood and lives on to inhibit the free expression of his impulses. In particular, his sexual and aggressive impulses are inhibited by taboos on incest and parricide, or in a wider form, endogamy and the murder of a kinsman. The repressed sexual impulses reappear in a variety of forms.

One of these is homosexual. In so far as this is also repressed, it gives rise, in combination with the repressed aggression, to two apparently opposite attitudes to other men. Unconscious homosexuality combined with a certain degree of inverted aggression takes the form of self-sacrificing devotion. This is the usual attitude to one's own group, who are protected by taboos, and especially to its leader, who is identified with the good aspects of the parental Imago. On the other hand, unconscious homosexuality combined with direct aggression takes the form of a desire to kill. This is the attitude to strangers, who are unprotected by taboos inhibiting aggression and who are identified with the bad aspects of the Imago.

Furthermore, such an attitude is paranoiac in the sense that it results from a distorted picture of the stranger. He is the depository of one's own repressed aggression, and is therefore thought of as wholly evil and quite free from the friendly sentiments characteristic of one's neighbour. But in so far as the stranger's attitude to one's own group is also paranoiac, each delusion makes the other true.

This, in rough outline, is a psycho-analytic account of man's warlike disposition. The precipitating causes of actual wars are numerous and differ with the degree of civilization. But the unconscious factors that produce the disposition are probably much the same in the most cultured people as they were in primeval times. What is new, however, is a conscious dislike of war, which is widespread though by no means universal. Whether or not this conscious attitude will succeed in controlling the unconscious factors is a matter that only the future can decide.

POSTSCRIPT

This conscious dislike of war is a product of restitutive mechanisms which, on revising my proofs, I see I have neglected. The unconscious fear of having destroyed or injured our good objects in infancy, gives rise to a strong desire to repair the damage, which is largely responsible for constructional work in general, and for pacifist activities in particular. But if internal conflicts or external events, or a combination of the two, convince us of the futility of our desire for peace, we are apt to

THE DEVELOPMENT OF WAR

defend ourselves against self-accusations by believing that our good objects are injured, not by us but by certain bad objects on to which we have projected our aggression. These we are apt to attack in the persons of the real or supposed enemies of peace – armament firms, capitalists, bolsheviks, autocrats or foreign nations. From this point of view, peace with its constructive work is the normal condition; war, with its sudden outbreak of destruction, an abnormal interlude due to a large-scale breakdown of restitutive functions. If, by analysis or some other method, our own unconscious guilt, that is, fear of having injured or destroyed our good objects, is lessened, we shall have more confidence in our powers of restitution, and, in particular, our pacifism will be more rational and stable.

10

The Psychology of Propaganda*[1]

I. INTRODUCTION

Propaganda has always been the means by which different political or religious bodies sought to make their wills prevail; but in the past its range was short and its spread comparatively slow. Its range – at first no greater than that of the orator's unaided voice – was only gradually enlarged by the use of written circular letters, like the Epistles of St Paul, and then by the invention and slow development of printing. But in the last few years, with the coming of cheap newspapers, of the cinema, and above all of wireless, audiences or readers of a few hundred have suddenly swelled to many millions. Its range now covers the whole world, and no one outside a desert island can escape its influence. For this reason, the psychology of propaganda, or what is perhaps the same thing, the psychology of mass suggestion, has suddenly developed an enormous practical importance.

If man were wholly rational, and influenced only by such propaganda as told the truth, the whole truth and nothing but the truth, there would be no problem. But unfortunately evidence and judgment are by no means the sole determinants of his beliefs and feelings. He has always been a credulous animal, easily convinced and easily inflamed by oratory. Sometimes he can be almost hypnotized into accepting anything that is asserted with sufficient authority and force. Our problem is to discover why.

* B. J. Med. Psych., vol. XIX, 1941–42.
[1] This paper was originally intended as one in a series of three lectures on the Psychology of Propaganda, which were to have been delivered by Dr Adrian Stephen, Dr Hargreaves and myself, but which were cancelled owing to the war. The greater part of it was written in the two months immediately before the war, and has only been corrected in minor details. One or two paragraphs, as indicated in footnotes, have been added subsequently; but pressure of work since the beginning of the war has unfortunately made it impossible for me to undertake any complete revision, or to bring my examples up to date.

To say, as psychologists were rather fond of doing, that he is suggestible merely names the quality we are trying to explain. We want to know why some people are more suggestible to propaganda than others, and why the degree of their suggestibility depends both on their relation to the propagandist and on the nature of his propaganda.

II. DIFFERENCES IN GENERAL SUGGESTIBILITY TO PROPAGANDA

Take first what may be called individual differences in general suggestibility. It is obvious that, other things being equal, educated people are less easily influenced by propaganda than uneducated ones – they have more knowledge against which to weigh what they are told. But apart from this, one of the main factors seems to be the attitude towards authority. The independent type of man, who feels little need for authority outside himself, is in general less suggestible than the dependent type, who needs the support of authority and the security that comes of feeling that he is a member of some group.

At first sight, such character qualities appear to be innate. Certainly they do not alter much between childhood and old age. A very dependent child, for example, seldom outgrows this disability. If, in later life, he is pushed into a responsible office, he is more likely to become dependent upon his subordinates, or to develop a sense of inferiority, than to evolve a self-confident independence hitherto foreign to his nature. But in spite of their apparent immutability, dependence and independence of character are now known to be not so much innate qualities as the results of very early experience.

Everyone starts life as a dependent individual, that is, as a child dependent on his parents. Some people grow up and become independent, but others remain psychologically children all their lives, always dependent on parent substitutes – either human or divine. Their development has been arrested.

In normal development (normal in the medical, not the statistical, sense), the child imitates and ultimately absorbs the characters of those persons in its environment whom it especially admires. Thus the boy admires and gradually absorbs the character first of his own father and then of the various father substitutes he finds at school. In this way he may develop an independent character, that is, he may become psychologically a parent rather than a child.

But this smooth development is easily disturbed. If, for instance, the boy's father is a drunkard who ill-treats his mother and himself, he may be unable to absorb this character, because to do so would endanger the chief object of his love. Having no model to imitate, he will fail to grow up, and may remain psychologically a timid but secretly rebellious son.

All this is a matter of common observation, which can be discovered without the aid of a psychoanalytical technique. What would not have been discovered without analysis, however, is that even the most model father may be pictured as a brutal and sadistic being in the eyes of his small son. This early picture is, of course, soon forgotten, and replaced by one that probably exaggerates all the father's actual virtues. But it survives in unconscious memory. Moreover, it is 'incorporated', that is, the small boy unconsciously feels it to be inside himself – like a demon who has taken possession of his body; the almost universal primitive belief in possession by evil spirits being in fact nothing but a slightly distorted version of this unconscious belief.

Now it is quite as, if not more, difficult for the child who has a false unconscious picture of a bad father to absorb this character as it is for the child who really has a bad one.[1] It will remain therefore distinct from his personality as a ghostly and unconscious persecutor throughout his life. To deny such a figure and to replace it by more friendly mentors will then become an imperative necessity for his peace of mind. Even an actual tyranny will seem preferable to this inner persecution. He will be happiest under authority, and will feel most secure as a member of some disciplined and powerful group. By identifying himself with it and with its leader he may get that sense of potency which is denied him as an individual. But his peace of mind will be secured at the sacrifice of his independent judgment. He will become a yes-man, uncritically accepting the views of his own group and will fall an easy prey to its propaganda.

[1] [1977 Even a real bad father owes as much to projection into him of the child's 'bad' sadistic self. It can also be internalized.]

III. SUGGESTIBILITY DEPENDS ALSO ON THE SOURCE OF THE PROPAGANDA

A man's suggestibility to propaganda, then, depends upon the degree of independence of his character, and this again upon the degree to which he can build his own character on the model of his father's character, not necessarily as it really is, but as he imagined it in early infancy and still unconsciously imagines it. But obviously suggestibility to propaganda also depends upon its source.

A few decades ago, when reading was still something of an accomplishment to the average labourer, uneducated people often managed to combine a high degree of scepticism to anything their neighbours told them with an astonishing credulity to anything they saw in print. 'It must be true, I saw it in print', they said; for the written word still possessed a magical authority. Now, however, if we have not become discriminating, we have at least become selective. We are at once over-credulous to newspapers of our own political party or nation, and over-suspicious to those of our political or national opponents. If the Axis press says that the French are persecuting the Italians in Tunisia, we tend to reject such statements almost as automatically as the Italians and Germans apparently believe them. Or if *The Times* says that our foreign policy has always been both wise and honourable, the Germans laugh at our hypocrisy to the indignation of our government's more loyal supporters. It is not merely that we disagree with the other side – this would hardly be irrational – but we can seldom even give them the credit of themselves believing what they say. Thus suggestibility and contra-suggestibility are not incompatible qualities. We possess neither or both at once. If we are suggestible to one authority, we are also contra-suggestible to its opponent.

Since credulity and suspicion so often go together, their cause is probably the same. The dependent suggestible type of person, as we know, needs support because he is not at peace within himself. He seeks protection against an internal enemy, in much the same way as the medieval villain sought the protection of a king, however tyrannical, against the local baron. But there is this difference, that whereas the villain knew his baron only too well, the dependent man is usually quite unconscious of his internal enemy. Had he lived in the age of faith, he might have been afraid of being possessed by the devil; but even then he would seldom have admitted that the devil of his unconscious fantasy was already inside him. In nightmares, or when for instance he is alone in the dark, something of the unconscious sense of persecution may become momentarily conscious, but for the most part he will successfully deny it. The denial, however, is seldom absolute. The internal enemy seems to reappear outside; in technical language, it is projected.

This mechanism of projection, by means of which internal enemies are as it were banished into the external world, is of very great importance in psychology. It is the main cause of the delusions of persecution in paranoia. The paranoiac is intensely suspicious; he sees the hidden hand of some enemy in almost everything that happens, and interprets the most friendly gesture as part of a deep-laid plot to encompass his destruction. But such symptoms are not confined to certifiable lunatics. Indeed, under conditions of sufficient stress, most people seem capable of producing them. In medieval Europe a paranoid form of witch-hunting was endemic; and, during the last war, this country developed a spy mania, which almost reached paranoid proportions: anyone with the remotest connection with Germany was certain to be suspected. Even in peace time, there are many otherwise sane people who attribute all the ills of the world to some one evil and mysterious source, which they identify, according to their religious or political prejudices, with the Jesuits, the Jews, the Bolsheviks, the Capitalists or the Germans. And similarly, to many Germans, Britain is the hypocritical and cunning enemy, who is ceaselessly plotting to destroy them.

We now begin to see why over-credulity and over-suspiciousness, or suggestibility and contra-suggestibility, so often go together. The same inner conflict that makes a man seek leadership outside himself, and then trust it blindly at all costs rather than give up this necessary support, also drives him to project his inner enemies on to outer ones whom he can hate and whom he inevitably distrusts.

When two groups become paranoid about each other in this

way, it becomes almost impossible to distinguish between false and true suspicions; for the false suspicions of each side soon breed counter-measures in the other and so justify themselves. The Germans believe, what Dr Goebbels tells them, that we are plotting their destruction, and disbelieve us when we tell them that at most we are only planning to protect ourselves. Similarly, we are inclined to believe that Hitler is plotting to destroy us and to dominate the world. Is this a true picture?

IV. SUGGESTIBILITY DEPENDING ON THE NATURE OF THE PROPAGANDA

So far we have considered two determinants of suggestibility to propaganda: the character of the propagandee, and his relation to the propagandist. We have now to consider the third, and perhaps the most important, determinant: the nature of the propaganda itself.

It is obvious that people are far more suggestible to some themes than to others. They have a selective credulity, which is determined by their unconscious fantasies. They tend to reject what does not, and to accept what does, correspond with their unconscious preconceptions. That this is so is best proved by the analysis of a few examples of successful propaganda.

I remember being taken to hear Hitler speak shortly before he came into power. He was preceded by Goebbels, and both orators said the same things in the same order. The repetition did not bore the audience, but, like the repetition in Ravel's *Bolero*, seemed only to increase the emotional effect.

It was not easy to keep one's balance; for if one was unable to identify oneself with the crowd and share its intense emotions, one almost inevitably personified it as a sinister and rather terrifying super-individual. To me, at least, the speeches themselves were not particularly impressive. But the crowd was unforgettable. The people seemed gradually to lose their individuality and to become fused into a not very intelligent but immensely powerful monster, which was not quite sane and therefore capable of anything. Moreover it was an elementary monster, something from the pleistocene age, with no judgment and only a few, but very violent, passions. Yet there was something mechanical about it too; for it was under the complete control of the figure on the rostrum. He evoked or changed its passions as easily as if they had been the notes of some gigantic organ.

The tune was very loud, but very simple. As far as I could make out, there were only three, or perhaps four, notes; and both speakers or organists played them in the same order. For ten minutes we heard of the sufferings of Germany in the thirteen or fourteen years since the war. The monster seemed to indulge in an orgy of self-pity. Then for the next ten minutes came the most terrific fulminations against Jews and Social-democrats as the sole authors of these sufferings. Self-pity gave place to hate; and the monster seemed on the point of becoming homicidal. But the note was changed once more; and this time we heard for ten minutes about the growth of the Nazi party, and how from small beginnings it had now become an overpowering force. The monster became self-conscious of its size, and intoxicated by the belief in its own omnipotence.

So far, there was no essential difference between Goebbels and Hitler. They played the same tune, with only minor variations. But Hitler ended on a peroration which was absent in Goebbels' speech. This was a passionate appeal to all Germans to unite. The monster became sentimental and far more human than it had been before. But this sentimentality ended on an almost masochistic note. Hitler ceased; and in the deathly silence, the Commander of the serried ranks of uniformed Nazis cried out a single sentence as a sort of Amen: 'Germany must live; even if we must die for her.' No one asked who threatened Germany; and why the supreme sacrifice should be necessary. That this was so seemed to be beyond dispute. At a single word from its leader, the monster was ready, indeed anxious, to immolate itself.

As propaganda, these speeches were an immense success. If, therefore, our assumptions are correct, they must have appealed to something already in the unconscious. To each successive theme, there must have corresponded some pre-existing unconscious fantasy.

The first of these themes was the sufferings of Germany. Now it is quite true that Germany had really suffered. She had been humiliated; the depreciation of her currency had wiped out the value of the savings of her people; and she was in the depths of an unprecedented economic depression. These surely are sufficient to explain at least the first part of the response, without looking for unconscious factors. But when we remember how easily a skilful agitator can create a burning sense of grievance, for example, in a factory, among people who had previously been quite contented, we see that there must be something in us that makes us peculiarly sensitive to any suggestion that we are ill-treated. The unconscious, in fact, usually does feel ill-treated, because most people, although they seek to deny it, carry an imaginary enemy within themselves; and for this reason they are often over-ready to believe in a grievance of external origin. Some people indeed go so far as to provoke one in order to lessen the sense of inner conflict. These are borderland psychotics. But the average person is somewhere between the two extremes of perfect sanity and madness. He is not easily stirred by propaganda to believe in wholly imaginary grievances, but he is very ready to overestimate any real grievances there may be. At the time of the speech I have described, conditions had already begun to improve a little. But under the influence of propaganda the people became far more conscious of their sufferings than they had been before. The unconscious imaginary sufferings were evoked by it to reinforce the conscious real ones.

The next step was to point out the authors of these sufferings. In reality, the main enemy was the great slump, which had started in America. But the concept of an impersonal force as the cause of our misfortunes is a late and precarious acquisition of the human mind. To primitive savages, calamities are never the result of impersonal forces. If they suffer from famine, disease or sudden death, they look for the sorcerer who, with his evil magic, has done these things. From our own more lofty standpoint we are apt to ridicule such primitive superstitions. But they tend to survive in our own unconscious minds. The unconscious is aware of its internal enemies, and begins by attributing any new calamity to them. But if someone points to an external author, we are very ready to believe him; for to fear and hate an external enemy at once lessens the internal tension. There is usually a small element of real truth, which is enormously exaggerated. Some people profited by the great slump, even if they did not create it. Some of these were Jews or

Social-democrats. The orators had but to accuse them and to the audience in its semi-hypnotic trance, they were already proved guilty and convicted.

But self-pity and hatred were not enough. It was also necessary to drive out fear, which might otherwise have made the Party too cautious to defy the State. So the speakers turned from vituperation to self-praise. From small beginnings the Party had grown invincible. Each listener felt a part of its omnipotence within himself. He was transported into a new psychosis. The induced melancholia passed into paranoia, and the paranoia into megalomania. Put in psychoanalytic language, it was not enough to substitute an external enemy for an internal one. It was also necessary to convert the internal persecutor into a mighty ally, which remained terrible indeed, but which would become terrible only to one's enemies, and no longer to oneself. The devil became the German (phallic) war god, and each listener felt him arise and throb within his breast.

Still there remained something unsatisfied in the unconscious; for it contains not only fears and hates, but also an intense yearning for a sort of Paradise, where injuries are put right and all men love each other. So Hitler made his great appeal for unity. This seemed to me to be the secret of his success. If, like some of his disciples, he had nothing but thunderbolts to offer, he could hardly have remained the god he is. But he also stirred the unconscious longing for the ideal family, in which no one should be injured and everyone should be at peace. This Paradise, however, was only for true Germans and true Nazis. Everyone outside remained a persecutor, and therefore an object of hate.

V. A PATTERN OF INDUCED PSYCHOSES

Nazi oratory, as I have tried to describe it, seems to follow a pattern or theme that is common to many other, and apparently quite dissimilar, types of propaganda. Viewed in an unfavourable light, propaganda often seems to be a method of inducing a series of temporary psychoses, often starting with depression and passing, via paranoia, to a state of manic bliss. But it may also be viewed favourably, as having in a sense a curative effect, if it finds the propagandee depressed and leaves him in a state of not too unbalanced enthusiasm. In both cases the fundamental pattern seems often to be the same.[1]

(a) *The Depressive-paranoid Phase*

The true propagandist very often feels himself to be a messiah who has discovered the road to salvation – whether this is a new faith or only some patent medicine. But his remedies will remain untried, unless he can first persuade people that they are in need of help. Sometimes they are already anxious or depressed. But if they are not, his first step must be to evoke these feelings from the unconscious. For this reason Nazi propaganda started with the sufferings of Germany – sufferings which were real enough, but which were exaggerated until people felt that they were indeed on the edge of an abyss from which Hitler alone could save them. For exactly the same reason the religious propagandist usually starts by evoking the anxious strain of guilt and the terror of damnation; while even the commercial advertiser appeals to the hypochondria, or the social sense of inferiority, that is often latent and fairly easily aroused, before trying to sell his patent medicines, cosmetics or clothes.

Political propaganda often follows the same pattern. We are told that the other political party, if it gains power, will destroy the value of our savings or lead us into war, or alternatively that it will cut down wages, fail to raise pensions or the dole, and so do nothing to relieve the worker's latent fear of destitution. But if the suggested threats are too unreal for us to grasp, or if we have little confidence in a party's power to save us from the calamities it predicts, such propaganda usually miscarries. The election cry of 'Safety First' in 1931 aroused the fears only of those few who had great possessions. Moreover, the appeal to fear was purely negative, and was not followed by any call to action.

An apparent exception to the rule that propaganda begins with an appeal to fear is afforded by the very common type that begins with an appeal to righteous indignation. The indignation may be for our own wrongs or it may be vicarious. The revolutionary mobs of Paris or Moscow were stirred to a white heat of fury by those who told them that they had been deprived of

[1] This paragraph was rewritten in April 1940.

their rights to liberty and equality. But our own indignation was only slightly less stirred, in the time of Gladstone by Bulgarian atrocities, in 1914 by the rape of Belgium, and in September 1938 by the threat to Czechoslovakia; while the Germans felt much the same about the Jameson raid and the Boer War. But I believe that the absence of anxiety in indignation is more apparent than real. The propaganda theme opens with a chord, rather than a single note, and anxiety is drowned in the louder clamour. That it is really present seems to be proved by those cases in which the indignation is thwarted of its outlet. If nothing is done to save the threatened object, anger subsides and we are apt to be left with a very great anxiety, either on our own behalf or on behalf of those who have been deserted to their fate. This, rather than relief, was the reaction of most pro-Czech Englishmen after the settlement of Munich.

The fear beneath the indignation is, I think, still clearer in Nazi propaganda. This began by evoking a state of 'group paranoia' among the German people. It made them feel that they were persecuted by enemies both inside and outside their country. It raised the sleeping bogeys of the unconscious and identified them with Jews and Democrats and Communists. Now bogeys from the unconscious are always primarily objects of fear. But fear can be submerged by hate, and Nazi propaganda has hardly been surpassed, even by medieval witch hunters, in the ferocity with which it attacked the bogeys of its own creation. Had it not done so, it might have produced a mass hysteria (such as the hysteria of the year one thousand when the end of the world was confidently predicted) but not the mass mania it actually produced. Indeed in Nazi psychology, as in the psychology of many pathological individuals, fear and hate seem to form a sort of vicious circle. First fear is stirred up, then hate to keep it in check; but the hate expects retaliation and thus increases fear, which has to be drowned by more hate and so on. The system needs *effective* hate – hate which can be satisfied – in order to preserve its life. If the hate were to become impotent, it would collapse into the hysterical anxiety which is its unconscious foundation.[1]

There is one type of propaganda that not only opens on a

---

[1] This paragraph was added in January 1940.

note of fear, but persists on this note throughout. This is terrorist propaganda aimed at the destruction of the morale of an enemy before or during a war. A good example is that part of Nazi propaganda which is designed for export rather than for home consumption. The Nazis have certainly been trying to terrify the world, and to some extent, it must be confessed, they have succeeded. To many people – and not only political opponents in Germany – the Nazi leader has become a dark and diabolic power, that hangs over the whole world, which they dare not resist and which they cannot escape from. This figure is taken straight from the unconscious. It is identical with the furies of Greek imagination, with the avenging God of the Old Testament, or the cloven-hooved Satan of medieval superstition. And in every case, incredible as this may seem, its prototype is one of the two unconscious and incompatible pictures the child forms of his own parents, in particular his father. For even the most admirable father becomes the prototype of his children's devils as well as of their gods. In unconscious fantasy this demon may be kept in check, or submerged by more friendly pictures of the same parent figure, which may appear as a loving god or guardian angel. But the more sinister picture remains dormant, like a ghost that has been only conditionally laid, ever ready to rise again out of the depths. Terrorist propaganda is like some medieval incantation; it seeks to raise this diabolic figure from the unconscious, not as an awful ally, but to paralyse all opposition. It can be remarkably successful, but only if the opposition has no leadership as resolute as its own.

(b) The Manic or Enthusiastic Phase

Except in the case of deliberate terrorism, no propaganda stops at fear. Having aroused, or at least intensified, anxiety, its next step is to awaken hope in its particular brand of salvation. This may be historically trivial, such as a patent medicine, or some item in the programme of a political party that does not differ greatly from its alternative; or it may be historically fundamental, such as a new creed, either religious or political.

Often the hope of salvation is thought to lie in one man. The sinner, who has first been made vividly aware of the awfulness of guilt, is exhorted to turn to God. Similarly, in the secular field, those who are, or who have been made, either anxious or depressed are told to seek their salvation in some national or party leader; and even in the trivial case of patent medicines, it appears to be a good sales point to give the name of the discoverer. The same appeal to an individual leader is also made when the object of propaganda is to restore the morale of a people which has been badly shaken. Here the first step, the awakening of anxiety, has already been made by the other side. The tune one country starts in order to terrorize its opponents into submission is completed by them for the opposite purpose of arousing their resistance. Thus in 1914, England and Germany responded to each other's propaganda, among other ways, by giving an enormous publicity to their own generals, especially Kitchener and Hindenburg.

The heroes or gods of one people are often the devils of another, Napoleon and Hitler being outstanding examples of men who have played this double role. To foreigners they symbolize the bad father and are therefore incarnations of all the powers of evil and destruction. To their own countrymen they are saviours and symbols of the good father figure, which like the bad one is preserved in unconscious fantasy.

But although the saviour hero is predominantly a good father, he may be also a 'combined parent', that is, a father and mother in one person; and if he is a revolutionary leader, he is likely to be a symbol of an elder brother, who leads the family against the tyrannical father, as well. That he can be all three at once, a trinity in one person, is no contradiction, for symbols are often overdetermined, that is, they stand for more than one unconscious figure.

The need to find in the external world such symbols of the good internal figures of unconscious fantasy is in proportion to the degree to which a man feels himself threatened by the bad ones. If he is not anxious, he does not turn to any saviour. But once his anxiety is aroused, he tends to lose faith in the powers of good within himself, and so seeks a symbol of them in order to reassure himself that they are still alive.

To become a hero-leader, it is usually not sufficient for a man to preach a gospel. He must be supported by a group. For a long time he may preach in vain; but once the group begins to form, it grows like a snowball, because each increment increases his symbolical authority. One people, one leader, he is identified with his group and gains the overwhelming power which sheer numbers give. Those outside the group can no longer regard him as an ordinary individual. He must be either god or devil; and if they have no stable god within themselves, or are isolated and have no alternative external leader, they must either endure unrelieved the sense of inner and outer persecution, or surrender to him and accept him as their god. To do this is an enormous relief from anxiety and inner conflict. He is all-powerful and must protect them. He is their conscience; and what he thinks is inevitably right. He begins as the saviour from real troubles, which he has probably exaggerated. He ends as the saviour from the anxiety which isolation outside his group may alone be sufficient to produce.

The discovery of a hero does more than merely reassure the unconscious that the inner persecutors are opposed by no less powerful friends. It also releases the capacity for reconstructive work, which may have been lost during the previous period of depression. The unconscious contains not only fears, hates and loves, but also a strong restitutive urge. In the unconscious fantasy of the child, so much is destroyed by his own aggression and by those upon whom he has projected it, that he can only be saved from utter despair by a belief in his capacity to restore the damage. This belief, and the urge that goes with it, seem basic elements in all constructive work. If external conditions are bad, for instance, after an unsuccessful war or during an economic depression, this belief may be temporarily lost, and a whole people plunged into an inactivity bordering on despair. But when they discover a hero and have confidence in him, they regain confidence in an inner power for good, which can deal successfully with their difficulties, however great.

At this moment, 25 August 1939, this country is faced by dangers greater perhaps than any it has faced since the Napoleonic wars. But the announcement of the Russo–German pact did not unnerve us because its effects were counterbalanced by our Government's resolute reaffirmation of our pledges to Poland. The firm leadership, which many of us sought in vain during the previous crises, enabled us to face the greater danger with more courage and more confidence in our capacity to defend, or, in the long run, to restore the values we stand for in the world. If, instead of this, we had deserted these values – as some of us feel we did at Munich – I think we should have been plunged into an inert despair unrelieved by the temporary removal of the threat of war. The threat to these values of freedom, justice and democracy had seemed so great that many of us were losing our capacity for constructive work. But it was quickly restored as soon as we felt the resolute leadership we had waited for so long.

In Germany also, leadership restored the people's belief in their capacity for constructive work. But there the unconscious urge to restitution found a different symbolic outlet. Nazi official values are not Freedom, Justice and Democracy, as we understand these words, but only the Hegelian State. Since the German State as a primary value can have no appeal to those outside Germany, while Freedom, Justice and Democracy must still make some appeal inside her, the moral advantage is with us. She will be less wholehearted, and will not enjoy the sympathy of neutral countries. Moreover, in the long run, the common values which unite us to our allies are likely to prove a stronger bond than the self-interest of opponents which, at any moment, may cease to correspond.

I suggested just now that propaganda might be regarded either as a means to evoke a mass psychosis, ultimately of a manic type, or as a means to cure a mass depression. To some extent the choice of aspect is subjective: there are curative elements in Nazi propaganda, just as there are no doubt manic elements in ours. But there is, I think, a vast difference in the degree in which the sense of reality is preserved. The German or Hitlerian war god, which the Teutonic people have incorporated and which has lent them, temporarily, so great a strength, seems too fantastic for our minds to comprehend at all. Like the Old Testament Jahveh, He is a good father figure to his people, but, to us at least, almost unrecognizably distorted by attributes from the imaginary bad one of unconscious fantasy. Our own national gods, those spirits of the unconscious on which we try to model our behaviour, are less unified and less distinct, but also more human and more real. They are based on parent figures that seem far less distorted by infantile aggression.[1]

[1] This paragraph was added in April 1940.

VI. SUMMARY

To summarize briefly the main features, as I understand them, in the psychology of propaganda:

(a) There are variations in people's general susceptibility which depend upon the degree of independence, that is, the degree of maturity, they have attained. Character is developed by imitating an ideal, not so much consciously as by an unconscious process of assimilation whereby the qualities of ideal characters – ultimately ideal parent figures – are gradually absorbed.

If the imaginary parent figures of early infancy are predominantly good and helpful, they can be absorbed without difficulty to form the basis of a well-balanced and independent character. But if these parent figures are predominantly evil, their absorption is hindered by anxiety; they remain in unconscious fantasy as internal persecutors. Therefore the resulting character, having little support within itself, will be excessively dependent on, and easily influenced by, others.[1]

(b) Suggestibility depends not only on the degree of independence of character, but also on the *source* of the propaganda itself. People are especially sensitive to the influence of those symbols of good parent figures they seek in the external world to protect them from the persecution of the bad ones.

(c) Lastly, suggestibility to propaganda depends upon its *nature*. To be effective it must correspond with, or symbolize, unconscious fantasies that are already there.

The most effective propaganda probably begins with an appeal to fear. It first points out symbols of the bad parents and so raises these sleeping demons of unconscious fantasy; and then erects compensatory symbols of the good parents, heroes who are strong enough to defeat the demons, and who can restore the people's lost belief in their power to do creative work, and give them courage to face real dangers often in fact far greater than the more or less imaginary ones they were first made to fear.

---

[1] [1977—It should never be forgotten that both the good and evil figures owe their characters in large measure to projection into them of the child's own love or sadism.]

11

Towards a Common Aim: A Psycho-analytical Contribution to Ethics*¹

I. INTRODUCTION

1. *Ends and means.* Two relatively distinct problems have always faced individuals, societies, and humanity at large: the problem of choosing the best means to achieve a given end, and the problem of choosing the end to be achieved. I say relatively distinct, because what from one point of view is an end, may be a means from another. For instance, good housing is an end from the point of view of the Ministry of Reconstruction, but a means from that of the Ministry of Health. From the point of view of the physiologist, the only ultimate ends are perhaps the satisfaction of the primary instincts,² and the psychologist would probably agree that all other 'ends' are the result of sublimation and are therefore, in the last analysis, indirect 'means' to the satisfaction of these instincts. But the word 'end' is commonly used in a much wider sense to denote any conscious aim which is not obviously and consciously a means to some other more remote end. It is only in this wider sense that we can distinguish between the two problems: choice of means and choice of ends.

2. *Science and ethics.* The choice of the best means to a given end is a practical problem of applied science. If as a society we agree that the greatest material comfort shall be our end, the best means can be deduced from empirical generalizations

---

* B. J. Med. Psych., XX, 1944.
¹ This paper was originally read at a small informal meeting of psycho-analysts in November 1942, and has been subsequently revised. As it was written under conditions which precluded access to a library, there are very few references to the relevant literature, and these were made from memory.
² Since the organism reacts when stimulated, and ceases to react when the stimulus is removed, it is convenient for some purposes to regard the removal of stimuli as the only ultimate ends.

of engineering and economics.¹ There may of course be heated disputes, for example, between the protagonists of rival means to end slumps; but such disputes are the result either of faulty logic or insufficient knowledge, and can be decided by more careful deduction or by further research.² But the choice of the end itself seems to present an entirely different type of problem. The protagonists of the rival ends of material comfort and let us say military dominance and glory for its own sake can only agree to differ, fight it out, or appeal to the one discipline that claims to decide such issues, namely, ethics. The choice of ends therefore is a problem of ethics.³

3. *Lack of progress in ethics.* Now it appears to be a fact which has often been stressed by positivist philosophers, that while applied science makes enormous strides in each decade, ethics has made none in several thousand years. We have much better means than our fathers of obtaining material comfort; but the world is no more certain whether it wants comfort or dominion, butter or guns – or something else – than it was in the time of Plato. Professional moralists still give different answers. No moralist can yet give an answer that can convince his rivals. The unresolved conflict of rival ideologies has

¹ The following is a rather academic example of the kind of problem which would be involved. Since an additional unit of wealth gives more comfort to a poor man than to a rich one, the average comfort value of a unit of wealth in a society will vary inversely with the degree of inequality of distribution. But since the effort put into production depends partly on the hope of reward, the total wealth to be distributed will, within limits, vary directly with the degree of inequality of distribution. The two functions may be represented by two curves sloping in opposite directions. Their product will give a curve representing the total comfort in a society (i.e. the average comfort value of a unit of wealth multiplied by the total number of units) expressed as a function of the degree of inequality of distribution. Within broad limits, it should be possible for economists to discover the equation of this curve and so to determine the degree of inequality of distribution at which it will reach its maximum value.

² In the opinion of Professor, now Lord, Keynes, the delay in relieving the great slump was due, not to the malice of bankers, but to ignorance, not only in bankers but also in economists, of a part of the field of economics which had been insufficiently explored. For this reason, he wrote, I think, in his *Treatise on Money*, that this was one of the rare occasions in which the material prosperity of the world depended on the solution of a purely intellectual problem – a problem which he and his colleagues have since then done much to solve.

³ Ethics is not concerned with means as such. Ethical arguments about whether or not an end justifies the means may occur, however, when an unethical end, e.g. political murder, happens to be a convenient means to another ethical end, e.g. the prevention of tyranny.

engaged the lives of many of the world's most brilliant thinkers; and being so far insoluble by argument, has never been more than temporarily disposed of, and then only by force. It has therefore cost immense effort and still greater suffering. The aim of this paper is to discover how far, if at all, psycho-analysis can contribute to this unsolved problem of the choice of ends, and so help society as it has already helped the individual.

II. ETHICS AND THE CONCEPT OF MORALITY
The Problem Reformulated

4. *Unanswerable questions.* As a first step, however, it seems necessary to reformulate the problem; for whenever a question has remained unanswered for thousands of years, this is usually because it has been expressed in such a way that it is either logically or empirically unanswerable.

5. *The metaphysical form.* To the metaphysician the question 'what ends ought we to seek' demanded an answer based not on experience but on pure logic – a synthetic judgment *a priori.* All attempts to do this failed because logic, which is essentially analytic, cannot get more out of a proposition than has been put into it. Like the conjurer, logic cannot produce rabbits out of a hat unless they have been put there first. The question was so framed that it was logically unanswerable.

6. *Theological form.* To the theologian in the age of faith, the question meant simply 'What does God want us to seek?' Here there was no logical contradiction in the question. Anyone who knew God could answer it. Unfortunately, those who did gave different answers, so that either there must have been several gods, or the prophets of the one God must have erred in their claim to know his wishes. In this form, in fact, the question was empirically unanswerable.

7. *Psychological form.* To the psychologist, I suppose, the nearest equivalent to the theological question 'What does God want us to seek?' is 'What does our superego want us to seek – or to avoid?' This can be answered empirically. But as the answer is different for different superegos it is only relative and subjective, not absolute and general.

8. *An empirical and general solution required.* What is required evidently is a restatement of the question in a form that admits

an answer that is both empirical and general. Subject to agreement on the meaning of the word 'normal' I would suggest that 'What does the normal individual feel he ought to seek?' may come near to satisfying these conditions.

The Concept of Normality

9. *Definition.* Normality in the psycho-analytical sense is not an average but an optimum, an optimum freedom from neurosis. It is something which is never quite achieved; but which some people approach as the result of a favourable educational environment, and others as the result of a successful analysis.

10. *Possibility of common ethical characteristics.* In this sense, of course, there is no reason to suppose that two different individuals would approach the same normality. In fact it is obvious that each would have his own optimum character, which would be different from other people's. Nevertheless, we should expect to find certain characteristics – both positive and negative – which would be common to all normal people. And among these we may find something like a common pattern of ethical values.

11. *Negative characteristics of normality.* It will perhaps be easier to begin with the negative attitudes that are present in abnormal people, but absent, or at least present only in a small degree, in normal ones.

12. *Paranoia.* Take, for instance, the aggressive self-righteousness of the paranoiac with delusions of persecution. Here, as Freud long ago discovered, it is really the paranoiac who is the persecutor, for the hate by which he feels himself pursued is his own hate which he first disowns and projects upon, or attributes to, its object and then readmits in what seems justifiable self-defence. In Mrs Klein's view, however, this projection of affect is only one stage of three in a vicious spiral of development. In the first stage, the infant projects his unconscious sadistic impulses upon his parents and so forms an unconscious picture of sadistic, diabolic or 'bad' parents, which is in sharp contrast both to his equally exaggerated picture of ideally benevolent, divine or 'good' parents, and to his conscious picture of the real ones. In the second stage, he 'introjects', or in unconscious phantasy incorporates, these bad figures and so feels himself

to be persecuted by inner enemies.[1] In the third, he seeks to escape the sense of inner persecution, by projecting[2] these internal bad objects outside himself and identifying them with external persons who thus become his imaginary enemies. We all recognize at least the results of such mechanisms in Nazi leaders, who have made their followers believe, and who, incredible as it may seem, probably themselves believe, that Germany is fighting a defensive and therefore a righteous war against a world plot to destroy her. We can all recognize the same paranoid features in a lesser degree, appearing from time to time in our own domestic politics. Every party is apt to form a distorted picture of its political opponents, and to depict them as wholly selfish, dishonest and tyrannical, when in reality these qualities are leavened by at least the average amount of constructive humanitarianism. Therefore any political end that is based on a paranoid distortion of its opponents, and, because of this distortion, justifies their actual or symbolic destruction, is abnormal.

13. *Denial and appeasement.* At the opposite extreme to delusions of persecution, is denial of danger when it is only too real. While paranoid mechanisms seem to have been one of the main determinants of German political ends in the eight or ten years before the war, the mechanism of denial – or 'scotomization' as it is sometimes called – seems to have been one of the main determinants of ours. Most of our politicians, together with the people as a whole, were quite unable to believe that the Nazis were really the implacable enemies of peace they seemed to be and indeed actually were. Therefore we substituted appeasement for a wholehearted preparation for inevitable war.[3] No doubt this attempt to appease an unappeasable, because paranoiac, enemy may have been

---

[1] This mechanism is described by Freud in *Mourning and Melancholia* (1917), where he shows how the melancholic's self-reproaches were originally directed against an external figure who has been introjected and now persecutes him from within.

[2] It will be observed that the word 'projection' is used both for the projection of affects, e.g. hate, and for the projection in unconscious phantasy of internal objects.

[3] In the early stages of the Nazi rise to power, appeasement was a substitute for preparation for war; in the latter stages, it was partly the effect of our delay in preparing. But even after Munich, many people believed it would prevent, and not merely postpone, war.

facilitated by a sense of guilt – whether justified or not – over reparations, and also perhaps by some degree of unconscious inversion towards an enemy who to the unconscious seemed magnificent because he was sadistic. But it would not have been possible without the mechanism of denial. Denial of this kind is probably more than the simple repression of fear of an external danger. From Mrs Klein's observations it would seem likely that both paranoid exaggeration and the denial of external danger originate in a hypochondriacal sense of inner persecution; but anxiety is reduced in the one case by the projection, and in the other by the denial, of the inner enemy. The paranoiac politician admits the 'badness' of the bad internal father figure and of other internal persecuting objects, but denies their location, and so projects them into the external world as imaginary or at least exaggerated enemies, and feels that he is justified in destroying, indeed, that it is his moral duty to destroy them. The political 'scotomizer' goes further and is unable to admit that there can be such 'badness', such implacable enemies either inside or outside himself, and therefore deludes himself into the belief that he can placate his enemies even when they are implacable. If he were not so convinced of the badness and implacability of his own bad internal figures he would be more able to accept the possibility of unreconcilable enemies in the external world. Therefore his political aims are based nearly as much on persecutory delusions as are those of the paranoiac type.

14. *Pacifism.* Allied to the ostrich-like attitude of denial and appeasement, but distinct from it, is that of pacifism. Here the 'badness' of the enemy is usually admitted; no attempt is made to appease him, but neither is he attacked. There is no open submission, but neither is there any active resistance. Clearly the original aggressive impulse is inhibited by guilt and anxiety, and replaced by some degree of inversion towards the enemy. But to be complete, an explanation in terms of instinct vicissitude must be accompanied by some account of the vicissitudes of the objects of the instincts. The objects of the child's early impulses of love and aggression – objects which determine the development of these impulses – were not only the real parents, but also the parent imagos, the parents as the child unconsciously imagined them to be. He retains these

imagos in his unconscious memory throughout life, and, as Freud has shown, they reappear both as the introjections which constitute his superego, and as the projections which he identifies with external persons. It is clear from Mrs Klein's observations of children, no less than from analogous conscious superstitions of primitive peoples, that such figures, in their introjected form, are not merely psychological parts of the child's personality, but are unconsciously felt to be physical persons spatially located within his physical self. They are of two types: good and bad, that is, friendly and hostile. Usually the good and bad are kept distinct; but sometimes both incompatible aspects are combined. The result is a mixed good and bad figure which is very different from a true picture in which friendly and hostile elements are toned down and fused into a consistent whole. In a mixed figure, the good and bad, friendly and hostile elements remain fantastically exaggerated although they are combined in one person – rather like the Calvinistic version of the Old Testament Yahweh who is capable of the extremes of love and hatred, and who, while selecting a few of his worshippers for everlasting bliss, preordains the majority to torments eternally prolonged. If the external enemy which the pacifist is unable to attack stands for this mixed inner figure, his attitude of absolute pacifism would be explained, for he cannot attack the bad or hostile element without at the same time attacking the good or friendly one. This attitude, no less than that in paranoia or denial, would be clearly recognized as pathological.

15. *Negativism*. Another attitude, which I think would be recognized as pathological in type, may be called moral negativism. This is the attitude of the disillusioned cynic, the man who feels that no end is worth striving for, fighting for, or still less dying for. It was rather common in this country in the period between the two wars, and found its philosophical expression in ethical relativity – a system which quite rightly saw through the logical flaws in metaphysical ethics, and in view of the diversity of actual moral codes, concluded quite wrongly that no code was worth defending. This attitude seems to be an end-product of another mechanism described by Mrs Klein. If the bad or hostile figures in unconscious phantasy are felt to be so strong that the good ones cannot be defended, the

despair that would otherwise occur is sometimes evaded by denying that the original good objects are good or worth defending. Negativism is thus a defence against depression.

16. *Summary of abnormal moral attitudes.* We have considered four examples, and no doubt many more could be found, of pathological characteristics that help to determine the choice of ends by individuals and societies. The paranoiac type of individual is militaristic and self-righteous. He sees enemies where none exist. His major aim is to destroy them. At the opposite extreme is the 'scotomist' who denies the existence or at least the implacability of the real enemies of the values he believes in. This is because he is unconsciously so afraid of them that his major aim is peace at almost any price. Unlike the 'scotomist', the pacifist is not incapacitated by fear of internal bad objects, but by an inability to separate them from internal good ones. The destruction of real enemies, which are identified with these mixed objects in their projected form, is therefore excluded from the ends he strives for. Lastly, an individual of the negativist type is so afraid of the internal persecutors of his unconscious phantasy, and of the external enemies identified with them, that he abandons the values he believed in as soon as they are threatened or attacked. He has no positive ethical ends, no values to protect. Since these four attitudes are all pathological, they would be absent from the attitudes that help to determine the ends of the normal individual. It may now be easier to outline some of the positive characteristics the normal man does possess.

17. *Positive characteristics of normality.* He has greater freedom from inhibitions and compulsions both in the sexual impulse and its derivatives – in short a fuller capacity for work and pleasure. He is more free because he has less unconscious anxiety: and he has less unconscious anxiety because his unconscious picture of the world is less distorted.[1] This picture still contains the good and bad internal figures of early phantasy. But since the barrier between unconscious phantasy and real experience is more porous, they are less exaggerated and correspond more closely with their prototypes and current representatives in the external world. The bad internal figures

[1] Optimum normality might be defined as optimum freedom from distortion in unconscious phantasy.

are less bad and the dangerousness of their external representatives is less likely to be either overestimated or denied. Similarly the good internal figures and their representatives are less threatened and easier to defend. All these differences will be reflected in the way in which the normal individual selects his ends. Unlike the negativist, he will have certain values, aims or ends which will be of supreme importance, and which he will feel able to defend or restore. Unlike the pacifist, he will be able to attack the enemies of these aims; unlike the scotomist who denies real danger he will be able to recognize these enemies; and unlike the paranoiac he will not imagine enemies where none exist and will reserve this aggression for those who are real. His aims will be characterized by a kind of militant constructiveness.

III. A PSYCHO-ANALYTICAL THEORY OF ETHICS

18. *The four problems.* Having established at least a *prima facie* case for the existence of such a thing as normal morality, we are now in a position to attempt an outline of a psycho-analytical theory of ethics. I propose to subdivide it under four questions: How does morality originate and what is its primary form? How do moral aims deviate in the course of development? What degrees of deviation are normal and what abnormal? What are the prospects for the future?

Origin and Primary Form of Morality

19. *Guilt.* The origin of morality in the individual is of course closely connected with the sense of guilt. The word 'guilt' is sometimes assumed to be synonymous with fear of the consequences of disobedience to authority, in particular the authority of the superego. But this definition does not quite fit the concept: for on the one hand, defiance of an unloved authority may be accompanied by great anxiety but is felt to be virtuous and heroic and by no means guilty; and on the other, injury to a helpless loved object, which has no authority, always causes guilt. It would seem best, therefore, to use the word, as Mrs Klein does, to denote the peculiar blend of anxiety and despair that follows aggressive acts or phantasies against a loved object. It is this aggressiveness, or rather the

sense of having actually destroyed or injured the loved object, which gives rise to the impulse of reparation, which is in turn largely responsible for nearly all forms of humanitarian and creative work. There are therefore at least two forms of morality; negative morality which aims at the avoidance of a repetition of aggression against the loved object or its symbols; and positive morality which aims at the reparation of the damage done. There is also a third form, aggressive morality which aims at the defence of the loved object against a threat by a third party. Here, a great part of the aggression against the enemy seems to be derived from aggression which was originally directed against the loved object itself, but which was later diverted into the service of its defence and reparation.

20. *Introjection and projection.* But the development of these impulses cannot be fully described without following the history of their objects, which appear to be located sometimes inside and sometimes outside the self. It is therefore necessary again to consider – and in greater detail – the roles of introjection and projection.

21. *Primitive faculties of the organism.* The simplest organism has only two modes of response to the external world: it can incorporate the particles with which it comes in contact, and it can eject what it has incorporated. Its descendants which have evolved the power of movement can also approach or avoid objects; and its still more remote descendants which have evolved limbs can grasp them, push them away or destroy them. But incorporation and ejection remain the most primitive faculties, in the service of which all other faculties may indeed have been evolved.

22. *Love and hate in incorporation and ejection.* It is therefore not surprising that Mrs Klein and her co-workers have found that incorporation and ejection, or their equivalents in phantasy, introjection and projection,[1] play an enormous role in the child. If the simplest organism, from which the child is descended, has any rudimentary feelings at all, it would seem

---

[1] These words are used in different senses by different authors. For the purpose of this paper it seems convenient to use incorporation and ejection for the physical acts, and to reserve introjection and projection for the phantasied act. This will at least avoid the suspicion that when we talk of introjected figures we are accusing their owner of actual cannibalism.

probable that what it feels when it incorporates a particle as food, or another cell with which it unites, is the prototype of love, and that what it feels when it ejects anything is the prototype of hate. But if so, the development of the mouth as an organ of aggression as well as of incorporation, and the development of a combined genital and excretory apparatus, must have ensured that in the higher animals incorporation and ejection can be used indiscriminately in the service of either love or hate. However this may be, we at least know that in phantasy a child can incorporate an object or a person either lovingly or destructively. If the child introjects an object or person through love, he feels that the resulting internal object or person is helpful, nourishing, and friendly, and gives him a sense of inner well being, qualities which may be summarized by saying that it is *good*. Conversely, if the child introjects an object through hate as a means of destroying it, the resulting internal object or person is felt to be itself aggressive, dangerous, hateful, an implacable enemy, in short, a persecutor, that is, *bad*. Similarly, objects that the child has projected or in phantasy ejected into the external world are felt to be good or bad according to whether they are good internal objects projected lovingly as gifts, or bad ones projected aggressively to get rid of them, or as missiles to injure some external object or person.[1]

23. *Good and bad objects and acts.* Thus the primary concept of a good or bad *object* is of an object cathected or charged with the love or hatred which motivated its introjection or projection. From this the most primitive concept of a good or bad *action* is at once derived. It is felt to be good to love a good object; bad to hate or attack it. Then, since the object derives its quality from the act, secondary objects (or persons) are conceived as good or bad according to whether their effects (actions) are good or bad, that is, according to whether they are helpful to primary good objects, or injure and threaten to destroy them.

24. *Fundamental principles of primary morality.* Thus are built up the three fundamental subjective principles of primary

[1] Since all acts of judgment may be modelled after the primitive acts of taking in and giving out, it seems possible that all external objects of which we have formed any concept at all have been subjected to the same imaginary incorporation and ejection, and for this reason are all painted as in some degree either good or bad.

morality: It is bad (i.e., it arouses guilt) to injure or threaten a good object; it is good to love, repair and defend a good object; it is also good to hate, attack or destroy a bad object, that is, any thing or person that threatens to destroy a good one.[1]

25. *Empirical universality of primary morality.* These three principles are empirical discoveries of analysis, and are general, not specific to certain individuals. The basis of morality is therefore neither *a priori* and universal as the metaphysicians claimed, nor empirical and relative as critical philosophers and anthropologists maintain, but empirical and universal in the sense that it is a quality, like binocular vision or an articulated thumb, which is found to be common to all mankind.

Deviation of Morality

26. *Developed morality relative not universal.* But if the primal basis of morality in the child, and in the deeper layers of the unconscious, is universal, it is obvious that the developed morality of the adult is relative. It is different in different societies and in different individuals in the same society.

27. *Divergence of content.* One obvious cause of divergence is that different people choose different symbols for the good objects they wish to defend and restore. But this does not alter the fundamental pattern of primary morality. In some cases, although the pattern seems to remain constant, the elements that compose it are unstable. In paranoia, good objects continually turn bad, and the world is peopled with imaginary persecutors who have to be destroyed although they are innocent of any hostile intent either against the paranoiac or against such of his objects as at the time happen to be good.

[1] This paper is concerned with political morality. But the same principles apply to sexual morality. To both the prude and the rake, intercourse is an act of aggression rather than of love, because unconsciously both feel themselves to be possessed by phallic devils; and to both, it is something guilty because it involves uncontrolled aggression against loved objects. But while the prude avoids guilt paranoiacally by projecting the phallic devils on to the rake, the rake avoids it manically by identifying himself with them. Therefore the prude disapproves of the rake, and the rake despises the prude. In the normal individual, whose internal figures are more assimilated and correspond more closely with their real prototypes and current representatives, the aggressive element in sex is under the control of love. Intercourse is creative and reparative rather than destructive. Therefore it arouses little or no guilt and is felt to be not only pleasurable but also good – except in situations which might really injure the loved object.

28. *Divergence of form.* But the whole pattern itself can be changed. What to the unconscious are certainly bad objects can be admired and even worshipped, and good objects can be left unloved and undefended, if not actually attacked. The cause of this rather astonishing transformation or even reversal of values can only be anxiety – an uncontrollable terror of bad internal figures and a compulsion to propitiate them at all costs.[1] If the attempt to protect the primary good seems hopeless, it is given up and an attempt is made by propitiation to turn terrifying bad objects into something good. Much of the ruthless morality of the Old Testament Yahweh and of the classical superego seems to be of this type. If the superego is a collective name for internalized objects both good and bad, its diverse qualities, both in the same and in different individuals, are understandable. It can give comfort and support, as well as forbid aggression against good objects. But it can also forbid acts of love towards good objects and their symbols – acts of love that have a reparative meaning to primary morality; and it can even require the persecution of these objects.

29. *Degrees in surrender of a good object.* There are many degrees in the surrender of a primary good object. Some part of the love impulse may be inhibited; the loved object may be still valued, but there may be a pacifistic inability to defend it; it may be treated with complete indifference, or it may be persecuted, not as the Inquisition thought for the love of God, but from the fear of the Devil.

30. *Nazi ideology.* It is difficult to retain an objective judgment in the middle of a war. But it does seem as if some such complete reversal of values is afflicting the Nazis at the present time. No doubt they still have good objects, which they feel they are defending, but the most conspicuous feature in their unconscious make-up appears to be a kind of sadistic phallic worship, the surrender to the 'bad' phallic deity symbolized by a loud-voiced but probably impotent fanatic.

Normal and Abnormal Degrees of Deviation

31. *The problem.* Having briefly outlined the way in which the primary morality common to all mankind can be distorted into many widely divergent forms, we have next to consider

[1] See paragraphs 12–15 above.

the extent to which such divergencies would occur in a normal society; that is, in a society with an optimum freedom from neurosis.

32. *Identity of form.* Normal development does not imply freedom from guilt. (If it did a normal society would be devoid of a reparative impulse, which is one of the main sources of all creative work.) Man has a primordial impulse to devour, and so to destroy, the things he loves, which inevitably produces anxiety or guilt. It is this primary oral aggression, augmented by aggression from other sources, which turns good phantasy objects into bad ones and blurs the distinction between the two. But in normal development, the tendency to distort the inner picture is corrected by reality testing. Reality testing proves that good objects have not been destroyed or converted into persecutors, and so permits the rediscovery of love. The remaining guilt, the product of primary aggression, is felt only as a protective constituent of love and a motive for pleasurable acts of reparation. Similarly, reality testing proves bad objects to be less hostile or dangerous than they seemed, so that aggression towards their current representatives is neither exaggerated nor inhibited by fear. Apart therefore from other characteristics of normality, all individuals whose inner picture of the world is not distorted will display a common pattern of primary morality: love for and the desire to promote certain values, and hate in their defence of real but not fictitious enemies. This morality is militant but without paranoid exaggeration.[1]

33. *Differences of content.* But it is only the form of the pattern which in normal development remains the same. The content, that is, the symbols of the primary objects of the emotional pattern, of course develops differently, and is sometimes incompatible in different normal individuals. Therefore even in

[1] Unlike empirical propositions, which can be measured by the absolute standard of real experience, ethical propositions seemed to be relative as long as there seemed to be no logically sound reason for choosing one standard rather than another from the many which different cultures have adopted. But what we have called the primary pattern of morality has some claims to be absolute in two senses. First, because everyone has it in infancy – and not merely an arbitrary few. Secondly, because the condition for its survival into adult life is the retention or restoration of a true inner picture of the world; and an inner picture is true or false, in an absolute and not an arbitrary sense, in proportion to the degree of its correspondence with real experience.

a completely normal world some conflict of ideologies which are both right – that is, both psychologically normal – would inevitably remain.

34. *Empirical view compared with absolutism and relativism.* This point of view is distinct both from ethical absolutism and ethical relativism. According to the absolutist, if there is a conflict of ideologies, one must be right and the other wrong. According to the relativist, they are both equally right. According to the empirical psychological view, one is better than the other if its emotional pattern is less distorted. But if the pattern is the same and only the content is different, both are equally right.[1]

35. *Limits of convergence.* We may now try to determine, in the light of a few examples, how far the conflict of ideologies, on which the world, since the beginning of civilization, has used or misused its energies, result from neurotic distortions of the primary pattern of morality, which are at least theoretically avoidable, and how far such conflicts result from differences of content in a normal emotional pattern and are therefore unavoidable.

36. *International conflicts of ideologies.* Among the symbols of the internal good objects, which in the normal emotional pattern are loved, and of the bad objects against which the good ones have to be defended, few have played a greater role in the history of the world than the concepts of one's own country and of its enemies. It is perfectly normal for a man to love his country, to wish to develop or restore it, and to hate its real enemies. Must we then conclude that the wars from which we have so often suffered were psychologically inevitable, and will continue until some one country conquers and absorbs the rest? This conclusion would follow if the patriotisms which have actually led to war were of the normal variety. But in reality they appear to have been far more often abnormal. To take the most recent example, I do not think that either the patriotism of the average German, or the patriotism of the average Briton, was normal in the period between the two world wars.

[1] The distinction between a common ethical form with different contents is clearly made by Mrs Klein in her contribution to *Science and Ethics*, edited by Waddington.

37. *Nazi patriotism.* The German's intense love of his own country, in so far as it was a symbol of the good parents, and his desire to repair the damage done to this good object was normal enough; but his hatred of the rest of the world was clearly paranoid. In the early nineteen-thirties, when this same world was almost totally disarmed and more friendly towards Germany than it had been for many years, he felt it to be a persecutor against which his own country could only be defended by war. 'Germany must live even if we must die for her' was an accepted Nazi slogan even before Hitler became Chancellor, and at a time when Germany had no real enemies at all. Moreover, Germany was not only the good mother but also the father land – and a father whose characteristics were by no means only good. It had many elements of the 'bad' father – a sadistic, phallic god – who was so terrifying that he had to be obeyed, admired and imitated even in his sadistic attacks upon what were primarily good objects, symbolized, for example, by the humanitarian ideals the Nazis now so violently repudiate. Thus, the whole pattern of the primitive or 'normal' morality is distorted. The Nazi identifies himself with a father figure, who to his own unconscious is largely bad, and so attacks many objects which to his own unconscious are largely good.

38. *British patriotism in the pre-war period.* In Britain in the same period, the average intellectual, who perhaps wrongly claimed to represent his less articulate countrymen, went to the opposite extreme. He denied the obvious threat to his good objects – his country and his ideals of freedom – and had so little confidence in his power to defend them that he often denied that they were good and worth defending. As he was unconscious of any urge within himself to fight for freedom against tyranny wherever it was found, he believed that his ancestors, who had acquired the empire as an accidental by-product of this urge, used it as a mere cloak for acquisitive self-interest, and ridiculed those of his contemporaries who still believed in these ideals.

39. *War result of abnormal forms of patriotism.* If both had been normal, if their patriotism had corresponded to the emotional pattern of primary morality, both would have been prepared to defend their country if really threatened, but neither would

have hated imaginary enemies who did not really threaten them at all. As the same pattern would have had a different content, some unavoidable conflict of interests would have remained. But they would almost certainly have settled these by a less disastrous means than that of war.

40. *Domestic ideologies.* Another conflict of ideals, which in future may become as important as the strife of nations, is the conflict of different social ideologies within one nation. During the war these are to a great extent submerged by the more immediate issue. But as soon as it is over, the old conflict between socialism and individualism, radicalism and conservatism, are likely to break out with renewed zest. Here again it is perfectly normal for each side to defend its own ideals and to attack the enemies of these ideals. But just as there are normal and abnormal forms of patriotism, so there are normal and abnormal forms of each type of political ideology.

41. *The paranoid type.* Perhaps the easiest abnormality to distinguish is again the paranoid pattern, which turns the most pleasant and well-meaning opponents into tyrannical oppressors on the one hand, or traitors on the other, fit only for the lamp-post or the firing squad. No party has the monopoly of such types, which are indeed to be found in all of them: in the socialist agitator, in the Blimp-like individualist, in the ultra-radical to whom anything that already exists is necessarily bad and in the ultra-conservative to whom anything that is new is necessarily worse.

42. *The appeaser type.* In sharp contrast to the paranoid type is the appeaser, I do not mean the man who is prepared to accept reasonable compromises but the man who is ready to sacrifice what he regards as fundamental values because he feels impotent to defend them. Closely related to him is the political invert, or quisling, who joins what in his heart he regards as his enemies in the persecution of the values he unconsciously still wishes to protect. He is always to be found in whichever appears at the moment to be the more formidable camp. In the last century there were pseudo-conservatives: men who suffered and who had seen their relations suffer under the unrestricted competition which then prevailed, but who were yet reactionaries for fear of their employers. Similarly, in

this century these are pseudo-socialists: men who, for instance, have inherited family businesses which to their fathers were not so much sources of income as good objects to be fostered and developed, but who work for the downfall of all private enterprise because they feel impotent to maintain their own.

43. *The cynical type.* Lastly, there are the cynical types, who, having no belief in their power to defend their good objects, deny that anything is good. Their politics are determined solely by material self-interest; as they have no ideals themselves they are unable to believe that ideals can be more than a cover for self-interest in other people. Part of the discredit into which individualism has fallen is the fault of its own theoretical apologists – the economists of the classical school – who imputed this motive only to their economic man.[1]

44. *Remaining normal conflicts of ideologies.* If such abnormal types are removed we are left with the normal partisan, who without exaggerating the defects of his opponents believes in and is prepared to work for his own system. The normal Socialist who sees in State Socialism, not only a structure of pleasing architectural simplicity, but a degree of justice and a hope of prosperity never before realized upon earth; the normal individualist, who while accepting the desirability of some control, is convinced that individualism offers the widest and most varied scope for human creativeness; the normal radical who is impatient to remove the less rational elements in our social structure; and the normal conservative, who, while not opposed to progress, is anxious to preserve everything that seems to him to be of value in the living structure of the present and the past. Such normal types, although they would often disagree, would at least be able to cooperate in the construction and preservation of a world which all of them would like, even if none of them felt it to be perfect.

45. *Ultimate aims.* They might even agree on the ultimate aims. The child seeks objects that aid, and tries to destroy those that frustrate, the satisfaction of his needs. But as the

---

[1] In reality, the fact that the average successful entrepreneur spends far more thought and time on building up his business, than on spending the profits, suggests that the actual motive contains a higher proportion of creativeness and reparation than of greed.

same objects sometimes do both, he also tries to protect them against his own aggression. Failure leads to depressive anxiety, or guilt, which may be more painful than unsatisfied desire. But in normal development, the primary 'egoistic' aim – to possess and enjoy good objects – is qualified by an 'altruistic' one – to protect and restore them; and aggression which first served the primary instincts, partially changes its allegiance. So man is an animal with a dual aim, and the society that satisfies him best must offer, not only material comfort, but also the best and most varied scope for creative and reparative work. If this were once agreed, the remaining conflict would cease to be ethical, that is concerned with ends, and would become practical, that is, concerned with means, which it is the business of applied science to discover.

Prospects for the Future

46. *Reduction of conflicts.* Turning now to our last problem – the prospects for the future – it seems improbable that a very high degree of general normality can be achieved for many centuries to come. We must therefore expect a long period of conflict of ideologies that differ in form as well as in content. But there are three ways in which the bitterness of such conflict may and probably will be reduced: by direct analysis, by improved early education, and by the general diffusion of psycho-analytic insight.

47. *By direct analysis.* As far as direct analysis is concerned, it is reasonable to expect not only that the number of people who are analysed will increase, but that improved technique will enable a higher degree of normality to be achieved; and also that an increasing number of individuals who have thus acquired normality will obtain responsible positions.[1]

48. *By improved education.* It is also reasonable to hope that an increasing knowledge of analysis will steadily improve the early education of the child, and that this will be reflected in a gradual raising of the standard of average normality.

49. *By diffusion of insight.* Lastly, by the general diffusion of analytic insight, it is to be hoped that pathological individuals

---

[1] [At the moment (1977) the trend seems to be rather in the opposite direction. Fewer people are able to pay the fees for five-times-per-week analysis and more analysts are compelled to do only half-time analytic work.]

in high places will be more easily recognized and their ideologies treated with the suspicion they deserve.

50. *Towards a common aim.* While therefore we can hardly expect the present war of ideologies to be the last on this planet, there are good psychological reasons to expect that the probability of such extreme forms of ethical disagreement will gradually diminish – and that our descendants will build a world in which constructive and reparative impulses will eventually predominate.

POSTSCRIPT: GUILT, MORALITY AND THE
OEDIPUS COMPLEX

1. The primary aim of this paper was to offer the outline of a psycho-analytic theory of ethics in place of the theological and metaphysical theories of the past – not to compare later psycho-analytical theories with earlier ones. But as Ethics is sometimes supposed to lie outside the proper field of psycho-analytical research, it may be desirable to add a note on the relation between the theory here developed and Freud's views on morals as expressed in *Totem and Taboo*, *The Ego and the Id* and other writings. For these works are the formations of our empirical knowledge of this subject.

2. In the classical psycho-analytic theory, morality appeared as a product of the Oedipus complex. The small boy desires his mother for himself and hates his father as a rival and wishes to kill him. But opposed to the hate of the father is fear and also a genuine love which combine first to suppress and then to repress the hatred, and so to maintain the two primary taboos of incest and parricide. In the early life of the boy, and in the early history of the race, the authority imposing these taboos is external – the actual father. Later, however, in the development both of the individual and the race, the father is introjected as the superego, so that the authority imposing these taboos – from which in Freud's view all morality is derived – becomes internal. In particular, guilt is explained as the result of tension between the ego and the superego.

3. Nearly all of this is retained in the later theories of Mrs Klein and her co-workers, but there are many additions and some modifications. The essentials of the Oedipus complex –

sexual impulses towards the mother, hatred of the father and the repression of the hate by fear and love, as well as the 'incorporation' or 'introjection' of the father – these are all retained. But it is now clear that the father is hated not only as a rival but as the persecutor of the mother. To Freud, if I understood him correctly, the small boy depicted his father as a persecutor mainly in order to justify his hatred, and to deny that it was based on jealousy. Certainly he does so for this reason; but the primary reason now seems to be that he projects upon his father all the oral, anal and genital aggressiveness which he originally directed towards his mother in the sucking and biting period of his early life. The difference is one of emphasis rather than of interpretation. Freud was familiar with all these mechanisms; but while he regarded jealousy as the main motive of the hate, Mrs Klein would I think give to jealousy and sadism an almost equal importance.

4. More far-reaching additions have been made in the concept of the superego itself. This is no longer only the father, which the brothers of the Primal Horde actually and the child in phantasy incorporated, but both parents – indeed at least two aspects of each of them – as well as various 'part objects', bits of the parents which the child begins to introject in a period before he has learnt to form clear and permanent concepts of whole persons as such. All these can be either friendly or hostile according to whether they were introjected lovingly or aggressively, and are felt to be either 'good' or 'bad' internal objects.

5. These additions necessitate a modification in the theory of guilt. In the classical theory, guilt was the result of tension between the ego and the superego. But the superego is no longer a single personality. It is a collection of many, often mutually incompatible personalities and part objects, and many relationships, including different forms of tension, can and do subsist between its various members and the ego. We therefore want to know which kind of tension gives rise to guilt. It would be misleading and contrary to the current usage of the word, to regard fear of a wholly bad internal object as guilty fear. In the common meaning of the word, as I understand it, guilt stands for that peculiar blend of anxiety and despair which follows aggressive acts or phantasies against loved

objects. Guilt therefore does not result from all forms of tension between the ego and the superego, but only from aggression against loved objects whether external or internal. This is equivalent to what I called the first law of primary morality; it is bad, that is, it arouses guilt, to attack or threaten a good object. The second and third laws follow from the first: it is good to restore, repair and defend a good object; and it is good to hate and attack a bad object, since this is necessary to the defence of a good one.[1]

6. If guilt is defined in a wider sense as the result of any tension between the ego and the superego, we are at once confronted with a great variety of consciences. In particular we should be compelled to admit that the man who out of fear of his bad objects deserts or even persecutes his good ones is acting in accordance with his conscience. In the newer theory, however, there is only one type of conscience; and the man who deserts and persecutes his good objects does so from fear, and not because of, but in spite of, his guilt. The first view leads to a relative, the second to a universal, system of Ethics.

[1] Guilt as opposed to fear (persecutory anxiety), and good objects as opposed to bad ones, are of course limiting concepts to which the corresponding feelings and ideas only approximate. Since all the various inner objects of the child's phantasy are ultimately derived from the same two parents, they are never wholly, but only predominantly, good or bad. Therefore aggression against predominantly good objects arouses some degree of fear (persecutory anxiety) as well as guilt; and conversely, aggression against predominantly bad objects arouses some guilt (depressive anxiety) as well as fear. In the depressive individual, good and bad objects tend to be confused; in the paranoiac individual, they are kept separate; but in neither do they correspond with their original or current external representatives. In the normal individual, they are neither exaggerated nor confused. He does not attack the good ones because they are not so mixed up with the bad ones; and he is much less afraid of the bad ones, partly because they are less omnipotently bad, and partly because, being much more separated from the good ones, he can attack them with much less guilt.

12

Social Conflict and the Challenge to Psychology*

1. THE PSYCHOLOGIST'S DILEMMA

For more than three decades, psychologists have been saying that the problems of the world are not purely economic, but also partly psychological. They have been saying, in effect, that it is ill. And behind their words, there may have been a phantasy that it ought to come to them for treatment. At first there was no sign of the world recognizing its illness, or of accepting the implied advice. But, by degrees and especially since the Second World War, there has been an increasing tendency to turn to them with rather more attention. It is this new attitude of a society, now more than ever aware of its discomforts, which presents psychology with its present challenge.

The challenge may be felt both as an opportunity and as an embarrassment. We may feel that our bluff has been called, and that we have much less to give than we unconsciously imagined. But this is perhaps not our major difficulty; for it does not prevent us from giving what we can. A greater difficulty, at least in my view, is that the challenge seems to raise – and in an acute form – the old problem of the relation of science to ethics, and in particular to politics. The conflicts which threaten the future happiness, and even the existence, of society are ideological. How are we to intervene? If we use our specialist learning to defend our own ideals, have we departed from the narrow path of science? If we remain 'scientifically' neutral, have we evaded the challenge? I do not know how widespread this feeling is; but it may be sufficiently general to deserve some preliminary investigation. I will call it the psychologist's dilemma.

* Read before the Medical Section of the British Psychological Society on 17 December 1947. Published *B. J. Med. Psych.*, vol. XXI, 1947–48.

SOCIAL CONFLICT AND CHALLENGE TO PSYCHOLOGY

The dilemma is itself partly psychological and partly logical in origin. The psychological aspect raises the whole question of what our politics means to our unconscious. As I shall be coming back to this subject later, I will give only an ideally simplified example here to illustrate the kind of conflicts involved. As we know, the defence of an ideology – for example, humanism against totalitarianism – may often mean the defence of a good mother figure against a bad father. But if at a deeper level other motives are at work, such as jealousy of the imaginary bad father, admiration of him, and even the desire to be as tyrannical as he is, doubts about the genuineness of the primary motive may arise; and these may reinforce the feeling that partisanship is unscientific. On the other hand, if there is also a desire to be neutral just because this bad father figure is too dangerous to attack, then neutrality may be felt to be a cowardly evasion. To take sides and not to take sides may thus seem equally impossible – or can be achieved only by splitting the personality into a partisan citizen and a neutral scientist.

Coming now to the logical, as opposed to the psychological, aspects of the psychologist's dilemma, I shall try to show both that partisanship need not be unscientific and that neutrality need not be evasive.

The argument of those for whom there is an impassable gulf between science and ethics begins by pointing out a supposed confusion between statements of fact and statements of preference. If I say I believe in psycho-analysis,[1] I affirm my conviction that a certain body of empirical propositions is true. My conviction can be proved or disproved by experience. My statement is a statement of fact. But if I say I believe in humanism, I am, according to the ethical relativists, merely stating a preference, and preferences are not propositions that can be either true or false. By generalizing this reasoning it seems to follow that all ethical or political attitudes are scientifically indefensible.

Nevertheless, the feeling persists that values can sometimes

---

[1] The term psycho-analysis now has a double meaning. It can denote either a method of treatment and research or the body of facts and theories in various stages of confirmation obtained by this method. I am here using it in the latter sense.

be defended by argument. And indeed they can be under one condition: when our good objects are bad to our opponents only because they do not know enough about them. In other words, we can give a valid defence of an ideology if we can prove that it is the unknown cause, or the effect, of something already generally desired.

If, for example, we want to defend humanism by argument, we should seek to prove that people tend to be happier in a humanist than in an authoritarian world, or healthier or more mature. Or conversely, we might seek to prove that the more mature and integrated a person is, the more likely he is to understand his neighbours, to feel a sense of responsibility towards them, and to be humanist in his general attitude to politics. It is obvious that an argument of this kind consists of factual, not preference, statements; and that it can be proved or disproved empirically. So far, therefore, as happiness, health or maturity are already desired, it does provide an empirical defence of humanism.

The same reasoning that justifies the defence of an ideology also justifies the defence of, or attack on, separate acts of legislation. Almost every act of legislation has consequences, some of which are economic and others psychological. Economists try to predict the economic consequences. And as what they predict is either desirable or undesirable, their prediction is a form of partisanship. But no one accuses them of being unscientific. In fact, to make such tendentious predictions is a recognized part of their job. In exactly the same way, it comes within our province to predict the psychological consequences – especially those concerned with mental health.

To take a current example, the control of employments order has so far been considered mainly from the economic aspect. Some economists believe that compulsion, others that inducement, are the most efficient means of effecting the redistribution of labour required. But, as far as I know, the question has not been considered very seriously from the point of view of mental health. My own forecast is that compulsion – especially in peace time when people feel less closely identified with a national cause – will tend to confirm and strengthen unconscious phantasies of inner persecution, which, in very varying degrees, are at least latent in all of us. If so, the end result would be an increase in typical schizoid feelings both of persecution and of apathy.

We are so accustomed to stress the effect of early environment that we are perhaps apt to underestimate the effect of adult environment on dormant phantasy in this way. My own impression is that very large numbers of people, who have always appeared to be well, can maintain their health only so long as they can enjoy the affection of their own circle and the satisfaction of congenial work. To deprive them of these two reassurances may be to deprive them of their mental health.

Of course such psychological consequences are not the only ones to be considered. But if they are what I suppose, and if they were generally known, they would be weighed with the economic consequences, and perhaps a different decision would be made.

But a partisanship of this kind, however legitimate, does have three limitations. In the first place, our knowledge of the psychological consequences of social changes is still too slight to enable us to predict them with much confidence. In the second place, even if we could predict them, the extent to which such predictions could influence policy must depend on the extent to which policy is determined by conscious anticipations of its results. In fact we know that policy is largely determined by unconscious motives, so that a greater knowledge of its *consequences* unaccompanied by a greater knowledge of its *motives* might have little influence upon it. And in the third place, to be too partisan would be to risk antagonizing and so losing the social patient.

For all these reasons an alternative technique which disregards consequences and confines itself to the analysis of motives may often be a better way of meeting the challenge to psychology. This, in fact, is the method almost automatically adopted by every analyst who has entered the field of sociology. It is unlike the analysis of individuals in two respects: since its medium of approach is by books, lectures, broadcasts and discussions, it is directed extensively to many individuals instead of intensively to one. And it is directed not so much to the whole of their personalities as to the most socially significant parts of them – to what we may perhaps call their political egos. But it is a method which is like the analysis of individuals in one essential: in confining itself to the analysis of motives, it preserves a strict ethical and political neutrality.

If this neutrality may sometimes be felt to be evasive, reflection will show us that it is not a withdrawal from participation in events. Indeed analysis should be the form of participation most likely to influence events; for society cannot become more conscious of its motives without altering its actions. It is true that by this method we should be renouncing any direct attempt to influence the direction of social movement. But there may even be an incidental advantage in this renunciation; for it enables us to suspend our judgment on many political questions about which we still know too little – or feel too irrationally – to give reliable advice. We do not have to form any precise idea of what a patient will be like when well in order to help him overcome his illness. For, we may be sure that as he learns to understand himself, he will find his own path to better mental health. Similarly, we may be sure that, so far as we can make society more conscious of its motives, the direction of its movement will be more in accordance with its welfare.

If this kind of non-partisan analysis of social motives is, in fact, often the best way of meeting the challenge to psychology, we can see at once that it has by no means been ignored. Freud himself, Ernest Jones, Flugel and many others,[1] both of the psycho-analytic and of allied schools, have all increased our understanding of such motives. And in some countries there has been a fairly widespread infiltration of the insight gained. But this has occurred at a time when its social-therapeutic influence has been obscured by other factors. The decline in the old sanctions of religion and class, which gave our society a precarious stability, has released enormous forces, both of construction and of destruction. In the ensuing upheaval, which has surpassed in scale all previous social readjustments, it has been difficult to see the operation of a new factor – the emergence of a new kind of self-consciousness, which includes some understanding of the forces that have been re-

---

[1] E.g. Freud, *Group Psychology and the Analysis of the Ego*, 1921; *Civilization and the Discontents*, 1930. Jones, *Essays in Applied Psycho-Analysis*, 1923. Flugel, *Men and their Motives*, 1934; *Man, Morals and Society*, 1945. Hopkins, *The Psychology of Social Movements*, 1938. Money-Kyrle, *Superstition and Society*, 1939.

leased. But perhaps the dissemination of recent psychological discoveries has already had some positive effect, not only in such fields as health and education, but also in our politics. I think we have become a little more conscious of our political motives, and a little wiser in our political behaviour, than we should have been without it.

If so, this is at most a barely perceptible beginning. An enormous amount remains to be done, both in acquiring and in conveying insight. Moreover, there is a sense of urgency about this work lest it should be too late to prevent some fresh deterioration or disaster.

II. THE ANALYSIS OF POLITICAL MOTIVES

There are good reasons why the political arena should be the happy hunting-ground of every conceivable unconscious motive. In the ordinary business of life we are dealing with concrete things and people, and our actual acquaintance with them is a constant check on our tendency to identify them with the figures of unconscious phantasy. Our feelings for our neighbours are conditioned by a realistic appreciation of their characters; and as these are neither wholly white or black, our loyalties are not fanatical, and we have some understanding, and therefore sympathy, even for those we dislike. In politics, however, we are dealing with the abstractions of nation, party, class or ideology; and there is little to prevent our unconscious phantasy from using these to express itself – in much the same way as a child will use its toys. In this field, therefore, our thinking tends to be much more unrealistic, and our passions correspondingly disproportionate to actual situations.

Some of the most important distortions seem to arise from the persistence of very early thought processes, which we are learning to understand, thanks largely to the pioneering work of Melanie Klein. Among these are the processes by which the child's earliest concepts of objects are duplicated in two ways: as external and internal, and as good and bad.

The intellectual pitfall arising from the first of these duplications is one into which all of us who care about the future of society are sometimes apt to fall. For what exactly do we mean by this troubled society which challenges our science? Factually, we may mean a collection of individuals troubled by tensions between them which we feel could be reduced. But emotionally we may mean the projection of some good but injured object within ourselves. If these two, the inner and the outer object, do not closely correspond, society becomes for us something other than the individuals in it; and if the gap between them is a wide one, we may abandon the individuals for the abstraction; or rather seek to control them, in a compulsive and omnipotent way, for its supposed benefit. In an extreme form, this lack of conformity between the inner and the outer object leads to the totalitarian fallacy that the welfare of the abstract state is best served by sacrificing the welfare of all its concrete citizens.

The other duplication, into good and bad, is the infant's earliest response to the intolerable conflict of both loving and hating the same object at the same time.[1] But it survives throughout life, in varying degrees, as a distorting influence on thought. The distortion, of course, has two aspects: the idealization of symbols of good objects, and the blackening of symbols of bad ones.

The widespread necessity to idealize something is very striking. In the past religion provided the ideal. People felt that, if they could not believe in it, life would be unthinkable; there would be nothing left to live for if God were dead. Now, a political creed often plays the same role. People feel that they must believe in it, that is, in its goodness and vitality. And if they have once chosen it as the symbol of their good object, to lose faith in it is to suffer a major psychological catastrophe.

In Germany in 1946, I saw several individuals who were in the throes of exactly this catastrophe. Incredible as it may seem to us, many kindly and otherwise intelligent people had believed in a 'good' Hitler – a Messiah of infinite benevolence who was to bring peace and unity to Europe. Some of them managed to maintain this picture to the end, against all the accumulating evidence, with a desperate ingenuity which exaggerated the

---

[1] Corresponding with the basic distinction between pain and pleasure, we are accustomed to make a basic distinction between those impulses which seek to annihilate and those which seek to preserve their objects. It may be a peculiarity of man, and to a lesser extent of all mammals, that, at the beginning of life, when they are least controllable, these opposite impulses should both be directed to the same object – the mother's breast.

faults of underlings in order to maintain the Führer as a spotless ideal. In such cases, the final disillusionment at the time of the war trials brought an utter despair which seemed immeasurably greater than the grief they felt at the actual loss of dearly loved relations.

These, of course, are exaggerated illustrations. But the need to cling to the belief in a good object, as an alternative to being left with nothing but the bad one, can be found, in varying degrees, in everyone – even in the disillusioned cynic who has consciously renounced it. Moreover, to many people the object must be spotless; for if a flaw is once admitted it may cease altogether to be good. For this reason, they defend it not only against destructive attacks, but also – and sometimes even more ardently – against constructive criticism. Obviously, this kind of idealization can be a very serious bar to objectivity in politics.

The converse of idealization, the blackening of the bad object, is the other side of the same medal. The bad object tends to be a depository for all the faults of the good one as well as its own. And in addition, it is the depository of our disowned aggression towards the good one. So far as this mechanism operates in our political thinking, we are unable to see any good points at all in other philosophies of life – or any good intentions to those who support them.

Clearly this splitting mechanism exerts a constant influence on party politics. The party system may be the only practical method of democratic government. But in most people there is an element of unreality in the idealization of their own side and the blackening of the other which makes it difficult for them to consider each social problem, as it arises, objectively and on its merits.

To split one object into an ideally good and an ideally bad aspect is perhaps the most primitive defence against anxiety and depression – anxiety at the sense of destructive persecution by what is hated, and depression at destructively hating what is also loved. But many other defences soon come into play; and they too can be recognized in later life – especially in our political thinking where the collective concepts used cannot be easily compared with the actual people represented.

Among the defences against persecutory anxiety, projection,

denial and what may be called transvaluation seem particularly important.

So far as the source of persecution is ultimately felt to be within the self, the anxiety can be lessened by projection. It is often a positive relief to feel persecuted by an external power – whether by a foreign nation or one's own government – and for this reason there is a tendency to exaggerate the extent to which either is hostile or oppressive.[1]

But if the fear of an external tyrant is too strong, the further defence of denial may come into operation. Instead of exaggerating a small degree of tyranny, a large degree is underestimated. We would see this defence very clearly before the war, when the majority of people, not only in this country but even more in Germany, succeeded in convincing themselves that Hitler was much less implacably malicious than he looked.

Such denial seems to be half-way to the defence by inversion, or transvaluation, in which the dreaded persecutor becomes fanatically admired. By exploiting this defence Nazi terrorism converted many social-democrats into ardent worshippers of Hitler, in much the same way as a small boy, under pressure of his terror of his father, may desert his mother and adopt a sadistic father image as his ideal. In fact domestic transvaluations of this kind, which were especially common in the German patriarchal home, seem often to have paved the way for later political transvaluations. Henry Dicks stressed the importance of such factors in the development of the Fascist character.

Turning from persecutory anxiety to depression, we find defences which perhaps belong to a slightly later stage of development; for depression presupposes the concept of a whole object which is both loved and hated at once. Depressive grief or guilt, for the two words are almost synonymous, gives rise to that impulse of reparation which is so important a factor in all creativeness. But if the damage done in phantasy is too great, and there is too little confidence in reparation, guilt becomes intolerable and has to be dealt with in some other

---

[1] It was a relief, when the war began, to project all the bad objects in our national ego onto the German nation, which seemed peculiarly well suited to receive them. But now the war is over, they are reappearing within this ego, where they have also become more diffuse and more intangible. It is as though the external dragon which was slain was rematerializing in bits which permeate our own society.

way. If it is dealt with by denial and projection, the result is a self-righteous and censorious character which feels itself to be never in the wrong and exaggerates the faults of others.

Now this trait, like many others, seems to be much more conspicuous in what might be called our political egos than in our individual egos. Even people who are normally both modest and charitable in private life, and easily forgive their enemies, find it much harder to criticize the party or nation with which they identify themselves, and may be implacable in their moral condemnation of its opponents.

The effect of the denial and projection of guilt on the exacerbation of all national and political animosities can hardly be exaggerated. We could see it most clearly in Germany, where the necessity to repudiate guilt for the first war was one of the major causes of the second; and we can see it there still in the relentless hatred with which the German people pursue those of their countrymen on to whom they have projected the whole guilt of the third Reich. It is more difficult for us to see how the same mechanism – less only in degree – has influenced our attitude to Germany after both defeats. The peoples of neither country wanted war; but while the Germans wanted many things which made war inevitable, the British wanted to avoid responsibilities which might have prevented it. Both nations therefore feel unconscious guilt – on the one side more of commission, on the other more of omission – to deny and to project upon the other; and the fact that they do so makes it still more difficult for this other to become conscious of their share.

In the political, as in the individual, field, those who are unable to admit any share of blame are never able to forgive their enemies. And conversely, those who are never forgiven find it still more difficult to become conscious of their guilt. Thus, the denial and projection of guilt is one of the main factors in national and political vindictiveness, and so in the perpetuation of all feuds.

Another consequence of the denial of collective guilt is political callousness. The victim of almost any tyranny tends to stand for some persecuted good object which we feel ought to be defended. If we are unwilling, or even unable, to do so, some guilt is inevitably stirred. But so far as we deny it, we make the victim correspondingly more responsible for his own misfortune, and become indifferent to his fate. Thus even those who are not themselves vindictive may show a marked degree of callousness to the fate of those, whether individuals or minority groups, who are the victims of legalized persecution elsewhere.

III. THE SOCIAL EFFECTS OF ANALYSIS

There are, of course, many other ways in which the unconscious may influence people in their political thoughts, feelings and actions. Sometimes the influence is near the surface and already widely recognized. Sometimes it is much deeper and will not be understood for many years to come. There is even a risk that this new movement of discovery and enlightenment may be checked, before it has had time to be effective, by the return of one of those psychotic episodes of which Germany has provided the most recent and terrible example. But we may hope that society will continue gradually to become more conscious of its motives, and in conclusion inquire how its political life is likely to be affected by the increasing insight.

It may help us to begin by distinguishing between two kinds of political cleavage: that between different political parties and that between different kinds of political conscience. For our purpose the second of these cleavages is much the more important. All parties contain individuals of three well-known types which, for clarity, I will describe in exaggerated contrast: the egoists, the authoritarians and the humanists. The political egoists are conspicuous for their apparent lack of conscience. They care little for ideologies except in so far as these express their positive self-interest, or their negative animosities and spites. The authoritarians have rigid principles, and are unyielding in their obedience to their code or party, in the service of which they are entirely callous. The humanists are devoid neither of self-interest nor of principles; but they are characterized by a certain warmth and understanding for their fellow-men, and by a capacity to be deeply stirred by suffering or injustice. They can be courageous in their opposition to tyranny; but they are not vindictive.

If examples of these three were subjected to character analysis, we should find that the excessive egoism of the first was partly a reaction to anxiety, and that it was made possible only by the denial of great quantities of depressive guilt. The egoist is greedy because he is anxious, and feels guilty because of the potential destructiveness of his predatory greed. But because his anxiety is more frightening than his guilt, it is the greed which becomes conscious and the guilt which is denied. We should also find much unconscious depressive guilt in the authoritarian. But the decisive factor in his make-up would turn out to be an excess of persecutory anxiety as the motive for surrender to a tyrannical superego. Here again, it is the anxiety that gets the upper hand. The guilt which results from the surrender of all other good objects when their welfare conflicts with the superego's categorical imperative is denied and replaced by an apparent callousness. In the humanist we might find some minor distortions of thought of the kind we have been considering, but there would be much less persecutory anxiety and much less denial of guilt. If, in fact, they were all successfully analysed, the humanist would undergo least change, and the characters of the other two would tend to move in his direction.

We cannot hope that the methods of collective analysis open to us – books, broadcasts or group discussions – will produce comparable results. But we can at least expect that a larger number of people will make a smaller movement in this direction.

It would not, as the utopians have hoped, be a movement towards universal concord. People will always compete, both egoistically for the possession of the same good objects, and altruistically (morally) in the defence of different ones. And they will always combine in different political parties for this purpose. But we should expect these conflicts to be conducted with more consistent realism. And we should also expect the political consciences of the rival parties to become rather more consistently humanist in outlook.

13
Varieties of Group Formation*

Forenote [1977] – I now find this paper, written in 1939 and published in 1950, a meticulous deduction from slightly obsolescent theories and rather dull.

INTRODUCTORY NOTE

This paper was originally given as an open lecture at the British Institute of Psycho-Analysis in the spring of 1939. (It was one of a series of six, delivered by different analysts which, but for the war, would have been published in book form.) The examples I chose to illustrate my particular thesis were the events and attitudes most familiar to an English audience at that critical period. The fact that they can now be considered in retrospect may in some ways be an advantage and, for this reason, I have not brought them up to date – except occasionally by adding an explanatory note in brackets.

As to the thesis itself, this is an elaboration of Freud's theory as expounded in his *Group Psychology and the Analysis of the Ego* (1921). He then described a primary group as 'a number of individuals who have substituted one and the same object for their ego-ideal (later called the superego) and have consequently identified themselves with one another in their ego'. This formula, which I accept as fundamental, has been my starting point. But while Freud was concerned mainly with the paternal imago, we know that both parent figures must play some rôle. Moreover, they must do so in each of the two aspects – ideally good and ideally bad – into which they are split in the child's early unconscious fantasy. (This splitting of an object as a defence against the anxieties aroused by ambivalence towards it has been especially stressed by Melanie Klein.) Some elaboration of Freud's formula to include the rôles of

* From: *Psycho-analysis and the Social Sciences*. I.U.P., New York, 1948.

both parent figures, in their bad as well as good aspects, in the formation of groups does therefore seem to be required. To supply it is the primary aim of this paper. Of course, many other factors, both psychological and social, would have to be included before our theoretical picture or model of a group could be regarded as anything like complete. I have concentrated only on filling what seemed to me a particular gap.

THE FAMILY AS THE PROTOTYPE OF ALL GROUP FORMATIONS

Man creates the society he lives in. Can he, like God, look upon his work and find it good? Sometimes he is complacent when it functions very badly. Sometimes he dislikes it even when it functions fairly well. But he seldom blames himself for its defects. He blames his ancestors, or those who seem to have imposed it on him, and overlooks his own share in the work.

The truth is, that in building his society he is influenced by unconscious as well as conscious motives, which are often incompatible with each other. For this reason he does not know exactly what he wants or why he fails to get it. If this is really so, some understanding of these unconscious motives is a first condition of the success of the societies he builds.

To uncover these unconscious motives we must go back to his early childhood. Here, in his relation to his parents, we shall find the model of all the varieties of social structure he will build in later life.

To be more exact, the basic model of all group formations is not quite the family as it really is, but the family as it appears in the child's imagination. Perhaps most of the troubles of society result from the fact that the two are by no means the same. The real family contains two parents; the imaginary one contains at least four – two good ones and two bad ones – who are the prototypes not only of divinities and devils but of our more abstract ideas of good and evil. This, of course, is not remembered, and some of it is never conscious, but it can be discovered by Freud's method of analysis, which Melanie Klein and others have applied to the direct study of very young children. We know, too, why it is that the child forms these contradictory pictures. When he loves his parents, he forms a good picture of them. But when they arouse his hate, he fears them and forms a picture of vindictive bad parents, who are different people altogether.

Moreover, in his efforts to disown his dangerous aggressiveness against one parent, he tends to attribute it to, or project it upon the other. Then to reassure himself against these imaginary dangers he exaggerates his picture of the good parents into perfect and omnipotent beings. But paradoxically enough, they not only give but also need protection; for they are threatened by the child's aggressiveness which he projects upon the bad parent figures. Lastly, they are not only persons to be obeyed and followed; but also persons to be admired and imitated. To the boy, it is more especially the mother who has to be protected and the father who is both followed and admired.

These figures of the good and bad parents are incorporated in the child's unconscious fantasy and so give rise to that sense of inner goodness and inner badness, almost of spiritual possession, of which some people are quite conscious. But throughout his life he will also seek to rediscover the pattern of his imaginary family in the outer world. In particular, he will seek to impose it upon all the varieties of group formation he will enter, and so help to mould.

TYPES OF GROUP VALUE

We may start our search for the elements of the family pattern in the group by looking for representatives of the good mother figure. In the person of a Queen Elizabeth or a Queen Victoria she may appear as the actual ruler of the group. Such queens have inspired a degree of self-sacrificing devotion that can hardly be explained in terms of the excellence of their real characters alone. A large part, at least, of this devotion must have sprung from their symbolic characters – although it is also true that each succeeded in identifying herself with the role she was cast to play.

But in masculine groups, at least, the good mother figure usually appears in a less concrete form. To most modern nations, for example, the concept of the Motherland has an enormous emotional appeal, especially when it is in danger. Frenchmen (in 1914) forgot their normal party quarrels and united as one

VARIETIES OF GROUP FORMATION

man when France was threatened. And a French soldier, even when routed, returned immediately to the attack, if someone reminded him of his country. A scene from the last war (1914–18) was once described to me by an eyewitness. A French battalion had been attacked in the early morning before they were properly awake. At first they bolted crying, '*Tout est perdu*', and it seemed that the Germans were certain to break through both the front and support line of trenches. But soon the routed battalion came charging back shouting, '*Vive la France*', and attacked with such desperate vigour that they not only captured their own lost trenches, but the German front line as well. It was simply the recollection of their country as a symbol of the good Mother in danger, that produced this astonishing return of valour. With such clear recollections of French patriotism in our minds, most of us were unprepared for the collapse in 1940. We did not realize that in a decisive minority of Frenchmen two fundamental changes had taken place: the good mother figure symbolized by their country was already so threatened that its defence seemed hopeless; and the bad father figure was being symbolized more by communism within, than by the national enemy outside their country.

But the figure who is threatened may be a father as well as a mother, and is perhaps always, to some extent, what analysts call a 'combined parent'. To the Germans, Germany is the Fatherland more than the motherland – a fact that may explain some of the psychological differences between them and the French. Perhaps because the son's attitude is always more ambivalent towards the father, the Germans are overapt to think of their Fatherland as threatened even when it is not. If the internal figure of the father is not quite trusted there is a constant unconscious effort to keep him in check and hem him in. In dreams, for instance, he may appear as a dangerous lunatic who has been kept for years in a strait jacket, but who at any moment may be expected to break out. A people who identify their country with such a figure are certain to be oversuspicious of plots to encircle it and to prevent its natural expansion. Their sense of claustrophobia will breed a compulsive desire to break out, which will naturally alarm their neighbours, who are then likely to form just those encircling alliances they fear. Whether and under what circumstances the neighbours of such a state would be wise to try appeasement rather than encirclement is an old problem, to which we shall return.

Another form in which the idea of a persecuted good figure who should be protected appears is in the concept of a small nation threatened by a big one, or of an oppressed minority fighting to be free. We all know the enormous influence of this concept on the history of the world. We remember the national enthusiasm and sympathy at the time of Byron for the Greeks, or of Garibaldi for the Italians. We remember how Gladstone, in his Midlothian campaign, fired the country and altered its whole political complexion by his accounts of the Bulgarian atrocities. We remember the determined fury aroused in us by what is described as the rape of Belgium (1914). And, at least until recently, we liked to think that our pride in our country rested not in the size of its dominions, but in its constant preparedness to fight in the old battle of Freedom against Tyranny. On the other hand, we find it more difficult to realize that to Americans the Irish, and to Germans, the Boers (1899) have played this same rôle of a damsel in distress. We may think, too, that the concept of persecuted Germans in Czechoslovakia, or of persecuted Italians in Tunisia is pure moonshine. But whether or not such concepts have been artificially created for a sinister purpose, they belong to the same psychological category as those that have often led our own country into war. Since tales of atrocities against defenceless peoples correspond with a pattern in unconscious fantasy, we are over-ready to believe them. But it by no means follows that they are always false, or that our indignation is irrational when they are true.

The same concept of a good figure persecuted recurs in still more abstract form. Some groups are bound together, not by common blood and common land, but by a common ideal, which may be religious or secular. I believe that such concepts as the Mother Church, or the Gospel which gives spiritual nourishment to mankind, are the psychological equivalents of the mother goddesses of earlier religions, and therefore of the good mother of unconscious fantasy. Even goddesses needed, as well as gave, sympathy and protection. Iris, Astarte and Aphrodite, no less than Mary, were represented as mourning for their loss; though by a curious twist of unconscious fantasy it was not the goddess but her divine son or lover who had been directly injured. Similarly, those religious ideals – which I suggest are more abstract symbols of the same figure – have usually been threatened, or persecuted, ideals – at least during their periods of most vivid life. Many of their adherents have gladly suffered death and torture in their defence; and seem sometimes to have provoked persecution in order to reproduce in the external world the central pattern of their unconscious fantasy.

Something rather similar to a gospel, but still further sublimated into a system of principles, is also the aim of political parties as we know them now. It may seem far fetched to claim that an abstract political ideal for which men sometimes give their lives is a symbol of the unconscious picture of the good mother. But it is no accident that Liberty, for example, is represented by a statue of a woman. Nor indeed is it strange that this should be so; for whatever is valuable on rational grounds tends to become associated with the earliest values, which we preserve in our unconscious, and from which it derives a great part of its emotional force.

Human history is largely an account of the conflict of groups each striving to defend their own values or ideals. Whether concrete or abstract, these symbolize good parent figures to be protected, and from this source derive their power. But can we tell whether this power is likely to be used for the benefit or for the destruction of mankind?

It is no part of psychology, or indeed of any science, to choose between ideals. Each, so far as it is neither based on falsehood nor contains an inner contradiction, is the equal of its fellow. But the attitude to ideals can be either pathological or sane. The dividing line is extremely difficult to draw. But the individual or the group who imagines attacks upon his ideals when they do not exist, or who provokes such attacks in order to realize his unconscious fantasy, is clearly on the wrong side of this line; for his inner life is full of unreal conflicts which he is compelled to reproduce in the external world.

But if the fanatic is unbalanced, it does not follow that the group or individual who abandons ideals too easily is necessarily more sane. If the good values we stand for are so threatened that we feel it hopeless to defend them, there is sometimes a tendency to devalue them, or even to feel that they are bad. I will try to make this clear by an example which is fresh in my mind. In the September (1938) crisis, it seemed likely that Czechoslovakia would become another Belgium in our minds. People who had hardly heard of it before were deeply stirred by the old ideal of a small nation in distress and prepared to take up arms in its defence. But as soon as they heard it was to be abandoned, many of these same people suddenly lost all interest in the Czechs. In some the change of feeling went further and they found themselves actively disliking the very nation they had been so anxious to defend. This seems hardly credible; but I saw the change occurring in several of my friends.

The tendency to abandon ideals too easily may result from the same internal disharmony as the tendency to propagate them with too much fanaticism. If in the internal picture the good parents are too much threatened by the bad ones, these symbols must either be defended with an undiscriminating zeal or abandoned altogether.

Which of these two alternatives is chosen by a given group is partly determined by the type of leadership it gets. If the leadership is fanatical, there is likely to be a fanatical response. If it is defeatist, there is usually a defeatist response. If it is resolute, and neither fanatical nor defeatist, there may be a balanced response. But, in the long run, the stability or lack of stability of the group depends upon the inner harmony or lack of harmony of the members that compose it. They tend to get the leaders they deserve.

TYPES OF GROUP ENEMIES

The concept of a good parent figure persecuted implies, as we know, the concept of an enemy; and we know, too, that this enemy is the bad parent figure on to whom the child has projected his aggressiveness. Because this enemy is part of the unconscious pattern, there is always a tendency to rediscover him whether he is there or not; and for this reason he is a constant factor in almost all group formation.

In tribes or nations he is often real enough and takes the form of some other tribe or nation. If two groups live in an area that only provides sufficient food for one, it is perhaps inevitable that they should fight – unless they mutually agree to restrict their populations. Such examples once led us to believe that all wars were ultimately economic, that they were special products of the struggle for existence. This theory, of course, contains a partial truth. But it also serves to cloak the irrational motives, which are at least equally important.

To the extent to which as children we have unconsciously incorporated an imaginary enemy, we shall tend to find him in the external world. In extreme cases we may suffer from obvious delusions of persecutions and be classed as paranoiacs. If we are more normal, and so long as we are behaving as individuals, the slight degree of over-suspiciousness that may remain will be counteracted by the different attitude of our friends. If you do not share my irrational distrust of a mutual acquaintance I am likely to revise my view. But when we are acting not as individuals but as a group there is no such check. When two groups begin to distrust each other, the suspicion of the individual will be confirmed first by the similar suspicions of the members of his own group, and then by the defensive reaction of the other. To each the other becomes the personification of evil, and tension increases which may eventually explode in war.

For a nation to permit its suspicions of another nation to grow unchecked may therefore produce an actual danger which would not have otherwise arisen. But there is another tendency, which is also dangerous. This is to repress or deny suspicions that are well founded. There are in fact two ways of dealing with unconscious anxiety produced by unconscious aggression. One is to project the aggression and become excessively distrustful. The other is to deny it and become too trusting. It is not easy for individuals, and still less for nations, to keep the balance between these two extremes.

To take a concrete example, there is no doubt that Germany's sense of claustrophobia, and determination to break out before the war (1914–18) was fostered by the encircling alliances made against her. But can we be certain that by repressing our suspicions we should not have fallen into the opposite danger of denying and failing to protect ourselves against an actual threat? Or to come bluntly to our present problem, can we be certain that appeasement rather than collective security is likely to keep peace? Hitler's own answer is that it was tried six years too late.[1]

Psychology can only give an answer in more general terms. If owing to the conditions of their infancy or to some other cause a particular people have a very large fund of aggression which they must project, as the only alternative to internal disruption, they are likely to be militant whatever the attitude of their neighbours may be. If, on the other hand, the fund of aggression is small, much provocation will be necessary. To determine whether and at what time a nation is in one rather than the other of these categories is a problem of practical statesmanship, which practical statesmanship has often failed to solve.

So far we have discussed only one type of group enemy – namely a rival group. But this element in the unconscious pattern may take many other forms. Sometimes the enemy may be felt to be inside the group itself. From time to time during the Middle Ages the terror of witchcraft seized hold of nations. The group became as it were hypochondriacal, and like the individual hypochondriac, sought to cut out the supposed evil within itself. The vague and roving terror of internal enemies would be periodically focussed on some poor wretch, and momentarily relieved by his or her destruction, only to return once more to seek fresh victims. The witch, of course, was a symbol of the unconscious image of the 'bad mother'. But since she was endowed with phallic attitudes, a broomstick, a beak-like nose and chin, and was moreover possessed by the devil, she was also what psycho-analysts call a 'combined parent' figure.

This same tendency to group hypochondria seems also to have been responsible for the burning of heretics as well as witches. The Church, and State united to it, could tolerate no foreign body within itself, and turned ferociously upon any that it found.[2]

[1] When British statesmen said that all problems were capable of solution by discussion, his answer was that there were 'fifteen years for that before he came to power'. Report of Hitler's speech in the *London Times*, 3 April 1939.

[2] [Possibly the present (1977) trade union insistence that non-unionists should not be employed to work with their own members is partly an example of the same mechanism and not merely the result of a rational desire to maximize their power.]

VARIETIES OF GROUP FORMATION

Coming to more modern examples, the same mechanism may, I think, be seen in those persecutions of minorities, both political and racial, of which we have heard so much. That the Nazi attitude towards Jews and Social-Democrats is, at least partly, a symptom of group hypochondria seems to be confirmed by no less an authority than Hitler, who described them, in a speech I heard, as a cancer in the body of the State that must be ruthlessly cut out. But lest I should be accused of seeing faults only in our neighbours, I would suggest that in our own country there are many people for whom the wicked Bolshevik or the wicked Capitalist are overcast to play this rôle. Moreover, I do not wish to suggest that all dislike of minorities within a group is irrational, but only that the irrational component is often larger than it seems.

Among primitive peoples throughout the world, perhaps the commonest anxiety is that of physical possession by evil spirits or forces. All illness, when not caused by the loss of some good internal object, such as the soul, is caused by possession by a bad one. Thus primitive medicine consists mainly of magical rites to restore the good or drive out the bad. We now know, thanks mainly to the work of Melanie Klein, that such superstitions are not confined to savages, but form part of the unconscious fantasy of every child. We know, too, that those in whom the sense of inner evil is near consciousness, often find the presence of a real external enemy a positive relief – for this relieves the much greater terror of the imaginary internal one who cannot be destroyed except by suicide. For much the same reason, a real external enemy is often a condition of the solidarity – sometimes even of the continued existence of a group. If therefore some nation is ever driven by this motive into the conquest of the world, the result might be, not external peace, but speedy disintegration and collapse – that is, unless it could find an abstract enemy to take the place of the external concrete ones it had destroyed.

Some groups do have abstract or at least spiritual enemies. The Church, for instance, used to be vividly aware of the enmity of Satan; and although he has now been largely ousted by more abstract concepts such as sin, impurity and vice, these have much the same meaning to the unconscious. To primitive man guilt (at least that part of guilt which may be identified with persecutory anxiety)[1] is quite consciously treated as something invisible but concrete, which can be washed off, driven out by an emetic, or removed by some other purification. It was therefore quite clearly identified with the internal 'bad objects' of the child's unconscious fantasy.

Since (persecutory) guilt is an internal 'bad object' to the unconscious, we may expect to find the same principles of denial and projection at work as we have found elsewhere. Perhaps these principles may account for the excess of zeal with which such bodies as watch committees endeavour to discover vice outside themselves.

In this connection, it is interesting to speculate whether human freedom has gained or lost by the decline in the belief in Satan. To a degree varying with the intensity of their inner conflicts men have always sought relief by projecting the devils they feel within themselves into the external world. So long as they believed in the reality of Satan, there was less need to seek for more abstract evils in their neighbours, where minor foibles were not so much attacked. Perhaps more people were comparatively free; but those who were suspected of intercourse with Satan, were burnt as heretics or witches – instead of being merely prevented from drinking, or betting or undressing on the beach.

Flugel once suggested that the future safety of the human race depends upon its ability to find the right object to attack. Some groups do in fact find their enemies in things that almost everyone regards as bad. To councils for the preservation of rural areas, the enemy is ugliness in many forms, which they sometimes attack with a commendable fanaticism. A similar, though perhaps even more abstract rôle, is played for the medical profession by 'illness', and for educationalists by 'ignorance', which both seek to banish from the world.

Like other psychological forces, the tendency to attack an inner evil projected into the outer world can be applied to ends that are generally acknowledged as either useful, useless or pernicious. To a great extent, no doubt, later education

---

[1] The sense of guilt seems to be a compound of two elements: a persecutory element aroused by the sense of having offended a feared object, and a depressive element aroused by the sense of having injured a good one. While the response to the first is propitiation that to the second is reparation.

VARIETIES OF GROUP FORMATION

determines the choice. But the less exaggerated the unconscious picture of the inner evil, the more likely shall we be to find its symbols only in those things which on rational grounds seem to deserve attack. The real test is not whether one can think rationally as an individual, but whether one can also do so as a member of a group.

But is an enemy – abstract if not concrete – a necessary part of every group formation? A society without enemies, and in perpetual peace, has been the dream of the Utopists – a dream which is at least approximately realized by the Society of Friends. Not only are they pacifists who do not fight; but they do not even proselytize or attack other people's religious views. The whole emphasis seems to be on the control of their own conduct. As Rickman has pointed out, they do not, like other groups, project their inner sense of evil, but attack it only where it is – within themselves.

TYPES OF GROUP LEADERS

So far I have said nothing about the leader whose presence often distinguishes the group from a mere crowd. The leader, of course, is the good parent figure – but in another rôle, for we have already found this figure beneath the values that the group defends. In masculine groups, at least, these values usually symbolize the mother, while the leader is a father symbol, whose main function is to lead the group in their defence.

Since the sons' attitude to their father is always ambivalent, that is, a blend of love and hate, many groups have tried to dispense with leaders altogether. Nowhere has this attempt been more successful than in Central Australia, where the tribes are ruled not by chiefs but by committees of old men. Fathers indeed are brought so low that they are even denied their share in procreation; children being conceived, not by natural means, but by the entry of an ancestral totem. But although the father figure is in this way banished from the earth, it is not difficult to recognize him in the spiritual form of these very totems who play an enormous part in the beliefs and rituals of these people.[1]

[1] Cf. Roheim, *The Riddle of the Sphinx*, London, 1934.

Although in very small communities the father figure may be dispensed with, or rather banished into the spiritual realm, in larger communities this has always been impracticable. In a common type of primitive autocracy the father is still projected into the spiritual realm to become the tribal god; but the god exercises his authority through some man who is more or less identified with him. Extreme forms of such theocracies developed in Babylonia and Egypt, in China and Japan and in the old civilizations of Mexico and Peru. The king was not only the priest of the god, but often also the actual god in human form. This theory was revived by the Roman Emperors to strengthen their prestige, and lingered on in a weaker form in the doctrine of the divine right of kings. But with the secularization of monarchy, the old ambivalence became conscious once more, and some nations returned, not indeed to the leaderless democracy of Central Australia, but to a system of leadership by election rather than inheritance.

Intermediate between the inherited leader and the elected leader is what may be called the appointed leader, that is, a leader who is elected by a ruling oligarchy. The so-called Greek democracies, containing as they did large numbers of voteless helots, had leaders of this type. Among other examples is the Pope who is elected not by the whole Roman church but by the College of Cardinals; and a manager of a company who is elected by the board.

A fourth type is the elected or at least popular leader who becomes an autocrat. To distinguish him from the other three we may call him self-imposed.

From the point of view of the stability and efficiency of the group, each of these four types of leaders have their peculiar merits and defects. The hereditary leader may be badly adapted to this job – that is, he may fail to resemble the kind of ideal father his particular group desires. But if he does satisfy this condition, his own security and the stability of the group is likely to be greater than in any other kind. For both in his own unconscious belief and in that of his followers, he already incorporates the spirit of his father and remoter ancestors, that is, of the previous leaders or father symbols of the group. Unlike other types of leader he inherits, as it were, a fund of prestige, which he can either squander or increase, but which certainly gives him a very great advantage. To the unconscious at least, he still has something of the past divinity of kings.

An appointed leader is probably more likely to be competent than a hereditary one, but he does not start with the same psychological advantages and must be a better leader in order to achieve an equal prestige for himself and therefore of stability for his group. Sometimes, especially in religious groups, this disadvantage is overcome by a ceremony of investiture, which symbolically transfers to him the prestige, spirit, or *mana* of his predecessors.

An elected leader, for example, the President of a Republic, a Prime Minister or even an ordinary Member of Parliament, is usually more likely to start his career with the requisite prestige than an appointed one; but it is usually more difficult for him to keep it. If he did not start with the requisite prestige, that is, if he did not possess the qualities of a 'good father' symbol, he would never have been elected. But unlike hereditary or appointed leaders, he is never free from rivals, to one of whom his group is apt to turn at the first sign of failure. Then, having ceased to symbolize the good father, he often comes to symbolize the bad one, and finds that the reverence he so lately enjoyed is turned to hate. These groups are often less loyal to leaders they chose themselves than they are to leaders thrust upon them. But the inconvenience of more frequent revolutions is offset by the fact that they are also bloodless. Our own constitution, as the late David Eder and also Jones have pointed out, has some of the advantages of both the hereditary and elective systems. For the fact that the Prime Minister has to take the blame for all misfortunes enables the King to remain a focus for the country's loyalty. This is probably one reason why a change of government is less of an upheaval here than in other democratic countries.

The difference between the elected leader and what I called the self-imposed one is of degree rather than of kind. At one end of the scale is the man who is elected by a group to preserve its existing values and ideals; at the other, the man who preaches an ideal and rallies a group in its support. He creates the group which follows him. To this type belong the founders of religions: Buddha, Christ, Mohammed; the founders of new political ideals and systems: Lenin, Mussolini, Hitler; and also religious or political revivalists.

Such leaders, so far as their ideals are agressively promoted, may become the victims of their own creation. Napoleon III started as the popular hero destined to revive the lost spirit of French Nationalism. The enthusiasm he had himself inspired pushed him, it is said against his better judgment, into the disastrous war that ended his career. We have yet to see whether Hitler or Mussolini can check their expansive policies before these lead to war – that is, assuming that either wants to do so.

How far then is a leader the cause or the effect of the psychology of his group? If the inner conflict in the members of the group is severe, they are likely to be melancholic, or to quarrel among themselves, unless they have an external enemy to identify with the bad figure of their unconscious fantasy. They are likely to turn against a pacific leader, and to replace him by one who gives them that exaltation which is for them the only alternative to melancholia. If, on the other hand, they are at peace within themselves, they will still be capable, and perhaps with less anxiety, of defending their values and ideals; but they will not be compelled to create enemies who would not have otherwise existed. They will not be easily influenced without due cause, and are likely to choose a leader who is resolute rather than aggressive. In intermediate cases, however, when the members of the group have an average amount of inner conflict, the leader may have a very great effect. If he seems weak in the defence of their ideals, they will soon be plunged in defeatist gloom. If he is aggressive they may become fanatical. And if he is resolute he may keep them balanced between these two extremes.

TYPES OF GROUP STANDARDS

So far we have found three types of symbols of the various figures in the child's unconscious picture of his family. The 'good parents', and more particularly the mother in her rôle as a figure to be defended, reappear as the values of the group. The 'bad parents' in their rôle of persecutors reappear as the enemies against whom the values have to be defended. The 'good parents', more particularly the father, in his rôle of defender, reappears as the leader or leaders of the group. But the 'good parents' and to the boy more particularly the father, have one other rôle. As we said before, he is not only someone to follow but also someone to admire and imitate. He remains throughout life an unconscious model for his sons' behaviour – a model which is only within limits modified by the later incorporation of other father figures. To the extent to which education and the treatment of young children by their parents in a given group is homogeneous the models of behaviour that different members erect within themselves will be similar, and the group will have what Roheim calls a well marked group ideal. This group ideal is the standard of conduct the group tries to live up to and must not be confused with the ideals the group defends. The group ideal of the Spartan, for example, was fortitude and courage; the ideals he defended comprised everything he meant by Sparta.

Small primitive tribes, who have had little contact with other types of culture, each develop characters, or rather standards of behaviour, peculiar to themselves. So also, though to a lesser degree, do larger nations. The group ideals of different sections of the English population differ widely from each other; but there is a common element, hard to define perhaps, which is distinct from the group ideals of Frenchmen or Italians. Artificial groups, too, such as the medical or legal profession, the army or the church, have their typical group ideals of conduct, which are often very rigid.

Each group naturally feels that their own standards are superior, and often disapproves of those of other groups. It is not the business of psychology to make moral judgments which are necessarily subjective; but it can make medical judgments and say that one group ideal is pathological and another sane. Among some of the North American Indians described by Margaret Mead in *Sex and Temperament*, the ideal man was he who destroyed the largest quantity of his own possessions. He amassed wealth in order to prove that he could destroy more than his neighbours; and in his anxiety to defeat a rival, he destroyed not only his boats, his blankets and his oil, but sometimes even his wife and family as well. Without analysing these people it would be difficult to say in detail how they developed this singularly masochistic ideal. But we know that one of the ways of dealing with inner conflict and anxiety is to develop a neurotic character, of which there are many forms. Something both in their treatment of their children and in their innate disposition must favour a form of inner conflict most easily relieved by the development of a masochistic character; and the very prevalence of this character, by making it a source of pride rather than of shame, must make it still easier to acquire. The tribe by its treatment of its children causes a mental illness, and then provides a rudimentary cure.

There is no guarantee that a man's actual character will correspond with the group ideal of his tribe or nation. If it does not, he will be maladjusted and probably unhappy. But he can sometimes join a congenial sub-group. If he has a strong need for reparative work he can become a doctor. If he has a sense of inner poverty, which can only be relieved by constant acquisition, he can become a predatory type of businessman. If he can only deal with his unconscious anxieties by extreme asceticism he can become a monk. And if he is not happy in a community at peace he can join the Foreign Legion. Some societies tolerate a rich variety of sub-groups of this kind. Others, those who cannot endure divergent minorities within them, seek to mould their citizens in the image of one chosen type.

Since the group ideal and the group leader are both ultimately based on the unconscious image of the good father, we should expect a close connection between the two. To a limited extent the group ideal is modified to conform with the actual character of the leader. He sets the fashion in small matters if not in great ones. In the pre-war (1914-18) period, for example, there was an astonishing profusion of Kaiser Wilhelm moustaches in Germany and of Franz Joseph whiskers in Austria. Sometimes, indeed, he seems to transform the whole character of his group. But he cannot do more than bring out what is already latent in its members; and usually they refuse to follow him if he differs too much from their existing group ideal. Henry VI, for example, had he been an abbot would by his piety have won the devotion of his monks, but as a king he failed to live up to the bellicose standards of the time and was deposed to make way for the more aggressive Edward IV.

VARIETIES OF GROUP FORMATION

The group, therefore, must accept the main responsibility for its own character. If some of its members find this character too aggressive, or too acquisitive, or too ascetic, or marred by some other defect, they are unlikely to change much even by a successful revolution against its leaders, unless they can vary the conditions that form character in the early life of the child.

SUMMARY

To sum up the main points in the argument: The child forms an imaginary picture of his family, which is more or less distorted and which he preserves in unconscious fantasy throughout his life. This picture contains good parent figures to protect, to follow and to imitate, and bad parent figures against whom they have to be protected. Moreover, he tends to reproduce this pattern in the external world.

When a number of individuals find common symbols for the elements in this unconscious pattern they form a group. They have common values to defend, a common enemy, a common leader and a common standard of behaviour.

These four features recur in a great variety of group formations. The values a group defends may be its concrete possessions, its motherland or some abstract religious or political ideal. The enemy it defends them against may be another group, a suspected minority within the group, or some abstract but more or less personified principle of evil. Few, if any, groups have no real or imaginary enemies at all. The leader they follow may be of many types. Some groups have tried to do without him; but in a new form he nearly always returns. He may be an ancestral god, a priest or king who incarnates the god, or a hereditary monarch. He may be elected, appointed or self-imposed. And lastly the group ideal standard of behaviour, depending as it does on education, may take any of an infinite variety of different forms.

A group like an individual may be either pathological or sane. If the individuals who compose it have severe internal conflicts they are apt to create enemies for themselves by suspecting enmity where none at first existed or to become depressed if they fail to get the fanatical leadership they need. Or they may relieve their inner tension by a character formation corresponding to a neurotic group-ideal. But if, as a result of a favourable environment in early life, or of later treatment, the individuals who compose a group are at peace within themselves, the group itself, whatever its form, will certainly be sane.

14

Some Aspects of State and Character in Germany*

Introductory Note – This paper may still be of some interest as showing the attitude of people like myself just after the Second World War. But I now feel that, because of its selection of only a very few determinants out of a vast number of neglected and unknown ones, it is too oversimplified to be a reliable guide to action.

PREFACE

This paper, based as it is on some 'field work' in the Germany of 1946, may today in 1951 seem to have no more than an academic interest. I believe the results of work of this kind, incomplete and selective as they were, should be recorded, and from the point of view from which they were then obtained. But I also think they should be related to the very different practical problems that have arisen since. I have therefore added a postscript for this purpose.

It has always been known that character is the combined product of heredity and environment. But, before the psychoanalytic discoveries of Freud, almost the only environmental influences considered were the example and deliberate pressure of parents, teachers or companions. And as these often failed to produce their expected or desired results, the relative importance of the hereditary factors (which could always be postulated if only in the form of some long dormant but now reawakened trait) was much exaggerated. It was left to Freud to discover the enormous influence of those forgotten experiences of early childhood that so often far outweigh the influence of both heredity and deliberate education.

* From: *Psycho-analysis and Culture* (Wilbur and Munsterberger, Eds.). I.U.P., New York, 1951.

Roheim was the first to apply this discovery of Freud to anthropology. If the specific character of an individual is largely the result of specific experiences in infancy, the typical character of a people – previously dismissed as racial or hereditary – might well be the result of certain typical experiences in infancy. Roheim may have had such a hypothesis in mind before he began his field work in Australia, or it may have been suggested to him by the homogeneity of character and of infantile experience he found there. But, at any rate, it was a hypothesis he was the first to verify by detailed observations in contrasting cultures.

Whether his own influence on other anthropologists was direct or indirect, his work was soon followed by several studies – such as those by Margaret Mead and Ruth Benedict – in which the early environment of children was brought into relation with the general character and pattern of a culture. And before long, the old idea of so-called racial character as an innate ethnological endowment, like the type of hair or the colour of the skin, had been supplemented, if not replaced, by the newer concept of a 'social' character, mainly determined by the whole pattern of a culture and especially by that part of it that most impinged upon the children.

The newer point of view was well established among most sociologists by the time of the Second World War and affected the attitude of the Western democracies to the German problem.[1] Twice in a generation, Germany seemed to have forced war on peace-loving, and indeed pacifistic, neighbours, and the practical problem – as it seemed at the end of both World Wars – was how to ensure that she would not do so again. Of course the problem really had two aspects. It should have included the question, 'Why had the pacifist democracies allowed or perhaps provoked German aggression?' as well as the question 'Why was Germany aggressive?' But although there was some self-criticism, it was with the second question, and so with the criticism of others, that the democracies were most concerned. At the time of the First War, two alternative theories – one crudely biological and the other as crudely sociological – held the field, which attributed German aggres-

---

[1] The influence of social environment may indeed have been overstressed as a reaction against the extreme racialism of Nazi philosophy.

siveness, on the one hand to a Tartar strain dating from the time of Attila, and on the other to her feudal and autocratic institutions. Both theories can still claim much popular support; but, by the time of the Second War, the sociologists, who had always inclined to the sociological theory, no longer held it in its originally crude form. They still believed that German institutions had influenced the German character, but they no longer believed that a simple change in institutions would produce an immediate change in character. For, in the meantime, the importance of the early home environment had been more adequately assessed. The influence of institutions affecting adults was no longer conceived as direct and immediate, but as indirect – through its influence on the home – and therefore slow.

This brings me to the work of a branch of the Control Commission called the German Personnel Research Branch which operated in Germany in 1946. It owed its existence to the vision and energy of Professor Henry Dicks who made it an instrument for the testing and development of social theories as well as for their application. As its name implies, it was to be concerned with research into the nature and origin of character in Germany. But of course it would not have been these unless it had a practical function as well, and something should be said about this aspect before returning to its more purely scientific work.

It was divided into two sections, one dealing with social surveys and the other with the assessment and recommendation of individual Germans, mainly for high-grade posts within the administration the allied authorities were trying to remould. Thus both sections, while complementary in research, had separate practical functions to fulfil. That of the Assessment Centre was to give preference to persons of 'democratic' over persons of 'fascist' character.

The mere statement of this aim touches an issue of such importance that it cannot be passed over without some comment. This is the difference between the prevailing anthropological and the psycho-analytic concept of the norm. To the anthropologist, a normal individual is one who is well adjusted to the society he lives in, so that the same individual can be normal in one society and abnormal in another. And from this it follows that it would be meaningless to speak of degrees of normality as between societies themselves – except with reference to some purely arbitrary standard. Expressed in concepts of this kind, the aim of the Assessment Centre could be described as the replacement of officials who were perhaps 'normal' with respect to the culture they worked in by others who were 'normal' with respect to a very different culture. And, so long as we have no independent standard with which to assess these different norms, such replacement must seem a wholly arbitrary procedure – as arbitrary, for example, as would be the replacement of medicine men by Baptist ministers, or, for that matter, of Baptist ministers by medicine men.

But when the psycho-analytic concept of a normal individual is introduced, the appropriate analogy changes. Admittedly, the psycho-analytic concept is not easy to define precisely. But, at least, it is not that of an individual well adjusted to the society he lives in; for, if it were, we should have to conclude, for example, that paranoids were normal in a paranoid society. The concept of psychological normality or health is structurally more similar to that of physical normality or health. We do not regard a man with tuberculosis as normal or healthy if he lives in a tubercular society, nor should we do so even if this illness were universal. What exactly does constitute mental health may be best arrived at by first defining what we mean by mental illness. Perhaps as good a definition as any is that it is a state of mind in which feeling, and sometimes perception too, is disturbed by unconscious fantasy. If so, the basis of all mental illness could be compared with a hysterical defect of vision, which at least restricts, if it does not otherwise distort, the perception of psychic reality. Of course, on this definition, no one is entirely healthy – for no one's psychic vision is entirely free from blind spots. But we can still form the limiting concept of a mind free from such disturbances and define this as normal or healthy, or, what is the same thing, as being mature in the sense of being fully integrated. And when we have got so far, we shall be inclined to reverse the anthropologist's definition of a normal individual as one well adapted to the society he lives in, and to define a normal or 'healthy' society as one well adapted to, and favourable to the development of, normal or 'healthy' individuals.

Now without going into further details at this stage, no analyst could doubt that at least the extreme type of fascist character, with its obvious paranoid and manic traits, was less normal in the psycho-analytic sense than the more democratic type. For by this we understood a type of mind that, as the result of insight, had some understanding of, and therefore sympathy with, others and so treated them with consideration. The aim of the Assessment Centre was to fill some key posts in the new administration with persons who were in this sense healthier or more normal than those who had held them before. By so doing it hoped to contribute in some small degree to the development of a healthier society – for, if it could not directly influence the infantile situation, it could still create, as it were, pockets of environment in which normal persons could thrive. Such an aim may have been uncongenial to those whose primary concern was with the cure of individuals – for little could be done for rejected candidates who were often obviously in need of treatment. But at least it was therapeutic in the social sense and not arbitrarily political. Thus a better, though still an imperfect, analogy to its work than the replacement of medicine men by ministers would be the replacement of both by scientifically trained doctors or teachers.[1]

After this short apology for the Assessment Centre's practical aims, I will return to its methods and some of the results of its researches.

Its method was rather similar to that of a War Office Selection Board. It applied the usual tests and, among them, a long 'psychiatric interview'. This was originally conducted by Dicks himself, and then by Lt. Col. Brangham. But when both returned to England, I was asked to carry on this part of their work and did so for about five months, first alone and then with the help of Mrs Margot Hicklin. These interviews provided most of the data for the conclusions put forward in this paper.

Dicks had classified about a dozen character traits to look out for, but I soon became especially interested in one, which in fact entered into most of the others. This was the structure of the conscience, or rather the structures of two contrasting types of conscience.

[1] The analogy becomes a close one if insight be regarded as an important form of knowledge.

I should explain that most of our candidates had not been very active Nazis (who were at that time debarred from administrative employment anyhow), nor did they have the fanatical manic or paranoid character we should have expected to find in active Nazis. They were for the most part permanent civil servants who had achieved high rank in their profession, and had been well established in it, before the Nazi domination.

The two character groups I want to discuss here may be called 'authoritarians' and 'humanists'. The authoritarians seemed to me to be at least five times as numerous. They had all the traits associated with the strictest type of paternal superego. They were obsessionally painstaking and meticulous in their work and their sense of duty to authority outweighed whatever other moral feelings they had. In fact they often gave the impression of being unable to conceive of any morality other than the morality of unquestioning obedience. This attitude was vividly expressed by one candidate who described the growing sense of guilt he had had because he did question, and inwardly rebel against, the increasingly ruthless policy he was called upon, and therefore he felt it his duty, to support.

The humanists, members of the smaller group, were comparatively free from the domination of so strict a paternal superego and were much less obsessively concerned with the duty of unquestioning obedience to its external representatives. And for this reason, they were able to be much more conscious of the extent to which those positive feelings of love and concern for their fellows, which exist as one constituent in everyone, were being outraged by the state they served. They felt guilty, not because they had questioned its authority, but because they felt they had not opposed it enough.

The two groups clearly displayed two quite different kinds of guilt. If we did not make the distinction between these two kinds of guilt we should be tempted to explain the difference in reaction merely in terms of different external representatives of the superego, the one linked with an authoritarian and the other with a democratic ideology. But this would be to miss the essential point. Melanie Klein was the first to introduce a most important distinction between two kinds of anxiety – persecutory and depressive. There is no doubt that both enter into that complex feeling known as the sense of guilt. But they can enter into it in very different proportions. The more the internal superego is feared, the more the persecutory element predominates. But when the superego is less feared, the other depressive element, which tends to be evoked whenever the ego turns against or merely deserts any object of sympathy and love, can become conscious as the stronger feeling of the two. Now the authoritarians experienced a predominantly persecutory form of guilt, when they questioned the edicts of the external representative of a feared internal figure. The humanists, to whom Germany was the 'fatherland' no less than to the authoritarians, experienced some of this kind of guilt too, but in a much smaller degree. And because they experienced it in a much smaller degree, they were able to be conscious of a different, and this time predominantly depressive type of guilt at having failed, or been impotent, to protect the victims of a tyranny.

As was to be expected, the two types of conscience were clearly correlated with two different types of home. With a few exceptions to which I shall return, the authoritarians when speaking of their early background, which they did readily enough, spoke of their fathers with the most exaggerated respect. And to these fathers, to whom they had invariably succumbed often after remembered conflict, they gratefully attributed their own regard for discipline. It was sometimes also possible to catch a glimpse of earlier, directly oedipal conflicts, not merely for the possession of the mother, but also for her protection against a domestic autocrat. But these had ended in defeat and the acceptance of the father's view that mother was only good so long as she was subservient and that father was always in the right. And in such episodes it was not difficult to recognize the prototype of a later conflict with Nazi ideology, which so often began with a desire to side with the oppressed and ended with the conviction that the oppressed had been justly punished and that the Führer, who was too dangerous to defy, must be infallible.

The humanists, almost without exception, stressed the atypical nature of the homes they had been brought up in – homes with much more freedom for the children and much more equality between the parents. For this reason, they were much less dominated by the stricter kind of paternal superego represented by the German state, and were therefore much less obliged by fear of conflict with it to repress their sympathy for its oppressed opponents. They were in fact much more mature, integrated and healthy people.[1]

All this was so much in accord with psycho-analytic experience that it may seem hardly worth recording. Indeed, if anything was surprising, it was that there seemed to be so few exceptions. Since the introjected father imago itself contains much of the child's own aggression projected into it, I should have expected to find more cases of ferocious superegos in persons whose actual fathers had been kind and easygoing. But I very seldom found them. Of course there must always have been some exaggeration of this kind. But, as far as I could see, the main structure of the paternal superego in its final form as it had been since the end of the oedipal period, was seldom a gross exaggeration of the actual father.

This does not of course imply that no relics of more ferocious and unrealistic superegos belonging to the earliest periods of infancy could be found in persons whose actual parents had been kind and understanding. That such relics in fact existed provides part of the explanation of another correlation. While most of the members of authoritarian professions, such as the army and the civil service, were also authoritarian in character, most of the humanists were to be found in the more liberal and independent professions. In part this was because each had tended to choose a career congenial to his character. But some had been thrust into an uncongenial occupation and often seemed to have been modified by it. Now, as far as I could see, such modifications were more conspicuous in the authoritarian than in the humanist direction: those who had come from patriarchal homes and later had external independence thrust upon them did not seem to have gained much inner freedom. But a good deal of such freedom, together with the humanism associated with it, seemed to have been lost by those who had once had it and then been subject for years to the influence of an authoritarian profession. To explain this last result, I think we must assume three stages of development, of which

---

[1] A disturbance of the introjective-projective mechanisms on which sympathy is based may be compared to a defect of vision. It may be general or specific. Insight into others may be generally 'myopic', or specifically disturbed by 'blind spots'.

STATE AND CHARACTER IN GERMANY

only the last two can be detected without a deep analysis. In the first stage, which has been stressed by Melanie Klein as common to all children, a superego with many ferocious and quite unrealistic traits was formed by the projection and reintrojection of the child's own aggressiveness. In the second this unrealistic superego was submerged rather than replaced by a more realistic one based to a great extent on the actual character of tolerant and kindly parents. And in the third, the earlier and more ferocious superego was re-awakened by the prolonged influence of an authoritarian environment.

The developmental histories of those individuals whose character, as originally laid down in their home environment, had or had not been modified by their professional environment seemed to me to be of great sociological significance. For they give some indication of the extent to which forces operating from without, or from above, can or cannot modify the character of a people.

To avoid the accusation of having grossly over-simplified the course of events in the history of an actual nation, I will illustrate my point by what does not claim to be more than an imaginary example. Suppose an isolated people to be at first in a state of stable equilibrium with very little change in either character or social structure. They are divided into two casts or classes: a large class of independent peasant farmers and a small class of civil and military officials who owe their allegiance to a king. In the homes of the peasants, economic and other responsibilities are divided fairly equally between the parents and there is less of that sense of masculine superiority which is conspicuous in the homes of the officials, where the prestige of the father is more stressed and a stricter type of patriarchal discipline is more rigidly enforced. So on the whole the children of the officials develop a stricter type of paternal superego and become more authoritarian in character as did their fathers and grandfathers before them. (From the psychoanalytic point of view, we can also say that the official classes are less 'normal' or 'healthy', not only because there is in fact a higher incidence of neurosis among them, but also because their less sympathetic and more obsessively disciplined character is the result of a greater fear of persecution by a less realistic, internal figure.) Now when, as nearly always happens among this imaginary people, the sons of farmers become farmers, and the sons of officials become officials, each finds the environment which is on the whole most congenial to himself. His character is confirmed, not modified, by it; and when he marries he recreates for his children the same sort of home environment as he enjoyed or suffered in his own childhood. In other words, he completes the circle of forces which preserves the stability of his culture.[1]

Now suppose that a king of unusually dynamic and despotic personality comes to the throne and not only tightens the discipline of the civil and military services, but also greatly extends them. Then a large number of individuals of the farmer cast, who may be attracted by what looks like opportunity, will find themselves in service professions which are more authoritarian than is congenial to their more independent characters. If there were no submerged traces of the stricter type of superego within themselves, the authoritarian profession would remain uncongenial and would not modify their character. But such traces, dating from the early persecutory position of infancy, are always there and may be reawakened. So in the end the character may be modified until the profession becomes congenial. If the characters of many individuals become more authoritarian in this way, we can hardly doubt that the home atmosphere they create for their own children will be affected. This too will tend to become more authoritarian; and the children when they grow up will be better adapted to an authoritarian profession from the beginning. It will be more congenial to them, so that they will maintain its nature and probably modify it still further in the authoritarian direction. In other words, the sequence of forces that maintained stability will no longer follow precisely the same tracks in each new generation. The old circle of forces will have become a helix or spiral.

[1] That under such conditions character tends to be transmitted from generation to generation will be readily admitted. But apart from individual exceptions, there often also seems to be a tendency for character to oscillate between each generation within a given family. When a class as a whole is considered, these oscillations are seldom apparent because they cancel each other out. But the swing between periods of relative puritanism and periods of relative licentiousness, which has been a feature of our own social history, may be in part the result of such oscillations being approximately in phase.

Suppose further that after some generations of authoritarian development, the political structure of the state is again changed and becomes democratic, and as the result not of any general pressure from below but of some external influence. There are certain to be a minority who will find this change congenial. These will on the whole be those whose home background has been humanist rather than authoritarian and who, as the result of the more liberal social environment, will be more likely to remain humanist in character. But the majority, at least of the official classes, will feel lost without the external counterpart of the stricter type of superego they have acquired in childhood. The precise effect on them may be very varied, but at least the change will have come too late in life to enable them to become psychically mature. They are likely to give the impression of being neurotically undisciplined rather than capable of freedom; and, perhaps after an unsatisfying orgy of artificial independence, they may be ready to welcome the return of some non-democratic system that offers an external discipline.

I do not in the least suggest that the above imaginary example offers an exact parallel to what happened in Germany from the time of Frederick the Great (or his father) to the time of Hitler. Still less do I wish to fall into the facile error of making the Hohenzollerns the only scapegoat. The forces involved in the real sequence of historical changes must have been vastly more numerous and complicated. But I do suggest that it provides a rough parallel to the operation of one or two of the more important of these forces. The imaginary society may be regarded as an enormously over-simplified map which stresses a real distinction between the official classes in Germany and the rest – for both the character and the home background of these classes did seem on the whole to be markedly more authoritarian than among most other sections of the people. And a great expansion of these classes from the time of Frederick the Great (when society was still favourable to the development of independent humanists like Goethe) to the time of William II did take place, and largely under the direct influence of the Prussian court. That this expansion, and the tightening of discipline accompanying it, could have influenced the German character is suggested by the case histories of individuals whose characters did seem to have been modified by authoritarian professions at first uncongenial to them, and who could hardly fail to pass on some of the modification to their children at an earlier age. The map, or model, depicts such a change as having taken place, and in this way. It also suggests a reason why the change should be more easy to produce than to reverse. In both respects it does no more than provide a possible explanation for what was widely believed by many of the most intelligent of the German candidates at the Assessment Centre. They believed that the Prussian Monarchy, and the philosophy that supported the Prussian State Ideal, had helped to form an authoritarian character which was well adapted to the autocratic system of the Hohenzollerns. And they believed that an inability to adjust this character to the liberalism of the Weimar Republic was the predisposing – though not the precipitating – cause of the rapid spread of fascism. Such beliefs seem plausible and were held as much by the apologists as by the critics of the Prussian system. But they must remain a little suspect until the links have been filled in between the supposed first cause and its apparently remote effect. The map, or model, by suggesting a way in which some of these links could have been filled in, increases the plausibility of these beliefs.

A specific and serious limitation of the model is that it includes no parallel to the development of the fascist as distinct from the authoritarian character. The one is often thought to be only an extreme version of the other, and this is perhaps what the German Personnel Research Branch expected to find when it first went to Germany. But as far as I could judge from the few of them I saw, the typical fascist or Nazi was more often the product of a disturbed or broken than of a patriarchal home. He was born just before, or during the First World War, and brought up by a mother who had become neurotic in the absence of her husband who, as often as not, never would return. So he developed the kind of instability that in another culture might have made him a delinquent – especially in the then prevalent conditions of widespread unemployment. This indeed is in a sense exactly what he did become, and with unusual ease because the Nazis institutionalized delinquency in pursuit of their political ideals.

What is at first sight surprising is not that so many people of this type should have developed after the First World War, nor that they should be canalized into the Nazi party by unemployment and the humiliation of defeat, but that the majority who were not fascist in temperament should have so easily surrendered to them. This can be explained only by the unsatisfied craving for leadership among the rest. Hitler spoke with an authority he had been careful to legitimize, and the authoritarians of the old order, who did not like his party, nevertheless joined it and obeyed. Moreover, he offered satisfaction for another craving of those who surrender their own freedom: the craving for vicarious power in identification with the all-powerful father state.

In conclusion I should like to make two general points.

The first concerns the influence of individuals, especially of those described by Hegel as *'welthistorische'*. The court historians of the past wrote as if the events described were determined solely by the acts of kings, statesmen and generals. These were the players and the rest exerted no independent influence. Then, in revolt against this disdainful attitude, social historians began to go to the opposite extreme. The people determined everything; the kings, the statesmen and the generals became their pawns, chosen or forced to express their latent but evolving purpose.[1] The truth, I think, lies somewhere between these two extremes. Since each generation, if left to itself, tends to reproduce the same home environment that formed its character, the character of any national group tends to be perpetuated. But an individual with great political authority can bring about changes in the external environment which may indirectly influence character; and, if his prestige is equal to his power, his own aspirations or ideals, and something of his character as well, may be widely 'introjected'. In both these ways, he may effect changes in the character of the group which, if only superficial among adults, may influence their homes and so become more deep-seated in their children.

It is not only widely believed, but seems probable on psychoanalytic grounds, that Frederick the Great and his father had

[1] It is worth noting that those who most firmly deny the influence of leaders, or of leading groups or classes, on social evolution seem often to be the most anxious to exonerate the people from any responsibility for whatever social calamities occur. But this, of course, is only an example of the more general rule that everyone tends to be biased by his own identifications.

this kind of influence and were partly responsible for the wide prevalence of the authoritarian character in Germany. (That this belief may be held more firmly because it provides a scapegoat for war guilt – because, like the myth of original sin, it projects guilt backwards onto a Primal Father – does not disprove its truth.)

But it would be wrong, I think, to suppose that the authoritarian character demanded a Hitler to fill the void left by the Hohenzollerns. It did not find him congenial. But, by its demand for a leader of some kind, it enabled Hitler to consolidate his power. In this sense only was it responsible for him. Had his system endured, he would perhaps have also succeeded in consolidating a further shift in character, this time from the authoritarian to the fascist type. What he actually did was to disrupt more families than anyone has done before with characterological effects on future generations that no one can foresee. But these will be the result of his failure and not of his intentions.

The last remaining point concerns the direction in which such changes are more easily made. What I saw in Germany of those whose occupation had been at first uncongenial suggested that the change in the authoritarian direction was easier to make than to reverse. And as what I have described, too vaguely perhaps as the 'humanist', 'democratic' or what used to be called the 'liberal' character was more integrated, mature and therefore healthy, the easier change to make was in the direction of illness. There can be no doubt that the rather different changes resulting from the whole-scale disturbance of family life in both World Wars was in this direction too. There is nothing here which would not be expected on general grounds; for we know that it is easier to cause a deterioration in those who are comparatively healthy by exposing them to the stresses of an unfavourable environment than it is to cure those who are already ill merely by improving their environment. And it is still easier, by changing the social environments of adults in one direction or another, to injure than to improve the home environment they create for their children. It can be made possible or impossible for them to create favourable homes; they cannot be made to create them.

So the imposition of a 'bad' society – one ill-adapted to

'normal' individuals – might be expected to lower the mental health of a people, and to fix it at this lower level in two generations. But, as far as can be seen, we have no right to expect that a reverse change would do more than permit the slower growth, through several generations, of maturity and health. In the long history of civilization, the mental health and maturity of peoples, and the political structure most favourable to it, may have been subject to many slow upward movements, each culminating perhaps in a period of brilliant output, and each followed by a much more rapid fall. It is to be hoped that the new science of psychoanalytic anthropology, which owes so much to Roheim's pioneering work, may eventually provide us with the knowledge needed to maintain such upward movements and to reduce the probability of falls.

POSTSCRIPT

The above analysis and attempted derivation of some aspects of German character was, as I have explained, based on observations made in Germany in 1946. At that time they also seemed relevant to a major problem of international security. This problem, as I have tried to indicate, was not merely the protection of our own form of society against the possible recrudescence of a hostile form. It was the protection of a liberal–democratic form which, with all its imperfections, did provide a more favourable environment for the development of integrated, mature and normal character than its fascist competitor. But now, in 1950, the threat comes from a different source. I feel, therefore, that I cannot take leave of the German question without adding a word to bring it up to date – especially as this will enable me to end on a rather more constructive note.

To do so, I must first go back to another observation of 1946. This was the obvious manifestation, if only in the over-emphasis of its denial, of a widespread sense of collective guilt of a genuinely depressive kind. It was quite apparent, behind a truculent defence which often easily collapsed, even in the most hardened authoritarians and fascists. Of course it had been brought nearer to the surface by failure. But it was not created by failure and would have been stronger, though less conscious, in success. There could be no doubt that the tragedy of such men was that they felt they had devoted their aggressiveness, and with a tenacious heroism, to the defence of something which in their inmost hearts they themselves felt to be mainly sinister and evil. It was therefore often of great therapeutic importance to them as individuals – and probably also for the future of their society – to be allowed to participate in the protection of what they could feel, both consciously and unconsciously, to be a better object. The idea of Western culture threatened from without had already begun to play the rôle of an object of this kind, and in the idea of its defence they had begun to seek an outlet for an unconscious reparative impulse. But there was also a tendency to turn against these new ideas in moods of fresh despair. In other words, very many Germans in 1946 were in a depressive phase which could be succeeded either by an impulse to constructive reparation or, if this failed, by a renewed paranoidal attack on the objects they had injured. Much, therefore, depends on whether, and how soon, they can feel allowed to share in the defence of these objects with other Western nations.

15
Towards a Rational Attitude to Crime*

The official attitude to crime, that is, the attitude implemented in the actual treatment of criminals, has undergone enormous changes in the last hundred years. Some people think the movement has gone too far; others that it has not gone far enough. It has certainly been a movement towards greater humanity. Has it also been a movement towards greater rationality? Or to make the question more comprehensive: what is a rational attitude to crime?

First we must be clear about the sense in which any attitude may be described as rational or not. A belief is rational if it is probable upon the evidence. But an attitude – for example about sentences, that they 'should be' stiffer (or milder) – is not the same as a belief; it is a desire at most conditioned by a belief – for example, that stiffer (or milder) sentences diminish crime. So it can be rational only in a derivative sense: namely, when it is conditioned by beliefs and when these are themselves rational.

We all know that attitudes are often not rational, but merely 'rationalized'. This is the case if the belief that stiffer (or milder) sentences diminish crime is held without evidence to justify an attitude based only on vindictiveness (or sentimentality). What is less obvious is that the same mechanism, which operates so clearly in this example, may operate again at deeper layers of the mind. If we have an impulse which expresses feelings we do not like to admit, we become over-ready to believe it to be merely instrumental to some more acceptable desire. In other words we embrace an irrational belief about the external world (that the impulse is instrumental to this acceptable desire) in order to maintain a false one about ourselves (that we do not have these unacceptable feelings). But at the next level of

* Pamphlet: *The Howard League for Penal Reform*, London, 1953.

analysis, we must expect to find that these feelings (of vindictiveness or sentimentality), which may not be so very deeply hidden, are in turn only there as defences against the acceptance of some still more unpalatable fact in our inner world of 'psychic reality'.

Once we are prepared for the discovery of such determinants, we shall have no great difficulty, in the case before us, in guessing where to begin our search. For irrational attitudes to crime and punishment must surely spring from the various defences everyone in varying degrees erects against his own unconscious sense of guilt.

At least there can be no doubt that this is true of extreme vindictiveness towards criminals, the origin of which is exposed in the parable of the mote and the beam, and was thus rediscovered, rather than discovered, by Freud. We can feel guilty about the predatory and sadistic impulses in ourselves, yet admit their existence. Or we can falsely deny that we have them, and be over ready to exaggerate and hate them in others – especially if these others arouse our unconscious envy by their freedom from the moral restraints we impose upon ourselves. So it is the denial and projection of something that exists in us – of part of our 'psychic reality' – which is the 'false belief' that conditions an irrational attitude of extreme vindictiveness towards those who manifest our latent defects.

The opposite attitude of extreme sentimentality may seem more rational by contrast. But it too needs examination. People who have it do not deny that they are potential sinners. But I suspect that they cannot easily tolerate the element of irreparability in regretted actions. Perhaps, in identification with the criminal, they cannot bear what they feel to be his load of guilt, and wish, by diminishing the legal punishment, somehow to make the crime less real. Or, for the same reason, they transfer the blame to his heredity or environment and make him entirely innocent. If so, they too deny reality – the reality of the guilt he does at least unconsciously feel.[1]

These and many other irrational attitudes could of course be

---

[1] Where over-sentimentality passes into indignation at the idea of punishment, the reformer may share the criminal's revolt against authority of any kind because he is at war with an over-strict conscience (superego) within himself.

TOWARDS A RATIONAL ATTITUDE TO CRIME

studied in much greater detail. But we are primarily concerned to discover what attitude could now be classed as rational. We have defined it as being based only on such beliefs as are probable on the evidence available. Thus what is rational today may not always remain so in the light of future knowledge. But at least we know enough to amend some former views.

As far as psychological knowledge is concerned, our attitude to a crime and its punishment will be rational if we can correctly imagine, and understand the origin, so far as this can now be inferred, of the feelings of everyone involved in it. A condition of this is that we should understand our own.

To begin with the victim of a crime (or anyone closely associated with him): his resentment and wish to retaliate was always dismissed as a primary, unanalysable response which, if consistent with the Sermon on the Mount, needed no explanation in itself. We now know, however, that some part of it is not so primary, but results from an identification of the criminal with past bogey figures, 'persecutory objects', of the infantile unconscious, which are themselves formed by the 'projection' of aggressive impulses. Moreover, there is always some unconscious relic of the child's feeling that every injury he suffers is inflicted on him by them as a punishment for his own misdeeds. So, paradoxically enough, a crime may arouse latent guilt in the victim, who will then seek to restore his sense of innocence by transferring the 'punishment' to the person who has inflicted it.[1]

The intuitive sensing of such elements – never wholly absent – has led to the accepted rule that no man should be judge in his own cause. And so far as he senses them himself, he will indeed prefer to leave it in the hands of a judge whom he feels to be impartial.

For reasons of this kind, the primary response to injury, which is perhaps no more than a self-preserving outburst of aggression, is developed into a prolonged anger that festers like a sore if denied all satisfaction. But for the same reasons, its intensity and duration depend less on the nature of the injury than on the

---

[1] This need not prevent them from unconsciously feeling responsible for it; for, by a process of 'projective identification' people commonly regard those they love, especially their children, as external bits of themselves.

state of mind attributed to the injurer. If he is believed to have become penitent, that is, if he will accept the guilt, he will tend to be forgiven.

It should not be forgotten that there are other innocent victims – if not of the crime itself at least of its consequences. These are the criminal's relations who really share his punishment without participating in his crime.[1] And if they are so often ignored in discussions of the subject, this can only be because we do not wish to remember what we inflict upon them.

Turning to the criminal himself, what is most relevant to understand about him is the degree of his capacity for consciously experiencing the moral feelings of 'normal' people. By normal I do not mean average but integrated, that is, without dissociated elements. No-one can claim to be wholly normal in this sense. The concept is of a limit of mental health to which we more or less approximate. It is obvious that the capacity for moral feeling varies very widely. Some people are incapable of consciously experiencing a sense of guilt at all. This is because it has become dissociated, so that in the above sense they are very far from normal. They are unable to feel consciously that what they do is 'wrong', though of course they nearly always know it to be illegal – an important distinction which seems to have become blurred in recent case law.[2] They may again be subdivided into those who are, and those who are not, capable of anticipating punishment, and, what is not the same, into those who are and those who are not capable of being deterred by it. For, while some are incapable of imagining unpleasant consequences, others both fear and seek them because of an unconscious sense of guilt which precedes and often causes the actual punished crime.

Of course, the above main group of those incapable of normal moral feelings are not separated sharply from their fellows. There are innumerable gradations between a complete dissociation of the sense of guilt and a full capacity to experience it, and so to be deterred by its anticipation.

---

[1] See footnote 1 p. 247.
[2] A person who can make no distinction between what is felt to be wrong and what he knows to be illegal is without a conscious conscience and in this sense 'morally insane'.

Not only the quantity, but also the quality, of the guilt feelings of different people differ very widely. The sense of guilt is not an elementary feeling but a compound of at least two – one 'persecutory' and the other 'depressive' – one or other of which may markedly predominate. Anyone with a 'persecutory conscience', as its name implies, fears retaliation from an authority within himself, his 'superego'. As he tends to identify external authority with it, he is usually law-abiding – sometimes to an obsessional degree. But there are exceptions. The internal authority may have different laws which can be kept only by breaking the external ones. Or, the strain of internal persecution may be so great that – as in the case of some of those not even conscious of a conscience – the substitution of an external punishment may be sought as a relief.[1]

The persecutory conscience in its law-abiding form is very common, especially in authoritarian societies. But as it is the expression of a pronounced split between the ego and a ferocious superego – itself formed by the projection of much of the ego's disowned aggression – it is not clinically normal.

The other type of conscience, as we know, is that in which the capacity for depressive guilt predominates. The word depression in ordinary speech is often understood to mean self-pity. But self-regarding sentiments are perhaps always secondary derivatives of affects towards external objects, which later become internalized. At least the self-reproaches of melancholia have been shown by Freud to result from an identification with a disappointing, and so discarded, love object.[2] And now analysts – especially those influenced by the first child-analyst, Melanie Klein, to whom we owe most of our later knowledge of the origin

---

[1] Those who unconsciously (or even consciously) seek external punishment as a relief from inner persecution may also seek it as a means of controlling ungovernable impulses in themselves. The existence of this motive, which often amounts to a masochistic craving (e.g., to have the devil beaten out), may seem to justify a return to the more sadistic severity of earlier justice. The masochist certainly despises softness; and sadistic severity may satisfy him for a time. But his craving for punishment is likely to return; since he is unable to find permanent satisfaction in anything that does not annihilate what at bottom he regards as his 'bad self'. Unfortunately, the 'good' and the 'bad' self share the same body, so that it is impossible to kill one and leave the other still alive.

[2] A good example, quoted by Abraham, was of a woman who accused herself of being a thief after becoming disillusioned about her father who was really caught stealing.

of such conditions – use the word depression primarily to connote a sense of despair at having done irreparable damage to a loved object. It is a response to unconscious aggressive impulses as well as to acts; and to the extent to which it results from an unconscious equation of the two, it is disproportionate (or irrational) and can be analysed away. But the capacity to feel it consciously, without exaggeration or denial, is one of the basic characteristics of a normal integrated mind. So only such offenders as are capable of conscious depression, not merely on their own behalf, but on behalf of those they have intentionally injured, can be classed as clinically normal. And since the anticipation of these feelings, in people capable of having them, is the most effective deterrent against crime, normal offenders are not very common.[1] But ordinary normal people may of course have lapses if subject to abnormal strains.

There remain two groups of persons who are affected, though less directly, by a crime and its punishment. They are the general public and other potential criminals.

The so-called public attitude might be defined as the average attitude of the public's more vocal members. But this ignores an important distinction between their attitudes as detached individuals and their attitudes when they feel themselves to be members of a group of good citizens faced by crime. The first is more varied, sophisticated and tolerant. For, whenever individuals feel themselves to be formed into a group, by being together in one place for one purpose, or merely by being addressed as a collectivity by a newspaper, extremely primitive attitudes tend to emerge.[2] It is often said, with truth, that the group of good citizens treat the criminal as a scapegoat. But I think that over and above the collective projection into him of their own 'bad selves', the situation inevitably arouses some of the still more primitive sadistic excitements of the hunting pack. So the individual in the crowd demands this pleasure, which he might blush at admitting when he is alone, and if, as a member of a crowd, he gets none of it from the courts in the long drawn

---

[1] To the rule that normal people are unlikely to commit crimes, I can think of only two exceptions: they might do so either if they were members of a submerged group which is in reality badly treated by society, or where the law makes 'criminal' what is not normally felt to be immoral.

[2] These have been especially studied by Dr Wilfred Bion.

out 'hunt' of conviction and sentence, he might conceivably demand a reversion to lynch law.

But although the public when feeling collectively may demand these things, their real need is for protection. So the extent to which 'making an example' deters the same and other potential criminals is of much more realistic importance to them. From what has been said, this is not so easy to determine. Many people – especially those who in any case tend to be law-abiding – are of course deterred. But some, those with a strong unconscious need for punishment, are positively enticed by the promise of increased severity; and others are incapable of anticipating it. We should remember, too, that criminals form a sub-group, the solidarity of which may sometimes be increased by punishment – especially as they often idealize what seems to them to be heroic.

From even so sketchy a review of the psychology of the parties concerned with crime and its punishment, or treatment, at least one obvious conclusion stands out. The primary aim of a rational attitude – that is, one based on an understanding of their several points of view – must be the 'repentance' of the criminal. For this assuages the victim of the offence, as well as being a sign of the offender's 'cure', that is, the reintegration of his dissociated conscience. And, although by itself it may disappoint the public's craving for a circus spectacle, it best helps to preserve their safety.

But unfortunately this is easier said than done. The tragedy of so many offenders is that the psychic injuries they have suffered in childhood have left them abnormal in this one point. It is precisely because their capacity to care for, and so to respect the interests of, others is so restricted that they prey upon their fellows. And for the same reason they cannot easily regret the injuries they cause. Though responsible in the sense that they consciously choose what 'normal' people call evil, they choose it because they are the victims of a moral disease. Once the disease is recognized as such, those who suffer from it begin to be thought of, less as mere enemies, than as people needing help. And if such help were quickly curative, there is no doubt that this therapeutic attitude would soon predominate. But unfortunately the disease is peculiarly difficult to cure and the therapy so far available is quite inadequate, both in quantity and quality, to give effective help to more than a small fraction of those who need it.

So for the time being, and until our therapy becomes more adequate, it is not easy to propose any radical alternative to the existing official attitude, itself a compromise of several conflicting ones. The criminal had declared war on society; and society, through the medium of all the forces of the law, treats him as an enemy, and enjoys retaliating on him when it can. Then, whether he is bound over on probation or goes to prison, attempts are made to help his return to a more normal frame of mind. I do not believe that punishment in itself is often curative.[1] Indeed, it would seem more likely to harden than to melt a frozen conscience; and, as a deterrent, it is double edged. The most it does with certainty is to isolate a few of society's enemies for a time. But an originally accidental concomitant of punishment by prison sentence is the opportunity it gives for the therapist, following the priest, to get in touch with these people who are enemies only because they are morally ill. So long as the therapist's technique falls short of the magnitude of his task, the rest of society can hardly be expected to forego its satisfaction in the punishment of crime, for the sake of those who cannot yet be helped to respond to generosity. But as his technique improves – as it will with increasing knowledge – cure rather than punishment will tend to become acknowledged as the overriding aim.

Postscript (1977) – Where the crime is of a purely destructive nature the chief motive is likely to have been envy, either conscious or unconscious. Envy seems to be curable only when it is either delusional – that is, for assets the victim is falsely imagined to possess – or unconscious, in which case making it conscious brings it under the influence of such conscious generous impulses as there may be. But primary envy is thought to be innate and therefore incurable, although Melanie Klein thought that its virulence might be attenuated.

---

[1] It has been argued that punishment might be more curative if it included some compulsory reparation to the victim. Certainly 'cure' involves the awakening of a desire for reparation, so that punishments which exclude the possibility of reparation discourage, and may prevent, recovery. But I am not sure how far making people do what they ought to want to do helps them to want to do it.

16

The Anthropological and the Psychoanalytic Concept of the Norm*

Any major new idea in one branch of science is nearly always fertile in many other branches too. But just because it is so potent, it seldom escapes the fate of being occasionally fertile in fields where it is not appropriate. So, for example, the nineteenth-century idea of evolution contributed in no small measure to the crude philosophy of twentieth-century militarism – a bastard Titan, by Darwin out of Hegel, which perhaps both parents would have indignantly repudiated.

One of the major new ideas of the twentieth century is that of relativity in physics. It has certainly been fertile in other fields in which perhaps it too has sometimes been applied without enough discrimination.

The application to be considered here is that which has led to a theory of social, and in particular ethical, relativity (Westermarck, 1932). Often the opposite and older view, which assumed the existence of some absolute standard or norm of attitude or behaviour, is now felt to be not only false but illogical. For, just as it was once assumed that an absolute, or unique frame of reference not only did, but must, exist in physics, so now it is often assumed that such a frame not only does not, but cannot, exist in either physics or sociology.

But so far as this conclusion is based on the analogy of physics, it is important to remember that Einstein's theory of relativity was first developed to explain the results of a negative experiment. If Michaelson and Morley had found, as they expected, that there was a difference between the velocity of light moving in one direction and that of light moving in another, they would have had evidence of the unique frame of reference which had always been assumed. Thus there was

* *Psycho-analysis and the Social Sciences*, vol. IV, 1953.

nothing illogical in the assumption that a unique frame existed: it might have been discovered. But it was not, and Einstein abandoned the assumption that there was one.

What the analogy of physics does teach us, therefore, is not that absolute standards in sociology cannot exist – an assumption that bars the way to any further enquiry – but that we ought not to make any *a priori* assumptions about them. So with a more open mind we can again approach the problem of whether, and in what sense, absolute standards can be found and usefully employed in sociology.

We all begin with an uncritical acceptance of what is approved in our own culture as an absolute norm of reference, and so regard the attitude or behaviour of typical members of other cultures as deviations to be pitied or condemned. Except that closer acquaintance bred a more tolerant superiority, this was also the standpoint of nineteenth-century explorers; and the comparative anthropologists of that period, who for the most part worked in libraries at home, do not seem to have departed much from it.

That anthropologists no longer occupy this standpoint may be the result of at least two factors neither of which might have been alone decisive. For, while intensive field work has increased their insight and capacity to identify themselves in thought with people of very different cultures, they might have retained their sense of superiority if there had not at the same time been a widespread internal collapse of many previously unquestioned values in their own society. At any rate their standard ceased to be a fixed one, and the new idea from physics seemed aptly to express, and perhaps to rationalize, this change. The existence of any absolute norm of attitude or behaviour was denied, and a doctrine of cultural, including ethical, relativity proclaimed.

So far as our old parochial standpoint was based on the assumption that what is approved by us must be approved by others, its abandonment represents a clear advance on understanding. At least at the conscious level, others do not accept but disobey our code; they accept and obey a different one of their own. Moreover, so far as we can find nothing unique about our code except its cultural distance from theirs, the problem of pin-pointing it is strictly analogous to the problem

THE CONCEPT OF THE NORM

of pin-pointing the position of the earth, which can be determined only with respect to other sidereal bodies and not with respect to a non-existent aether.

Nevertheless, this relativist point of view is by no means wholly satisfying – though for different reasons – to at least two groups of people: missionaries and psycho-analysts. For both seem to believe in some standard that is absolute, or at least independent of the arbitrary choice of some specific culture. To the missionaries this standard is God, and they believe that he exists. To the psycho-analysts, it is a vaguer concept they call mental health.

The difference of viewpoint between most anthropologists and most psycho-analysts is especially apparent in the different meanings they attach to the word 'normality'. To the anthropologist, a normal person is one who is well adapted to the society of which he is a member and who finds its culture congenial. This of course is a relative norm, applicable only to an individual with respect to his society and culture. And those who use it would probably dismiss as meaningless any question about whether the society itself was normal. To the analyst, however, people can be normal even if they are maladjusted to the particular society they live in and dislike its culture. Moreover, if the analyst's norm for individuals is really independent of their society, its meaning can be extended and that society defined as normal which is congenial to normal individuals.

To this of course the anthropologist has his own reply. He does not believe that the analytic concept of the norm is really independent. He suspects that analysts have taken it 'unconsciously' from their society and culture; in short, that they have never got beyond the naive parochialism we all begin with.

The accusation is a serious one, and must be taken seriously. It compels us to examine the way in which we have in fact arrived at our standard of normality or mental health.

This standard is something we have developed gradually. It is more precise and also narrower than it was fifty years ago; but it is still by no means as precise as we should like, and, even if we have a fairly clear idea of it, we may be dissatisfied with our attempts to formulate it in words. Fifty years ago, anyone free from gross hysterical, obsessional or psychotic symptoms would have been classed as mentally normal. But people came for treatment for much more nebulous complaints, such as a sense of frustration in life or because they felt unhappy. Freud's own definition, which excluded such cases as well as those with more clear-cut symptoms, equated the normal with a full and uninhibited capacity for both work and pleasure. But this standard is not quite independent of the social setting. It presupposes at least a tolerable environment for the person concerned. So strictly speaking, it should perhaps be used more as a test, than as a definition, of normality. And this is probably all that Freud intended it to be.

We may get further if, for the moment, we divert our enquiry from the concept of normality or health to its opposite, that of abnormality or illness. For the only reason why the concept of health has been narrowed is because the concept of illness – which is the analyst's primary concern – has been so much widened.

In logic, of course, the definition of a concept is no more than a rule about the use of a word. It is not a proposition, and conveys no knowledge. Yet there is a sense in which the definitions of science epitomize accumulated knowledge. They hold it, as it were, in a latent form ready to be brought out at will by the assertion that something corresponding to them exists. Thus, for example, a class of animals with some common feature is first named, then other common features are discovered, and in time these come to be regarded as part of the definition of the class. The resulting concept of an animal with such and such a size and shape and habits says nothing in itself; for it may refer to an object of mythology. But as soon as we assert that such an animal exists we convey a good deal of detailed knowledge. In much the same way, the present analytic concept of illness epitomizes the accumulated discoveries of fifty years' research.

Put schematically, the sequence is as follows: we began with a list of symptoms, that is, with a definition by enumeration. We discovered some of the mechanisms that brought about these symptoms, and, in the process, found ourselves redefining and reclassifying illness in terms of the mechanisms that caused it. We then found that the same mechanisms could give rise to many traits of character not previously on the list of symptoms but which now had to be added to it. In this way the concept of the pathological was steadily enlarged, and that of the normal correspondingly narrowed. Indeed, if we were consistent we should admit that the analytic norm is now that of a limit of freedom from pathological mechanisms and symptoms – a limit which can never be achieved in practice.

Such a result must at first sight seem pedantic. If these mechanisms are found in a person who would have previously been classed as quite normal, why cannot we regard him as normal so long as they are present in him only in a slight degree? For practical purposes, this of course is exactly what we do. We are content if they are sufficiently diminished in a patient to allow him success and happiness in life, and we set no higher standard for ourselves. So the standard that satisfies us in practice is a quantitative one depending not on the presence or absence of these mechanisms but on the extent to which they operate. And this of course would have to satisfy us in theory too if no qualitative distinction could be found.

But, although we do regard any individual as normal, in the practical sense, in whom these mechanisms operate only in a slight degree, we continue to regard the mechanisms themselves as pathological. So there is an inherent paradox in our practical definition, which takes us back again from the individual to the mechanisms that operate in him. Why do we label some of these as pathological? Merely because if they operate with a high degree of intensity they do give rise to symptoms? Or because of some peculiarity in themselves? And when we ask this question we begin to see the answer: because they all involve some functional disturbance in the capacity for rational thought.

This is a general proposition which I think every analyst would accept. But it is not easy to prove it in detail, or even to say exactly what it means. For to do so we must be able to form a picture of the way in which the function of reason develops and of the disturbances it is liable to undergo.

The function of reason is to accumulate a kind of knowledge supposed to be peculiar to the primates and typical of man. But it is perhaps best to begin by distinguishing a more primitive kind of knowledge which can be acquired by most species and is innate in all. To take an example of what I mean: suppose an edible object to be characterized by a certain taste and smell; suppose further that some species of animal reacts to any object having this smell by first tasting, and then eating or rejecting it according to the presence or absence of the taste; then the species may be said to have at least an 'imageless expectation' that the one will be normally followed by the other. What I called primitive knowledge consists of such imageless expectations so far as they are in fact correct.[1]

An enormous amount of our knowledge is of this kind. But many of our expectations are also expressed by images which may be anything from almost exact copies of the expected sensations to merely verbal symbols. And these images expressing expectations (or beliefs) are fitted together into what we call our picture or model of the world. This is in itself an extension of our immediate field of view. It includes what we should see behind us if we turned our heads, or in other times and places if we went there. And science extends it further to include those structural qualities of the universe which we can never verify directly because they are too large or too small for us to see or feel (Schlick, 1948).

I do not mean of course that more than a fraction of this picture or model is conscious at a time. But so far as our imagination is uninhibited, we can move about in it, as it were, quite freely in thought or bring up any part of it we like from our latent store.

Its scope and accuracy, that is, the extent of its correspondence with the possibilities of sensory experience, depends on the operation of two tests: that of congruence with past sensory experience, and that of consistency with itself. And, if this were all, we should indeed be what, before Freud, we too proudly called ourselves, rational beings whose beliefs were solely the result of evidence and logic. But unfortunately both these tests are often interfered with.

To gain a clear idea of how this comes about, it would seem best to begin with a distinction between the factors that produce our picture of the world and those that tend to correct it. Philosophy used to regard it as the product of observation and

---

[1] [What I then termed an innate imageless expectation corresponds to what Bion calls an 'innate preconception' which is, I think, a much better term (1977).]

reason. But, in fact, observation and reason would seem to do little more than apply the tests of congruence and consistency to the product of an imagination which, in itself, is much more concerned with the anticipatory fulfilment of desires than with the forecasting of probable experience.

Indeed, at the beginning of post-natal life, imagination often takes the form of positive and negative hallucinations which, on the one hand, assert the presence of what is pleasurable and satisfying and, on the other, deny the existence of what is painful. In other words, the pleasure principle predominates.

We know, of course, that in spite of it the child's first picture of the world is often far from pleasurable. He is the prey of many painful and destructive feelings which seem to threaten his very being from within and which he cannot deny. And, since his impulses are incompatible with each other, their hallucinatory gratification involves him in almost as much distress as he escapes. But by means of various defence mechanisms he tries to make his imaginary world less painful than it would be without them, and, in the process, distorts it still further into a gross caricature of his perceptual (real) one.

What is specific in defence mechanisms is the employment of a mental process, which may have other functions too, in the service of the pleasure principle. Sometimes we have a special name for it when it is so employed, as when we distinguish between the 'forgetting' of ideas not momentarily required and their 'repression' because they are painful. But this is not always so. We do not always, as perhaps for clarity we should, make a verbal distinction between 'projection' as the basis of all our understanding of our fellows and the defensive projection of what we are unable to tolerate within ourselves.

Projection of course is what gives life to our picture of the world. At first it is all animate, until under the influence of corrective testing the objects in it are felt to be sentient only when they are, in some measure, like ourselves. So projection in the service of the reality principle tends to give us a picture that, so far as we can compare it with perceptual experience, is accurate or true. But projection in the service of the pleasure principle tends always to distort it.

This defensive, or, as we can also call it, paranoid, projection, which may be hallucinatory in degree, is perhaps the most basic, as it is surely the most extensive, distorting influence there is. In the early period, the child continually projects his own aggressive feelings, which are aroused or increased by every discomfort or frustration, onto their objects, so that these affects seem to threaten him from without. And then, since he imaginatively devours or 'introjects' these objects – perhaps in order to destroy them – they also threaten him, and in a still more terrrifying way, from within, until he projects them again. In this way, a vicious spiral of aggressive introjection and defensive projection is set up which seems to make them worse. Such states of mind – and they are frequent in early childhood – are characteristic of what Melanie Klein, to whom we owe most of our knowledge of them, has aptly called the 'persecutory' or 'paranoid' position.

As Melanie Klein has also found, the paranoid position tends to be followed by a depressive one, in which the child feels that it has destroyed its 'good' figures together with its 'bad' ones; and then, in turn, by a hypomanic defence in which he denies his sense of guilt. But since paranoid defences are at the base of so many other disturbances, and have sooner or later to be dealt with in any successful analysis, I need perhaps not go beyond them for illustrations of the point I hope to make.

In their case, at any rate, the conceptual distinction between what is healthy and unhealthy, or normal and abnormal, is comparatively clear. It depends not on the extent to which projective mechanisms are operating, but on whether or not they are operating defensively. Without them we could not form a live picture of the world. But so far as they operate defensively this picture is distorted and does not correspond to perceptual reality in points where the two can be compared.[1]

In other words, so far as projection operates defensively at all, the capacity for rational thought is interfered with. And this, I think, could be shown to be also true of every other defence which analysts class as pathological.[2]

Now the significance of thus linking the pathological with the irrational, and by contrast the normal with the rational, is that it gives us something to measure by a standard that does

---

[1] If we cannot compare the feelings we project into people with their actual feelings, we can compare their expected with their actual behaviour.
[2] I have tried to show this more fully in my book (1952).

seem to be absolute. For in this respect rationality is analogous to truth. A man's beliefs do not have a relative degree of truth measured by their approximation to the prevalent beliefs of his own or some other culture arbitrarily chosen as a frame of reference. They have an absolute degree of truth measured by their approximation to the facts which alone can prove or disprove them. And in the same sort of way – though this is a little more complicated – his beliefs have an absolute degree of rationality measured by their approximation to what is probable on the basis of such facts as come within his experience.

So in the concept of a mind that is rational because undisturbed by defence mechanisms we have found what may lay some claim to being itself a fixed point of reference from which all actual minds, with their varying degrees of irrationality, have, as it were, a measurable distance.

But the qualities so far ascribed to such a mind are purely cognitive and therefore too meagre to form a standard of much use in practice. We must therefore inquire what other qualities, of an affective kind, if any, such a mind would also have. This is an empirical question. No mere juggling with words can give us the answer. But recent advances in analysis do now suggest an answer – and one which could not have been foreseen. They suggest that a rational mind conditions some quite specific affective traits of character.

We may begin by reminding ourselves that every defence mechanism tends to produce a corresponding character trait, which is called paranoid, schizoid, manic or obsessional after the defences embodied in it. So a rational mind, which is free from these defences, must also be free from the traits produced by them.

But we can make positive statements about it too. The character changes that take place in a successful analysis, as defence mechanisms are weakened, are often very striking. Paranoids become friendly, schizoids human, hypomanics modest, and obsessionals adaptable. In other words, they all become 'nicer' as well as happier and more efficient people.

One change of special interest is in what may be called moral character. From Melanie Klein's work (1948) we have learned to regard guilt as a compound rather than as an elementary feeling, in which at least two 'elements', one persecutory and the other depressive, are involved. Since these can be combined in almost any proportion, the guilt feelings of different people range over a whole scale, the dominant element being persecutory at one end and depressive at the other. This also is true of the response to guilt, which ranges from propitiatory sacrifice to creative acts of reparation.

Now the effect of a deep analysis is always to weaken the persecutory element and to bring out the depressive one where it has been previously denied. In this way people who had previously been concerned only with avoiding or offending something feared within themselves come to care more about not hurting but rather helping something loved. And, since their understanding and therefore sympathy with others is also widened, they tend to become more helpful and considerate toward all those with whom they have to do in the outside world as well. If we may give the convenient names 'authoritarian' and 'humanistic' to the extreme opposite types of moral character, we may say that analysis, by weakening paranoid defences, tends to promote a shift in moral character toward the humanist end of the scale. In other words, this type of character would seem to be something else which a rational mind would always have.

We began by considering the point of view, often adopted by anthropologists, that the only norm applicable to individuals is the one defined by their society or culture. There is a sense, of course, in which this must be wrong, for one can always arbitrarily choose an independent norm. But the one we chose – that of being rational, or of being undisturbed in the capacity to form true beliefs on the evidence of sense perception – does seem both to correspond with what is already implicit in the analytic concept and to have the same kind of independence of social standards as we ascribe to truth.

We then found good reasons to believe that rationality, in this strict sense, conditions a specific type of character, or, to be more precise, that it conditions the presence of certain traits in character.

It is worth noting that the two points of view promote very different attitudes to therapy. A psychotherapist who is a relativist would be almost inevitably concerned only with the problem of adapting errant individuals to the society of which they happen to form a part. A social therapist with the other point of view would be as inevitably concerned with the adaptation of society to normal individuals.

BIBLIOGRAPHY

Klein, M. (1948), A Contribution to the Theory of Anxiety and Guilt. *International Journal of Psycho-Analysis*, **29**, 1948.
Money-Kyrle, R. (1951), *Psychoanalysis and Politics*. London: Duckworth
Schlick, M. (1948), *Grundzüge der Naturphilosophie*.
Westermarck, E. (1932), *Ethical Relativity*.

17

Psycho-analysis and Ethics*

I. THE TRANSFER OF AN ETHICAL PROBLEM FROM PHILOSOPHY TO SCIENCE

Philosophers are now divided into two main schools of thought: those who try to ask and answer metaphysical questions, and those who try to show that all metaphysical questions are meaningless.[1] But if logic is on the side of the second school, we still need not dismiss all speculative philosophy as a sterile pursuit. The questions it formulated may often have been grammatically meaningless, but those who formulated them were clearly wrestling with some problem which they felt to be important. What was wrong was not that there was no problem, but that there was a failure to formulate it in such a way that an answer would be possible. So the essential difference between science and philosophy would seem to be, not that science deals with significant and philosophy with meaningless problems, but that science deals with those that are clear cut and philosophy with those which have not got beyond the stage of being only dimly felt.[2] Many centuries of philosophical endeavour may be required before such questions get beyond this stage, and when they do they cease to be philosophical and are immediately transferred to science. In other words, the task of philosophy is perhaps always a preliminary one: that of formulating new problems for science.

Among the oldest questions of philosophy are: What is a good individual? And what is a good society or state? It is not difficult to see what the philosopher who asks, and tries to answer, these questions is trying to do. He is trying to defend

* From: *New Directions in Psycho-analysis*, Tavistock, London, 1955.
[1] According to Wittgenstein, the right method of teaching philosophy would be to confine oneself to propositions of the sciences, leaving philosophical assertions to the learner, and proving to him, whenever he made them, that they are meaningless. *Tractatus Logico-Philosophicus*, 1922.
[2] Professor Jerusalem of Vienna expressed this well by saying that philosophy begins with an 'intellectual discomfort'.

his moral and political preferences – both from doubts within himself and from the hostility of others – and he is trying to do this in a particular way, by argument rather than by force.

It is clear that success in these tasks would be a very notable achievement. It would – at least in theory, though not necessarily in practice – transfer the ultimate arbitrament of moral and political disputes from the arena of force to the court of rational discussion. But is it even theoretically possible?

If what is being sought is a 'proof' of a 'preference',[1] this is certainly a futile quest, which would never have been attempted but for a confusion between two senses of the word 'belief'. We may say, for instance, that we 'believe in' democracy when what we really mean is that we desire it and may thus mislead ourselves linguistically into treating our desire as if it were a belief which could be 'true' or 'false'. But strictly speaking, a desire or preference is not an object of belief, can be neither true nor false, and is therefore not susceptible to 'proof'.

The discovery that preferences cannot be proved may be an important negative achievement of 'positivist' philosophy. But I no longer think that this disposes of ethics. It would do so if beliefs and preferences were entirely independent of each other. But they are not. We know that our preferences affect our beliefs; and it is equally true that our beliefs affect our preferences. As we acquire knowledge – and this consists in the substitution of true beliefs for false ones – our moral and political preferences undergo a change. Now consider the way in which such changes could occur in different individuals, whom we may suppose to start with very different preferences. There are three possibilities: the preferences may remain divergent, or they may converge, or they may converge in some respects and remain divergent in others. There is no *a priori* means of knowing which of these three alternatives is correct. If the first, then such preferences are relative, and all attempts to find a rational argument to justify some one against the rest must necessarily fail. If, however, either of the remaining two alternatives should prove to be the case, if preferences converge,

---

[1] Many ethical arguments can be shown to have been circular. For instance, a preference for a particular moral code or political system is first expressed in a definition. Then the definition is treated as a proposition and an attempt is made to prove it 'true'.

either wholly or in part, with increasing knowledge, then such preferences, or at least some aspect of them, could be justified as being held by all wise men. Moreover, since knowledge, that is, true beliefs, can be proved and communicated, it would be logically possible, though not perhaps feasible in practice, for the wise to convert others to their preferences.

Some such possibility as this must have been in Plato's mind when he formulated the basic problems of ethics. His question, in effect, was not 'What is a good man or a good society?' but 'What are the morals and politics of the wise?' We may try to reconstruct from a trivial example some of the background of his thought. If a man prefers pork pie to caviare, this may be either because, while acquainted with both, he really prefers pork pie, or because he is unacquainted with caviare. Plato seems to have taken the second alternative for granted, and proceeds to inquire about the taste of the truly wise who are acquainted with everything.

Now this question could have a unique answer only if Plato's assumption is correct, that is to say, if differences of aesthetic or moral and political taste result solely from the limitations of our knowledge or experience. But whether it has a unique or a multiple answer, it is a significant question of a kind which could transfer ethics from philosophy to science.

Unfortunately he does not seem to have tried to find an empirical answer. Instead, he became enmeshed in the coils of a concealed tautology. For his answer – that the wise prefer the good – results solely from his definitions: that the good is what is most desirable, and that what is most desirable is what we should desire if we were acquainted with everything.

Moreover, for Plato, wisdom did not consist in any empirical knowledge, but in acquaintance with the ideal prototypes of things.

Nevertheless, there can be no doubt, I think, that Plato's formulation of the problem as one about the morals and politics of the wise is the only formulation that can lead to significant and important results. Unlike the question 'What is a good man or a good society?' which can only be answered by a definition, the question 'What are the morals and politics of the wise?' is, at least in theory, capable of an empirical answer, which may or may not prove to be unique.

PSYCHO-ANALYSIS AND ETHICS

To make it also a practical question, we must modify it a little further. In the first place, we must specify the type of wisdom we refer to. Obviously some kinds of knowledge are more relevant than others. Neither our moral nor our political preferences are much influenced by our knowledge of motor-cars or aircraft. But both are modified, often profoundly, by our knowledge of what is broadly called the humanities – or, more specifically, by our understanding of ourselves and so of other people, that is, by our knowledge of psychology. Our politics, if not our morals, must also be influenced by other forms of knowledge, for example, of economics and the technique of production and of general sociology. But since these influence our choice of means to a pre-determined social end, rather than of the end itself, we may ignore them for the moment, and begin by considering only the influence of our knowledge of ourselves.

In the second place, wisdom – which for our immediate purpose we have now equated with psychological insight – although increasing, is always incomplete. No one can claim to be all wise, or even very wise, though if he studies he may hope to be becoming wiser. If, therefore, the ethical question is not to be purely academic, we must stop asking about the ethics of the wise, and ask instead about the changing ethics of those whose wisdom is increasing. Taking account of these modifications, our question now becomes: How do our moral and political preferences change with increasing psychological insight? Do the preferences of different people remain divergent? Do they tend to converge? Or do they converge in some respects and remain divergent in others? If so, what is the type of morality and ideology towards which they converge?

These questions, or so it seems to me, have always been latent in ethics. The task of philosophy is to make them manifest by so formulating them that an empirical answer is possible. From then on the task of answering them belongs to science – in this case, to psychology.

II. PSYCHO-ANALYSIS AS A METHOD OF PSYCHOLOGICAL RESEARCH

Plato put his question nearly two and a half millennia ago; and even had he put it clearly, that is, in a form admitting an empirical answer, we might have had to wait until now before a correct answer could have been given. The relevant science might not have been sufficiently developed.

Suppose this question to have been asked in this form at some previous time. We should have seen that the moral and political preferences of any individual usually changed, at least to some extent, as his knowledge of the sciences of man increased. But I do not think we should have been able to observe any certain convergence between the preferences of different individuals as they each advanced in learning. Indeed, it would have seemed clear enough that an equally profound knowledge of history, of economics, and of every other branch of the humanities was compatible with the widest moral and political divergencies. We should therefore have been forced to the conclusion that there was no rational means by which one set of values could be defended against others. The essential relativity of values would have seemed well established – each being right only for those who held them and wrong for others.

Almost within the last half century, however, a new branch of learning has developed which is particularly relevant to our inquiry; for more than any other it profoundly affects all our feelings and desires. This science investigates a field the very existence of which was only recently discovered – namely the field of our own unconscious minds. We may therefore reopen the old question in a new form and ask: How are our morals and politics affected as we become more conscious of ourselves?

The technique that enables us to widen the boundaries of our consciousness is psycho-analysis. That the effect it has on our emotions and desires is solely the result of the knowledge it conveys, and not of some other influence, is a point vital to the argument to be developed. To prove that we meet our obligations to the patient we need only show that these changes diminish his distress by helping to restore his capacity for both work and pleasure. To justify them to any society that sets itself above the individual, we might also have to show that they make him a more efficient functioning unit. But these are both arbitrary counts. To justify them to science, which is not arbitrary, we have to show that they are the result of having helped him to see the truth about himself. To increase in him this kind of wisdom is the analyst's overriding aim.

Everyone knows that analysis is a form of therapy for mental illness. But there is some uncertainty – perhaps even among analysts – about its aims and the way in which they are achieved. If the analyst has a sense of responsibility towards his patients – and it is impossible to imagine a competent analyst who has not – he certainly desires to lighten their distress. If he has a sense of responsibility towards society – and this is a less important asset – he may wish to improve their adaptation to it. But if either of these were his primary aim he might sometimes have to use a different method. He might have to prevent his patients becoming conscious of some troubles which they had hitherto successfully evaded. Or he might have to prevent them from becoming wiser than the society they lived in, lest their adaptation to it should be worsened rather than improved.

In general, however – and in the long run perhaps always – the hedonic interests of the patient, and the utilitarian interest of society, are best served by the pursuit of truth. That this should be so is very far from obvious. The content of the unconscious consists of insatiable libidinal desires, passionate destructive hatreds, terrible anxieties and all the abysses of depression and despair. What hedonic, what utilitarian, purpose can possibly be served by bringing these to light? That it does serve such purposes has been proved by every analysis that has succeeded in its primary purpose of raising the iron curtain of repression. But how are we to explain so unexpected a result? One part of the explanation is that opposite impulses, which have been dissociated from each other, are necessarily modified when brought together in the light. But I think a more important part is that some of these impulses are diminished in intensity by the discovery that they are reactions to imaginary situations, which they themselves created, rather than to real ones.[1] The patient, in fact, learns two sorts of truth about himself: first, that he has many impulses and emotions which he had previously denied. And secondly, that these impulses (which seemed omnipotent at a time when there was no distinction between sensation and idea) have first created, and

---

[1] The therapeutic process has been examined in detail by James Strachey in two papers: 'The Nature of the Therapeutic Action of Psycho-Analysis' (1934), and 'Symposium on the Theory of the Therapeutic Results of Psycho-Analysis' (1937), *Int. J. Psycho-Anal.* vols. XV and XVII.

are now maintained by, an unconscious phantasy world which is a gross distortion of the conscious world of sensory perception. It is, I think, this last discovery that most changes his emotional behaviour.

Of course the emotional and the intellectual aspects of the process react reciprocally upon each other. An interpretation that lessens a patient's anxiety improves his emotional relation to his analyst and this in turn removes an impediment to further insight. But if the emotional change is achieved by a 're-assurance' rather than an interpretation, there is no durable advance. So it is always the increase in insight – the successive flashes of self-knowledge awakened by interpretation – that initiates and maintains the therapeutic process.

A grossly over-simplified example may best serve to illustrate this single point. A young man complains of exaggerated nervousness in the presence of authority. This soon shows itself in his relation to his analyst. Consciously, he regards him as helpful and sympathetic, and indeed over-estimates the extent of his skill and benevolence. But he begins to behave as if he believed him to have the exact opposite of these qualities – as if he believed him to be a sinister, almost a diabolic, figure who had both the power and the wish to injure him. This, in fact, is what he does unconsciously believe. If true, such a belief would amply justify his symptoms, which are neurotic only in so far as it is contrary to all the evidence. His analyst's task is to help him free himself from it by showing him how it was developed. They begin by discovering that all authoritative figures in his life, from his present analyst to his father, of whom he was once extremely jealous, have been consciously admired and loved, but unconsciously hated. This goes some way to explain his fear, because he naturally expects to be hated in return. What reduces the fear, however, is not, I think, the mere discovery of the hatred, but the discovery that the hatred has distorted its object. A vicious spiral had been in operation: his unconscious hatred had painted his father blacker than he was, and this increased blackness had in turn increased his hatred, until he had built up, in unconscious phantasy, a truly diabolic figure of which he lived in mortal dread.[1] Meanwhile,

---

[1] As is well known, such figures are unconsciously felt to be internal persecutors, which are projected into the analyst and other figures in the external world.

at the conscious level, all this was not only denied but actually reversed; for he had tried to defend himself against his dread by over-idealizing its object. Consciously, he had painted every authority, from his father to his analyst, much whiter than they really were, and so had sought to turn them into wholly benevolent guardians of himself – into gods to protect him from his devils. With these discoveries, the two opposite pictures begin to converge to a reality which is somewhere in between the two, and the fear, together with the exaggerated admiration, is appreciably diminished.

Even in an over-simplified example, I cannot pretend that this is the end of the story. Hatred based on jealousy does not fully account for the sadistic malevolence of that phantom of his unconscious imagination of which he stood so much in awe. The sadism was originally his own. Its first object was his mother. He had later projected it upon his father whom he had thus made its agent in his early quarrels with her; and he had then become terrified of the Frankenstein monster which his omnipotent phantasy seemed to have created. So what we ultimately arrive at is the fear of a destructive impulse within himself – and here perhaps remains a nucleus of ineradicable conflict and anxiety.

All this and more has to be laid bare by slow and painful steps before his fear of authority can be reduced to that rational minimum which is justified by the extent to which any given authority has the power and will to do him harm. But perhaps I have said enough to show how analysis achieves its results. The patient's emotional behaviour is irrational. It is not justified by the situation he is really in. He behaves as if he were in different situations. He unconsciously believes he is in them; he is in them in unconscious phantasy; he is unconsciously deluded. Analysis seeks to show him what are these beliefs, these phantasies, or these delusions, and how they are produced. So far as it succeeds in this, it frees him from them; he may still have conflicts, and he may still have some fear of his own aggressiveness, but he no longer has delusions, and no longer fears the phantoms his aggressiveness created. So far as he ceases to believe in his phantasy world, he behaves rationally in the world of his perceptions. Thus analysis is a rational process which operates solely by exposing error and replacing it by truth.

We know from the records of many past analyses a good deal about the various types of unconscious belief or phantasy we are likely to meet, and experience is continually adding to the list. As several usually operate at once, the art consists, not only in seeing which are there, and one's own rôle in them, but also in choosing which to interpret first. Different analysts, even when they belong to the same school and have the same degree of technical ability, may perhaps take them in rather different orders; but, if these analysts are relatively free from individual blind spots, no important theme is likely to be missed, and the end result will be very much the same. For what has been pieced together is the truth, of which there can be no two versions.[1]

III. TWO TYPES OF CONSCIENCE

Among the various changes of feeling and desire that occur in analysis, as the patient gradually learns the truth about himself, are changes in his moral attitude. A moral impulse may be defined as an impulse to do, or to refrain from doing, something because to refrain from doing, or to do, it would arouse a sense of guilt. Obviously such impulses can change their object, or increase or diminish in intensity. But what is less obvious, and was for a long time overlooked, is that there can also be a qualitative change in the guilt which is their motive.

We are accustomed to think of guilt as an elementary feeling. We now know that it is a compound of at least two elements. In a deep analysis, there is a fundamental change in the relative intensity of these components, or, to be more exact, in the patient's relative capacity to feel them; he becomes less sensitive to one and, on the whole, more sensitive to the other. But this

---

[1] As to the wider differences between different schools, it is not always easy to distinguish between those which are real and those which are apparent. The real differences, which are considerable, are between the different contents attributed to the unconscious. The apparent ones are between different conceptual systems used to represent the same content.

[1] [I would now (1977) lay greater stress on the discovery of another truth – that, in unconscious phantasy, the patient has hated, attacked, injured, perhaps killed people or objects he loves both in the outer and still more in the inner world. This brings about mourning followed by the sense of resurrection of the objects in the inner world.]

distinction, which we owe to Melanie Klein, is comparatively recent. In earlier analyses, which did not penetrate into the deeper levels of infantile experience, only the diminishing component in guilt attracted much attention. We will consider separately the moral changes brought about by these earlier analyses and compare them with the changes occurring in the more recent and fuller analyses which those influenced by Melanie Klein's work on the very early levels of infantile experience endeavour to conduct.[1]

Unlike psychopathic delinquents and some psychotics, who often give the (incorrect) impression of having no capacity for guilt at all, most neurotics and especially obsessionals are extremely conscientious. And it was with neurotics that analysis was at first concerned. Their guilt seemed to have been first aroused in early childhood by certain primitive sexual wishes and to have subsequently become attached to, and so interfered with, many non-sexual sublimations. The result was a crippling, and often progressive, inhibition of whatever activities they tried. They seemed to be suffering from an excess of guilt, so that the diminution of this guilt appeared as the ultimate aim of their analyses.

A prolonged study of such over-conscientiousness in neurotics led Freud to the discovery of the superego – one of the major achievements of analysis. The first step, and by no means a small one, was to recognize the guilt motive at all in what to the patient seemed a meaningless symptom which gratuitously condemned him to impotence in whatever he strove to undertake – indeed often in whatever his conscious morality bade him undertake. And when this was done, the way in which such a crippling, and often self-defeating, morality could have been developed remained to be unearthed. Freud's well-known explanation is certainly true, but is no longer generally believed to be the whole truth. It may be briefly stated thus: the child's Oedipean jealousy brings him into conflict with the parent of the same sex as himself, whom he may have loved and admired but now also, though less consciously, hates and wishes to mutilate and to destroy. His sense of guilt is originally his fear of a talion punishment from this parent, and in

[1] Of course the terms 'deep' and 'shallow' are relative. What seems deep today may seem shallow enough to our successors.

particular his fear of being castrated by him. After a period of conflict, of varying intensity and duration, he succeeds in repressing his jealousy, and good relations with this parent are once more restored. But the change is brought about in a very special way. The image of the loved, hated, and feared parent is split into two. The more realistic aspect continues to be identified with the external parent of perception. But the less realistic and more terrifying aspect is incorporated in phantasy as an unconscious part of the self. To this 'introjected' parent Freud gave the name of superego. In his view, it is the necessary guardian of morality; but when over-developed, it condemns its possessor to mental illness, and by so doing defeats part of its own purpose which is to transmit the positive as well as the negative demands of the society we live in.

Freud by no means ignored, indeed he stressed, the fact that the same parent who is feared and hated is also admired and loved.[1] Nevertheless the superego morality described by him is predominantly a morality of fear.

Moreover, it is an essentially relative morality. Its primary taboos – those on incest and parricide – are of course common to all mankind; but since its basic aim is to appease, by obedience, a feared authority, it is as varied in its superstructure as the will of the authority to be obeyed. Its immediate sanction is the introjected parents whose moral code was in turn derived from their parents and so from the traditional mores of the society in which they lived. And since the superego is readily identified with the sanctions of this society, it is further strengthened by them, and becomes both indirectly and directly the precipitate of these mores. Thus the superego morality of a 'good' German Nazi is very different from that of a 'good' British Socialist, and still further removed from that of a 'good' Trobriander or Dobuan. There is indeed only one common element in the superego moralities of different societies or sub-groups; they all alike demand the same unquestioning obedience, but to codes of very different kinds.

If we next inquire about the changes effected in superego morality by the self-knowledge which analysis endeavours to extend, there can be little doubt about the answer. So far as this morality is based on irrational fears, for example, on a

[1] 'Humour', *Int. J. Psycho-Anal.*, vol. IX, 1928.

castration anxiety which is no longer, as it may have been in primal times, justified by the actual situation, the effect of analysis is to weaken the fear and the morality based upon it. Of course the process is never complete; a varying amount of 'persecutory guilt' remains. But the direction of the change is always and inevitably the same – towards the liquidation of a morality based on an irrational anxiety.

No special analytic knowledge is required to convince us that there must be another aspect of morality based not on fear but love. Yet its unconscious ramifications have proved even harder to unravel. What we have now learnt about them we owe to Melanie Klein's discovery of early persecutory and depressive states in the development of children, which we must now examine.[1]

Those analysts who accept her results are quite as concerned as those who have not yet done so with the exposure of the phantasies underlying the persecutory element in guilt. Indeed, they seek to carry this process much further; for in their view the superego, which Freud discovered, does not begin as he believed, about the age of five, but is already at that age approaching its final form after five years of previous development. In its earlier stages, however, it consists of unintegrated phantasy objects, by which the infant believes himself to be persecuted from within, and has not yet acquired its final character of an integrated internal mentor. The phase in which these persecutory anxieties reach a maximum intensity has been called by Melanie Klein the 'paranoid position'. Its discovery has of course greatly increased the chances of successful treatment of adult paranoiacs. It has also enabled us better to analyse the paranoid elements in all patients – including 'normal' people – and so further to diminish the persecutory elements in their conscious and unconscious sense of guilt.

Now sooner or later, in any deep analysis, as the sense of persecution is diminished, depressive feelings begin to appear. As these are analysed in turn they are always found to express grief and remorse for injuries to a loved object for which the patient feels himself to be responsible. This grief and remorse constitute the other element in guilt which we may describe

[1] Melanie Klein, *The Psycho-analysis of Children* (London, 1932), and *Contributions to Psycho-Analysis*, 1921–45 (London, 1948).

as depressive as distinct from persecutory. In order to understand its origin, and its relation to the persecutory element, we must try to reconstruct the first stage in the intellectual and emotional development of a newborn baby. This is the association of percepts with memory images to form concepts of enduring objects. Since to him the most noticeable attribute of any percept or memory image is the pain or pleasure it provides, he begins by linking all similar percepts and memory images that are pain-giving or frustrating to form one object and all similar pleasurable or gratifying ones to form another. Thus, for example, his first concept of the breast is not of one object but of two, which are as wholly incompatible with each other as night and day. Moreover, since he attributes to, or 'projects' upon, the frustrating breast all his own rage at the frustration, it is felt as persecutory as well as disappointing. And, similarly, by the projection of his love, the gratifying breast is also felt to be actively benevolent.

That these ideally 'good' and ideally 'bad' objects are different aspects of the same one (and the same child both loves and hates them)[1] is a discovery which is delayed because it is so intensely painful. But sooner or later this discovery is made, and with it comes the first onset of depression, which later forms the depressive element in guilt.

Since the good object which is injured, either in phantasy or fact, tends to turn into a persecutor, the two elements are, perhaps from the beginning of the depressive phase, almost inseparably combined. But they can be combined in very different proportions, and the proportions in which they are combined in any given individual will determine the type of his conscience, the kind of situation that arouses it and the nature of the action it impels.

All true guilt, as Freud long ago discovered, is aroused by what is basically the same situation, namely conflict with the inner representative of an integrated parental figure. But the two elements in it will be combined in proportions determined by the extent to which this figure is felt to be bad and persecutory or good and beneficent. And from this it follows that the external situations that arouse guilt can be very different for different

---

[1] See W. Clifford M. Scott, 'A Psycho-Analytic Concept of the Origin of Depression', *Brit. Med. J.*, 1949.

individuals. Those whose superegos are predominantly persecutory will experience guilt, and of a predominantly persecutory kind, in situations where they are tempted to defy this figure or some external power which represents it. But the situations that will arouse guilt in those whose inner figures are predominantly good, will be such as imply an injury to, a betrayal of, or a failure to protect, the people or values that symbolize their good internal objects.

There will also be a fundamental difference, not only in the quality of the guilt and in the type of situation that arouses it, but in the reaction to the guilt aroused. Those with predominantly persecutory consciences react by propitiation. Those in whom the persecutory element is slight and are in consequence relatively more sensitive to the depressive element react by reparation.

It is obvious that these two types of conscience, which are characteristic of different individuals, can coexist in the same one. To some extent they always do so. Every child, especially in the Oedipean phase of his development, is faced with situations that evoke a direct conflict between them. In the boy, for instance, to disobey an autocratic father is felt as wrong because it arouses great quantities of guilt in which persecutory feelings predominate. But to obey this father may involve the desertion, not only in phantasy but also to some extent in fact, of a defenceless mother. Then obedience too is felt as wrong because it arouses the other type of guilt in which the predominant feeling is depressive. In some people this kind of conflict persists throughout life. But in the majority, it is settled one way or the other fairly early, and with it the subsequent pattern of their consciences.

We have next to inquire about the way in which the depressive element in guilt is affected by a deep analysis. In the case of the persecutory element, as we have seen, the effect is to diminish it. And the theoretical limit of this process – never of course achieved in practice – would be a state in which the patient feared only real dangers in the external world and had ceased to fear, because he had ceased to believe in, those existing only in unconscious phantasy. He might still fear the disapproval of his fellows, or the long arm of the law, but he would have ceased to be afraid of being castrated or eaten by his superego. In the case of depressive guilt, however, the effect is somewhat different. Since much of this guilt arises from acts performed in unconscious phantasy, the exposure of the phantasy as distinct from fact certainly relieves it. But phantasied acts imply a desire to commit them. That the patient has wished to destroy, to injure, to desert or to betray his loved objects is itself a fact, which analysis cannot disprove but rather exposes to the light of day. Thus a substantial reduction in this kind of guilt cannot be achieved merely by showing that the destructive impulses have not in reality achieved their aim – unless these impulses themselves are also reduced. What analysis does do is to weaken these impulses indirectly; for aggression toward loved objects, while partly primary and irreducible, is greatly increased by the persecutory anxieties the phantastic basis of which analysis does undermine. It also helps to free the reparative response to the irreducible destructiveness that still remains.

Thus analysis, while diminishing the conflicts that lead to depression, increases rather than diminishes the capacity to feel guilt of a depressive kind whenever a 'good' object is in any way injured or betrayed.[1]

IV. HUMANISM AS AN ATTRIBUTE OF INSIGHT

We can now see what must be the end of at least the first part of our inquiry – that concerned with morals. We have discovered that there is a causal link between the possession of a certain kind of conscience and the possession of a certain kind of wisdom. This gives us, in broad outline, the answer to our question. All that remains is to fill in some of the more salient details.

We may begin by classifying people into four main groups according to their attitude to morals. Of course some people will belong to more than one group, and indeed everyone will do so to some extent; but this is a complication which for simplicity we may here disregard. In the first group are those who do not appear to have any morality at all. They do not consciously experience either form of guilt themselves, and regard those who claim to be influenced by moral obligations or scruples as hypocrites or weaklings. But this is because they

---

[1] [1977 Perhaps the most important discovery is that the 'bad' object owes its badness to the splitting off and projecting of the 'badness' of the self.]

deny their unconscious guilt, not because they do not have any to deny. They pride themselves on being super-normal; but in reality they are hypomanic, for their freedom from anxiety and depression is achieved at the cost of their capacity to understand themselves. The second group contains those who are at once self-righteous and censorious. Their guilt is for export only. They deny it in themselves, but see it most clearly in others on to whom they project their own share as well. So they live in a state of moral indignation with the scapegoats for their own offences. They too believe themselves to be normal people, who indeed excel others in virtue; but they are really hypo-paranoid and live in terror of discovering the truth about themselves.

The two remaining groups are composed of people who are conscious of a conscience. The distinction between them is not so clear cut, for it is formed, as it were, by the middle point on a scale stretching between two theoretical extremes. At one end of the scale are those in whom the persecutory element in guilt predominates. They are concerned mainly with obedience to an exacting superego or its external representatives. They tend to be self-disciplined but hard. Their consciences may be described as authoritarian. The other end of the scale contains those who have little sense of persecution and in whom the capacity for the depressive element in guilt is relatively unimpaired. Such people are less afraid of disobedience; but they are more consciously distressed by any disloyalty to the values or persons who symbolize their good internal objects. In practice they may be less law-abiding citizens, but they are more kindly and more ready to take up arms in the defence of other people's wrongs. In short, they have more freedom within themselves and more responsibility towards their neighbours.

These distinctions may be illustrated by different attitudes to the morality of war. The hypomanics have no guilt about attacking neighbours they despise, and may do so with elation. The hypoparanoids are over-anxious to start crusades against neighbours on whom they have projected their own unadmitted crimes. Unlike either of these, the attitude of those with an authoritarian conscience will depend on the nature of the inner authority they serve. If it tells them to fight, they will do so with obedient zeal irrespective of the real issues involved.

If it tells them not to, they will remain obstinately pacific, and will not even defend the people or values they love. In this they are in sharp contrast with the humanists who are prepared to fight whatever threatens what they care for, but who do not initiate aggression.

Similar differences characterize the attitude of these last two groups to sexual morality. The authoritarians conform with the conventions of society; the humanists are influenced more by positive loyalties than by restrictive codes.

Passing from descriptive to causal differences, we have already seen that the humanist conscience is possessed by, and only by, those who are relatively free from blind spots and capable of feeling what is in themselves. They surpass all other groups in the insight which, on the one hand, diminishes their irrational persecutory anxieties, and, on the other, enables them to feel grief if they injure or abandon what they love. Thus a movement away from the authoritarian and towards the humanist type of conscience is the moral effect of any increase in that kind of wisdom which consists in insight or self-knowledge. And this is true, however the increase in insight is brought about – whether by a formal analysis or by some other means.

But the humanist consciences of different individuals are by no means necessarily identical. Being based on love rather than fear, they do not display the almost limitless variability of the authoritarian conscience, which springs from a pliable subservience to whatever code has been imposed. But they do differ from each other in so far as the current symbols of good objects to be cherished and defended are different. This gives the answer to the first half of the question we began with; as people become wiser in self-knowledge, their morality converges in some respects and remains divergent in others. Their consciences become more humanist in form, but this common form is compatible with a certain variety of content.

V. THE INFLUENCE OF INSIGHT ON POLITICAL OPINION

There still remains the second half of our question – that concerned with politics. Can we also say that increased insight would bring about some convergence in the form or content of our political preferences?

That it would do so at least so far as insight influences morals and morals influence politics must be already clear. I do not think, for example, that a humanist politician could tolerate the guilt of attacking a comparatively harmless neighbour, as Germany did in 1939, or of abandoning a friendly one, as Britain did in 1938. So both active and passive forms of non-humanist political behaviour would tend to be reduced. And, in general, a predominance of the humanist type of conscience would modify the political behaviour of any group, whether nation, class, or party, to other groups in much the same way as it would modify the private behaviour of individuals to each other. Since each group would be likely to be the priority 'good object' to its own members, they would still be likely to put its interests first, which, if threatened, they might indeed defend more stoutly than at present. But they would not be able to ride rough shod over the interests of another group, or to desert those of a friendly one, without a sense of guilt; nor would they be so prone, in resisting an aggressive group, to project their own guilt feelings upon it and so to paint it blacker than it is. In other words, our political behaviour would not only be more consistently loyal to our own values, but also less callous towards its rivals and less vindictive towards its enemies. In short, there would be a measure of convergence towards a humanist standard of political behaviour.

There would also be some convergence in our political beliefs, by which I mean our beliefs about political affairs. Such beliefs – for example, those expressed in our idea of other nations, parties or classes, or in our sociological, including economic, theories – are by no means solely determined by our contacts and our studies. They are often very greatly influenced by unconscious phantasies surviving from early childhood which distort our conscious inferences and deductions. So insight by reducing these impediments to social science would help to bring us nearer to a common truth.

But can we go still further and say that increasing insight would bring about some convergence in political ideology, that is, in the different 'ideal' states or societies which different individuals would like to live in?

Anthropology has taught us that any fairly homogeneous people tends to create a society congenial to itself, and that many different kinds of society exist each of which is 'good' to its own members, but 'bad' to members of the others. The anthropologist, who himself has a specific character, will naturally prefer some kinds of people and some kinds of society above the rest. But, in the absence of any independent standard against which to measure his own subjective one, he will usually dismiss such judgments as relative and therefore outside the bounds of science. This attitude may be in itself a healthy reaction against a too naïve assumption of superiority by earlier travellers. But it seems to me to be carried much too far in the relativist denial that any independent standard can be found.

The relativist position culminates in the relativist definition of normality, according to which a normal person is one well adapted to the society he lives in. Definitions cannot be false; but they can be ill chosen, or they can fail to fit the pre-existing concept they are endeavouring to express in words. Now the clinical concept of normality may be vague. But it certainly does not depend on adaptation to society; for, if it did, some people whom every clinician would class as ill would have to be classed as normal in some societies. A verbal definition of normality that both fits the clinical concept and is absolute in the sense of being independent of the standards of any arbitrarily chosen culture may be difficult to find. But it seems to me to emerge, at least in outline, from the following considerations. What we call illness, whether this is a specific symptom or a 'character defect' is something we try to cure, or at least to lessen, by analysis, that is, by helping the patient to achieve a higher degree of insight or self-understanding than he had before. Sometimes the task is beyond our present technical ability. But this does not lessen our belief that insight, if we could only awaken it, would still effect the cure. In other words, we believe that what we call health is something that can be achieved by insight. Now, if this causal connection between health and insight exists, we can use it to give a verbal definition of normality that does fit the clinical concept and is independent of any arbitrarily chosen cultural standards. We can define a normal – that is, a healthy – mind, as one that knows itself.[1]

Since in reality self-knowledge is always incomplete, it follows from our definition that there can be no completely normal person. But this conclusion, with which no analyst will quarrel, does not lessen the value of a term to denote a limit to which real people approximate in various degrees.

Having reached a definition of a normal mind as one that knows itself, we have next to inquire about its other attributes. These are not included in the definition and can only be discovered empirically. Some of the moral attributes we have already found: they comprise what we called a 'humanistic' as opposed to other forms of conscience. Two qualities which Freud used to define normality in a wider sense are certainly attributes of anyone who is approximately normal in the narrow one. These are a well-developed capacity for both work and enjoyment. But, for our present purpose, the most comprehensive and significant attribute is perhaps maturity.

We can now re-word our question about the ideological effects of insight in rather different terms and ask what kind of state would be most congenial to people who, as a result of insight, are humanist in conscience and have also attained a fairly high level of psychological maturity in other respects too. There can be no doubt that such people would be most unhappy (and maladjusted) in any state that sought to dominate their consciences or to control their labours. They would therefore be opposed to totalitarianism in all of its many different forms. But neither would they be content to thrive in a *laissez faire* society which accepted no obligations towards those who were less fortunate or less efficient in the economic struggle for existence. So their political aim would be a state that accepted responsibility for welfare without curtailing independence.[2] This also gives us the answer to our question

---

[1] The two expressions: 'A mind that knows itself' and 'an integrated mind' are I think equivalent. Integration as a criterion of mental health has been stressed by Marjorie Brierley (1947) in her paper 'Notes on Psycho-Analysis and Integrative Living', *Int. J. Psycho-Anal.*, vol. XXVIII. Chapter VI in *Trends in Psycho-Analysis* (London, 1951).

[2] The political cleavage in this country since the war has been roughly between those who stress the first to the partial neglect of the second, and those who stress

in its original form. The effect of increasing insight would be to bring about some convergence in political ideology towards what may still be called, in spite of totalitarian attempts to misappropriate the term, the democratic aim.

VI. CONCLUSION

How little, or how much, have we achieved by this inquiry? Certainly there is nothing new in the conclusion that wise men are humanist in morals and democratic in their politics. Most people in democratic countries believe it already. But to prove it empirically has, I think, only been made possible by the more recent discoveries of analysis – in particular by those we owe to Melanie Klein's pioneering work which she began with children. These discoveries, as I have tried to show, enable us for the first time to construct an argument capable both of confirming this belief in those who already have it, and perhaps, in the long run, also of convincing those who at present hold a contrary opinion.[1]

---

the second to the partial neglect of the first, of these two desiderata. But in the last few years each party seems to have borrowed – if without acknowledgment – from the other a good deal of what it had previously neglected.

[1] The argument briefly outlined in this paper is developed further in my book *Psycho-Analysis and Politics* (London, Duckwork, 1951).

18

An Inconclusive Contribution to the Theory of the Death Instinct*

Before coming to my main theme of the death instinct, a few words on the concept of instinct in general may not be out of place.

If, as external observers, we study any animal, we note that it has certain dispositions to behave in certain ways in certain situations.[1] We say these dispositions are partly innate and partly acquired, but a difficulty arises when we try to say which part is which. At least in the higher species, and especially in man, every behaviour pattern is the joint product of heredity and environment. We know that the two contributions are not separate entities like the foundation and superstructure of a building, but we often speak of them as if they were, and so become involved in such misleading dichotomies as that between what is there at birth and what develops subsequently, or between what develops in a 'normal' environment and what deviates from it in an abnormal one. We should come nearer the implied distinction if we regarded what is innate as a range of potentialities, and what is acquired as an actuality selected from them under the influence of a particular environment. Thus we have an instinct to eat and acquire specific eating habits.

The range of potentialities comprised by instincts has widened in the course of evolution. The instincts of lower forms of life are relatively stereotyped; those of the higher animals are much more plastic, and include mechanisms for modifying themselves in accordance with the experience encountered. Both the stereotyped and the plastic dispositions could be

* From: *New Directions in Psycho-Analysis*, Tavistock, London, 1955.
[1] The term 'situation' here includes an internal stimulus to appetitive behaviour as well as an external pattern eliciting consummatory behaviour.

described by conditional statements of the form, 'if a then A, then if b then B, etc.', where a and b are patterns of stimuli – both internal and external – and A and B are patterns of response. But in the case of the higher plastic instincts, propositions giving the precise way in which such patterns are progressively modified by their own outcome would have to be included. In other words, a complete description of a higher plastic instinct would take the form of a pyramid of conditional statements giving the widening alternative developments in every conceivable environment. Then the actual development in the actual environment would be represented by one line from the apex to the base. In man the instincts are particularly plastic, and the 'width' of the pyramid needed to describe them, correspondingly great. Biology has not got beyond a rough and uncertain classification of some of the main forms common to our species. Future work may also list the racial and individual differences – for it may be presumed that we differ innately from each other as much in our instinctive potentialities of function, which express the minutiae of cerebral structure, as in our more easily recorded, overt structure.

So far we have considered instincts from the external, biological, point of view – that is, behaviouristically. But as psychologists we are not only concerned with behaviour. Indeed, strictly speaking, we are concerned with behaviour only because we depend on it to infer states of mind, which it is our business to study and describe. By a process of controlled identification we imagine we have these before us. We can then again abstract what I have called the dispositions. But we seek to go beyond the behavioural factors to the underlying tendencies to think and feel, either consciously or unconsciously, in certain ways in certain 'perceptual situations'.[1] In other words, we are concerned with the phantasy responses which may precede and initiate behaviour.[2] In this field, the analytic technique invented by Freud has reaped a steady harvest. He

---

[1] The term 'perceptual situation' is taken to include the conscious or unconscious perception of an inner need, such as hunger, as well as the perception of a pattern of external objects. It denotes the psychological equivalent of the biological definition of 'situation' in the footnote to page 285.

[2] To be precise, what the psychologist studies are the psychic correlates of those cerebral processes which the biologist assumes, though cannot observe, to be the 'effects' of stimuli patterns and the 'cause' of behaviour.

and those who have followed him have listed a number of innate phantasy patterns and can describe how they are likely to develop under the influence of different environments. The psycho-analytic study of these phantasy patterns is the study of instinct in man.

One unforeseen result of this study was that old classifications of a number of distinguishable instincts tended to break down. Not only did apparently homogeneous instincts turn out to be the expression of a number of component phantasies, but the same primary phantasies, divided and recombined in an extremely complex way in the course of their development, were found expressed in a number of apparently unconnected instincts. But from the beginning, Freud saw conflict to be a basic character of the inner world of phantasy, and was therefore led to believe that all instincts must at least be divisible into two main groups. The classification he at length evolved into life and death instincts is still highly controversial. But it is not a mere metapsychology divorced from practice[1]; for the view we take of it profoundly affects our working theories and our clinical technique. This is because we are basically concerned with anxiety, the origin of which the theory of the death instinct may possibly explain.

While many analysts are unable to follow Freud and accept this theory, Melanie Klein goes further than he did. She not only accepts the death instinct, but believes the fear of death to be at the root of persecutory, and so indirectly of all, anxiety. Against this, both Freud and Ernest Jones had already argued that one cannot fear what one cannot conceive of, and that it is psychologically impossible to form a positive idea of anything so negative as being nothing. I used to be much impressed by this argument, which corresponded with my own epistemological approach, but I have since come to feel it to be something of a quibble; for if we cannot form an idea of being dead, we can certainly form an idea of, and fear, the experience of dying.

Now Freud's theory of a death instinct and Melanie Klein's view that there is also a basic fear of death are conceptually

[1] Or perhaps it would be more correct to say that the metapsychological and the empirical aspects of the theory are so interwoven, in analytic thought, that it has become difficult to distinguish between them.

distinct. The first postulates a primary impulse to seek death; the second a primary impulse to fear and to avoid death. There is no *a priori* reason why we should not have both; for though they conflict, they do not logically exclude each other – indeed the first may be supposed to stimulate the second. But neither do they necessarily imply each other. Let us therefore consider them in turn, beginning with the second.

The old analytic argument against the existence of a basic fear of death rests, implicitly if not explicitly, on the discovery that what is consciously thought to be a fear of death often turns out to cover other unconscious fears, such as the fear of castration. But it is now fairly generally agreed that there are fears more basic than the fear of castration or loss of love (Freud), or even the loss of all capacity for pleasure (aphanisis, Ernest Jones). There is, for instance, the terror of disintegration.[1] It may not be easy to be sure – still less to convince the doubters – that such anxiety attacks express the fear of dying. But there are other pointers, of a more general kind, which are perhaps easier to follow. Why, if there is no fear of death, are nearly all religions so concerned with immortality? Why, in our ambitions, are we so passionately anxious for something of ourselves, a work of art, a scientific contribution, a business, or just our good name, to be accepted and to survive? Why, not only for our pleasure but for our peace of mind, do we need children who should create grandchildren, and so on? Why, in short, do we so strive for immortality – or at least for immortality by proxy? Or how better can we describe those moments of deep despondency, which no one altogether escapes, than as a feeling that there is no joy in fighting an enemy who must ultimately defeat us – no joy in living if death or destruction must surely overtake us and all our works, those offshoots of ourselves we try to save?[2] And why, if there is nothing in it, have the biologists so much stressed an instinct of self-preservation? We may not be able to form an idea of our own annihilation, but in common with other animals we are

---

[1] The terror of disintegration may perhaps be equated with Freud's concept of traumatic anxiety.

[2] We feel these moments to be cowardly, to be the antithesis of that courage which can find joy even in fighting for lost causes. This is the theme of Russell's *A Free Man's Worship*, that people should enjoy striving for what they value without the consolation of myths that deny the ultimate destruction of the world.

certainly predisposed to anxiety at threats of it.[1] If we were not, our line would have died out long ago and we should not have existed. Indeed, it is a mere tautology to assert that the only instincts that can be developed by selection are such as tend to promote the survival of offspring to inherit them. So the instinct to preserve ourselves to produce offspring must be basic; and the instinct to protect them, if necessary before ourselves, must be a derivative of it to improve the survival prospects of the species. In other words, all the striving that fills life is the expression of a ceaseless battle against death.

But it is still a long way from the acceptance of the fear of death – or at least of situations likely to cause death – as a basic instinct, to the acceptance of Freud's theory of a death instinct. Indeed, the very arguments in favour of the one seem, at first sight, to militate against the other. Since instincts, in the Darwinian sense, are developed by the selection of such mutations as favour the survival of offspring, and so of parents to produce them, how can we imagine the development by selection of an instinct of self-destruction? Of course this argument, by starting with the Darwinian conception of instinct, really begs the question. But the Darwinian conception, which certainly holds for all of what Freud called the life instincts, has been immeasurably fertile in biology, and is not something to be lightly thrown away as a general explanatory principle. So before accepting the death instinct, that is, the existence of an instinct with a self-destructive aim which cannot have been evolved by selection to promote survival, we must do our best to see how far the analytic facts can be explained without it.

The following theory seems to me to go some way to explain most of these facts on Darwinian lines without the assumption of a death instinct. But I shall also argue that it does not go quite far enough.

To every organism another organism has three basic

[1] Perhaps the nearest we can get to the idea of our own annihilation is the idea of the annihilation of all our good objects, both internal and external, and of being left with nothing but the bad ones – the containers of our own destructiveness. But then this is terrifying because these bad impulses threaten to destroy us. So the ultimate object of fear, if it is not the idea of being nothing, is at least the idea of the painful process of being reduced to this condition – if not of death, of dying.

potential meanings. It is something to eat (or reject),[1] something to be eaten by, or something to unite (or reunite) with. And it is tempting to suppose that the corresponding impulses aggressively to desire and consume the first, to fear and avoid the second, and to love and preserve while combining with the third, may have been developed, both phylogenetically and ontogenetically, from each other in this order. According to the theory of the death instinct, the aggression in the first of these impulses has been, as it were, diverted from an originally self-destructive aim, and used in the service of the life instincts. But let us, for a moment, consider the contrary (Darwinian) hypothesis, that it was originally evolved as an appropriate response to the threat of death by hunger. Assume further that aggressive greed towards the outer world when under the influence of hunger is the primary impulse, and let us try to imagine how the next impulse, that to fear and avoid other organisms when they are dangerous, can have been evolved from it. In evolving something new, Nature tends to make use of what is already there. So it is not unlikely that an organism's capacity to 'recognize' the danger from its potential enemies results from the evolution of a tendency to project into them the aggression felt within itself. We know from analysis and especially from Melanie Klein's work with children, that this is the way in which persecutory anxiety either originates or is at least augmented in human beings. And such facts of analytic observation suggest the hypothesis that the paranoid mechanism, which is so fundamental in our lives and which we see so clearly in its exaggerated forms, may be the innate mechanism through which self-preservative behaviour in the face of external danger is achieved, at least in the higher, and perhaps in every species. If so, the fear of death in this specific form would be not the fear of a death instinct originally directed against the organism itself, but the fear of a projected aggression originally evolved in the interests of self-preservation.

Coming to the third stage, the evolution of the sex impulse to unite and reproduce: as we experience it, we can detect, in addition to identification and protective love, a not altogether

[1] The impulse to reject or discard what is unpleasant or disgusting provides, as it were, another thread to be woven into a complete account of the development of object relations. But for simplicity I have ignored it here.

stable fusion between a sadistic impulse to mastery and a masochistic impulse to surrender.[1] Each partner is, as it were, at once the eater and the eaten, yet both are preserved from actual damage. And we may reasonably suppose that the safety of each partner is somehow achieved by a partial turning of aggression against the aggressive self – for this, too, is in accordance with analytic findings. And we may again conclude that a tendency to such inversion has been evolved to protect the partner – and later the offspring and whatever we identify ourselves with – against an original predatoriness which, if unchecked by such a mechanism, would endeavour to consume the world. This seems plausible enough. If we accept it, we have a hypothesis which may seem at least to lessen the need for a theory of a death instinct. For the assumption of an aggression, originally evolved to secure our own survival,[2] and now partially turned inwards to secure the survival of those we identify ourselves with and love, is sufficient to account for at least some of the self-destructive impulses we find.

Such a mechanism would seem necessary to the survival of any species that reproduces sexually; and could have been further evolved to protect the offspring. It could even – though this is a digression from my main theme – have been used to produce in each species some acquiescence in its optimum longevity. In bacteria and insects, and in all those forms of life which, when faced with a changing environment, rely for their survival more on improvements through mutations in germ plasm in successive generations than on adaptation in soma, the life span of individuals is relatively short. In those which rely more on learning, and the transfer of acquired knowledge to other younger members of the species, the life span is relatively long. We must suppose this to be because, in each species, an optimum longevity has been selected. We can go further and suppose that in our own species our life span is determined by a neurological limit to our capacity to acquire and store knowledge, and that we are predisposed to die when,

[1] The common view that sadism is masculine and masochism feminine may be qualified by the consideration that this applies only to the phallic component. The allocation of the active and passive aspects of the oral component tends to be reversed: the active oral component being more conspicuous in female genitality.

[2] Both directly by the active pursuit of prey, and indirectly by warning us of danger by other predators.

this capacity having been exhausted, we begin to become more a liability than an asset to our fellows. An innate tendency for the progressive transfer of concern for survival from ourselves to those of our products with which we identify ourselves could promote the survival of our species in two ways: positively, by making the old protect the young; and negatively, by helping the old to acquiesce in their extinction instead of harmfully competing.

There is therefore much to be said for a phylogenetic hypothesis which derives the fear of objects from the projection of aggressive greed, and self-destructiveness from the need to divert this greed from loved objects, that is, from objects at once desired by, and projectively identified with 'good' parts of, the self. And ontogenetically, we are familiar with an inverted aggressiveness of this kind. But we believe we can also detect a primary threat to the self from within the self which is not derived from anything. It is indeed this apparent fact of observation that is the analytic basis of the theory of the death instinct, and that must be capable of being explained in some other way before that theory can be discarded as empirically redundant. To do so, it might be thought sufficient to remember that, ontogenetically, the distinction between self and object is only gradually achieved. It is a philosophic truism that we can never be aware, in the sense of being directly acquainted with, anything beyond our own sensations and ideas. So in fact the dualistic conception of self and outer world expresses a rather arbitrary, and by no means constant, distinction between those sensations and ideas which we define as constituting ourselves and those we define as constituting the outer world. In the new-born infant the distinction is rudimentary, or still non-existent; so fear of death by hunger, aggressive greed, and fear of aggressive greed in a projected form, are played out between entities not yet separated into self and outer world. This, so it seems to me, might well give rise to that primary sense of being threatened from within which we assume in infants and which perhaps recurs whenever the boundaries between self and outer world are again disturbed.

At first sight, the conclusion to be drawn from such considerations is that the theory of the death instinct is not necessary to account for the facts observed. But before discarding it other more general arguments in its support have still to be assessed. Freud himself, as we know, based it not only on analytic studies of masochism and the compulsion to repeat the past but also on a wide philosophical survey embracing, if not the universe, at least the whole of life. And although we are accustomed to think of his philosophy as a superstructure designed to explain his discoveries, it perhaps deserves to be taken more seriously on its own account.

In this philosophy or 'metapsychology', he derived the destructiveness he found in man from a conservatism in organisms which reacts against the forces that brought them into being. If it is not too fanciful to link this concept of conservatism with that of catabolism in biology and entropy[1] in physics, Freud's metapsychology of the death instinct could perhaps be restated in the following terms.

If we revert to the behaviouristic standpoint and use the word behaviour in its widest sense, we observe a basic conflict of forces. The organism is threatened both from within and from without by the forces of destruction – that is, by catabolic processes as well as by external enemies. It reacts against them in such a way as to maintain its integrity as a system. And we may add that, as an additional precaution, the system also tends to multiply itself. From the point of view of physics, no new laws have to be introduced to explain why this should be so. If chance once produced a boundary-maintaining system of molecules which reproduced itself in a limited environment, competition and selection would automatically ensure the evolution of ever more adaptable systems capable of maintaining themselves in an ever wider range of possible environments. Thus, given the existence of reproductive organisms in a limited environment, logic alone should have led us to expect the biological part of the universe to run counter to the entropy of the whole.[2]

---

[1] Entropy can perhaps be personified as a kind of 'levelling' principle in nature.

[2] Perhaps Darwin's main contribution to science was not the empirical discovery of evolution, but a piece of pure deductive reasoning: that, given the well-known facts of inheritance with variation in a limited world, evolution must logically occur. Whether these facts alone are sufficient to explain the pace of the evolution that has actually occurred, or whether the inheritance of acquired characters must also be assumed is, on the other hand, an empirical question which was left by him, and still remains, without a certain answer.

From the point of view of psychology we attribute at least to the higher systems in this small part something we deny to the inorganic part of nature, namely awareness and the will to live; and this would seem to be the psychic correlate of the forces which maintain them as organic systems. We are directly acquainted with the will to live in ourselves and have no hesitation in projecting it into our picture of our fellows, as well as into other animals so far as they behave as we do. But at what level in the organic hierarchy are we to draw the line? And are we to attribute psychic equivalents only to the system-maintaining processes, and not to the disruptive processes they counteract?

Where we are acquainted with a psyche in ourselves we believe it to be conditional on the integrity of the particular and highly complex system of our brains. And as brains, like other organs, are presumably evolved to preserve and multiply their owners' lives, it is not easy to associate a primary self-destructive impulse with neural processes in evolved cerebral structure.[1] For these reasons, the body-mind correlations we assume in scientific thought tend to be restricted, on the one hand to such organisms as are possessed of brains, and on the other to such psychic processes as are correlated with self and species preservation. But the limits we thus impose on the spontaneous animism of pre-scientific thought begin to seem arbitrary as soon as we remember that imperceptible links of evolution connect the complex neural system of a brain to ever simpler patterns of reactive tissue. We can find no obvious place to draw a line below which mind should disappear and only matter remain. So after all the old animistic conception of the world, which scientific people pride themselves on having outgrown, may have erred only in attributing complex mental processes to simple systems; and perhaps we should be prepared to follow Leibnitz in attributing some *petits perceptions* even to the simplest systems of all. And our hesitation in doing so may be diminished when we remember that there is a sense in which the mental world with which we are alone acquainted, and

---

[1] N. Tinbergen, *The Study of Instinct* (Oxford, 1951) defines an instinct as a hierarchically organized nervous mechanism which is susceptible to certain priming, releasing, and directing impulses of internal as well as external origin, and which responds to these impulses by co-ordinated movements *that contribute to the maintenance of the individual and the species* (my italics).

which includes what we call our perceptions of the external world, is more 'real' than this external world of physics which physicists themselves now regard as only a mathematical construction.[1]

The argument we have embarked on may lead to conclusions repugnant to our current thought, which is still predominantly materialistic. But we cannot escape these conclusions without abandoning our belief in continuous development.[2] We can observe that our own behaviour 'expresses' psychic impulses, and we attribute such impulses to other organisms so far as they are like ourselves in structure and behaviour. Then, having made this initial step, the principle of continuity forces us to attribute some psychic correlate, of however indefinite a kind, to all observed behaviour.

But can we, at the risk of becoming altogether lost in the fogs of mysticism, venture to be more precise in such a revised animistic conception of the universe? If behaviour in the widest sense is any guide, we see the two opposite tendencies which so impressed General Smuts and led him to write *Holism and Evolution*: on the one hand entropy, on the other the organic development of ever more complex and adaptable systems. The principle of continuity suggests that we may have to attribute psychic correlates to both.[3]

At least there seem good biological as well as analytic reasons for regarding the fear of death[4] – either our own or that of those with whom we are identified – as the basic motive in life. And when, in analysis, we meet this fear in its more primitive forms, it seems to be linked with the awareness of a self-destructive force. Whether our awareness of this force can be explained as the awareness of aggression at a time when the distinction between self and outer world has not been achieved or has broken down; or whether it can in some way be

[1] Clifford Scott's concept of the 'body scheme' (which is in part derived from Schilder's concept of the 'body image') includes the external world.

[2] The alternative to the principle of continuity would seem to be some form of 'emergent vitalism' – a doctrine which I find much harder to accept.

[3] It can be argued that in conceiving a model of the universe in which events are the resultant of these opposing forces, we are merely 'projecting' the forces we experience within ourselves. But this argument, while attacking animism, implies the admission that both forces are in fact within us.

[4] To avoid logical difficulties, we can always substitute the 'fear of dying' for the 'fear of death'.

conceived of as a psychic representative of entropy – of the catabolic process in our brains and bodies – seems to me an open question. But as a major cause, and an effect, of anxiety in man it is a force that certainly exists.

In conclusion, I should like again to stress my point that the fear of death, or of dying, and the death instinct are logically distinct. Empirically we know that the fear of death is either derived from, or at least greatly increased by, our own aggression. But an aggression felt to threaten the self because it has been projected or inverted, or, still more fundamentally, because the distinction between self and outer world has not yet developed, or has disappeared, is not the same as the death instinct conceived by Freud. If no such instinct exists, we must assume that the fear of death (e.g., by hunger) is primary and that aggression (e.g., aggressive greed) is an instinctive response to it which, if not clearly directed against an external object, serves only to increase the sense of danger. If, however, there is a death instinct we can hardly doubt that the fear of death is a response to it. As Paula Heimann says: 'Danger arising primarily within the organism provides the stimulus for the human being's innate capacity for fear.'[1] The difficulty consists, not in how the death 'instinct' works if it exists, but in seeing how it can exist at all. It cannot be an instinct in the ordinary sense – something evolved in the interests of self- and species-preservation.[2] It can therefore hardly be conceived except as a kind of psychic correlate of entropy – something prior to the instincts proper which were presumably evolved to counteract it.[3]

[1] 'Notes on the Theory of the Life and Death Instincts' in *Developments of Psycho-Analysis* (London, 1952).
[2] An instinct to secure no more than an optimum longevity (p. 291) might conceivably have been evolved. But, if so, it would be something far more specific and limited in scope than the general death instinct envisaged by Freud.
[3] If we do accept the death instinct in some such terms as these, there still remains the possibility of a further open question: that of the relation of the death instinct to aggression. With Freud, we can imagine the one as the outward expression of the other. Or we can imagine a secondary aggression as evolved, in the interests of self- and species-preservation, to counteract a primary self-destructive force, and then becoming inverted and so confused with this 'death instinct' when in fact it was only the death instinct's temporary ally. But if there is no difference between the observable effects of these two hypotheses, the distinction is perhaps unreal.

19
Psycho-analysis and Philosophy*

Most sciences have their roots in philosophy, and academic psychology is no exception to this rule. It was, in fact, the last to break away and become an independent discipline. But psycho-analysis – that new science created by Freud – sprang from medicine rather than from academic psychology. Probably for this reason, philosophers and psycho-analysts have so far taken little interest in each other's work. And what interest there was at the beginning tended to be more hostile than co-operative. Of course there were always exceptions; but, on the whole, philosophers, so far as they took notice of psycho-analysis at all, condemned its basic concepts as muddled and self-contradictory. And analysts silently responded by dismissing philosophy, or at least classical philosophy, as a symptom of obsessional neurosis.

I think both criticisms exaggerate an element of truth which each side has gradually become more able to admit. If so, perhaps the time is ripe for more co-operation. I believe philosophy can be useful to the analyst – particularly in his attempts to reconstruct the development of the child's picture of the world. And a psycho-analytic approach to some problems of classical philosophy could be of interest to the philosopher. So I should like to say something – if only tentatively – about both, beginning with the second.

A PARADOX IN THE DEFINITION OF PHILOSOPHY

As my point of departure, I will take a question which has the deceptive appearance of being simple: What is philosophy as distinct from other disciplines? A good historical definition, from Russell's *History of Western Philosophy* (1946), is that

* From: *Psycho-analysis and Contemporary Thought*.

philosophy lies between science and religion. Scientific questions demand empirical answers, and scientific statements are designed to be tested by observation. The answers to religious questions, on the other hand, though supported by empirical arguments, are primarily based on faith and revelation. The problems of classical philosophy would seem to differ from both of these. They were not expected to be solved by observation; or, if they were, they ceased to be philosophical. Nor were they to be solved by acts of faith, but by reason.

Now, philosophy is much concerned with paradoxes, so that we need not be surprised to find one already in its definition. But this first paradox is certainly startling. For while most classical philosophers would probably have agreed that philosophy consists in the pursuit of synthetic knowledge by pure reason, the logical positivists claim to have proved that there can be no such thing. In other words, according to some of the most distinguished of modern philosophers, there can be no such thing as philosophy in the classical sense. This was the view of my own teacher, Moritz Schlick. It was still more uncompromisingly expressed by Wittgenstein [1], in whose opinion a teacher of philosophy should leave philosophical propositions to the learner, and content himself with pointing out that they were meaningless. Of course, this should not be taken to imply that classical philosophers accomplished nothing. They contributed enormously to logic and mathematics on the one hand, and to all the sciences, especially psychology, on the other. But in the narrow sense in which we have been trying to define it, this would seem not to be philosophy.

We can evade the paradox by redefining philosophy as a kind of advance-guard to science engaged in constructing, criticizing, and clarifying our overall pictures, or models, of the world – for this is what most philosophers have actually done. But such a definition would not have satisfied those whose aim it was to prove *a priori*, and without reference to experience, that their models were necessarily true. It is precisely this which has been the aim of so much classical philosophy. And it is precisely this which, according to the critics, is not only an impracticable but an illogical demand.

I have stressed the point because it inevitably raises a problem of interest to psychology: Whence came this craving for synthetic *a priori* knowledge; that is, for something logically impossible?[1]

MOTIVES FOR PHILOSOPHY

Most professions have motives peculiar to themselves, and we may suppose that philosophy is no exception to the rule. Curiosity, one would think, must play a major rôle. But so it does in science – and also in other matters which philosopher and scientist alike would regard as merely trivial. We have therefore to inquire whether there is anything specific about philosophical curiosity.

The first point to notice about curiosity in general is that it often gets inhibited. Even the proverbial curiosity of children is already diverted from its original aim – not so much because it is rebuffed, as because it is unconsciously derived from a kind of aggressive intrusiveness, akin to greed, for which they unconsciously expect retaliation from their parents [2].

That curiosity is unconsciously felt as dangerous seems strange to modern man, but the ancients took this for granted. They consciously believed it impious to know more than the gods had chosen to reveal. For this impiety, for eating the fruit of the Tree of Knowledge, Adam and all his descendants are said to have deserved eternal punishment. Perhaps the fear of it was greater among the people of the Old Testament than among others. At any rate, they concentrated on religion, and avoided both philosophy and science till comparatively recent times. Then they made up for the delay by producing men like Spinoza in philosophy and Freud or Einstein in science.

Meanwhile it was the early philosophers of Greece who first had the courage to face the mysterious dangers of cosmic and moral speculation. And the risks were not altogether fanciful. For if the gods themselves did not exact the expected punishment, the faithful were apt to exact it on their behalf. Indeed,

[1] As a friendly critic, Mr Paul Segal, has rightly pointed out, I here tacitly assume the correctness of logical positivism without subjecting it to the same kind of psycho-analytical examination as I have attempted in the case of classical philosophy. I agree with him that in its early days, logical positivism was by no means free from emotional bias (splitting), classical philosophy being its 'bad' object and physics its over-idealized 'good' one.

from Socrates onwards, philosophy has always had its martyrs. But to the unconscious mind, I think, the imaginary dangers were always greater than the real ones, and the fear of these can still be an unseen impediment to curiosity about ultimate things which perhaps stand for the first things the child was aggressively curious about.

I would tentatively suggest that science, in later separating itself from philosophy, also freed itself from some of these unconscious anxieties, and that it did so by means of a partial renunciation. This renunciation can be overt, as for example when a scientist leaves all 'ultimate questions' to religion, and confines his curiosity to what he may think of as the material world. But I believe a similar renunciation can occur unconsciously, even when it appears not to have been made at all. He may assert, for example, that all significant questions can be answered in principle by science, and that such metaphysical questions as appear to be unanswerable result from bad grammar and are not significant. This may be sound logic, but, psychologically, it suggests a sour-grape attitude towards some kind of ultimate knowledge which is renounced though still unconsciously desired. Perhaps, therefore, what was specific to philosophical curiosity was that it retained more of its original aim – the pursuit of a knowledge felt, in some sense, to be ultimate; and we may add total as opposed to piecemeal. But this does not explain why such knowledge was to be obtained by contemplation, by looking inwards rather than at the external world; nor why the quest should be illogical, as the critics claim it to have been, as if it contained some inner contradiction.

The characteristic of looking inwards to discover the secrets of the universe would seem to imply that the ostensible object of speculation, the cosmos, was felt to mirror, or to be mirrored by, an inner world of absorbing interest. Moreover, there was a perfectionist element in past philosophical activity which seems related more to art than science, and suggests that curiosity was, after all, of secondary importance – that the ultimate aim was less to know, than to create, the universe. Psychologically, such an aim is less absurd than it may seem. For what to an outside observer is our picture, or model, of the world is to us the very world itself. In this sense we can create it. And we can do so in many ways – for example, teleologically or mechanistically. And the apparent contradiction between two ways need not be real. If both correspond with experience at every point at which they can be tested, they represent the same phenomena – like two equations of a curve, one in cartesian, the other in polar, co-ordinates. (This was the theme of the first paper I ever published [3].)

But though the world can be conceived in many different ways, the common-sense picture of it most of us employ is not particularly original. It is influenced by, and largely copied from, that which is current in our time. And once completed, we seldom question it again. The philosopher is different in that he creates what others copy. Indeed, his determination to create would seem to imply a refusal to copy which may be linked with that contempt for observation of which the classical philosophers have often been accused. Hegel, for example, when told that history did not conform to his philosophy, is reported to have said, 'So much the worse for history'. Such denial of facts, combined as it is with great creative ability, can express, I think, an unconscious envy of the parental gods, whose work is so much admired that it has to be ignored and re-created [4]. What, of course, was ignored, or actively destroyed and re-created, was, not the universe as made by God, but the old models of it made by previous philosophers – especially that enshrined in commonsense philosophy. And what, in the end, was so much admired as the work of God was the work of the philosopher who created the new model – and this may really have been an intellectual achievement of the highest order.

The two motives so far discussed – a curiosity and a creativeness which express an unconscious challenge to parents, whose creativity may consciously remain the object of grateful admiration – could partially explain the demand for total as opposed to piecemeal knowledge, and the refusal to look for it outside. In some degree, too, the will to create rather than to copy could explain why many philosophers have condemned classical philosophy as futile; for, if science is right, the secrets of the universe are only discoverable by observation. But this does not solve what according to the critics is the greatest puzzle: that the basic aim of classical philosophy – the pursuit of synthetic *a priori* knowledge – was not merely futile, like looking in the wrong place for something, but illogical, like looking for a round square.

Perhaps we can get a little further if we examine a third motive for philosophy, and that is doubt. Philosophical doubt has become proverbial. What others take for granted, whether in morals or in the theory of reality, arouses doubt in the philosopher, and this may well be his initial motive. It should be confessed at once that doubt applied to the philosophy of common sense is often justified. For if the layman examines his own philosophy, he will probably find it to be full of inconsistencies. It may contain, for example, different codes of ethics – one for home, one for the office, perhaps another for Sundays, and two more for domestic and foreign politics – as well as different theories of reality, one materialistic and another theological.

Now, these discordant elements express different and incompatible aspects of personality, which co-exist peacefully enough only because they seldom meet. We are accustomed to associate splitting mechanisms with schizophrenia, but they are also the means by which ordinary people defend themselves against the anxieties aroused by internal conflicts. The hedonic gain is obvious if conflicting attitudes to the same thing at the same time can be replaced by different attitudes to different things at different times; and this is what splitting achieves – though at the cost of truth. I believe one of the main characteristics of the classical philosopher was that such evasion of conflict by means of a little splitting, which comes so easily to most of us, was very hard for him. For this reason, he started more conscious of inconsistencies in his initial picture of the world, and therefore more troubled by doubts which reflected his greater awareness of ambivalence. Simultaneously to satisfy both sides of any conflict, rather than to satisfy each separately by splitting, may have been the source of the illogical aim he is accused of.

I think he often did achieve a higher degree of integration, of harmony of system, than other people; but the essential inconsistencies of human nature would seem to preclude complete success. At any rate, it is perhaps doubtful whether a philosophical system which is both internally consistent and comprehensive has ever been created. Most classical systems have been shown by other philosophers, either to be self-contradictory after all, or to have gained their consistency at the cost of leaving something out which ought to be in, but is not in because it will not fit. Such defects are usually attributed to the immense complexity of the task. But they may also reflect essential inconsistencies in man which no system can resolve.[1] What at first sight may appear as an unusually harmonious personality, with no minor splits, is sometimes achieved at the cost of a major split elsewhere which involves the total exclusion of an important aspect of the self. And I think the same thing can happen to a philosophic system. As far as it goes, it may be a completely harmonious picture of the world; but some whole section of what ordinary people call reality – it may be matter or mind, or perhaps the concept of evil – is ignored.

I would stress that much of what I have just said is necessarily speculative. But at least we have some theories to test against examples.

DOUBT AND CERTAINTY IN ETHICS

That the stimulus to ethical inquiry comes from moral doubts and conflicts within the self seems highly probable. Those who 'know what is right' are not aware of any problem, though to others they may seem to have shelved rather than to have solved it. In contrast to people of this kind, the philosopher of morals is more likely to be found among those who, having lost faith in the code they started with, are in search of a consistent alternative. Our problem is to trace these doubts to their origin.

To the psycho-analyst, the first step at least seems comparatively easy. Everyone is by now familiar with Freud's explanation of conscience: that it begins with the child's fear of displeasing his parents and reaches its final form when he 'introjects' them, or rather his ideas of them, as far stricter

[1] I wish to imply, not that it is logically impossible to construct a system which, within its own level, is consistent and comprehensive, but that it may be psychologically impossible to achieve the hidden aim of complete self-integration by means of the construction of such a system.

and 'better' than they really were. But because this idea of an internal authority, or superego to give it Freud's term, is largely unconscious, it is to this extent unalterable, so that the conscious ego, which does develop and mature, may become increasingly in conflict with it. The initial impulse to ethical inquiry may well come from conflicts of this kind, and end in one of two ways: either the authority of the superego is bolstered up by the construction of systems that purport to be absolute, or undermined by a scepticism designed to rob it of its terrors. Kant's ethics, with its stress on the categorical imperative, would seem a good example of the first alternative; that of the Epicureans, who attacked superstition as the cause of fear, a good example of the second.

But below such ego-superego conflicts is another which is, I think, more fundamental. Freud's theory of a conflict between life and death instincts is still controversial among analysts themselves; and of those who accept it, some do so with reservations and others with additions. Thus, while Freud believed in a death instinct but not in a basic fear of death, Melanie Klein believes in both. Personally, I find the concept of a death instinct difficult. But I believe in innate destructive impulses which necessarily have the, at first solipsistic, self as their primary object, and so give rise to the fear of death. In a form which is relevant to ethics, I would put it thus: deep in the unconscious, the ultimate source of anxiety is our own aggression, especially aggressive greed, which, however, may seem to threaten us, either from within[1] or from without, like a foreign force. Then, as a defence against the resulting unconscious intensification of the fear of death, the aggressive component in the ego's will to live may be increased to such a degree that every external object tends to be unconsciously viewed as a kind of nourishment to be consumed or as a threat to be destroyed. But, in conflict with this completely predatory egoism, the ego has developed an opposite tendency to embrace and identify itself with other objects, which it then as desperately endeavours to preserve. So an insoluble unconscious conflict threatens to arise, and is averted in the first place largely by mechanisms of splitting which tend to divide the world into

---

[1] Thus, for example, we speak of hunger 'gnawing' as if it were a devouring enemy inside.

enemies to be destroyed and friends to be protected from the external replicas of our own aggression.

This solution, maintained as it is by some denial of unlikeable qualities in the friends and of likeable ones in the enemies, is stable only so long as it is not too closely examined. Those who do examine it, if only semi-consciously, may be faced with the ethical problem in what I think is its most basic form: whether to prey on others that we may thrive or to sacrifice ourselves that they may.[1] Of course the dichotomy is not so absolute as it appears to the unconscious, for our interests and those of others are often the same. But to a great extent an incompatibility of interests, and indeed a competition for survival, does in fact exist. The classical philosopher would seem to have been, at least pre-consciously, more aware of this dichotomy than others. Perhaps he also unconsciously exaggerated it.

The underlying problem of how to thrive without feeling guilty at doing so at the expense of others is primarily internal. Most philosophers have treated it as such; but some have sought to evade it by treating it as solely external. Rousseau, for example, blamed society for all our faults and tried to construct an ideal one in which we should all be good as well as happy. He substituted, as it were, a myth of primal innocence for that of original sin. Thus his system was achieved at the cost of leaving something out – namely, the whole problem of the individual's sense of guilt which is rooted in ambivalence. We can give him credit for helping to inspire those liberal movements which really reduced some social tensions and so lessened one external cause of internal conflict. But the consistent development of his denial of the individual's unconscious sense of responsibility for predatory aggression led in the end, not to the emancipation of individuals from their sense of guilt, but to the mass projection of conscience, in its most ferocious form, into totalitarian states which sought to control even the thoughts of individuals.

I do not wish to imply that the attempt to improve the external world is necessarily futile. But I do think that past

[1] Freud speaks of 'a carrying-over into the region of the mind of the dilemma – eat or be eaten – which dominates the organic world' ('Anxiety and Instinctual Life' in *New Introductory Lectures on Psycho-Analysis*, 1933).

attempts to do so have been disappointing. Those two dominant expressions of our innate aggressiveness, greed and envy, do not seem to diminish in proportion to a reduction in their apparent external causes. And the unconscious guilt they arouse remains a secret motive for a demand for scapegoats. It looks as if these impulses might have to be diminished through a better understanding of ourselves before the benefits of a more humane society can be fully realized.

In contrast to Rousseau, Kant was concerned to devise, or, as he thought, to discover, a universal code for individuals. According to his 'categorical imperative', we ought each to act in such a way that we could wish our own behaviour to become a general law governing the behaviour of everyone. Philosophically considered, I do not think, as he did, that this is a synthetic judgment *a priori*. But as a contribution to the psychological problem of achieving an optimum compromise between egoism and altruism, it would seem to have much to recommend it.

It is characteristic of philosophers, who demand consistency, that they are not content with a merely personal solution of the moral problem. Their aim is to find some one standard which everyone has only to understand to agree to. If there can be no such things as synthetic judgments *a priori*, the quest may seem a vain one, and, for this reason, the ethical relativists have abandoned it as hopeless. But I think there is a sense in which it may, after all, be partially achieved. Since Plato there has been, as it were, a persistent hunch among philosophers that wickedness is the result of ignorance, and that if we were all wise we should all be good; and by this is implied good according to some universally accepted standard. Now, if by wisdom we understand knowledge of ourselves, there is much recent analytic evidence that different people in fact approximate to a common type of moral character, which I have called humanist, as they advance in this kind of knowledge. In other words, the hunch about a common standard for all wise men, which so many philosophers have tried to prove by non-empirical arguments, begins to seem probable in the light of recent empirical discoveries – a theme which I have developed elsewhere [5].

THE THEORY OF REALITY

Turning from ethics to the theory of reality, the same passion for consistency is responsible for much which to the ordinary man seems palpably absurd. And, as before, the initial motive is doubt, this time directed towards the physical aspect of our common-sense picture of the world.

Take, for instance, the theory of reality as developed by Locke, Berkeley, and Hume. From the beginning, philosophers have been troubled by doubts aroused by apparent inconsistencies between what things seem to be and what they are. When the end of a stick is dipped in water, it looks bent. The ordinary man is not much troubled by such experiences. The stick looks bent but he 'knows' it is really straight and can 'prove' this by feeling it. The philosopher is less easily content. 'If', he will say, 'my sense of sight can deceive me, why should I be more sure that my sense of touch is telling me the truth? How, in fact, can I be sure that all my senses are not deceiving me with an "appearance" (hallucination?) totally unlike reality?'[1] Or, to put the question in another way: 'Are there any qualities which I can attribute to the "real" stick as opposed to those I can attribute to its appearance?' To this question common sense before the time of Locke would probably have answered that the colour belongs to the appearance and the hardness to the reality. Locke argued that there is no essential difference between the two, and that the hardness, the 'feel of' the stick, like its colour, is a sensual or subjective quality and belongs to the appearance. But as opposed to these secondary qualities, substantiality and extension belong, he said, to the 'real' objective thing. This division, which for a long time was good enough for science, still influences our common-sense conception of the world. But, in fact, Berkeley soon showed it to be entirely artificial. For, like colour, hardness, and so forth, substantiality and extension are perceptible qualities, though terminologically disguised, and belong to the appearance; so the whole distinction between appearance and reality, in this sense, disappears. To be consistent, therefore, Berkeley thought

[1] However valuable in philosophy, a doubt of this kind has unmistakable affinities with the distrust of the paranoid who, because of his own ambivalence, is unable to trust any other person.

of objects as being real only when perceived, and as existing only in the minds of their percipients. This, of course, threatened to leave him with a very discontinuous world, in which objects existed only intermittently. But he saved the situation with the aid of God, who is always perceiving everything, and so keeps it permanently real. It remained for the agnostic Hume cheerfully to remove the final prop, and to leave us, as it were, floating in a purely subjective world. In his philosophy, not only do objects consist only of their secondary qualities and therefore exist only when perceived, but we ourselves consist only of our sensations and our thoughts, and therefore exist only when awake. In Hume's view this is the only consistent way of thinking of the world. But he admitted that neither he nor anyone else could think consistently for any length of time.

Our psychological problem is to discover whether this is another case of consistency being achieved at the cost of leaving something out which ought to be in. What is, of course, left out is the concept of a substance, or matter, which can exist without being perceived. To both Berkeley and Hume such a concept is self-contradictory. As psychologists, we want to discover whether this was their sole objection to it, or whether for some other reason it aroused an unconscious animus in them.

In the case of Berkeley, at least, there are some grounds for supposing that it did. For J. O. Wisdom [6], in a recent book, has argued that to Berkeley, who in the end became hypochondriacally preoccupied with purging his own body, the very idea of matter had a persecutory significance and, as such, had to be eliminated from his picture of the world. No one, as far as I know, has attempted a similar analysis in the case of Hume, who appears to have been one of the sanest, as well as one of the most amiable, of men. But we do know that the force of his own logic led him to construct a picture of the world so strange and so repugnant to common sense that he himself could never hold it for any length of time. And what, I think, his logic did lead him to construct, or reconstruct, was the phenomenological world of the infant from which the common-sense picture is developed.

But whether Hume's philosophy was or was not influenced, in any great degree, by unconscious motives, the resistance to it certainly was. We take our common-sense picture of the world too much for granted, and so forget that it is a picture created by ourselves. Moreover, it can be lost or destroyed in certain states of madness, in which it can, as it were, disintegrate into its original elements, and so lose its comforting solidity. It is, I think, the fear of this disaster that Hume's philosophy so greatly stirred – a fear which Dr Johnson eloquently expressed when he stamped on the pavement to prove that it was real.[1]

THE CONSTRUCTION OF WORLD MODELS

This brings me to the contribution of philosophy to psycho-analysis. If we are not all philosophers, there is an important sense in which we all have a philosophy – that is, a general picture of the world – together with general rules of conduct. Thus the current philosophy of common sense is what a philosopher would call a naive dualism. To the psychic part belong our sensations, thoughts, and feelings, perhaps also an anthropomorphic concept of a psyche, mind, or soul which 'owns' them, and is itself saddled with a conscience. To the physical part belong the physical objects we 'perceive' and think of as ultimately analysable into non-perceptible molecules, atoms, electrons, and so on. (See also [7].)

Subjectivist philosophers, like Hume and his successors, Mach and Avenarius, have taught us not to take this common-sense world for granted. They have also constructed a monistic and subjective alternative which, at least in its cognitive aspect, is probably quite close to the world of the infant. By so doing they raised the psychologically important problem of how one is developed from the other. And I think that that branch of philosophy which is concerned with logic and the construction of language may have given us the outline of a model which may aid the solution of the problem.

The main difficulty in the subjectivist point of view is that most presentations of it do not make adequate provision for the concept of linguistic symbolism and external reference. If

[1] [Possibly their 'original elements' into which the world could disintegrate, may be what Bion calls beta-elements which cannot be remembered or thought and are fit only for evacuation by projection.]

all the qualities of a perceived object are subjective, the object as a transcendental entity does not exist. But applying the same argument to a remembered object, we might arrive at the conclusion that all its qualities belong to our *present* subjective experience, and that the past perception, of which it is the memory, does not exist. And this comes perilously near to the assertion that, since there is nothing, we cannot think of anything beyond our momentary experience; in other words, that ideas have no external reference and language, whether verbal or non-verbal, no meaning.

So what the extreme subjectivist seems to be depicting is the momentary world of a person who has no language, not even a language of pre-verbal thought, with which to refer to the objects of memory or expectation. Now, this does seem to approximate, though only in its cognitive aspect, to the world of the infant. For at the beginning memories and expectations, which later have external reference, are not yet differentiated from phantasies so charged with emotion that they have a hallucinatory vividness which makes them indistinguishable from perceptions.

But even the emergence of the distinction between present thought and its absent object, which enables the more integrated child to think of a permanent world, is probably not alone sufficient to enable him to think of a dualistic one. For to do this, he must not only be able to think and feel about permanent, as distinct from intermittent, objects, but also to identify with others and become able to think and feel, from an outside point of view – that is, self-consciously – about the relation of his own thought and feelings to them. The intermediate stage, of being able to think of permanent objects but not of the relation of the thought itself to them, reminds me of a limitation of language first pointed out by Wittgenstein, which Russell showed how to circumvent [8]. According to Wittgenstein, no language can express its own relation to what it represents. So that, according to Russell, if we do talk about this relation we must do so in a language of a higher order than the first. Of course it is difficult to say when the capacity to use a second-order language begins, especially as it is at first a language of pre-verbal thought. But its emergence would seem to be equivalent to the emergence of a capacity to identify ourselves with others, and so to think and feel, self-consciously, that is, from outside, about the relation of our thoughts and feelings to their objects. And this in turn would seem to be equivalent to the emergence of a dualistic picture of the world.

To the philosophers, therefore, we owe not only our first awareness of there being a problem about the development of our dualistic picture of the world, but also the suggestion of there being at least three stages in this development, which correspond with no language, first-order language, and second-order language. It remains for psychology to fill in the details.

This can be attempted by two independent methods: by the direct observation of children and by the psycho-analysis of children and adults. The first is used by Jean Piaget in his important work *The Child's Construction of Reality* (1955). I must leave it to others to correlate the observational and the psycho-analytic approach. My present aim is only to correlate the philosophical and the analytic one.

STAGES OF DEVELOPMENT

In other words, I shall try to combine the cognitive stages suggested by philosophy with the emotional stages, or positions, reconstructed by analysis. In doing so, I have been guided, in the main, by Melanie Klein's discoveries [9]. But I have also borrowed concepts from biology. The result is a five-stage model of development, the first three of which more or less correspond with the 'no language' stage suggested by subjectivist philosophy. I should add that my reconstruction does not claim to be more than tentative. It is also artificially schematic.

The first post-natal stage, just after what Freud described as the 'shock' of birth, is probably akin to the buzzing confusion imagined by William James; though we believe we can add that it is a persecutory confusion of a traumatic kind. Probably this is soon followed – perhaps within hours – by a stage in which certain *Gestalten*, or significant patterns of sensation, begin to emerge. We know from such students of animal behaviour as Tinbergen [10] and Lorenz [11], that certain patterns of stimuli evoke innate responses, for example, in newly hatched birds. And we have reason to believe this to be true also of the human infant. Moreover, just as the newly hatched gull responds by gaping to a red spot on cardboard in the same way as it would to the red spot on its mother's bill, so the human infant may not at first discriminate between different members of a class of objects having the same *Gestalt* – that, for example, of a breast. Nor does he distinguish between the percept and the hallucinatory memory of it.

We must try, then, to envisage this second stage as one in which there is little or no symbolism in either of two important senses. There is no symbolism in what may be broadly called the linguistic sense, because the idea, for example of the breast, has the hallucinatory vividness of a percept, and so cannot yet stand *for* past or future percepts not present at the time. For this reason, the 'object' has an intermittent rather than a permanent or 'objective' existence. And there is little symbolism even in the psycho-analytic sense. What we later call symbols are, rather, equated with their objects [12]; for no one member of the class of patterns having the same *Gestalt*, and evoking an innate response, is yet clearly distinguished as *the* object of which the other members later become symbols eliciting only a partial response. Nevertheless, there is one sense in which these *Gestalten* may be said to be significant: the baby behaves 'as if' he recognized them as objects of intense desire, or of destructive hatred and persecutory fear.

It is, in fact, these different affective responses which determine the only discrimination made at this stage: that between good or pleasurable and bad or painful experience. And this distinction cuts right through later identities. For the various appearances, whether sensed or hallucinated, of what will later be thought of as one object are at first classified into two groups, one good and beneficent, the other bad and persecutory. Sometimes the good, sometimes the bad, aspect comes into being and then ceases to exist; for they are not yet thought of as continuing to exist when neither hallucinated nor perceived.

The third stage in my over-schematic presentation is that in which one only of the members of a class of patterns having the same *Gestalt* elicits a total response, while the response to the others becomes partial. That is to say, they become symbols in the psycho-analytic sense. They can be *substitutes* for what we should call the real object; but they do not yet *represent* it in the way that an idea, or later a word, can represent an absent object. By this time the good and bad aspects of the same object have different symbols; and, since good symbols tend to become bad whenever they arouse anger or fear, they are continually being replaced by new ones. In this way the infant's world is rapidly enriched. But although it has many 'objects' in it, these are not yet 'objective' in the sense of being substantial and permanent.

Up to this point, therefore, the infant's philosophy is a subjective monism, akin to that of Hume – though it is emotionally split into good and bad. Only in the next or fourth stage, when 'good' and 'bad' phantasies become more integrated and so lose some of their hallucinatory intensity, can they acquire 'meaning' as referring to percepts which are 'external' in that they are not being actually perceived. Then, while much of phantasy remains an unconscious part of an immanent subjective world, conscious imagery emerges from it to form the thought-model of an external objective world which, unlike Berkeley's, continues to exist even when not observed. In other words, the child has a first-order language of pre-verbal conscious thought with which to make a model of experience. But his world is not yet fully dualistic. A subjective monism has been replaced by a predominantly monistic materialism; for although he now thinks of an external world in relation to himself, he does not yet think with full self-consciousness of his mental ego's relation to it.

Only in the final stage – and I should remind you again that I am describing a fluctuating process as if it occurred in steps – does the child more definitely project his observing self, at first into his parents – that is, identify himself with them – and so observe, as it were from without, his own emotional relation to them and to the external world in general.

From the beginning there has been an interplay between what we call 'introjective' and 'projective' mechanisms. And this implies that there has been some boundary, and a fluctuating one, between what is at first mainly a 'body-ego', controlled by phantasies, emotions and unconscious processes, and more objective perceptions. But what can belong alternately to the self or to the external world in earlier stages is not an integrated ego – and still less a self-conscious one. In these earlier stages it is, I think, more the primitive *Gestalten*, endowed with the simple affects of love, hate, or fear they arouse, that could at one moment be 'introjected' to form part of the self and at the next 'projected' outside. Moreover, at first the aim of these mechanisms was only, on the one hand, to get rid of, and ultimately to annihilate, all bad objects and feelings, and on the other to assimilate all the good ones into the self – in short, to preserve a blissful solipsism, all good, all one, all self. This, incidentally, would seem to be the aim of certain mystical philosophies. But in the stage we are now trying to reconstruct, introjection and projection are being used in a more complex way to form the concepts of one's own and other people's minds.

It would be difficult to say which comes first. For the two ideas seem to develop together and to enrich each other. But I will suppose that, as soon as objects come to be thought of as having a permanent existence, the former simple affective response to them develops into more complex sentiments, each of which might constitute a kind of part ego. Such a sentiment, once formed, can then be projected into, or attributed to, its object – for example, the mother – no longer to get rid of it if it is bad, but also to endow her with goodness if it is good. Moreover, it is felt to be expressed in her behaviour which can thus confirm and enrich it. In other words, his picture of her sentiment, originally based on identification, is more realistically developed. And then, by imitating, or re-introjecting his picture of her, his picture of his own mental self is in turn enriched. So, by an alternating process of introjection and projection, the concepts of his own and other people's egos are gradually built up.

This stage in which the child learns to think of himself and others as people, with similar feelings and desires, is the one in which he begins to feel concerned for them, and for himself, as people – in particular, concerned for the damage he may do them in imagination when he is angry. In fact, the most important turning-point in his early development is reached, the 'depressive position' discovered and so termed by Melanie Klein, when he is capable of being deterred, not merely by anxieties of a persecutory kind but by feelings of guilt. And from now on he is a moral being, with a moral conflict between love and hate and between egoism and altruism.

But the aspect of this stage I would emphasize here is the

child's greater capacity to identify with others, and so view, as it were from without, his own feelings in their relation to objects – to be self-consciously conscious of experience. To the infant, and in unselfconscious periods to the adult as well, perception, filled out by memory beyond the field of view, constitutes or *is* the world. But as soon as he can split off part of his observing self outside, this complex of perception and memory which a moment ago was the objective world itself, becomes a subjective picture of it. Such a momentous change in outlook is, I have argued, equivalent to the acquisition of a second-order language – a second-order thought-model of the world – which is dualistic because its object is the relation of mind to matter in the broadest sense.

Although I believe that the five stages I have described do roughly correspond to significant points in a developmental process, which ends in the dualistic philosophy of common sense, I do not wish to imply that there are only five or that they can all be clearly distinguished. The main ones can be. Others are inserted because they seem to be almost logically required – like the intermediate steps in an argument of which we are given only the beginning and the end.

Moreover, the last stage would seem to be at least intermittently reached, though not consolidated, at a very early age, after which there are only refinements to be made. For there is a good deal of evidence that the depressive position is reached about the middle of the first half-year, and this I think implies that the child, if only pre-consciously, can identify himself sufficiently with his mother to begin to imagine his own relation to her from her point of view. If so, he already has the essential rudiments of a second-order thought-model of the world, although he has not yet acquired a verbal language and is still incapable of verbal thought.

LANGUAGE AND VERBAL THOUGHT

Pure imagery, without the use of words, is thus, I think, sufficient to form, not only a first-order model but also a second-order one, and so to achieve the dualistic philosophy of common sense. But all the refinements in these models, which distinguish us from our pre-verbal ancestors, potentially perhaps no less intelligent, are the product of language in the narrow sense, and of the capacity for verbal thought.

Verbal language, which Hobbes called the greatest invention of all other, presupposes an imagery based largely on psychoanalytic symbols in a way first described by Ernest Jones [13]. But in the end this imagery is restricted to verbal signs, linked only by custom to what they represent. Of its many functions we are here concerned only with its use in recording and extending knowledge by the construction of word-models of the expected possibilities of experience. In accordance with the dualistic nature of the overriding model, knowledge is of three kinds: psychological, physical, and psycho-physical. It is on the rôle of language in psychological knowledge that I would like to conclude.

Psychology is in a sense a very ancient science. At least from the time when language acquired proper names, personal pronouns, and verbs to express emotions and other mental states, man has been, if intermittently, raising the level of his own self-consciousness – a form of progress which perhaps best deserves the name.

The chief credit for the advances of the past is due to the poets who, even before writing was invented, have been creating imaginary characters, personifying traits, which their hearers could then for the first time apprehend and recognize as existing in those around them or in themselves. Everyone, for example, is now familiar with Shakespeare's main characters. They have become part of our understanding of psychology because he created them. By doing so he raised self-consciousness and intuition to an appreciably higher level than before.

The philosophers, too, have done the same, though in their case it was more the intellectual than the emotional and unconscious aspect of our psychology that their work has helped us the better to perceive. To them we owe much of our knowledge of how we form at least the intellectual part of our picture of the world.

Moreover, this work of the poets and philosophers, so far as it has increased self-consciousness and intuition by putting into words so many states of mind which otherwise would have remained unnoticed, has to this extent already mastered some part of the unconscious. So psychology and psycho-analysis have ancient forerunners. What is new in it is the explicit recognition of unconscious processes and the development of a specialized technique for their exploration. This is the achievement of Freud.

It may be expected that, with the aid of this new technique, there will be an acceleration in the rate at which the level of consciousness, and so also the sense of personal responsibility, is raised. Something of the kind has already taken place. We cannot yet judge its full significance. But if the new insights are not lost in some calamity, the future historian may well look back on Freud's work as marking a decisive change in the tempo of human progress.

BIBLIOGRAPHY

[1] Wittgenstein, *Tractatus Logico-Philosophicus*, 1922.
[2] See Klein, Melanie, *Contributions to Psycho-Analysis*, 1948, especially the paper on Intellectual Inhibitions (1931).
[3] Money-Kyrle, R., 'Belief and Representation', which appeared in the first and only volume of *Symposion*, 1925-6.
[4] Klein, Melanie, 'A Study in Envy and Gratitude'. Read at the 1955 International Congress of Psycho-Analysis, and shortly to be published as a book.
[5] Money-Kyrle, R., 'Psycho-Analysis and Ethics', 1952 (republished in *New Directions in Psycho-Analysis*, 1955) and, *Psycho-Analysis and Politics*, 1951.
[6] Wisdom, J. O. (1953). *Unconscious Origin of Berkeley's Philosophy*. London: Hogarth Press.
[7] Money-Kyrle, R., 'The World of the Unconscious and the World of Common Sense', *British Journal for the Philosophy of Science*, VII, 25, 1956.
[8] See Russell's Introduction to the English Translation of Wittgenstein's *Tractatus*.
[9] See Klein, Melanie, *The Psycho-Analysis of Children*, 1932; *Contributions to Psycho-Analysis*, 1948; as well as the papers by herself and her colleagues in *Developments in Psycho-Analysis*, 1952, and *New Directions in Psycho-Analysis*, 1955.
[10] Tinbergen, *The Study of Instinct*, 1951.
[11] Lorenz, *King Solomon's Ring*, 1952.
[12] Klein, Melanie, 'The Importance of Symbol Formation in the Development of the Ego', *Contributions to Psycho-Analysis*, 1948.
Segal, H., Paper on 'Symbol Formation' to be published shortly.
[13] Jones, Ernest, 'The Theory of Symbolism', *Papers on Psycho-Analysis*, 1918.

20

The World of the Unconscious and the World of Common Sense*

I. AFFECTIVE AND INTELLECTUAL RESISTANCE TO INTERPRETATION

The basic procedure of analysis, due to Freud, is well known. The patient tries to convey his conscious thoughts and feelings to the analyst who, in virtue of his own previous analysis, believes that in many of them he can recognize the influence of other thoughts and feelings which are repressed. When he interprets this connection, the patient may himself recognize it as correct or he may not do so for one of two reasons: either he may understand the interpretation but reject it as untrue, or he may fail to understand it. In both cases, if the analyst still believes his interpretation to have been correct and lucidly expressed, he will attribute the patient's failure to accept it to an affective resistance which he will try to analyse in turn. But there are intermediate cases in which the sense of an interpretation, though verbally understood, will seem too 'impossible' to be vividly conceived; and here, at least, a specific intellectual problem may also be involved.

The contrast between two sorts of interpretation, one comparatively superficial and the other deep, may illustrate the kind of problem I have in mind. A woman patient[1] begins a session by saying she has just seen an overdressed person in the street, who looked like a prostitute and to whom she has taken an immediate dislike. From such material, if supported by previous evidence of a similar kind, the analyst perhaps infers that, unconsciously, she believes this person to be another, and

* B. J. *Philosophy of Science*, vol. VII, no. 25, 1956.
[1] The assumption of a woman patient being analysed by a man is a grammatical convenience which permits the substitution of pronouns for a tedious repetition of the nouns.

a preferred patient, who has just left and with whom he has been having an affair. She may accept the interpretation with embarrassment, or contemptuously reject it with the remark that he must be very conceited to imagine that she could have any personal interest in him or his other beastly patients. A rejection of this kind is clearly no disproof. But, whether true or false, the rejected interpretation is intelligible and has been clearly understood.

Now take the kind of 'deep' interpretation which is often given by analysts, such as myself, who have accepted Melanie Klein's theories on the early development of children.[1] Another patient, or the same one at another time, is anxious to be helped and for this purpose to accept almost any interpretation that may be given. For while yesterday she felt she had got a great deal from her analysis and became elated, she is now anxious and depressed. In particular, she has suddenly become anxious about money. So many demands are being made upon her, especially by the expenses of analysis, that she will soon be destitute. And to her anxieties on her own behalf is added depression about her inability to give adequate presents to certain friends to whom she now remembers she owes much.

Taken singly, these various worries may seem sufficiently explained in terms of their conscious causes. But their general pattern, coming as it does just after a period of elation in analysis, will suggest to the analyst the influence of a deep unconscious phantasy with which he is familiar, and can only be familiar, through his own analysis – a phantasy about an early feeding situation. He may therefore tell his patient that yesterday she felt as if she had swallowed some 'good thing' from him, represented by the 'good interpretations' she so avidly consumed, but that this now seems threatened inside (ultimately by her own dissociated greed which she attributes to everyone who may make demands on her, and especially to himself).[2] He may add that, at the same time, she feels overwhelmed with gratitude for the same good thing, is in despair about never being able to repay it and that this despair has increased her fear of its becoming a 'bad thing' which will eat

[1] Melanie Klein, *The Psycho-analysis of Children*, London, 1932; *Contributions to Psycho-Analysis*, London, 1948.
[2] The bracketed clause will, of course, be expressed in simple language.

her up (and the good one inside) in revenge. Finally, he may explain that these complex feelings repeat those she experienced in infancy in relation to her mother and that the 'good' thing, which may be lost or become 'bad', is a breast.

If accepted – and to be accepted it must first be understood – an interpretation of this kind may at once relieve the patient's distress. But, unless great care is taken to phrase it in terms of feelings of which she is already aware, it is likely not so much to be rejected as untrue as to fail to convey any clear impression of its content. For, though not logically meaningless, it may well seem to be factually nonsense.

If so, the lack of understanding may be attributed either to an emotional resistance in the patient or to the analyst's failure to express himself in appropriate terms. But, in either case, it cannot be denied that his difficulties are increased by the incompatibility of what he is trying to say with many preconceptions both of science and of common sense.

The patient may object that she has been bottle-fed from birth, so that her present feelings cannot possibly repeat those she once felt for her mother's breasts. And, in any case, if her sense of material reality is firmly established, she will find it hard consciously to conceive the idea of containing her analyst's breast – especially as he is a man and has not got one. Thus, what she does understand of the interpretation will seem to be scientifically impossible, and the rest will be inconceivable to her.

A comprehensive study of the intellectual implications of these two difficulties would take us far: one is concerned with biological theories of the nature of instinct and the other touches an ancient problem of philosophy – that of the nature of reality itself. I will try to deal with the first one first; for, though less fundamental, it is, I think, related to, and can serve to introduce a discussion of, the second.

II. INSTINCTS

The prevalently material trend of science has accustomed us to think of instinct in terms of innate behaviouristic reactions to stimuli rather than as innate, cognitive, affective, and conative responses to sensations. Moreover, the very suggestion that there could be an innate cognitive element in any response is apt to be repudiated as implying an impossible belief in the inheritance of memory. We therefore start burdened with two prejudices: one general against a subjective theory of instinct at all; and one specific against the suggestion that inherited memory, or anything like it, can possibly be found.

The case against the inheritance of memory rests mainly on our inability to imagine any biological process by which the acquisitions of an individual could so affect his germ cells as to become innate in his offspring. This is not of course conclusive evidence against Lamarck; but I accept it the more readily because I believe that something resembling racial memory, should it be found to occur, could be explained quite well without him. We confidently assume that the physiological concomitant of memory is a cerebral process conditioned by an acquired modification, perhaps in synoptic resistance, of some complex pattern of neurones. But it is possible to imagine that similar modifications could arise as the result of mutations in germ cells and that these would tend either to die out or to spread through the species, according to their value to it. If so, the psychic concomitant of cerebral processes determined by heritable modifications of this kind could be mistaken for racial memory, when in fact it was the result, not of the experience, but of the mutations of former members of the species. In other words, if such mutations have occurred and been selected, we could, for example, be born into the world with some capacity to 'recognize' the more important objects and situations we are likely to encounter without having inherited any 'memory' of them.

Now we know from the study of animal behaviour that there are many highly complex innate reactions to stimuli – for example, the 'gaping' response of the newly hatched gull to the red spot on its mother's bill[1] – in which animals behave 'as if' they 'recognized' an object or situation they had never experienced before. If, therefore, we were not afraid of interpreting our observations in psychic terms, we might conclude that some innate capacity to recognize what has never been experienced not only could be, but has been, evolved.

[1] See N. Tinbergen, *The Study of Instinct*, Oxford, 1951.

That we do not jump to such conclusions is the result of a determination to stick to what we can actually observe. So long as we are dealing with animals other than ourselves, this may be a wise restraint. But it leads to a paradoxical result when our own species is the object of study. For, while we are not yet able to do more than guess the nature of the cerebral processes which mediate between stimulus and innate reaction, their psychic concomitants can be observed in ourselves or described to us by others. To exclude this part of the evidence is, therefore, to exclude the only link between stimulus and innate reaction that we can so far observe.

These psychic processes may, indeed, be difficult to observe correctly. Different workers often disagree about what is there to be seen. But at least there is a technique, that of psycho-analysis as developed by Freud, which makes such observations its principal concern.

Of course the analyst is never presented with material that is entirely uninfluenced by learning.[1] But he habitually deals with psychic patterns that are both very early and very general, and in which even the individual variations appear to result as much from different heredities as from different environments. So he has no doubt that he is dealing with innate modes of thought which, though certainly evoked by experience, have hardly yet begun to be specifically moulded by it.

But if he tries to make a clear distinction between instinct in a primary form and instinct as moulded by experience, he will encounter a special difficulty which is itself significant. He will have to rely on external evidence since no internal difference, except in degree of precision, can be found. However far back he goes and however certain he may be on other grounds that he is dealing with instinct in the raw, he will still find in it, not only affective and conative, but also cognitive aspects which might have been supposed to be the hallmark of a learned response. So it begins to look as if what I have suggested as possible is in fact the case: that we are born into the world with the capacity to 'recognize' some of the objects and situations we are likely to encounter in it.

There is much psycho-analytical evidence that we are so

---

[1] Especially if pre-natal experience has to be considered.

born. And this is perhaps a sufficient basis for some further advance in the psycho-analytic theory of instincts – which is admittedly in need of much development. Here biology can help us; for it has already given names to certain elements in innate behaviour which would seem to have their psychological equivalents. The concepts of 'sign stimuli' in 'innate releasing mechanisms'[1] is particularly suggestive because it is as such that certain *gestalts*, having the characteristics, for example, of a breast, would seem to function in the human infant. I think we need a special term for these. The word 'symbol' in its analytic sense does not quite fit. When we say a child is responding to a 'symbol of the breast' we imply that he is responding to something other than the breast: but the term we need must include the object together with its symbols so far as these elicit an innate response. In spite of a slight risk of confusion, I suggest the term 'primary symbol' for this purpose.[2]

There seem to be several primary symbols. All are *gestalts* having the characteristics of some object or situation of major biological importance, such as breast, mouth, penis, vagina, and the act of intercourse. And there can be little doubt that the innate response to them is cognitive as well as affective and conative. That is to say, any sensory pattern having the *gestalt* of a primary symbol arouses a 'sense of recognition'. At least it is 'recognized', often, of course, wrongly, as something desirable or dangerous and, for this reason, evokes rudimentary emotions of love, fear, or hate, together with some striving, if only in imagination, to possess, escape from, or destroy it.

We must suppose that innate psychological responses of this kind have been evolved because they help the infant to adapt himself, almost without experience, to specific objects and situations he is likely to encounter. But, even if he does not encounter them, he will still respond, in much the same way, to some other object or situation of the same *gestalt*. So the analyst who interprets some pattern of his patient's emotional

[1] Tinbergen, op. cit.
[2] Jungian 'archetypes' and Platonic 'ideas' may have affinities with 'primary symbols' as defined above. In particular, Plato's theory of ideal forms laid up in heaven which are dimly remembered when we perceive their imperfect earthly copies, would seem to me to have its basis in that sense of recognition which I believe to characterize the psychic response to a primary symbol (innate release stimulus).

response towards himself as a repetition of her response to her mother's breast, is not much disturbed by the discovery that she was bottle-fed from birth. For it is still true that she was repeating her response to a primary breast symbol.

Yet there is perhaps a subtle difference between her and other patients which he might have noticed: a greater sense of having missed something which she ought to have possessed. Must we then suppose that there is also a specific innate idea of the breast? Biologists describe innate 'appetitive behaviour', in response to the stimulus of an internal need, which precedes the 'consummatory act' evoked by an innate releasing stimulus. The animal or baby seems to be 'looking for' something which it may never have encountered before. But the innate capacity to 'recognize' what is needed does not necessarily imply a positive innate idea of it. All we can be sure of is that there are graded acts of recognition of the form 'this is not it', 'this is nearly it' and 'this is it'. So if we speak of innate ideas we should perhaps regard them as being at first only negatively defined.[1]

III. REALITY

It seems a far cry from biological theories of instinct to philosophical theories of reality. But I believe instinct in the main creates our first world which survives in the unconscious, and that the common-sense world is developed from it under the influence of a few months' experience.

This common-sense world is so familiar that we think of it as something we have been born into and which will exist, independent of our thoughts and feelings, long after we have left it. But we can also think of it in terms of subjectivist philosophy as an ordered arrangement of sensations, including feelings and memories of them – that is, as something constructed by ourselves. And, in doing so, we can see in what sense it is objective and substantial too.

In the first place, it is egocentric.[2] We can certainly move

---

[1] But this is a matter about which it is perhaps best to suspend our judgment for the present.

[2] The concept here developed of the world as radiating from the body-ego is similar to Clifford Scott's concept of the 'body scheme' which is itself an extension of Paul Schilder's concept of the 'body image'.

about it in thought, viewing it from any point we choose within its space-time framework. But our bodily sensations normally remain fixed at its momentary core. So long as this remains, the ego is felt to be separate from its 'objective' surroundings. Thus, the egocentricity of the world prevents it from being solipsistic. But it may become solipsistic in states of 'depersonalization' when its egocentricity is lost.

In the seond place, it is dualistic. That is to say, the sensations and ideas of which it is ultimately built, are grouped in two different ways to form two different kinds of entity: 'solid' percept-objects, including animal bodies, and 'unsubstantial' minds which these bodies 'possess'. In it, therefore, three types of relation are distinguished: those between different objects which comprise the physical part of the world; those between different minds or different parts of the same mind which comprise the sociological and psychological parts; and those between objects and minds which comprise the psycho-physical part.[1] But the distinction between sensations and ideas can also occasionally be lost; and then the world becomes monistic.

Lastly – besides the two divisions between the ego and its surroundings, and between matter and mind – the division between subject and object occurs in a third and more fundamental way. For we can also think of the whole common-sense world as being only a 'subjective model' (which, within limits can be tested[2]) of an objective 'reality' (which within limits can be predicted or controlled). It is true that when we enquire what it is that we can compare with the model and predict or control, we find that it is no more than some future sensory experience which is only objective in the sense that it is not being experienced now. It is also true that the switch from thinking of the common-sense world as reality to thinking of it as a model of reality is only a change in the order of the model we are using – a switch from a first order model to a

---

[1] Strict behaviourists believe that only the first of these relations is a fit subject for scientific study.

[2] Thus, for example, the model contains memory images, and so expectations, of what lies beyond our field of view, and these can be proved to be either true or false according as they do or do not correspond with the extended field of view we obtain by moving. The model and what it represents coincide in present experience.

second order model of the relation of the first order one to what it represents.¹ But the fact that we make the switch at all has its roots in actual experience. If our expectations and our wishes were always automatically fulfilled, I do not think we should ever do so. It is the experience of surprise and disappointment that forces us to think of the 'real' world as something different from our conception of it – something discovered rather than created by ourselves. And this would seem to be the basic source of our sense of its objective independence.

We also discover the limits beyond which the world thought of as a model cannot be verified, as well as those beyond which, when thought of as reality, it cannot be controlled.

Thus, for example, we discover that the physical aspect of our world model is more easily tested than its psychological or its psycho-physical aspects. Subject only to the limitations of our movements in space-time, its physical aspect is always potentially testable and is, in fact, confirmed whenever perceptual experience coincides with our expectations about the behaviour of percept objects. The psychological aspect, comprising our picture of our own and other people's minds is, strictly speaking, only testable in the part that represents ourselves (and then only so far as this is conscious) since we cannot perceive the mental experience of others. But because we perceive a 'psycho-physical' relation between our own 'physical' acts and 'mental' processes, we expect other people's acts to conform with our picture of their minds and assume it 'true' until these expectations are disproved.

We also discover that the extent of our capacity to change the 'real' world depends on the section we are concerned with. If we observe ourselves from without, which we can do in thought, even our thoughts seem to be determined by heredity and environment.² But, experienced from within, our control over our own thoughts, feelings, and desires is restricted only by internal conflicts. Next absolute in degree is the control we

¹ Failure to distinguish between models of different orders is probably responsible for some ancient confusions in philosophy.
² The determinist view that the desires which determine action are themselves determined by heredity and environment is by no means the same as the fatalist view that our fate is independent of volition. As far as I know, Professor Moritz Schlick was the first to show that the two views are incompatible.

exercise over those percept objects which comprise the limbs of our bodies. The thought of moving them seems automatically to produce the 'real' movement, so far at least as they are uninjured and not in any way restrained. It is by means of our power to move them that such more limited control as we possess over the rest of the world is achieved. By pulling or pushing we move physical objects, perhaps also causing them to operate mechanically, chemically, or electrically upon other physical objects. Or, by moving our tongues in speech, we seek to influence the 'minds' of other people, either as an end in itself or to do something for us. This completes the list of modes of control we can certainly exert, though some people wish, and others fear, to believe that more direct and mysterious modes are also available to us: for example, by magic, by prayer, or by telepathy.

The above account of what philosophers call the naive world of common sense is clearly Humean (or Machian) in character. I have stressed this subjectivist approach because I believe that if we can think of the common-sense world, with all its objective solidity, as a psychological construction which mirrors the possibilities of sensory experience, we are also able to imagine that it might not always have had this solidity for us. In other words, we can imagine a world which is without those distinctions (between ego and its surroundings, mind and matter, thought model and what it represents) which characterize our relation to the world of common sense. And if we can do this, it may be easier for us to conceive the possibility of the strange world of the infant, and of the unconscious – a world in which, for example, ghostly breasts can be swallowed whole and bite back at their attacker.

This other world, which analysts are trying to explore, appears, as I said, to be the product of instinct rather than experience. At the beginning no pattern of sensation seems to be perceived at all unless it has the *gestalt* of some primary symbol; and, since grades are not yet distinguished, all examples of the same primary symbol are equated. So corresponding with the few innate needs of our species, the first world – so far as we have yet been able to reconstruct it – appears to have only a few types of object and activity: almost everything seems to be a breast, a mouth, or a penis, and almost every activity an eating, an evacuation, or an intercourse[1]; and even these few separate categories are often fused together. Moreover, there is no difference between the percept and the memory of things, or between situations that occur and situations constructed in imagination in what is not yet a dualistic world; and no stable boundary between ego and object in what is still predominantly a solipsistic one. There is, however, one clear distinction and this separates much that later will be treated as identical. Every object or situation has two forms, one good and the other bad, according so the affective response to it.

The affective response determines the conative. Something is done with the object or situation in phantasy; and, since there is almost no distinction between 'solid matter' and 'ghostly image', almost anything can be done with it. But it would be a mistake to suppose that this first world is therefore a place of blissful wish-fulfilment. Conative impulses are in perpetual conflict and not yet integrated in such a way that there can be a resultant of opposing forces. Indeed, there is not one child with conflicting feelings, but several 'bits of child', with different feelings which may temporarily unite only to be again split by the next conflict. And then the dominant bit, which most nearly has the sense of being an ego, will feel threatened and persecuted by the other bits which, like evil spirits, seem to be endangering its world.[2]

From this phantastic world, the world of common sense gradually emerges under the influence both of internal maturation and of external experience. Some degree of integration of conflicting impulses into one ego, as well as some recognition of the identity between good and bad aspects of objects and situations, would seem to occur in advance of a clear distinction between phantasy and fact. At any rate, there is an important phase of development – the 'depressive position' discovered and so named by Melanie Klein – at which a child begins to feel responsible for, and depressed about, all the damage he has

---

[1] These words stand, of course, not for our precise idea of the corresponding objects and activities, but for their primary symbols or *gestalts*. Whether or not there are really only so few objects or situations in the infant's world can, of course, only be determined by future research.

[2] Thus, unlike the world of common sense, this first world is not within limits controllable. It would seem rather to fluctuate between the two extremes of being omnipotently controlled and wholly uncontrollable.

done in phantasy; and these feelings are as acute as if he had really done it.

Before long, however, the two vital distinctions between the ego and other people and between phantasy and perceptual fact (mind and matter) are firmly established at a conscious level. Meanwhile objects previously identified in virtue of a common *gestalt* are being differentiated on the basis of their several uses, and new classifications on the basis of more practical similarities are being formed.[1] So, under the influence of perceptual experience, the world of common sense rapidly develops; and, by the middle of the first year, it is probably complete in all essentials like the world of any sane adult. Henceforth, it is clung to with a tenacity that impedes all efforts to form a clear picture of its forerunner. Nevertheless, the old world can reappear in dreams, and the new one can be lost in states of madness. Perhaps it can also be temporarily surrendered in philosophic contemplation.

But I doubt whether a course in subjectivist philosophy would have really done much to help the patient I quoted. Perhaps it is only because the philosopher is already a certain sort of person that he can think of the world in subjective terms. To the average layman, Hume's unsurpassed lucidity is as incomprehensible as a hieroglyphic. This is not, I think, because the layman is stupid, but because the subjectivist argument arouses a deep anxiety in him. It seems to threaten that sense of being a solid person, surrounded by a solid world, on which his sanity and life depend, and he clings to it the more tenaciously just because it is precarious. That this world is less indestructible than it may seem is perhaps a fact which both the philosopher and the analyst have been able to accept.

What the patient in analysis and the layman in philosophy really fear is the unconscious world of infancy which lies beneath it; and the fear of being engulfed by this 'mad world' must be lessened by interpretations of anxiety before interpretations of its content can be clearly understood.

[1] The original classification with a few primary *gestalts* is, however, never really lost. Our emotional response to objects is determined by their symbolic meaning as well as by their practical use.

21

Normal Counter-transference and some of its Deviations*[1]

INTRODUCTORY

Counter-transference is an old psycho-analytic concept which has recently been widened and enriched. We used to think of it mainly as a personal disturbance to be analysed away in ourselves. We now also think of it as having its causes, and effects, in the patient and, therefore, as an indication of something to be analysed in him [1].

I believe this more recently explored aspect of counter-transference can be used, in the way described, for example, by Paula Heimann [2], to achieve an important technical advance. But of course the discovery that counter-transference can be usefully employed does not imply that it has ceased ever to be a serious impediment. And as both aspects in fact exist, we may surmise that there may be a problem about their similarities and differences which still deserves investigation. Perhaps this problem may be put in the form of three related questions: What is 'normal' counter-transference? How and under what conditions is it disturbed? And how can disturbances be corrected and in the process perhaps used to further an analysis?

NORMAL COUNTER-TRANSFERENCE

As to the analyst's correct or normal attitude to the patient, there are a number of aspects which have been mentioned both in papers and discussions. Freud spoke of a 'benevolent neutrality'. This I take to imply that the analyst is concerned

* *Int. J. Psycho-analysis*, vol. 37, 1956.
[1] Read at the 19th International Psycho-Analytical Congress, Geneva, 24–28 July 1955.

for the welfare of his patient, without becoming emotionally involved in his conflicts. It also implies, I think, that the analyst, in virtue of his understanding of psychic determinism, has a certain kind of tolerance which is the opposite of condemnation, and yet by no means the same as indulgence or indifference.

Many analysts have stressed the element of scientific curiosity, and certainly we should not get far without this sublimation. But, by itself, it seems a little too impersonal. Concern for the patient's welfare comes, I think, from the fusion of two other basic drives: the reparative, which counteracts the latent destructiveness in all of us, and the parental. Of course, if too intense, they betray excessive guilt about inadequately sublimated aggressiveness which can be the cause of very disturbing anxieties. But, in some degree, both are surely normal. The reparative satisfactions of analysis are obvious and often referred to. So, in some degree, the patient must stand for the damaged objects of the analyst's own unconscious phantasy, which are still endangered by aggression and still in need of care and reparation. The parental aspect has been mentioned, in discussions, by Paula Heimann [3]. No one would suggest that the patient stands only for a child, and not sometimes for a sibling, or even for a parent. But it is with the unconscious child in the patient that the analyst is *most* concerned; and because this child so often treats the analyst as parent, the analyst's unconscious can hardly fail to respond in some degree by regarding the patient as his child.

Now, to a parent, a child stands, at least in part, for an early aspect of the self. And this seems to me important. For it is just because the analyst can recognize his early self, which has already been analysed, in the patient, that he can analyse the patient [4]. His empathy and insight, as distinct from his theoretical knowledge, depend on this kind of partial identification [5].

But identification can take two forms – introjective and projective – a distinction latent in Freud's concept, the significance of which Melanie Klein has recently brought out [6]. We may therefore expect to find both forms in the analyst's partial identification with his patient.

I will try to formulate what seems to be happening when the

analysis is going well. I believe there is a fairly rapid oscillation between introjection and projection. As the patient speaks, the analyst will, as it were, become introjectively identified with him, and having understood him inside, will reproject him and interpret. But what I think the analyst is most aware of is the projective phase – that is to say, the phase in which the patient is the representative of a former immature or ill part of himself, including his damaged objects, which he can now understand and therefore treat by interpretation, in the external world.

Meanwhile the patient is receiving effective interpretations, which help him to respond with further associations that can be understood. As long as the analyst understands them, this satisfactory relationship – which I will call the 'normal' one – persists. In particular, the analyst's counter-transference feelings will be confined to that sense of empathy with the patient on which his insight is based.

PERIODS OF NON-UNDERSTANDING

Everyone, the analyst no less than the patient, would be happy if the situation I have just described, and called the 'normal' one, would persist throughout the whole course of an analysis. Unfortunately, it is normal only in the sense of being an ideal. It depends for its continuity on the analyst's continuous understanding. But he is not omniscient. In particular, his understanding fails whenever the patient corresponds too closely with some aspect of himself which he has not yet learnt to understand. Moreover, some patients are much less co-operative than others. There are patients with whom the best of analysts find great difficulty in maintaining contact – with whom the 'normal' relationship is the exception rather than the rule. And even with co-operative patients, it is subject to fairly frequent breaks.

We recognize these breaks at once by our feeling that the material has become obscure, and that we have somehow lost the thread. Now whatever has in fact been missed, the fact of missing it creates a new situation which may be felt as a strain by the analyst as well as by the patient. Of course some analysts – for example, those who most crave the reassurance of continuous success – feel such strains more acutely than others.

NORMAL COUNTER-TRANSFERENCE

But, apart from individual differences, there is a peculiarity in the very nature of the analytic technique which must impose some strain on all of us – especially at moments when we cannot help a patient who is in obvious distress. For, if my argument so far is right, we all have some need to satisfy our parental and reparative drives to counteract the Death Instinct; but we are much more restricted in the ways in which we can do so than a real parent, an educationalist or any other kind of therapist. We are restricted to the giving of interpretations [7]; and our capacity to give them depends upon our continuing to understand the patient. If this understanding fails, as fail from time to time it must, we have no alternative therapy to fall back on. Here, then, is a situation peculiar to analysis, when lack of understanding is liable to arouse conscious or unconscious anxiety, and anxiety still further to diminish understanding. It is to the onset of this kind of vicious spiral that I am inclined to attribute every deviation in normal counter-transference feeling.

If the analyst is in fact disturbed, it is also likely that the patient has unconsciously contributed to this result, and is in turn disturbed by it. So we have three factors to consider: first, the analyst's emotional disturbance, for he may have to deal with this silently in himself before he can disengage himself sufficiently to understand the other two; then the patient's part in bringing it about; and finally its effect on him. Of course, all three factors may be sorted out in a matter of seconds, and then indeed the counter-transference is functioning as a delicate receiving apparatus. But I will discuss the first stage first, as if it were a lengthy process – as it sometimes is.

THE ROLE OF THE ANALYST'S SUPEREGO

The extent to which an analyst is emotionally disturbed by periods of non-understanding will probably depend, in the first instance, on another factor: the severity of his own superego. For analysis is also a form of work required of us by this inner figure – which, incidentally, a demanding patient may sometimes come to represent. If our superego is predominantly friendly and helpful, we can tolerate our own limitations without undue distress, and, being undisturbed, will be the more likely soon to regain contact with the patient. But if it is severe, we may become conscious of a sense of failure as the expression of an unconscious persecutory or depressive guilt. Or, as a defence against such feelings, we may blame the patient.

The choice of one or other of these alternatives seems to me to determine something else as well. For when that interplay between introjection and projection, which characterizes the analytic process, breaks down, the analyst may tend to get stuck in one or other of these two positions; and what he does with his guilt may determine the position he gets stuck in. If he accepts the guilt, he is likely to get stuck with an introjected patient. If he projects it, the patient remains an incomprehensible figure in the external world.

EXAMPLES OF PROLONGED INTROJECTION AND PROJECTION

An example of the first, that is, the introjective, alternative may be seen when the analyst gets unduly worried, both on his own and his patient's behalf, about a session that has gone badly. He may feel as if he had regained some of his own old troubles and become almost physically burdened with his patient's as well. Only when he separates the two can he see what he has missed and get the patient out of him again.

Often, it is something towards the end of a session, or of a week, which he feels he has missed, and then he has all the patient's supposed frustration in himself. This may look like a self-punishment for having unconsciously intended to hurt the patient. But we may wonder whether the patient has not contributed to the analyst's distress – whether the leaving of his analyst with an unsolved problem about himself is not his way of projecting himself into the analyst both to punish him for, and to avoid, the threatened separation.

In other words, there may be a symbiosis between the analyst's tendency to prolong the introjection of a patient whom he cannot understand or help and the patient's tendency to project parts of himself, in the way described by Melanie Klein, into the analyst who is not helping him. (This may be particularly disturbing if what the patient is most anxious to get rid of is his own destructiveness.)

In such cases the ultimate cause of the analyst's slowness in understanding and reprojecting the patient may be that the patient has come to stand for something which he has not yet learnt to understand quickly in himself. If he still fails to do so, and cannot tolerate the sense of being burdened with the patient as an irreparable or persecuting figure inside him, he is likely to resort to a defensive kind of reprojection which shuts out the patient and creates a further bar to understanding.

If so, a new complication may arise if the analyst, in projecting the patient, projects aspects of himself as well. Then he will have the chance to explore within himself the workings of those mechanisms of projective identification, which under the influence of Melanie Klein, Rosenfeld and others have so fruitfully explored in schizophrenic patients [8]. Nor need we be surprised at this, for the discovery of pathological mechanisms in mental illness is usually followed by the recognition of their less obvious presence in normal people too. A 'slow-motion' example of the kind of process I have in mind may be seen in another fairly common week-end experience. For a little time after he has finished his week's work, the analyst may be consciously preoccupied with some unsolved problem of his patients. Then he forgets them; but the period of conscious concern is followed by a period of listlessness in which he is depleted of the private interests that usually occupy his leisure. I suggest this is because, in phantasy, he has projected parts of himself together with his patients and must wait, as it were, till these return to him.

When this partial loss of self occurs within a session, it is often experienced as the loss of intellectual potency; the analyst feels stupid. The patient may well have contributed to this result. Perhaps, frustrated by not getting an immediate interpretation, he has unconsciously wished to castrate his analyst, and by treating him as if he were, has helped to make him feel castrated [9].

A complicated example taken from my own experience would seem to illustrate the simultaneous operation of all these processes. For while the dominant theme was my projection of a patient who wished to project his illness into me, I also experienced a sense of being robbed of my wits by him.

A neurotic patient, in whom paranoid and schizoid mechanisms were prominent, arrived for a session in considerable anxiety because he had not been able to work in his office. He had also felt vague on the way as if he might get lost or run over; and he despised himself for being useless. Remembering a similar occasion, on which he had felt depersonalized over a weekend and dreamed that he had left his 'radar' set in a shop and would be unable to get it before Monday, I thought he had, in phantasy, left parts of his 'good self' in me. But I was not very sure of this, or of other interpretations I began to give. And he, for his part, soon began to reject them all with a mounting degree of anger; and, at the same time, abused me for not helping. By the end of the session he was no longer depersonalized, but very angry and contemptuous instead. It was I who felt useless and bemused.

When I eventually recognized my state at the end as so similar to that he had described as his at the beginning, I could almost feel the relief of a re-projection. By then the session was over. But he was in the same mood at the beginning of the next one – still very angry and contemptuous. I then told him I thought he felt he had reduced me to the state of useless vagueness he himself had been in; and that he felt he had done this by having me 'on the mat', asking questions and rejecting the answers, in the way his legal father did. His response was striking. For the first time in two days, he became quiet and thoughtful. He then said this explained why he had been so angry with me yesterday: he had felt that all my interpretations referred to my illness and not to his.

I suggest that, as in a slow motion picture, we can here see several distinct processes which, in an ideal or 'normal' analytic period, should occur extremely quickly. I think I began, as it were, to take my patient in, to identify introjectively with him, as soon as he lay down and spoke about his very acute distress. But I could not at once recognize it as corresponding with anything already understood in myself; and, for this reason, I was slow to get it out of me in the process of explaining, and so relieving it in him. He, for his part, felt frustrated at not getting effective interpretations, and reacted by projecting his sense of mental impotence into me, at the same time behaving as if he had taken from me what he felt he had lost, his father's clear, but aggressive, intellect, with which he attacked his impotent self in me. By this time, of course, it was useless to try to pick up the thread where I had first dropped it. A new situation had arisen which had affected us both. And before my patient's part in bringing it about could be interpreted, I had to do a silent piece of self-analysis involving the discrimination of two things which can be felt as very similar: my own sense of incompetence at having lost the thread, and my patient's contempt for his impotent self, which he felt to be in me. Having made this interpretation to myself, I was eventually able to pass the second half of it on to my patient, and, by so doing, restored the normal analytic situation.

According to Bion [10], the capacity to make this kind of discrimination, and much more quickly than in the example, is an important part of the capacity to use one's counter-transference in the interests of analysis.

POSITIVE AND NEGATIVE COUNTER-TRANSFERENCE

Coming now to counter-transference in the narrow sense of an excess of positive or negative feeling, this too is often an indirect result of the frustrations arising when a distressed patient is not understood, and no effective interpretations can be given. For the analyst whose reparative impulse is thwarted of its analytically normal outlet may be unconsciously inclined either to offer some form of love instead, or to become hostile to his patient. Meanwhile, the patient may be facilitating the process by trying to provoke one or other of these affects in his analyst, who is the more likely to respond *to* his patient's mood just because he has lost his empathy *with* it.

Now, however scrupulously we may suppress an excess of positive or negative feeling of this kind, the patient is likely to sense it unconsciously. Then a new situation arises in which his response to our mood may itself have to be interpreted.

If, for example, the counter-transference is too positive, the patient may respond to our increased emotional concern by complaining that we have no emotional concern. We do not contradict him as he may wish. But it may be appropriate to tell him that he believes we are attracted to him and has to deny it in order to avoid the responsibility for a seduction. For an important early pattern may be involved. As a child, he may have been unconsciously aware that his caresses embarrassed one of his parents, for example, his mother, because she was afraid of being aroused by them; and the sense of being rebuffed may have rankled all his life, because it was needed to counteract his guilt for trying to seduce her. If so, the interpretation of the repetition of this pattern in the transference may enable the patient to reassess, not only his analyst's, but his real parent's attitude to him.

But if it goes unnoticed, and its effects unobserved, the unconscious offering of love in lieu of effective interpretations may disturb the analysis in many ways. For instance, the analyst may foster the split, directly in his own mind and indirectly in his patient's, between himself as a good parent and the real parents as bad ones. Then the patient may never become aware of his guilt towards them – a guilt which, paradoxically enough, is likely to be all the greater if they were really bad; for it is in proportion to his own ambivalence. If this guilt is not recovered in analysis, the patient cannot work through that early stage described by Melanie Klein as the depressive position, in which the developing infant begins to become aware of, and miserable about, the conflict between his hatred and his love.

As to the negative attitudes to a patient which may also result from a temporary failure to understand him, these would seem especially to arise when the patient becomes a persecution because he is felt to be incurable. Then, as before, the analyst's triple task is first to become aware of this defensive mechanism in himself, then of his patient's part in bringing it about, and lastly of its effect on him.

To take the last point first: The sort of paranoid patient I mentioned earlier, who hated me for years and seemed to make no noticeable progress, can easily come to stand for one's own bad and persecutory objects, which one would like to get rid of. Such feelings betray themselves in one's sigh of relief after the last session of the week, or before a holiday. One's first impulse may be to suppress such hostile feelings; but if one does not allow oneself to become aware of them, one may miss their influence on the patient's unconscious. For instance, I came to feel that the occasions on which this patient repudiated me with more than ordinary violence, followed rather

NORMAL COUNTER-TRANSFERENCE

than preceded, moments when I would really have been glad to see the last of him. And then my interpretation that it was he who felt rebuffed met with more success.

I also noticed more clearly that the times when I was aware of disliking him followed moments in which I had despaired of helping him. And I began to wonder whether he, on his side, was not trying to make me despair and, if so, what his motives were. Several seemed to be involved, of which perhaps the most important was that, in his phantasy, getting well was equated with the renunciation of an unacknowledged homosexual component in himself. He unconsciously wished to prove to me that this could not be done. Meanwhile, he attacked me consciously for not curing him, that is, for not removing the impulse; and unconsciously for not satisfying it for him.

CONCLUSION

If what I have said so far touches only the fringe of an immensely complicated subject, it at least suggests the possibility of approximate answers to the questions I began with: What is normal counter-transference? How and under what conditions is it disturbed? And how can disturbances be corrected and in the process perhaps used to further an analysis?

The analyst's motive is a blend of curiosity with parental and reparative drives. His equipment consists both of his theoretical knowledge about the unconscious, and of his personal acquaintance with its manifestation which he has gained in his own analysis. But it is with his use of the second that we are here concerned; that is, with his insight, for this consists in his ability, by means of a partial identification with his patient, to apply his acquaintance with his own unconscious to the interpretation of his patient's behaviour. When all is going well, this identification seems to oscillate between its introjective and projective forms. The analyst, as it were, absorbs the patient's state of mind through the medium of the associations he hears and the postures he observes, recognizes it as expressing some pattern in his own unconscious world of phantasy, and reprojects the patient in the act of formulating his interpretation. In this phase he may get that sense of helpfully understanding his patient from within which satisfies both his curiosity and his reparative drives. To some degree, his interest is also a parental one; for, to the parent, the child is his early self, and it is with the same child in the patient that the analyst is most concerned. His sense of being in touch with it, his empathy, comprises his 'normal' counter-transference feeling.

What keeps the process going is the analyst's repeated acts of recognition, in the introjective phase, that such and such a pattern of adsorbed emotion expresses such and such a phantasy in his own unconscious. And what causes a break in this relationship is a failure in this recognition.

The cause of a failure may be something still feared, because not yet fully understood, within the analyst to which the patient has come too close. But the result need be no more than a retardation in the analytic process, which enables us the better to observe its separate phases. This happens particularly when it is the first or introjective phase which is slowed down. The analyst then feels burdened with the patient and with some of his old immature self as well. He has to do more slowly, what at other times he does at once: become conscious of the phantasies within him, recognize their source, separate the patient's from his own, and so objectify him again.

But the analyst may also have to deal with two other factors, which are much less in evidence when the process is going quickly. These are the patient's contribution – in particular his use of projective identification – to the analyst's disturbed emotions, and the effect which these in turn may be having on the patient.

It may be, however, that the analyst does not succeed in sorting all this out within himself before he re-projects the patient as something not understood, or foreign, in the external world. Then, since his reparative impulses can find no outlet in effective interpretations, he may be tempted to fall back on some form of reassurance instead. Or, if he despairs of his reparative powers, he may defend himself against depression by feeling angry with his patient. In either case, his intuition has temporarily gone so that any interpretations he makes can be based only on his knowledge of theory, which by itself is likely to be a sterile substitute for a fruitful combination of the two.

NORMAL COUNTER-TRANSFERENCE

If we were omniscient analysts, the only counter-transference we should experience would be that belonging to those intuitive periods when all is going well. In fact, the less satisfactory states I have tried to describe, in which our feelings are at least in some degree disturbed, probably take up a lot more analytic time than we readily remember or admit. Yet it is precisely in them, I think, that the analyst, by silently analysing his own reactions, can increase his insight, decrease his difficulties, and learn more about his patient.

NOTES AND REFERENCES

[1] The use of counter-transference as an 'instrument of research' has been especially studied by Paula Heimann ('On Counter-Transference', *Int. J. Psycho-Anal.*, 1950, 31). That is to say, she has stressed its *causes* in the patient, while Margaret Little ('Counter-Transference and the Patient's Response to it', *Int. J. Psycho-Anal.*, 1951, 32) has stressed its *effects* on him. This, too, is clearly an important aspect. But, in interpreting the patient's response to our counter-transference, opinions differ about whether, as she thinks, we should occasionally be prepared to admit to him what our counter-transference was – instead of confining ourselves to interpreting what is in his mind, namely, his *beliefs* about our attitude.

[2] Heimann, Paula. *Ibid.*

[3] The sublimation of curiosity and of parental impulses have been stressed respectively by Clifford Scott and Paula Heimann in scientific discussions in the British Psycho-Analytical Society. But I have not found specific references to these points in any of their published papers. In 'Problems of the Training Analysis' (*Int. J. Psycho-Anal.*, 1954, 35), however, Paula Heimann does implicitly refer to the dangers of an excess of parental sublimation.

[4] Conversely, by discovering new patterns in a patient, the analyst can make 'post-graduate' progress in his own analysis.

[5] Annie Reich speaks of a 'short-lived identification' ('On Counter-Transference', *Int. J. Psycho-Anal.*, 1951, 32), and Paula Heimann of identification in both introjective and projective forms in her 'Problems of the Training Analysis' quoted above.

[6] Klein, Melanie. 'Notes on some Schizoid Mechanisms', *Int. J. Psycho-Anal.*, 1946, 27, and in *Developments in Psycho-Analysis*, 1952. I think the distinction between introjective and projective identification is implicit, though not very clearly brought out, in Freud's *Group Psychology and the Analysis of the Ego.*

[7] The extent to which we are in fact restricted to pure interpretations depends, in some degree, upon our school. We are all agreed that our main rôle is to give interpretations. No one denies that we also arrange a certain framework within which to give them: we provide

the physical comfort of a couch; and we preserve a certain courtesy of manner with minor variations according to the requirements of different patients, some wishing to shake hands before or after every session, others not, and so on. But opinions differ about whether the framework, once established, should be deliberately manipulated. Thus, Winnicott, if I understand him rightly, has argued that some psychotic patients can only form a relation to an ideal object which they have never had, and that the analyst may have to play this rôle before analysis proper can be started; in other words, that it is not alone sufficient to interpret the patient's efforts to force this rôle on him.

[8] Klein, Melanie, *Ibid.* Rosenfeld, H., 'Transference Phenomena and Transference Analysis in an Acute Catatonic Schizophrenic Patient', *Int. J. Psycho-Anal.*, 1952, 33.

[9] If so, the patient is also likely to introject him in this condition and then feel in more desperate need of external help than ever. At such moments, the analyst may become disagreeably aware that the patient is still more urgently demanding that which he is still less able to give – consciously, a good interpretation, unconsciously a breast or penis which now neither feel they have.

[10] Bion, W. R. 'Language and the Schizophrenic.' Ch. 9 in *New Directions in Psycho-Analysis*, 1955. Edited by Melanie Klein, Paula Heimann and R. E. Money-Kyrle. How exactly a patient does succeed in imposing a phantasy and its corresponding affect upon his analyst in order to deny it in himself is a most interesting problem. I do not think we need assume some form of extrasensory communication; but the communication can be of a pre-verbal and archaic kind – similar perhaps to that used by gregarious animals in which the posture or call of a single member will arouse a corresponding affect in the rest. In the analytic situation, a peculiarity of communications of this kind is that, at first sight, they do not seem as if they had been made by the patient at all. The analyst experiences the affect as being his own response to something. The effort involved is in differentiating the patient's contribution from his own.

22
The Process of Psycho-analytical Inference*[1]

Introductory Note – this paper rather puzzles me. I even remember being rather frightened of it in the middle of reading it at the Paris Congress!
I do not know whether some of the notions I tried to introduce in it – and have not developed further – frightened me because no one else had mentioned them before (such as the notion of a 'necessary adjunct') or whether I really recognized them as worthless.

According to methodologists,[2] a genuine is distinguished from a pseudo-science by the fact that it is possible to say, not only what evidence would prove its theories true, but also what evidence would prove them false.

Our critics argue that, like astrology, psycho-analysis fails to pass this test because we appear to them to have a limitless capacity to defend ourselves against negative evidence by means of additional hypotheses. There can be no disproof, they say, if a patient's denial of an interpretation can be taken only as evidence of a 'resistance'; if his assertion that the opposite of what is said of him is true can be explained away in terms of 'ambivalence' and the co-existence of conscious and unconscious impulses; and if the analyst, when himself convinced that he should have made a different interpretation, fails to withdraw the first one on the ground that, owing to 'over-determination', it is still right at a deeper level.[3]

* *Int. J. Psycho-analysis*, vol. 39, 1958.
[1] Paper read before the 20th Congress of the International Psycho-Analytical Association, Paris, July–August 1957.
[2] See J. O. Wisdom who, in 'Psycho-Analytic Technology' (*British Journal for the Philosophy of Science*), defends analysis as a science.
[3] We are also accused of being unscientific in our technique: of suggesting to patients what we claim to find in them; and, lastly, of remembering in the report of cases only such evidence as supports our theories.

Now since the technique of proof and disproof is most advanced in the physical sciences, it might seem natural to take them as our model in seeking to confound our critics. We might try, for example, to show that our theory of the unconscious, like the physicist's model of atoms, enables us to predict observable behaviour, the non-appearance of which would disprove the theory, that is, expose it as useless.[1] But, however successful such experiments might be, they would not I think provide an adequate defence of what is most vital to us: namely, that specialized form of anthropomorphic reasoning on which, I believe, the whole structure of analysis ultimately rests. This no longer has any parallel in physics – except in so far as models of atoms still contain faint traces of animistic projections of a tactual kind. To prove that, in psycho-analysis, anthropomorphic reasoning can still lead to reliable results is not, I think, sufficient. We have to examine the inherent conditions under which it is reliable or not.

The essence of all anthropomorphic reasoning is that, on the basis of our acquaintance with the link between motive and action in ourselves, we infer a motive from the action of others. That is, we imaginatively project it.

Since we cannot actually see – although we often feel as if we could[2] – into another mind, anthropomorphic inferences can never be directly tested by the person who makes them. But upon them depend all our social contacts; and I think it can be shown that only under three conditions do they rightly come under suspicion.

First, they are unreliable in proportion to the unlikeness of their objects to ourselves. We no longer apply them to

---

[1] It is perhaps better to think of theories, or models, as useful or useless, and reserve the words 'true' or 'false' for specific or general statements about observable phenomena (including mental phenomena which can be observed only by one person).

[2] Susan Isaacs ('Criteria for Interpretation', *Int. J. Psycho-Anal.*, xx, 1939) speaks of our intuitions as perceptions. Since the term perception denotes a kind of vivid inference which results from projecting past into present experience, the term is well chosen. But it does not imply that we actually see into a patient's mind to confirm an interpretation. He alone can do this, and then only if he becomes conscious of its content. Even his verbal agreement is only indirect confirmation for us. (It should be admitted, however, that, in the present state of our knowledge, the possibility of a more direct contact of a telepathic or extra-sensory kind ought not to be excluded).

nature and consciously infer that a thunderstorm expresses the anger of the gods. We have become cautious in applying them to our domestic animals. But we do, and must I think, assume them reliable when applied to persons like ourselves – provided neither of the other conditions of unreliability are there.

Of the two other conditions, one is the absence of a fairly large set of supporting inferences which combine to form a consistent and intelligible pattern.[1] It should be easy to show that, in our attempt to co-ordinate a great mass of material, we pay full regard to this condition in our work, and, in particular, that we distrust an interpretation if the inference from the response does not support the inference on which the interpretation was originally made.[2] In other words, we subject our intuitions to the control of our intelligence.

But we also know that the inferences, for example of a paranoiac, can be consistent and systematized in a highly intellectual way, and yet be quite distorted. Inferences, therefore, are unreliable – and this is my third condition – if there are grounds for supposing that the mental apparatus of the inferring mind is in any way disturbed.[3]

To say, as I think we must, that such grounds can often be detected only by analysis, so that only analysis can question the validity of the anthropomorphic inferences on which analysis itself is built, may sound like arguing in a circle. But the true analogy is with a spiral.

The analyst's whole technique might be described as a method of correcting errors in the anthropomorphic reasoning of patients as these come to light in the transference. And he does this, neither by giving them more evidence about himself, nor by pointing out their inconsistencies, but by analysing the projective mechanisms which disturb their inferences about him.

Of course, if my argument so far is right, all our ideas about

[1] Since we cannot see into a patient's mind, the test of consistency is the only one we have. We like our inferences to be consistent with each other and with our theory. As an analysis proceeds they come to fit more and more into a complete picture of the patient's personality.
[2] A point stressed by J. O. Wisdom in his paper referred to on p. 243, n. 2.
[3] Since a normal mind does not trust inferences made under either of the first two conditions, the third may perhaps be said to include the other two.

other people's minds depend upon projection,[1] which errs only when too compulsive to be checked by an adequate observation of behaviour. It is by remaining a blank screen, and so limiting the extent to which patients can use these checks on him, that the analyst can best study the distorting bias in their projections.

Biologically, the function of projection may be presumed to be that of enabling us to imagine, as a preliminary to recognizing, the various types of animal or person we shall have to do with in the world. But psychologically, it appears as the response to certain anxieties in us. It is this that gives it its tendentiousness, so that we become over-ready to think we recognize what we have imagined in advance.

As a provisional classification, I would suggest that it operates to people our world with three main types of object, which, however, are not mutually exclusive.

First, it provides us with friends in whom we believe we see the reflection of some conscious interest or trait of our own. They represent the multiplication, in fantasy and perhaps also in fact, of aspects of our egos, and are felt to need each other for companionship and support, that is, to counter both depressive and persecutory anxieties.

This group shades off into my second category which, for want of a better name, I will call 'necessary adjuncts' – people we unconsciously create, and perhaps discover, in order to complete ourselves. The admired qualities we put, or find, in them are such as we do not, or are unconsciously not permitted to, possess.[2]

Lastly, we want what in a broad sense may be called 'enemies' – people who are feared, disliked, or despised as the depositories of something feared, disliked, or despised in our-

---

[1] This may be disputed. But I believe it to be as impossible to imagine a motive in others which does not lurk somewhere in us, as it would be to imagine a colour we had never seen. I should stress too that I am using 'projection' in a wide sense not confined to its pathological manifestations.

[2] For example, a woman may desire to find in a husband not only the organs she lacks, but also some of the aggression she wrongly believes to be inseparable from them – aggression which she dare not have and is defenceless without. Conversely, a man may feel that the capacity to love is feminine, and that his marriage completes him in this respect. But many other types of 'necessary adjuncts' would seem to occur in marriage, in business partnerships and co-operative activities, and, in bizarre forms, in the perversions.

selves. For not only are aggressive aspects of ourselves split off and projected in this way, but also despised aspects. Thus every self-sufficient group would seem to have to contain some 'failures', as well as other forms of scapegoat, to preserve the rest of the members from feelings of inferiority, which cover what in a physically insecure society would appear as an exaggerated fear of death.[1]

All these types of defensive projection, if too compulsive, can do more than falsify one person's picture of another. If dominated by a powerful unconscious motive to do so, they can affect a recipient whose own ego is not sufficiently robust. For example, not only will a psychotic attribute his psychosis to others; they may feel in danger of having it imposed on them. It is to this and other aspects of a still rather mysterious process that Melanie Klein drew attention by giving it a special name: projective identification. So to the old question 'How is a patient perceiving us?' we sometimes have to add the new one, 'What is he trying to force on us?'; and no less important 'Why?' In terms of my classification, he may be trying to force us to be a 'friend', a 'necessary adjunct' or an 'enemy', or a mixture of the three. But of particular relevance is the anxious projection of that sense of failure – which may itself result from an unsuccessful effort to rob and appropriate success.

Now the analyst, both from his own analysis and the analysis of patients, has deepened his own consciousness, and has, in particular, become aware of these distorting mechanisms. His inferences about other people are, therefore, deeper – that is, they penetrate to motives which are still unconscious to them – and also more reliable than they were before. I do not mean that, when off duty in his private life, his inferences about others are not often disturbed by compulsive projections. But in the analytic session, he is oriented towards the unconscious and especially on his guard. Moreover, his patients usually give him much more data about themselves, on which to form his inferences, than anyone does in private life. He is therefore much less likely to make mistakes.

But he is not infallible, and to satisfy the methodologists, we

[1] Such scapegoats tend to be expelled or to leave of their own accord. Then new ones have to be discovered. Elliott Jaques has studied the rôle of projection in small groups in his book, *The Changing Culture of a Factory* (1951).

must also show how he discovers and corrects mistakes. We have to distinguish sharply between being slow to understand – because of limitations in our acquaintance with the unconscious – and making positive mistakes. Uncertainty and ignorance are not the same as error. But perhaps a prime cause of error, in analysis as in other fields, is intolerance of ignorance.

The biblical myth of the creation of the world out of chaos might be taken to represent the child's creation of an integrated world-model of things and people out of an original chaos of feeling and sensation. He does it by splitting and projection; for these mechanisms, which can produce such pathological results, are also the mechanisms by which every sort of intellectual mastery is achieved. But the greater the stress under which he builds this model, the less likely will it be to be altogether true, in the sense of fitting the actual possibilities of experience[1]; and the more tenaciously will he cling to it as knowledge, and fear ignorance as a return to persecuting chaos.

Moreover, the old association between the three values of truth, goodness, and beauty, which may seem to have no logical connection with each other, strongly suggests that knowledge is unconsciously equated with the first object to be known, loved, and admired – the whole good breast; and mental confusion with its attacked and so fragmented counterpart. If so, much will depend on how this first good object is felt to have been acquired. If with love and gratitude, the knowledge with which it is equated will be sufficiently secure for periodic revisions to be tolerated, although each necessitates, in some degree, a temporary return to chaos.[2]

So far as such revisions also involve a reassessment of the self, and the admission of bad or worthless aspects of it, the fear of ignorance is strengthened by the fear of truth.

At any rate, a capacity to tolerate both fears, or both aspects of the same one, is a measure of the analyst's normality, and an

---

[1] It will be noted that instead of conceiving an external world as something of which we make a model, I find it more consistent to think of 'experience' as the ultimate reality of which what we call the external world is our model.

[2] I am here generalizing from Rosenfeld's observations on confusional states which precede advances in the analytic treatment of schizophrenic patients. See his paper 'Note on the Psychopathology of Confusional States in Chronic Schizophrenias', 1951.

important part of his technical equipment. Much of his time is spent in the passive rôle of waiting till the patient's associations arouse a pattern in his mind which links with, and is completed by, a pattern of motive and behaviour which he can recognize as potentially operative in himself. This also involves, in the co-ordination of material, an intellectual task which, like all intellectual tasks, repeats the mastery of chaos. His power to tolerate a temporary confusion is especially important if he is faced with something new in the patient, which he may have to discover by the indirect route of finding a previously unrecognized parallel in himself. More often, the required pattern is something he is already familiar with from his own analysis. But even then, he has to wait for the 'bell to ring' in him before he can regain the security of knowledge, and is able, at the right moment, to assume the interpreter's more active rôle.[1]

It is only when he cannot tolerate the waiting period, in which he is exposed perhaps to the confusion in the patient's mind, that he may intervene with guesses based on theory. But unless he is so afraid of ignorance that he has become a doctrinaire, he does not seek to defend them at all costs as his critics suppose. For if he cannot, without knowing the whole of his patient's unconscious, prove such guesses to have been wrong, he is soon aware that there are no immediate grounds for believing them to be relevant or right.

I referred to such sources of error in my former Congress Paper ('On Counter-Transference'), and except to show our critics that we do not claim to be infallible, it would hardly be worth while to mention them again, were it not that some of Melanie Klein's more recent work does, I think, throw a very helpful light upon them.[2]

In her view, primal envy disturbs that grateful incorporation of the breast on which the child's sense of his own goodness and capacity to love ultimately rests – replacing it in some degree with a sense of having only got the fragmented,

[1] A factor to be mentioned here is the extent to which the analyst's own analysis has been emotionally, as well as intellectually, convincing to him. So far as only intellectual conviction was involved, he will be able to pass on to his patient only what he intellectually believes rather than also what he feels to be true.
[2] 'Notes on Some Schizoid Mechanisms' (1945); and 'Envy and Gratitude' (1957).

confused and dirtied object to which his own envious attacks reduced it. Now on such insecure foundations, an apparently normal and even generous personality may be built by means of a secondary, and perhaps rather greedy, incorporation of the breast and other good objects on the one hand, and on the other the forcible projection of bad parts of the self – especially the envy, the incapacity to love and resulting sense of failure – on to suitable scapegoats in the external world. Among the hallmarks of a personality of this kind are to be found, I think, both a strong desire for esteem as a defence against the fear of not being able to give, and so of not deserving love, and a particular sensitivity to the projection by others of that sense of worthlessness which so easily arouses an echo in the self. In other words, this type of projective identification is feared because it has been used.

Though everyone, in some degree, uses and fears such projective defences, several analysts[1] have pointed out that patients in whom they operate strongly are particularly difficult to analyse. To this we can add – since we are concerned with the reliability of inference – that it is these patients who are most likely to confuse the analyst by threatening to throw him back into that primal chaos from which in infancy his world was made. And perhaps it is those analysts who, without knowing it, have made most use of this same mechanism in the construction of their world who are most confused by it when used against them by patients.[2]

The situation may be illustrated by a patient's dream, which did not seem very promising to him at first as all he could remember was that there were two straws, one longer than the other. This reminded him, however, both of blow-pipes for poison darts, and of a story of a vet who was trying to give a

[1] Especially Bion and Rosenfeld.
[2] In *Group Psychology and the Analysis of the Ego* (1922) Freud discusses the links between identification, hypnotism, and being in love. As a subject for further enquiry, I would suggest that fear of the wish to fall in love or to be hypnotized is related to the fear of masochism and this in turn to fear of the wish to surrender to someone else's projective identification. Possibly this mechanism, although appearing earlier than genitality recognizable as such, may have an innate basis in it. At any rate, the wish to project (anal) parts of the self into, and so control, another person, and the opposite wish in this way to be controlled, have a suggestive similarity of pattern with genital impulses of a masculine and feminine nature respectively.

horse a stomach powder, by blowing it down its throat – when the horse blew first. He was not quite clear whether he was the vet or the horse, but he did realize, with a sudden shock, that this is how the analysis had always seemed to him.

He was one of those patients who compulsively try to control analysis, that is, make or remake their own order out of chaos. In particular, they wish to be unchallenged in their use of those mechanisms of splitting and projection which can be used to create either a true or a false picture of themselves in relation to others. They may seem co-operative and intelligent. But behind the compulsion to control analysis is a specific fear: that the analyst in trying to help them will only succeed in muddling them up. And perhaps below this is the greater one that he will expose an underlying sense of worthlessness. If, therefore, the analyst does not understand these fears, because they ring only an unconscious bell in him, he will only be aware that his own efforts to control the situation and make order out of chaos have miscarried, and that he is muddled up.[1]

It is with such patients, who may wish to muddle him both to conceal a painful truth and perhaps also out of envy, that the analyst, in defence against chaos and the sense of failure, may cling to and use theory in a mechanical and dogmatic way, which really muddles them and brings about the very situation they most fear: that of seeming to have their old defences of projection used against them to such a degree that they become unable to project at all, and now experience the real faults of others as their own.

But the recognition that such difficulties can arise is also equivalent to the discovery of a means to lessen them. What has to be analysed is a specific form of persecutory fear – the patient's fear of becoming the victim of projective identification emanating from the analyst – of the analyst's 'blowing first', and so of being overwhelmed with confusion, illness, failure and death. If this is brought into the open, it may be possible to show that the fear itself is the result of a projection. For it was

---

[1] Although any analyst may experience disturbances of this kind, their frequent or intense occurrence would suggest a weakness in his ego. In saying this, however, it would seem important to distinguish between an ego which appears strong because it has strong defences, and one whose strength is rooted in the acceptance of a true, and therefore indestructible, picture of itself.

originally they who used the defence of projective identification to control and overwhelm their mothers, who, as Bion has suggested, may, by resisting it, have lent some substance to the patient's fear of its being done to them. If this is accepted, much depression may be expected to emerge, which has to be worked through in turn. But perhaps a main barrier to progress has been passed.

23
On Prejudice – a Psycho-analytical Approach*

The dictionaries give more than one meaning of the word prejudice. In particular – and this, I think, is the only meaning we are concerned with – it is defined as a 'previous, premature or hasty judgment'. What seems to be implied is that it is an emotional judgment – either positive or negative – and that, while not necessarily wrong, it is the product of faulty reasoning, and so much less likely to be right than an unprejudiced one.

This seems a straightforward notion. But I think it contains the seeds of possible confusion, because two distinct types of judgment are mixed up in it: judgments of fact, which I will call beliefs; and judgments of value, that is, evaluations.

Take the case of a racial antipathy, and consider under what conditions we can, strictly speaking, call it a prejudice. Clearly both types of judgment are involved. There is a belief that a certain race has certain qualities; and there is a negative evaluation of these qualities – that is, they are disliked. So, in deciding whether the antipathy is a prejudice, two questions arise: Does the race really have the qualities attributed to it? And if it does, can dislike of them still be called a prejudice?

The classical Greeks believed all Cretans to be liars, and disliked them accordingly. But if, as is probable, this belief was unreasonable – perhaps a gross exaggeration of an element of truth – the antipathy based on it was clearly a prejudice. The difficulty in deciding what is, or is not, a prejudice arises only when a given race really has a quality for which it is disliked. For, at first sight, the decision might then seem to depend in a rather arbitrary way on the nature of the quality. Most people would say that it would be a prejudice to dislike a race because

* Delivered as part of the symposium on 'Prejudice', in a joint meeting of the Medical and Social Sections of the British Psychological Society, 23 March 1960.

353

of its colour, but that it would not be a prejudice to dislike it because of its arrogance – since we feel arrogance to be the kind of quality which can be quite 'reasonably' disliked.

We are faced, then, at the outset, with the problem of finding a criterion – if such a thing exists – for distinguishing between 'reasonable' and 'unreasonable' dislike of qualities which people really have.

A biologist might speculate on the possibility of an innate dislike of what is unlike ourselves – since something of the kind is sometimes found to inhibit breeding between closely related variants of the same species. If so, reason, whether faulty or otherwise, would not be involved at all. An anthropologist might point out that every society tends to feel it 'reasonable' to dislike what is unlike the specific cultural standards it has acquired. And here reason enters only in a relative way – in the sense that we feel it reasonable to conform with the prevailing attitude of our group – and provides only a relative criterion, which varies with the culture that applies it, of what is a prejudice.

But what is reasonable, in the sense of being based on reason, ought to be the same everywhere. So before giving up our search for a more absolute criterion, it may be worth our while to reword our problem, in psycho-analytic terms, as one about the difference between a 'normal' and a 'pathological' dislike. For what is normal in this sense is, not what necessarily conforms with the standards of any particular culture, but what is the product of a well-integrated mind; and this is a standard which does not depend on the culture we happen to belong to.

It will be remembered that we have been discussing 'dislike' arising from qualities which people really have, rather than from those they are wrongly supposed to have. And we have now set ourselves the problem of deciding when this is pathological. In fact, I think most pathological dislike does involve a distorted picture of its object. But an unconscious affect can sometimes reverse the evaluation of an object without materially distorting its perception. For example, a backward boy who unconsciously envies his cleverer school-fellows, may persuade himself that it is worthless to be clever, and so come consciously to despise them for their cleverness. Here there is no material falsification of his picture of them; he does not deny that they are clever. But he does deny that he envies and values cleverness. In other words, his contempt is pathological because it results from lack of self-awareness, he is not integrated enough to be aware that he envies what he professes to despise. For the same reason, his devaluation of cleverness is something that can be cured – if he can be made conscious of the underlying positive evaluation. We can also say that his contempt is 'unreasonable' because faulty reasoning is involved in it – though this affects only his picture of himself. Therefore it has the essential quality of a prejudice.

It seems clear then that, even when there is no material falsification of the picture of an object, there can be a prejudiced evaluation of it. The example I gave belongs to what might be called the 'sour-grape' type, because in it – by mechanisms described in detail by Melanie Klein – envy is felt to poison the object which is desired and not possessed.

Having I hope disposed of this difficulty, we can get on to those much clearer forms of prejudice in which there is a distorted picture of the object. If some national, or racial, prejudices start in a sour-grape way, by affecting to despise the active energy and wealth, or perhaps the passive serenity and wisdom, unconsciously envied in a neighbour, they seldom halt there, as dislike once stirred tends also to falsify the picture of its object. This can happen in either, or both, of two ways: the other nation or race can be denied a good quality which it has got, or given a bad quality which it has not got.

As to the denial of a good quality, this is a common alternative response to unconscious envy. If the envious boy had not denied that he valued cleverness, he might instead have denied that his schoolfellows were clever. At this point I must interrupt my argument to say that unconscious envy need have none of these effects. It may be covered by an over-idealization. In this case, there is a positive prejudice which exaggerates the good qualities of its object, and belittles the bad ones. Primitive peoples have sometimes over-idealized their own conquerors in this way. But such attitudes are, of course, unstable; and when they collapse, the underlying negative prejudice comes out – perhaps with explosive force.

To return to the more straightforward case we were about

to consider, in which unconscious envy distorts the picture of its object by depriving it of an envied quality. Here there need be no denial that what is envied is felt to be a virtue. But there is a denial – often in the teeth of overwhelming evidence – that others have more of it. So, in spite of the examination results, the envious boy may persuade himself that those at the top have no more intelligence – only better memories or better luck. What occurs here is really robbery in imagination; for he secretly claims the potent intelligence himself. So too, for example, some warlike peoples, who set a special store on, and envy, courage, have been in the habit of denying it to others, and claiming it all themselves.

This is often combined with the other, and I suppose commonest, distortion, in which bad qualities people have *not* got are attributed to them, or those they have, exaggerated. I am sure you are tired of the envious schoolboy, but I will use him once more as an example. He may start with a simple prejudiced devaluation of cleverness, go on to deny that his rivals are really clever, and end by accusing them of arrogance – whether they have this quality or not. In other words, he pictures them as both stupid and arrogant which of course is exactly what, without knowing it, he is himself.

The vast majority of prejudiced dislikes are, I think, based on 'projections' of this kind. There are many facets of ourselves; and when one or more of these cannot live happily with the rest, it tends to get split off and projected into other people – as in the parable of the mote and the beam. We do not, I think, do this quite fortuitously. It is more that we are, as it were, on the look-out for suitable targets into whom to project these alien aspects of ourselves; and so exaggerate what we perceive of them in others. The resulting 'mote and beam' type of prejudice has two aspects: one favourable to us, the other unfavourable to the person or group the disowned trait is projected into.

Defensive projection has a long pre-history in the individual, dating from the 'paranoid-schizoid' position of infancy described by Melanie Klein; and it follows patterns then laid down in him. Not only traits, or parts of the ego, can be projected in this way, but also superego and other internal figures; and not only what the rest of the ego regards as bad traits, but also aspects felt to be too 'good' to co-exist with the rest, so that the resulting prejudice may be either negative or positive.

Because of its pre-history, the kind of trait anyone is likely to project is specific to himself, prim people being prone to project sensuality to form prejudices about the supposed licentiousness of others, and so on. In general, I think the probable nature of any given individual's negative prejudices could be inferred from the nature of his superego and his ego-ideal.

Freud, who introduced these terms, never defined their precise relation to each other. But while a superego is an 'internalized', and probably exaggerated, aspect of a parental figure, which remains separate from the ego, perhaps we may say that an ego-ideal is a, probably exaggerated, aspect of a parental figure with which the ego has identified itself – in what is basically a hypo-manic way. Thus, while failure to please the superego arouses guilt, failure to live up to an ego-ideal arouses only shame. My point is that it is particularly those traits of ourselves which are liable to arouse either guilt or shame that are liable to be split off and projected into others.

Similarly, if such a thing as a group superego, or a group ego-ideal, can be defined, I should expect group prejudices to arise from the projection of qualities felt to be disapproved of by, or incompatible with, these parental figures.

It used to be said in the last century that, if any Englishman were asked to describe a typical Englishman, he described the Duke of Wellington. In other words, we tried to identify with him as our group-ideal. In particular, his imperturbability being much admired, it became shameful to get excited in a crisis. At the same time, it was rather generally believed that all foreigners invariably did – and this must have been an exaggeration of any actual difference which may have resulted from some foreign nations not having made imperturbability part of their own group-ideal.

What makes this a prejudice, is not only the exaggeration of the excitability of others, but also the exaggerated contempt for excitement, which the splitting process also brings about. Well-integrated people would still have their dislikes; but since faulty, and in particular schizoid, reasoning would not be involved, these could no longer be described as prejudices.

It might be as difficult to give a list of 'normal' dislikes, as to give a list of pathological, or prejudiced, ones. But I would regard it as normal to dislike those who really threatened our existence, or those who were really arrogant or treacherous, and so difficult or unreliable as friends. Moreover, I believe the dislikes of well-integrated people would turn out to be much more uniform than is usually supposed.

The defence mechanisms so far described – the reversal of a primary evaluation out of envy, the denial, also from envy, of qualities which others have, and the projection into others of qualities unconsciously possessed by us – these, and many variants of them, all play a part in the construction of prejudices. But I think there is also a more general defence mechanism which operates, in particular, to maintain them once they are formed. This shows itself as a general reluctance – sometimes amounting to an inability – to revise any system of beliefs to which we have become habituated.

To understand the resistance against revising any established system of beliefs, we should have to have a full understanding of the way in which these are constructed in the first place. And this is a fascinating problem by no means fully solved. But so far as a system of beliefs involves a system of classification, it includes the arrangement of things in accordance with their apparent differences and similarities. Now the acts of noting differences and similarities seem to be what might be called domesticated forms of more primitive, and much more emotionally charged, acts of splitting and integration. It is by means of these primitive violent mechanisms, which appear to be associated with hate and love respectively, that the infant constructs his first fantastic picture of the world. Moreover, the earliest classification is in the main concerned only with the separation of all 'bad' objects from all 'good' ones; and this is done far less in accordance with the actual qualities of objects, than as a defence against the intolerable anxieties which arise when the two categories get mixed.

In the course of normal development, these mechanisms gradually become less violent, and so able to be more realistically employed, till in what I called their domesticated form they build those systems of classification by which we orient ourselves – in particular with respect to what in ideals, people, classes, parties or nations are felt to be good or bad. But if the evidence on which we allotted objects to classes was incomplete – and this can be either because further evidence was not available, or because it was ignored from prejudice – the resulting system may be wrong. If so, there remains the risk, as it were, that new evidence may become available, or old evidence previously ignored may be thrust upon us, to suggest that the system ought to be revised. What happens then will depend both on the extent of the required revision, and on the stability of the person concerned. But if the required revision is at all extensive, it cannot be performed without passing through a period, between the collapse of the old system and the construction of the new, which is always painfully confusing, and in extreme cases, characterized by a kind of intellectual panic. So rather than face this confusional distress – this regression I would say to one of the most painful states of infancy – we may prefer to ignore such new evidence as runs counter to our accepted system of beliefs.

This might be called the 'dogmatic' type of prejudice. I would expect it to play a major role in maintaining group animosities between races, nations or parties, whose religious or political belief-systems are very different from each other. Since to overcome it would involve at least one, and perhaps both, sides in a massive revision of systems they had been brought up on, I would also expect it to be the most recalcitrant.

Such intolerance of confusion may be responsible, not only for maintaining a prejudice, but also for its formation. So far as people find the uncertainty of a suspended judgment disturbing, their judgment is likely to be hasty. And this, it will be remembered, is the dictionary definition of a prejudice.

In this paper, I have spoken – and that only in a very general way – only about the psychological factors which make us liable to prejudice. But, like a cold, a specific prejudice is something we can 'catch', if we are both liable to it and exposed to infection. So, for example, a preference by each of two peoples for biased and misleading history might not be alone sufficient to create a serious prejudice, unless all books easily accessible to each about the other were biased and misleading. In other words, if prejudice is to be adequately understood, it must be studied both from the psychological and the social point of view.[1]

Since no one can easily maintain a prejudice after discovering that it is one, any investigation – from either point of view – must tend to reduce the amount of prejudice to be investigated. And since the many problems that beset mankind are more likely to be solved by an unprejudiced, than by a prejudiced, approach, any such investigation must have a practical, as well as a merely theoretical, interest for us. If, as I believe, far more social conflict springs from prejudice than from any conflict for survival, a deeper and more widespread understanding of its psychological and social determinants is, indeed, a necessary condition for a more harmonious world.

POSTSCRIPT

Among the various types of prejudice classified above, I included those which correspond with what is disapproved of by an individual's superego. But as Mrs Klein pointed out, in the discussion following this paper, an individual may be at war with his superego, and in this case his prejudices are apt to be reversed. And Dr Winnicott, after reading the paper, wrote to remind me of the mechanisms by which people can develop prejudices against the prejudices they were – or imagine they were – brought up on. Since contrary prejudices of this kind are very common, and often quite as irrational as those they are directed against, they certainly ought not to be forgotten.

[1] This is particularly so in the case of those truly insane outbursts of prejudice to which groups are sometimes prone.

24
A Note on Migraine*

The patient who helped me to undestand her defensive use of this complaint and, by so doing, greatly lessened its severity in her, had long suffered, intermittently, from a typical form of it. That is to say, the attacks began with a sense of partial blindness, as if her view were obscured by a dark area, after which jagged, blinding lights appeared, and ended, after these had gone, in an acute headache which gradually wore off.

It had already become apparent, during the course of some years of analysis, that the migraine was affected by psychological factors, and, in particular, that it tended to become worse whenever the analysis itself was felt as, in a high degree, emotionally disturbing. I had once suggested – on what grounds I am afraid I no longer remember – that she felt her migraine to be analogous to the blinding light St Paul saw on his way to persecute the Christians and that it was therefore related to her own unconscious sadistic phantasies. But this was all I could discover, or guess at, until a particular dream gave a much more specific clue. This followed a period of unusually frequent and severe attacks during which she had been trying to face, and adjust herself to, an actual calamity in her life. In the dream, 'she was outside her own house. Her mother (who does not, in fact, live with her) was inside and calls her in. She goes in, with strong feelings of love (such as she could hardly remember actually feeling for her mother). Her mother is bending down by an electric wall plug, and seems to be small. But then she becomes small, too. Her mother looks at her and says she cannot bear the terror in her eyes. Then she looks down and, to her horror, sees that her mother is about to electrocute her with two wires.'

All I could at first see in this was a link with a dream of the

* Int. J. Psycho-analysis, vol. 44, 1963.

previous night in which 'she had been able to tell a woman, who was symbolically in the relation of a mother to her, about the actual calamity (I mentioned)'.

In fact, she had found it almost impossible to speak to anyone about this, though I felt both dreams reflected an increased ability to do so to me. I also noted in the incident about first her mother, then also herself being small, a characteristic confusion between herself and her mother as to who was the mother and who the baby. At the end of the session, I felt that the dream had been important, but was disappointed at having discovered so little of its meaning.

The next session began with my patient's being silent, and appearing to be resentful. I suggested this could be because she felt I had missed an opportunity to understand the dream. She then gave more associations to it. In particular, the electric wires reminded her of a curious object in an earlier dream of three nights before: 'a thing, like a fishing rod with a lump like an electric switch on it, seen lying under her damaged car, which seemed to have been torn away from the trafficator lamps.'

It then occurred to me that these torn off trafficator wires represented her optic nerves which she felt her internal mother had burnt out in order to protect her from seeing something terrifying. She was immediately convinced by this; and further confirmation was provided by the prolonged disappearance of the migraine – which has not returned, though of course I cannot guarantee that it will never do so. (In retrospect it seems possible that the fishing rod with the torn wire attached represented a 'rod' from the retina. It is not, of course, suggested that her infant-self knew anything of optic nerves or rods and cones. But she did seem to be using her adult knowledge to form a dream-model of an early pattern of emotional experience which had remained unmastered because she had never been able to begin to express it in symbols. That this can be a function of dreams is an idea I owe to W. R. Bion.)

The next problem was to discover what it was which, apart from the actual calamity, was unconsciously linked with it and too terrifying to be seen. Another dream, about ten days later, threw some light on this. 'She is driving her car away from a house. There is a wall on the left and, on the right, a green van parked well on the verge. A sports car is approaching and she slows down. But although there is plenty of room for it to pass between her and the parked van, it swerves away from the van on her right, across in front of her, and crashes into the wall on her left. A young man gets out; his eyes are mad, sightless, and glazed; he staggers over to her car and attacks her headlights with an enormous spanner.'

Here, again, is the attack on the eyes – both his and her own – represented by the headlights of her car. Furthermore, from the pattern of the accident, I suggested that it looked as if it had occurred because the young man (already familiar as her imaginary male twin) had seen something in the parked green van which she had not. She then remembered that the green van had appeared in an earlier dream about two months before, just after the actual calamity I spoke of. In that dream: 'the green van had been parked and a pack of hounds had poured out of it, each wearing a red coat as if they were huntsmen . . . . There had also been an accident involving three cars in this dream; and she had been afraid the ambulance or fire-engine, which was coming, would run over the hounds as they crossed the road . . .'.

It seemed probable, then, that what the young man had seen, and she had not, in the green van in the recent dream was linked with the red-coated hounds in the earlier dream. I suggested that the hounds which 'poured out' were faeces, that they were red because they were bloody, and that this represented the evidence of an internal calamity, probably to me as her internal mother. I also tried to link this with the miscarriage her mother had had in her infancy. However, there did not seem enough evidence to substantiate this at the time; and she, though thinking it plausible, did not seem to be emotionally convinced.

Meanwhile, as she had lost her ability to have migraine, other defences against the full perception of what I thought was an internal event began to take place. For instance, about four months later, I think after I had interpreted some oedipal material and used the word 'murder' in a way which had aroused in her an unusual sense of horror (unfortunately my notes are incomplete on this point), she arrived at the next session feeling quite disorientated. She told me she had dreamed that 'she was sitting where I sit, trying to show a book of paintings to three women: one who could hear but not see, one who could see but not hear, and one who couldn't remember . . .'.

It seemed clear that she had split herself in this way in order not to apprehend the full horror of the situation illustrated in the book.

Moreover, I got the impression that, like some patients described by Bion, her oedipal phantasies had been, and were being, split up before they developed. I felt as if she were requiring me to act as her imagination and tell her how her phantasies would have developed if she had been able to develop them. From the beginning there had been intermittent, and quite conscious, anxieties about accidents I might have at weekends in my car, which I had done my best to interpret as they arose. There had been persistent, but also scattered, references to car accidents seen, but not heard, in dreams, and waking experiences of noises associated with screams heard, when their cause was not seen. From these I constructed a more vivid picture of what I thought one phantasy, if it had not been disrupted at its inception, would have become: a phantasy of an accident to the car in which I was imagined to go off with my wife and children for the week-end, and that she would both see it and hear the screams. There was also evidence, from the intensity with which she seemed sometimes to listen for noises inside her body, that all this was felt to take place inside her, when her unconscious rage with me for leaving her was at its height. This, or something like it, seemed to be the horror in the green van – ultimately her envious self – against the apprehension of which she had originally protected herself by the migraine. (I also thought it had been hiding behind the actual calamity she had been unable to speak of.) She emotionally felt this interpretation to be right and experienced relief.

I should add that the greater integration she then achieved enabled her to be more aware, not only of terrifying phantasies, but also of good ones. On the next night she dreamed that my consulting room was an art gallery containing two objects of extraordinary beauty.

In this note, I have tried to isolate and follow one thread –

that of migraine – among many others interwoven with it. I am aware that I have done so very incompletely. I do not think I should have got on to this particular thread at all, but for the two dreams that made it obvious. Retrospectively, it became obvious that the migraine thread had been present in many earlier dreams, and other material about blindness in various forms, which I had not understood at the time. I have no evidence on which to justify a general theory that everyone with a constitutional liability to migraine would be likely to use it in the same defensive way. All I claim to have established is that it can be so used.

25

Politics from the Point of View of Psycho-analysis

[*Introductory Note*, 1977 – This paper was originally written in 1964 for and at the request of the *20th Century*. Then I was asked to shorten it for the *Observer* (under the same ownership). But in fact neither this paper nor the shortened version of it, appeared in either.]

If we wish to investigate the psychology of politics, it may help to start with a glance at the last half million years of human evolution. For it was in this period that man, having outstripped all other species, became his own chief rival in the struggle for existence. Such conditions, according to the late Sir Arthur Keith,[1] favoured in us the development of a double attitude towards our fellow men – an attitude which admirably fitted us to co-operate in groups for the purpose of war with neighbouring groups. In other words, while developing a capacity for love and loyalty, we lost the built-in inhibition against killing our own kind which most other species possess. In particular, this must have added a new bitterness to sexual rivalry, seldom lethal in other species, but potentially lethal in man wherever there is no law and order to keep him in check. At any rate, no psycho-analyst can have any doubt about the murderous ferocity which struggles in the unconscious against opposite feelings whenever jealousy or envy are aroused. That they are aroused already in infancy in relation to the child's own parents and siblings was one of Freud's least welcome discoveries.

One must suppose that our remote forbears were at first unaware of the problem which the simultaneous presence of both loyalty and ruthlessness in their relations with each other

[1] *Essays on Human Evolution*, 1946.

had in store for them: they could save a neighbour's life at the risk of their own one day, and murder him the next without any sense of conflict, if he became a rival. The split in their minds had not come together to make them aware of a contradiction: the friend they loved and the enemy they hated remained for them two different kinds of animal – as they may again become for us when we are engaged in war.

By degrees, however, man began to know himself, to become aware of his own psychology and of its contradictions. As a result he was threatened with a new complaint – that of a bad conscience which has plagued him ever since.

Against this new evil – for evil it must have seemed – he developed other psychological defences. It was no longer sufficient merely to maintain the split in the object of his ambivalent feelings. He began splitting off parts of himself – predominantly the lecherous and murderous parts – and putting them into scapegoats in order to evade his unconscious sense of guilt. As Freud has pointed out, convicted criminals may still serve this function; they help the law-abiding citizen to forget that he might be potentially as bad.

But, in spite of these defences, our forbears' developing capacity to be conscious of themselves left them no peace. At first this introspection, which brought them into contact with depression and the sense of guilt, seems itself to have been considered as the major sin. This, as Dr Bion has argued in a recent book,[1] can be inferred from several early myths. Man ate of the Tree of Knowledge of Good and Evil, knew that he was naked, and was cast out of Eden. Oedipus' punishment follows not his deed, but his *discovery* of it.

The myth of Oedipus can be thought of as the elaboration, with profound poetical insight, of the unconscious meaning of episodes that were presumably common in those days. A chieftain's son leads a raid, or perhaps a revolt, against a neighbouring chieftain, kills him and takes his wife. A less introspective prince than Oedipus would have had no sense of conflict in combining loyalty to his own parents, and respect for their marriage, with the murder and rape which destroyed another couple in the same position as his own parents, and so

[1] *Elements of Psycho-analysis*, 1963.

unconsciously symbolizing them. Or, if he were momentarily troubled in his mind, he would have simply eased it by a ceremony of purification which transferred the guilt to a scapegoat. Oedipus represents a man whose mind is not so easily set at rest. He pursues, as it were, the scapegoat till he unmasks it as himself. Then he tears out his eyes, which may represent, not only self-punishment, but also an attack on the very insight which brought him so much pain.

From this point of view, Oedipus epitomizes man at a critical stage of his development, when he was faced by a new sort of choice: that between self-knowledge and self-deception. The extent to which he chose self-deception is something I suppose the prophets and the poets have always been aware of. But only since Freud developed his technique of psycho-analysis has it begun to be systematically investigated.

I hope the relevance of this to my theme of psycho-analysis and politics will now begin to become apparent; for, if psycho-analysis is a method of exposing self-deceit, politics, in which self-interest is bound to come in conflict with our wish to believe in the disinterestedness of our concern for the common good, is a likely field for the discovery of self-deceit.

In order to investigate it, however, we need to know a little more about the general principles involved. In discussing man's development, we got to the point when he nearly became aware of his own conflicts, in particular of his bad conscience, and began to deal with it by various forms of self-deceit. To facilitate this, he seems, at least in recent centuries, to have redirected his curiosity away from himself, and fixed it more on the external world[1] – with the result that physics has achieved a disproportionate advance.

In addition, he further developed his defence mechanisms to protect him from disagreeable truth. These can be very

---

[1] What is perhaps a false dichotomy between mental and physical may, in part, correspond with the difference between, on the one hand, those sensations arising from autonomic and proprioceptive systems, which are linked with the awareness of emotion (or, in the James–Lange theory, *are* the emotions), and, on the other, those of our five senses from which we derive our notion of external objects. If so, the shift in interest from the inner to the outer world could be epitomized, for example, as a shift of interest from the gut to the eyes – in which, of course, not only a difference in sensation, but also in the phantasies aroused by sensation, would be involved.

complicated. But common to them all – except the most primitive – is a sort of hypertrophy of one aspect of purposeful thought at the expense of another. In order to survive, we are equipped with a capacity to imagine what we need as well as with a capacity to plan ways and means of getting satisfaction. It is the first half of this double process at which, in some fields, we seem to get stuck; so that, instead of making the effort to achieve our aim, we are content to imagine we already have it.

This can be more accurately expressed in terms of Freud's theory of two Principles of Mental Functioning. The first is the Pleasure Principle which aims at the denial of every form of unpleasant truth and its replacement by agreeable illusion. The second is the Reality Principle characteristic of a mature capacity to face all problems, both in the inner and in the outer world, and try to solve them.

Of course, if we did not operate at least mainly on the Reality Principle in our dealings with the outer world, we should soon cease to survive. But the penalties for operating on the Pleasure Principle in our dealings with our own psychology are less immediately apparent. To take a simple example, which at last brings us directly to the application of psycho-analysis to politics: If anyone chooses to believe that his political orientation is inspired by noble motives, when these are in fact largely contaminated by unconscious greed or envy, it is by no means obvious that his comforting delusion does him any harm. Why then should we seek to probe our motives? Those who, like Oedipus, desire truth at any cost will need no other justification for its pursuit. But most people, before making the painful effort, will wish to be assured of at least probable advantages. And, indeed, it can be shown that, if the effort is not made, the short-term gain in equanimity may be too dearly bought at the cost of long-term disaster.

To mention only one form of this, failure to understand our own psychology, because of the dominance of the Pleasure Principle in this field, inevitably involves a complementary failure to understand other people too. That this can be disastrous in private life is obvious: its effects, for instance, in unsatisfactory marriage and disappointing children are there for all to see. I suggest it can be even more disastrous, because on a larger scale, in politics where the relation of sub-groups to each other and to their government is psychologically analogous to intra-family relations. If for no other reason, then, an attempt at political psycho-analysis as a prophylactic would seem to be worthwhile.

A certain amount of information is already available. Psycho-analytic treatment, which is the same as psycho-analytic research, aims at disclosing the various ways in which a failure in reality thinking can come about in individuals; and, as their political thinking forms part of their thinking in general, analysts have opportunities for studying how this, too, can go astray. Making use of the concepts introduced, or elaborated, by Melanie Klein, as well as Freud's, I will try to list a few of the defence-mechanisms which seem to operate against reality thinking in politics. What, as always, is common to them all is that they interfere with the discovery of truth in the interests of a short-term gain in equanimity.

I will begin with the two splitting mechanisms against ambivalence and guilt I have already mentioned, and will add one more – the so-called manic-defence – which, like them, seems to me to be specifically human. For they represent primitive ways of dealing with man's ambivalence towards his own species – an unconscious loving and hating his neighbour at the same time – which has saddled him with internal tensions not shared, in anything like the same degree, by any other species.

That such tensions would be likely to be nowhere more present, even when we are unaware of them, than in the field of politics would seem likely; since politics is the continuation, in a more civilized form, of the inter-tribal warfare in which our forbears were perennially engaged during the latter stages of their evolution. The difference, of course, lies in the fact that, where there is a democratic constitution, a victory can be gained without actually massacring the defeated party. In spite of this, any political question in which we become involved is likely to arouse acute unconscious conflicts in which self-interest, perhaps heightened by the still more unconscious presence of ruthless greed and envy, struggles with consideration for the interests of others, reinforced by an unconscious conscience which requires us to put their interests before our own.

Moreover, to introduce a further complication, the parties and personalities, as well as the more abstract concepts involved, acquire an added emotional significance because they become unconsciously linked with the figures of the individual's own family as they appeared to him in early childhood – that is, not necessarily as they were, but as they appeared to be in his unconscious phantasy. Expressions such as 'Fatherland' or 'Brotherhood' are among the outward and visible signs of corresponding unconscious identifications. One consequence of this is that political conflicts are apt to structure themselves on one or other of two common patterns: a revolt by the children against the parents, and a squabble between the children for what the parents have to give.

If, therefore, politics arouse personal conflicts between altruism and egoism, not only at the adult level, but also at the infantile level where they are still more acute, it is only to be expected that defence mechanisms should come into play which work on the Pleasure Principle to conceal the complexity of the inner problems. By such means the discomforts threatened by the tensions of ambivalence, by the sense of guilt and by various anxieties, can be largely disposed of – at the cost of truth.

Ambivalence – the state of loving and hating one's neighbour at the same time – is, as I said, commonly dealt with by a primal kind of splitting. Members of one's own party are felt to be good, or at least better than they are, members of the other party can seem wholly bad – a different and nastier sort of animal. If we lose an election, we may be sorry for ourselves and for other members of our party who are felt to deserve our sympathy. If we win, we triumph, and are not sorry for the other side at all. In other words, we adopt an attitude which would be justified if our own side were wholly constructive, and our opponents wholly repressive or destructive. Perhaps an approximation to this state of affairs occurred in Germany in the 1933 election which brought Hitler into power. But the apportionment of motive is seldom as clear-cut as this. My point is that we tend to exaggerate the extent to which it is.

Some of the practical consequences of such splitting can be seen by comparing political debate with the sort of discussion that takes place among the members of any good board of directors. By good I mean not only that they know their subject, but that they are all concerned to reach the best decision, irrespective of who happened to think of it first. Private thinking, at its best, is of this nature: each point of view is, as it were, allowed to have its say before a decision is arrived at. But once the splitting characteristic of party politics has bedevilled our minds, our thinking degenerates from discussion to debate. One internal voice is concerned only to disprove the other's point of view without considering it seriously at all.

So much for defences against the tensions arising from ambivalence. Coming now to defences against the sense of guilt. The sense of guilt is a complex human emotion having a complex history, which involves such entities as the unconscious superego first discovered and investigated by Freud. Suffice it to say here – and this has been particularly brought out by Melanie Klein's studies of young children – that the chief sources of feelings of depressive guilt are greed and envy, which no human being is entirely free from. So far then as greed and envy influence our political opinions – and at least unconsciously they can hardly fail to do so – we are threatened with a sense of guilt. To evade it, the other sort of splitting defence comes into play, to reinforce the first one: we tend to split off the greedy and envious parts of ourselves and project them into the other side, with the result that, while becoming largely blind to the operation of these motives in our own party, we perceive them, as it were in double measure, only in our political opponents. This, incidentally, increases our lack of sympathy for them in political defeat – since we feel they thoroughly deserve it.

I am not suggesting that indignation with political opponents is never justified. But the extent to which it is justified cannot be objectively assessed until our picture of them is freed from the distorting influence of our own projections. And this is by no means easy for anyone, even trained analysts, to do.

A further complication arises through the fact that the two splitting mechanisms – and especially the one used as a defence against the sense of guilt – arouse a good deal of what is strictly speaking psychotic anxiety. For people cannot split-off and project bad parts of themselves without feeling persecuted by them. Of course, since our interests, and the causes we espouse, are likely to be affected by the result of an election, some anxiety is rational enough. But to this may be added a large amount of persecutory, or paranoid, anxiety which is itself the end product of splitting and projection. In other words, the penalty for easing one's mind with the illusion of being nicer than one is, is an exaggerated sense of being threatend from without by the very impulses one has disowned.

We have, therefore, two sorts of anxiety to contend with – one rational, the other not. Against these, further defence-mechanisms may come into play; and paradoxically enough, these seem often to be more effective in keeping us unaware of rational anxieties which, in our long-term interests, we ought to face, than in curing us of the irrational anxieties which we ought not to have at all.

As to the denial of real dangers, this comes about, not because they have not been foreseen by some part of the mind, but because they have been too frightening to be consciously faced. In other words, a short-term gain in peace of mind has been achieved by means of what is called a 'manic defence'. In my view, nothing else can explain how this country fell, almost unprepared, into two world wars, the approach of which ought to have been obvious many years before they became inevitable. Perhaps other dangers that ought to be equally obvious are being denied in the same way now. Some people think this is the case with the danger of over-population. But the point I want to make is the more general one: that, in order to evade worry about anything which is not immediately upon them, human beings are politically reluctant to take a long-term point of view. And this would seem to be the result, at least in part, of being too much worried, by the persecutory anxieties I spoke of, about the immediate present.

Apart from the defence mechanisms already mentioned – and there are many more – there is one which seems to me to be phylogenetically earlier, and more ubiquitous, than any of the others. Probably everyone is familiar with experiments on learning in animals: how, for instance, they can be taught to find their way through a maze by following certain signs associated with food, and avoiding others associated with a mild electric shock. But if the two signs are gradually made more similar, the unfortunate animal becomes confused and terrified in a way which is very suggestive of psychotic confusion in humans. This mental state is extraordinarily painful and appears to be in part 'paranoid-schizoid' (Melanie Klein) and part 'confusional' – that is, a mixture of persecutory and depressive feelings (Rosenfeld). And as it is experienced, though in different degrees by everyone in infancy, we are all liable, under different degrees, of stress, to regress to it again. The conditions, both innate and environmental, favourable or unfavourable to our successfully outgrowing it, have also been, and are being, studied. All I want to stress here is that outgrowing it involves learning to know our world. Or, rather, to be more precise, it involves developing theories with which we try to explain or anticipate anything that happens. Now as these are seldom, if ever, quite accurate, they are in need of occasional revision. But this cannot be done without some temporary return to that state of confusion from which we are always endeavouring to escape. That our capacity to think depends in no small measure on our capacity to tolerate such states of temporary confusion without too much anxiety is a point recently made both by Dr Jaques and Dr Bion. People who cannot tolerate this well are apt to cling dogmatically to any theory or opinion once formed in the teeth of new evidence that it ought to be revised – or perhaps discarded altogether. Of course, other motives, such as reluctance to admit one had been wrong, play their part in this dogmatism as well; but I think the fear of confusion is the primary motive.

For these reasons, we probably do tend to shirk, or at least delay, trying to re-think political problems when the old solutions – perhaps valid in their day – become outworn. If so, we achieve a short-term gain in peace of mind at the expense of holding opinions that are, or have become, inadequate and, therefore, might be dangerous.

I hope I have said enough to suggest that there is much in politics which could benefit by psycho-analytic clarification. But in recommending that this should be attempted, I should add two warnings. First, it is easy enough to use psycho-analysis polemically, to uncover flaws only in one's political opponents. But if we find ourelves doing this, without first applying it pretty rigorously to our own opinions, we should suspect a 'mote and beam' principle operating in us, and a 'scapegoat' motive. Second, if alternatively, in applying it to ourselves, we expect to find it easier to reach political decisions, I think we should be mistaken. Usually it makes them more difficult, as many more factors than one was at first aware of come into the picture. On the other hand, nothing can be more risky than to think we know where we are going when in fact we don't; and this, I believe, has been and still is common enough in the political life of any nation.

26

Megalomania*

Looking back from what, by comparison, may appear a more enlightened age, the extreme violence of the opposition to the simple, and now almost obvious, truths propounded by Copernicus, Darwin and Freud, seem almost inexplicable – or rather it would so seem if Freud himself had not explained it as the inevitable response to three major blows to human narcissism. The thesis I hope to develop here is that this narcissism, which is still with us though it may take other forms, is a psychotic trait so pervasive in our species that to possess it is commonly considered to be not merely 'normal', but essential to health.

A critical illustration of what I mean is to be found, in an easily recognizable form, in those patients whose illness appears to consist in a 'loss of confidence'. In such cases, analysis will probably reveal that their former 'confidence' had in it more than a just assessment of their capacities in relation to their tasks. It contained, in its affirmation of a special worth, a manic quality, as a defence against a sense of worthlessness, which differs only in degree, but not in kind, from a megalomanic delusion. To them this 'delusion' was a part of their 'health' which they hope the analyst will restore to them. Moreover, their friends and relatives entirely share their view. They had before been functioning successfully – perhaps even brilliantly – on the basis of a good, to the analyst an exaggerated, opinion of themselves which they have now lost. No wonder, then, that everyone, except the analyst, believes this 'good', in reality exaggerated, and so delusional, opinion to be an attribute of health.

---

* The title and to a great extent the theme of this paper was suggested to me by a phrase in Dr D. Meltzer's paper on prehistoric cave paintings, delivered to the Imago Group, London, in the spring of 1962. The present paper was read to the same group in the spring of 1963.

MEGALOMANIA

The delusional element in excessive self-confidence is, of course, clinically well-known. It springs from a particular kind of identification with admired figures. In its extreme and overt form, it expresses itself as a belief that one is some admired historic figure, or even God himself. In its unconscious, latent form, it originates in a particular kind of identification with the parents and, as Melanie Klein believed, ultimately with the feeding breast. Its delusional quality consists in that which distinguishes it from the internalization of parental figures as superego, between which and the ego a barrier remains intact. The delusion arises only when the barrier is obliterated by an envious penetration of the superego by the ego so that it can claim the greatness for itself. Or the ego can in phantasy consume the superego, as suggested by Freud in his reconstruction of the Primal Feast. In both cases, what is delusional is not the *desire* for the envied identification between what in the inner, as once in the outer world, was infant and parent (or part-object), *but the assertion that the identification is a fact.*

Some degree of this delusion I would suppose to be inevitable in infancy. The infant might well be unable to support the sense of its own helpless insignificance without it. My point is that it is something the human race as a whole seems unable fully to outgrow.

CLOTHES AND THE DELUSION OF DIVINITY

Anthropologically speaking, we seem to have been afflicted with it at least since we began to cover our nakedness with clothes. For while these were used as an alloplastic adaptation to cold, the idea of using them at all was almost certainly derived from the impulse to identify with admired animals, deified as potent parent symbols, by destroying them and putting on their skins – for something of the kind is still done, by primitive peoples in their rites, who do not use clothes for any other purpose. (The specifically human habit of ritual dancing in costume, to ape the creative acts of parental figures so appropriated, was probably acquired at the same time.)

There can be little doubt that clothes still have a similar significance for us – except that we now use them to emphasize the difference between ourselves and inferior animals, instead of our identity with animals once felt to be superior. In Greek culture, it is true, nakedness could achieve its own apotheosis, if it was the nakedness of an athlete or of a statue which idealized the 'human form divine'. But, in general, to be unclothed is to be reminded of our kinship with other animals, while to be clothed is to over-stress the gulf, and so implies a claim to be not merely the most clever sort of animal, but something more than animal. It is true that we are ambivalent about this delusion; for to cut adrift altogether from the animal in us would be to lose the physical basis of our sexuality. There are times when we wish to shed our clothes and the delusion they foster.

But to return to the delusion. This is still clearer in the case of clothes of office. The judge in his robes symbolizes, not merely a man learned in the law, but the very lawgiver in all his majesty. Whether, as an individual, he holds the delusion that he is this, and gains support from it, it is certainly held unconsciously by most people in the court. So they ease his task by giving him reverence.

This brings me to another point: the effect of clothes, not only on the wearer, but on those who see him in them. Clothes being an important, and perhaps the earliest, 'status symbol', two clothed people can hardly meet, at least for the first time, without a belief about their 'relative status' being aroused in both of them. There are many social occasions on which people take great pains to dress alike, and thus foster the belief that everyone is of equal standing. Then no one can be pushed out of a sense of superior importance. But in contacts between two people wearing clothes suggestive of different ranks, one of them may be confirmed in this sense of superiority, while the other may be pushed out of it. There may also be cases in which neither has it; but if a certain degree of megalomania is almost universal in our species, these must be rare. In the usual case, neither have much difficulty in adopting the beliefs expected of them in this situation. The one who is believed to be superior receives respect, is confirmed in his opinion of his superiority, and becomes gracious if a little patronizing. The other, just because he too believes the first to be in some sense a super-man, can idealize him as such, and find compensation for his own sense of having shrunk in stature in the enjoyment of reflected glory. There are, of course, other cases to consider. Sometimes the one who has the higher status deliberately steps off his pedestal, in order to spare the other the possible distress of having to step off his. (To do so is, indeed, part of traditional good manners.) Or, if the one with the lower status is disturbed by too much envy, he may try to stay on his own pedestal by trying to push the first one off. (And this, of course, is part of traditional bad manners.)

STATUS AS A GARMENT

What has been said above implies that status itself, whether symbolized by clothes or not, is a kind of garment – a garment which, though it remains intangible, is felt to change the very nature of its wearer.

The organization of society consists in the allotment of status rôles to individuals. It is a fact that a given individual plays, and is appointed to play, a given rôle – say that of judge. And it is a fact that he must have comparatively rare and specific qualities which render him competent to play it. It is also a fact that, on his appointment, he changes his rôle, say from Queen's Counsel to Queen's Judge. But it may be presumed that his competence to play this rôle has not significantly changed in the short period from just before to just after his appointment. These are the facts. Yet it is possible to infer, from the subtle change in the relation between him and his colleagues, the existence of a widespread belief, which is unconscious and delusional, that his new status has suddenly increased his stature. Though less blatantly expressed, this belief is of the same kind as that which once asserted the divinity of kings from the moment of their succession; and so it is, I think, with any rise in status. Even when there is no 'investment' of robes and insignia of office, the achievement of a higher status is felt to imply, not merely the taking over of a higher rôle, but a change of skin which converts the incumbent into a nobler sort of animal. In other words, the whole concept of status, as opposed to that of rôle, commonly implies an element of delusional belief.

COMPARATIVE STATUS AND THE DELUSION OF INFERIORITY

This, however, is still only one side of the picture. Since all statuses are relative, their comparison implies, I think, not merely a single, but a double delusion – a delusional inferiority on the one hand, and a delusional superiority on the other.

Of course, many possible emotions may be aroused between people when they become aware of the sense of a difference in status. Compassion towards the supposed inferior may be as common as arrogance and contempt; and, on the other side, pleasant feelings of admiration and gratitude may override painful feelings of inferiority, hate and envy. But it is the feelings of arrogance and contempt, and the response to their real or supposed presence, that I would first try to trace to their source. In doing so, we might start with the fact that the idea of inferiority is very often associated with the idea of dirt. The lowest and most despised caste in India is composed, I believe, of lavatory attendants, crossing sweepers, grave-diggers, and all those whose rôle is directly concerned with the disposal of dirt or corruption. And, in general, the 'proletariat', or the 'masses', whenever these terms are used with contempt, are always thought of as unwashed. The aristocratic nose is proverbially narrowed and held high in order to avoid their stench.

Such considerations are perhaps alone sufficient to give us the answer straight away; for, in fact, it is something we already know and only have to be reminded of. There is a moment in the life of every baby when the sense of being one with the good breast begins to be replaced by a sense of twoness. He is then threatened by the feeling that, while all goodness comes from his mother and her milk, he is capable of producing only dirt. To evade such painful feelings, various delusions may be adopted. Among the commonest of these is that the faeces are good after all, in fact the most valuable substance, without which nothing can be done. A patient, for example, dreamed that she gives 'dogs' to a policeman to give to two women who want them – which, on analysis, seemed to represent the phantasy that if her mother (represented by the two women, or breasts) wanted babies, she could have them only if the child gives her (dog) faeces to her father (represented as the policeman with his phallic helmet) for him in turn to give to her mother. But the delusion I am more concerned with here evades the unpleasant truth in a rather different way, by a direct reversal of rôles: the baby projects itself into the breasts and, in phantasy, becomes the person who alone is valuable. Thus, for example, the same patient dreamed that she was wearing a fur coat 'worth thousands', while the women on each side of her she described as two 'old cows'. But the fact that the coat had spots, which the patient herself associated to faeces, suggested a suppressed awareness that the grandiose phantasy was a delusion used to deny the unpleasant truth.

I have said unpleasant truth – for it is true that the mother's breasts give milk and the baby's bottom faeces, and not the other way about. But this truth, when operated on by the baby's suppressed contempt for itself, becomes an element in another and opposite delusion: that the mother arrogantly regards the baby as *only* an object of contempt. This, too, seems to appear in the dream, if the coat covered by dark brown spots represents the baby as nothing but a mass of dirty holes.

This mechanism is so important to my thesis that, before proceeding, I will quote another example of a baby's idealization of his own behind as superior to his mother's breasts. A male patient, who suffered from mixed feelings of arrogance and inferiority, as well as from some repressed passive homosexual trends, dreamed of a 'young "Regency Buck" who, when he went to the "Varsity", wore with great pride a special hat given him by his mother. This was curved like a bowler in front and square like a top hat behind and it was very large.' He associated the curved part at once to breasts and suggested that he felt his mother had given him these. But, on further inquiry, the whole shape of the hat reminded him more of a homosexual little boy presenting his behind for admiration. So it became clear that the arrogance of the little boy part of him was ultimately based on the delusion that his behind was better and more attractive to men (particularly, of course, his father) than his mother's breasts – or rather, that it *was* these breasts. But, in fact, he had a great contempt for passive homosexual undergraduates, whose vanity, he felt, was utterly unjustified. In other words, he had a great contempt for this part of himself, and believed it to be worthless: In the dream, he had tried to get rid of it by making the 'Regency Buck' look like another undergraduate – a friend to whom he was ambivalently attracted.

Perhaps enough has been said to illustrate the existence, and origin, of this sort of double delusion about this unique merits on the one hand, and utter worthlessness on the other, of the self. Of course, it becomes far more complex, in the course of its development, since the same envious mechanism which began by claiming the breasts goes on to claim all other envied objects too. And this, since the latent awareness of the falsehood of these claims persists, serves only to increase the underlying sense of worthlessness – which is further augmented by the fact that growth in the capacity to love has been sacrificed in the pursuit of adoration. Thus, to maintain the delusion of a special merit, and the sense of being adored, or at least admired for it, there must always be some other object on which to project the opposite delusion of worthlessness. A great deal of the jockeying for status which takes place in later life clearly serves this purpose. A periodic rise in status is required in order that the despised part of the self, which always tends, as it were, to catch up, can be left behind in the relatively low one just vacated.

THE PROJECTION OF INFERIORITY AND THE CONCEPT OF AN INSULT

If a hidden, but essential, function performed by the achievement of a higher status is passively to leave the despised or inferior self in the persons still occupying the lower status from which the superior self has successfully emerged, the same aim can be pursued by other means which, though more actively aggressive, involve much less real effort. For it can be done, without working to achieve a higher status, by anyone who has mastered the technique of projecting the lower one. And very galling it is for those who have sweated to achieve eminence, to be robbed of the psychological reward, and made to feel inferior, by someone who has never laboured to achieve anything at all.

MEGALOMANIA

It is true that, in the last analysis, the only figures that can rob an individual of the illusion of his grandeur are his own superego – usually that aspect of it into which envy has been intrapsychically projected – and his envious id. So those in the outer world who seem to do it deliberately are sometimes maligned. They may be persons who, because they have achieved a certain degree of serenity, are wrongly thought to be arrogant, and for this reason become equated with a superego which is determined to keep the ego in its place, or with an id-aspect which, for different reasons, is determined to do the same. But often the intention to do it – by behaving like what may be called an 'inferiority projecting superego' or an envious id, either consciously or unconsciously, exists.

This form of projective identification by which one person manages to dispose of his inferior ego by putting it in someone else, and causing this other actually to feel inferior, can be brought about in ways so subtle that not even the aggressor, let alone his victim, is conscously aware of what is being done – though both are aware of the effect upon their feelings.

It is done, I think, most effortlessly by those whose delusion of superior merit – of being identified with their own superegos – is so absolute that they are never consciously aware of the defects they unconsciously dispose of by arousing the sense of them in others. In fact, they behave in a manner which, if it were conscious, would be recognized as deliberately insulting, but which, being unconscious, is so well concealed that the victim can neither counter nor riposte.

In those with an equal desire for superiority, but without so firm a supporting delusion of it, the insulting behaviour by which they try to keep it can be more clearly recognized for what it is – even when it is not conscious – and provokes a clearer response.

I suggest that our usual response to an insult, when it is recognized as such, is specifically human, almost ubiquitous in our species, and itself evidence of the delusion of grandeur from which, with very few exceptions, we seem, in varying degrees, to suffer. Other animals react to an injury as we do. But with the possible exception of dogs, which have acquired so many human characteristics through selective breeding and close contact with man, I doubt whether any other animal reacts as we do to an insult which is not an injury. For in order to feel insulted it is first necessary to have pretensions. The words, 'Who the Devil do you think you are talking to?' spring to the lips of the insulted man, and thus betray his pretensions to be 'somebody', that is, something more than he would be without the mystic garment of his status. It was not so long ago that, among 'gentlemen', that is, persons of this status, insults which challenged could not be righted except by spilling blood; and many people still feel that an insult unavenged rankles for ever in their breasts.

By contrast with these, there are people who are incapable of feeling insulted, either because their vanity is unassailable – and this implies an element of unassailable delusion – or because they have really accepted themselves for what they are and have no delusions to be shattered. Since intended insults do them no harm, they have no compulsion to return them. Perhaps the 'meekness' praised in the New Testament was originally intended to apply to people of this type – and not, as the word now suggests, to those who are pacifist at any price. At any rate, what was being preached against was the pride which differs from normal self-respect in that it implies pretensions and can be maintained only by the prompt return of any insult aimed against them.

There remains the task of relating this jockeying for status in the outer world with processes taking place in the inner between the ego, the superego and the id. For much of the former can be expressed as an 'acting out' of an internal situation in which the ego enviously desires to usurp the grandeur of the superego, while the id endeavours enviously to destroy both. If this perhaps over-simple formula is in essentials right, the ego, so far as it has been successful in its aim, has to defend itself against not merely one, but two, potential enemies: the superego itself which, so far as it contains much id envy, behaves like a jealous god whose claim to be the sole possessor of omnipotence and omniscience has been challenged; and the id, which always, in some degree, remains the fount of destructive envy and so relentlessly attacks the ego for any success it has in equating itself with the envied superego. In this predicament, the ego's primary defence is by projection. It sees the hostile parts, both of its superego and its id, in the persons who it believes, often wrongly, to be hostile to its status.

Two dreams of a male patient illustrate the basic intrapsychic nature of these two dangers. In one, a young man, easily recognizable, I think, as an envious id-aspect of the dreamer, was behaving in a very boorish and insulting manner towards a very senior official, clearly his own paternal superego. In the other, a baby shark, which on analysis seemed to be the dreamer's baby self incorporated in, and so enviously identified with his father's phallus, was gliding rapidly over the sand towards the sea, which symbolized his mother. Before it reached it, however, two policemen, clearly superego figures, caught it and turned it inside out. Then, to the dreamer's surprise, nothing but the skin was left. So while, in the first dream, the envious id attacks the envied superego, in the second, the envious superego attacks the ego which has tried to identify with it.

The second dream also neatly illustrates my thesis about clothes. In it, status and the robes which symbolize it appear as what I maintain they often are, a skin which the wearer feels he has usurped.

THE STATUS OF INSTITUTIONS

If an individual is often prepared to defend his own status, if need be with his life, he can be still more touchy, and courageous – because other loyalties are also brought into play – in the defence of the status of an Institution he belongs to. For however carefully we may define an Institution in terms of the properties of its members, their rôles in it and of the relation of these rôles to each other, and to those of non-members, we speak and think of it as if it were a super-individual – that is, as something with pretensions to be upheld. The psychology here is more complex but has, I think, essentially the same roots. That is to say, the individual's megalomania appears to have been lost because it has been projected into the institution; but, in a subtle way, it is regained because the individual feels himself to be 'in' the institution and so, once more, arrogantly, and not merely proudly, identified with it. Therefore, he is also capable of suffering acutely through its shame if he fails to take quick vengeance on any one who seems to shame it.

This, of course, is particularly clear when the Institution is a sovereign state – a Hobbes' Leviathan. One wonders how many of the wars of history have been fought solely for self-defence or even aggressive self-interest, and not also to avenge what has been felt as a national humiliation. At any rate, the 'face-saving' devices still considered necessary by those anxious to preserve the peace suggest that the greatest danger is often felt to be just this. If so, this is evidence of arrogance, derived from the identification of individuals with their unconscious picture of their nation as a super-individual. Here, again, the distinction between injury and insult seems to be decisive. The impulse to defend one's country against enemies may symbolize the impulse to defend one's superego – paternal, maternal or combined – against hostile parts of oneself. But, so long as the impulse is to defend it against injury, no delusion need be involved. The element of delusion comes in, I think, only with the idea of an insult because this idea implies a delusional pretension – that of the individual who has projectively identified himself with his country as an external representative of his superego. It is this delusion, I maintain, which breeds national arrogance, a sentiment different in kind, and not merely in degree, from national self-respect based on a knowledge of actual national achievements.

This delusional element, and the arrogance it breeds, in our relation to the institutions we belong to is, I think, the cause of most institutional malfunctioning. This can be seen, not only in the behaviour of major institutions such as states, but in the workings of any ordinary committee – the sort of thing almost everyone has sat on. As an apparatus for arriving at the truth on any question, and so of deciding action, it has great merits, as well as less easily discernible defects. Much depends, of course, on its composition. It is at its best when all its members are sufficiently free from status-ambition for their desire to arrive at the truth to be undisturbed by the desire for personal ascendancy. The result of their collective deliberations is then likely to have a sounder and more ample basis than could have been achieved by any one of them alone. The danger lies in the possibility of delusional arrogance, which may be only latent in the members, manifesting itself as a group phenomenon. In so far as this happens, the committee is unconsciously thought of as a super-individual, and as such infallible. There is then an increase, beyond what is justified by probability, of confidence in the rightness of decisions and a corresponding decrease in the care with which they are arrived at. At the same time – and this has often been remarked on – there is a kind of moral degeneration: the members of the committee cease to have qualms about doing many things which, as private individuals, they would do only with reluctance, or not at all. In extreme cases, they can become – or so it appears to me – identified with the kind of superego described by Bion as concerned to maintain a moral ascendancy without any morals.

This can have serious consequences, for example, when the decisions of the committee affect other people's lives. In the past, people's lives were far more in the control of other individuals whose whim might make or mar them. But there was, as a rule, at least this remedy for the frustrated, that they could transfer their dependence to some other individual. We have largely discarded the system of control of individuals by individuals. But, as we are not prepared to return to an archaic struggle for existence, we have been forced to develop the system of control by committees – in particular, by selection committees. Now, committees are less subject to whims, but they also have less human feeling; and for those who are unjustly frustrated by them – and they are not infallible – there seldom exists some other committee to which they can transfer their application.

The conclusion to be drawn from this is not, I think, that such committees should be abolished, but that they should be improved; and perhaps the only way of doing this is by publicizing the mechanism of the defects to which they are prone. For if these spring from insidious influence of the *unconscious* arrogance of individuals acting as representatives of a committee, and in *unconscious* phantasy, clothed in the skin of a super-human monster, they have only to become *conscious* of this for the whole fiction and its consequences to collapse. Then it would function as a different kind of group: one in which the individuals do not lose their sense of personal responsibility and are, therefore, more careful in deciding what should be done, and more ready to admit and correct possible mistakes.

THE CONCEPT OF INJUSTICE – REAL AND FICTITIOUS

I would like to conclude with a word on the rôle of delusional arrogance, either individual or collective, as a major cause of what we call injustice. We often speak of 'injustice' as a denial of 'human rights', leaving a wide scope for argument about what these 'rights' may be. To avoid this ambiguity, I will use the word injustice to mean no more than the denial of recognition to the human qualities, including any special merits, which any one may have. If he himself claims more than he possesses, anyone or any institution which fails to recognize his claim will be believed by him, though falsely, to be unjust. A good deal of the supposed injustice in the world is undoubtedly of this type: it is a product of the delusional arrogance of those who suffer from the sense of injustice solely because they claim to be more, in some way, than they are. There remains, however, much genuine injustice resulting from the delusional arrogance of those who deny them such specific merits as they do possess, and often treat them as devoid even of their more general claim to be members of the same human species. That is to say, they use them to project their own sense of worthlessness.

Thus both the fictitious and the real sense of injustice, which embitters the lives of individuals, either on their own behalf or on behalf of the institutions they belong to, and which is the cause of so much actual strife, is attributable to delusional arrogance, or what is the same thing, to megalomanic insanity – either in those who suffer from fictitious injustices or in those who inflict real ones. I have argued that this kind of arrogance has been endemic in our species at least since we began to ape our animal gods by killing them and putting on their skins as clothes. The remedy, of course, is not to deprive ourselves of our actual coverings, but to perceive that, like the Emperor's clothes in the story, the grandeur with which we cover our psyches is a fictitious garment existing only in imagination.

27

Review

Elements of Psycho-analysis. By W. R. Bion.* (London: Heinemann, 1963. Pp. 110. 15s.)

This is a difficult book, not because there is any lack of clarity in exposition, but because the ideas defined in it are new. The reader cannot recognize them as belonging to categories of thought already familiar to him; for they are themselves unfamiliar categories, the members of which remain to be recognized by him. It is this process of filling the defined, but at first empty, classes with examples, perhaps from previously unnoticed patterns from one's own psycho-analytical experience, that gives them solid meaning.

It would seem to follow that there are at least two ways in which these new ideas can be misunderstood: they may, from the outset, be mis-recognized as special cases of familiar ideas; or they may gradually become distorted by the accumulation of inappropriate examples. In now giving an outline of what I believe to be the main theme of Bion's book, I hope I have not gravely erred in either of these two ways; but the difficulties of precise communication of psycho-analytic concepts are so great that some misunderstanding is almost inevitable.

The kind of attention an analyst accords his patients is peculiar in that it largely disregards conscious meaning in its search for patterns that fit psycho-analytic theories, and so permit what is unconscious to be recognized and interpreted. For this purpose, two things are necessary: knowledge of an adequate number of psycho-analytic theories and accurate observation. As to the first, Bion believes that comparatively few theories should be enough, provided they are formulated with sufficient generality (see his *Learning from Experience*). But, of course, if they are not adequate, there will not be enough

* *Int. J. Psycho-analysis*, vol. 45, 1964.

pigeon-holes, as it were, for all the observations. As to the second, if the observations are not accurate, they will be likely to be put in the wrong pigeon-holes in the network of theory even if, in itself, this is adequately comprehensive.

The importance of accurate observation is therefore paramount. Dr Bion's present book I take to be an exposition of a method he has elaborated to sharpen his own powers of observation, which he now offers to others. In essence, it involves a kind of preliminary sorting out of analytic material into categories, which do not themselves correspond with psycho-analytic theories, but which form what he calls the 'elements' of psycho-analysis. This is achieved by means of two co-ordinates: one representing the degree of sophistication of the thought expressed, the other representing the use to which the thought is put.

Although the categories formed in this way do not, as I said, correspond with psycho-analytic theories, the system by which they are formed is a product of theories of thinking which Bion has arrived at in the course of work with patients suffering from disturbances of thought. According to these theories, the formation of thoughts and the development of a capacity to think depend on two mechanisms: an oscillation between paranoid–schizoid and depressive positions (PS ↔ D), and a basic form of projective identification in which what is projected is felt to be received by an object that introjects it (mating of contained with container, ♂♀).

The passage from the confusion of the PS-position to the order of the D-position takes place by means of the selection of a fact. For instance, I would suppose that, for the new-born infant, the first 'fact' is the nipple, the discovery of which begins to bring order into his hitherto chaotic and therefore persecutory sensory and emotional experience.

But, if I have understood Bion rightly, this initial discovery of the nipple as the first 'fact' must also involve the first operation of the ♂♀ mechanism. For the breast seems to be initially experienced as an object that, by accepting, relieves evacuated distress. In other words, it is the prototype of all 'containers' ♀.

There seems to be no doubt that both the PS ↔ D and the ♂♀ theories do help to illuminate what takes place between infant and mother, as repeated between patient and analyst. One thinks, for example, of the way a temporarily confused and terrified patient will fasten on to a single comprehended interpretation as if it were the elixir of life; and of the enormous sense of relief, as if from an evacuation, when a withdrawn patient feels that his emotions have at last been understood. But whether the two mechanisms are separate from the beginning, or form two aspects of the same mechanism, perhaps remains an open question.

At any rate, on Bion's theory, it is by means of these two mechanisms that thought can develop through a series of stages from the crude to the sophisticated – or, by their reversal, can again degenerate, either temporarily when re-thinking is required, or permanently as in certain psychotic states. The earliest stage of all, which Bion thinks can be inferred though not observed, is one in which thoughts proper do not yet exist, but only the raw sensory and emotional experience from which thoughts emerge. At this stage there is no distinction between objects and their representation: thoughts and feelings are things, and neither have meaning. Bion calls these β-elements; and, as the baby can do nothing else with them, he endeavours only to project them.

The next stage depends on the existence of a good, receptive breast that can act as a container. Presumably, as I said, this has to be discovered by the operation of PS ↔ D – that is to say, from the welter of the baby's own confused sensations and projections, a breast or perhaps at first only a nipple has to be abstracted. For this to succeed, two conditions must be satisfied: the baby's projections must not be dominated by such an excess of greed or envy as to contaminate the container from the outset; and the mother, as container, must be adequately receptive.

If all goes well, the mother by understanding and adapting herself to the baby's needs, helps him to discover what they are – which he would not do if, for example, she were anxiously to stuff her nipple in his mouth when his immediate need is to be de-winded. In other words, she takes on his behalf the first and crucial step in the development of his thought. What in effect I think she does by responding correctly to his *most* pressing need, is to 'abstract' it from a welter of confused distress. For it is this abstraction which, on Bion's theory, converts the β-elements of raw experience into the first elements of true thought. These he calls α-elements. Only by internalizing a breast that does this for him can the baby begin to do it for himself.

From then on, α-elements (qualities, relations, abstracted from raw sensa) proliferate in his mind and become the basis of both unconscious and conscious thought. (The patient who cannot form α-elements cannot have unconscious fantasy or conscious thought and, linked with this, he can neither sleep nor be awake.)

Further stages in sophistication come about by successive repetitions of the same mechanisms. Thus, by means of PS ↔ D, patterns of α-elements are abstracted from the rest to become dream-thoughts or myths. These, in turn, function as preconceptions which, by the operation of ♂♀ mate with realizations to form conceptions (or concepts), and so on to still higher stages of sophistication.

Expressed in slightly different terms, I think what Bion is describing here is mental development through the construction and use of systems of classification. To form the idea of a class in the first place some quality, or some pattern of relations, has to be noticed, which is abstracted from what was previously a confusion (by PS ↔ D). So arises the general concept of a class of objects (whether physical or mental) having such and such a quality (e.g., being blue), or consisting of such and such a system of relationships (e.g., being triangular). This, in turn, functions (by ♂♀) as a container into which new realizations (further members) can be put. Again, by abstracting part only of the defining attribute or pattern from a class, or from a combination of classes, new sub- or super-classes can be formed.

If I have understood Bion rightly, what I have just called a 'class' (the result of abstracting, naming and so binding together a set of attributes or relations) is the same thing as what he sometimes calls a 'theory' (In *Learning from Experience* he alludes to the word 'Daddy' as the name of a theory that certain elements are constantly conjoined). He explicitly states, and this is entirely consistent with my equation between my 'class' and his 'theory', that a theory is neither true nor false, but only useful or useless according as it turns out to have, or not to have, realizations. For the same applies to classes, which are certainly neither true nor false, but may, or may not, have members. I confess this nomenclature has puzzled me, as something must express 'expectations' or 'empirical beliefs'; and if theories do not, what does? I suggest – and this is in accord with Bion's view that conceptions, produced by the mating of preconceptions with realizations, function in turn as fresh preconceptions – that development consists in oscillations between 'propositional' and 'definitional' uses of theory. Thus, when it is first noticed that blackbirds have yellow beaks, the corresponding thought has the character of an empirical proposition ('All blackbirds have yellow beaks') which might conceivably be false and have to be amended. By degrees, however, the yellow beak is thought of as among the defining qualities of a class of yellow-beaked blackbirds, and the occurrence of a bird which was black but which had a red beak would be dealt with differently, not by modifying the proposition (for it has become a definition), but by excluding the red-beaked bird from the class of blackbirds proper. But I am not sure whether this corresponds with Bion's thought.

In Bion's system for classifying thought, eight stages of sophistication are listed: β-elements; α-elements; Dream Thoughts, Dreams and Myths; Pre-conception; Conception; Concept; Scientific Deductive System; Algebraic Calculus. Though pre-conceptions, conceptions and concepts are listed in the middle, it is an essential point in his theory that all categories, except the first, can have these functions.

So much for the vertical co-ordinate, or axis, of the 'grid'. The horizontal axis gives the uses to which the elements can be put. To illustrate these, it will be convenient to suppose that an element, whatever its level of sophistication, is a statement that such and such an object (in virtue of its qualities or relationships) belongs to such and such a class – e.g., 'X is a cad'. In the first place, this can be a mere definition in which even attempts to argue the point lead nowhere, since they would be met by an impatient 'Well, anyway, he is what I call a cad'. Secondly, and this is the category the analyst is mainly on the look out for, it is a statement, either true or false in itself, used to keep out some true, but less pleasant thought, for example, the thought that the speaker has injured X and feels guilty about it. Thirdly, the statement can be used merely to note an observation for future reference. Fourthly, it can be made to invite attention and presumably discussion. Fifthly, it can be made under the influence of very strong curiosity, and then expresses a determination to discover the reason for X's caddishness, or perhaps the reason for the belief in it, at whatever cost. Lastly, it can represent an act intended to modify the world. Thus, if such a statement is made by a patient in a session, the analyst will perceive that he is expected to do something about X's caddishness. These are Bion's six categories of use, though he does not claim that there are no more, nor that those chosen by him may not be in need of modification.

With its eight stages of sophistication and six types of use, the grid contains forty-eight categories in all, with possibilities of further extension. With its aid, the analyst who is practised in Bion's method should be able to recognize a patient's statements as belonging to one or other of these categories. This should aid him in his further work of recognizing them as realizations of some psycho-analytic theory and formulating appropriate interpretations. For example, suppose the statement 'X is a cad' to be recognized (*a*) as belonging, ideologically, to a class of preconceptions about which curiosity is felt; and (*b*) as a realization of the psycho-analytic theory of splitting and projection. Then the analyst will know that the patient is ripe for an interpretation about his splitting off and projecting a part of himself felt to be caddish. But if it seems to belong to a β-element class used for action, it will itself be an act of evacuation by which the patient is ridding himself of his supposed caddishness. The interpretation will have to be adjusted to this different situation and the analyst will also probably expect a different response – namely, that, instead of its being accepted or at least considered as helpful, it is more likely to be felt as an affront (an aggressive projection by the analyst).

Anything that goes into a single grid category is what Bion calls an element of psycho-analysis. This I think is the same as what might be called a 'mental element' or an 'element of ideation'. As distinct from this, Bion's concept of a 'psycho-analytic object' is comparable to a molecule with a number of atomic elements. It must, he says, have dimensions in the realm of 'sensa', 'myth' and 'psycho-analytic theory', or, in terms of the grid, it must have its roots in three stages of sophistication, that of α-elements, that of dream thoughts or myths, and that of scientific deductive system. Suppose, for example, that the patient has communicated, verbally or otherwise, a feeling of being jealous of the analyst. This is the 'sensible' element, as both are aware of it. Suppose, further, that the analyst can infer, as the cause of the jealousy, an unconscious fantasy in the patient that the analyst has just been having intercourse. This is the element of dream or myth. Suppose, lastly, that the analyst can recognize this as being, for the patient, a realization of Freud's theory of the Oedipus complex. This is the element from the scientific deductive system. When these three elements are present, the object is a psycho-analytic object, and a complete interpretation can be made.

I hope enough has been said to show the value of the grid as an aid to observation. As to the theories that underlie it, these are concerned with the very origins of thought itself, and should be applicable, not only to psychotic patients, but to the minor disturbances of thought from which every patient – or, for that matter, every analyst – occasionally suffers.

I believe, too, that the theory once formed offers great possibilities for systematic development. For instance, Bion suggests that the first preconceptions are innate 'empty thoughts' waiting for 'realizations' to turn them into 'conceptions' (or concepts). It would seem to follow that the selection of cerebral mutations has predisposed the baby to be able, as it were, to 'recognize' and form concepts of the more important objects and situations likely to be met with in the world. In particular, I would suppose the baby to be innately predisposed to form concepts – or a succession of concepts of rising levels of complexity – of such objects as breast, mother, penis, father, parents and siblings. But environmental deficiency on the one hand, or some innate factor such as excessive envy or intolerance of frustration on the other, may interfere with the conceptual process and lead to the formation of misconceptions. If so, it should be possible to list the conceptions (both positive and negative) which we are innately predisposed to form, together with the corresponding misconceptions we often do form, and the symptoms liable to be caused by these. In this way, another kind of grid could be compiled to aid the analyst in recognizing the specific misconceptions it is his business to expose and, by so doing, enable the patient to correct them.

In conclusion, I would like to repeat what I said at the beginning: The difficulties in communicating psycho-analytic concepts, especially when new, are so great that I cannot guarantee not to have 'misconceived' some of Bion's. But even if my summary is correct, much has been inevitably left out. There is, therefore, no substitute for the book itself. In spite of its lucidity, the labour of understanding it may be considerable; but so, in my view, is the reward.

28

Success and Failure in Mental Maturations

[*Foreword*, 1977 – On re-reading this paper, most of which I still think approximately valid, I found some passages which I no longer understood. But as I assume I at least thought I understood them when I wrote it, I have given them the 'benefit of the doubt' and left them in.]

The facts gradually revealed by psycho-analytic exploration can be expressed in several different ways. If a new way does no more than express familiar truths in unfamiliar words, it is likely to be redundant or actively confusing. But sometimes the change involves the sort of shift in perspective which can be extraordinarily illuminating. Thus, for example, without exactly increasing the analyst's theoretical equipment, it may enable him to notice, in his patients, more realizations of psycho-analytic theory than he had done before, and to interpret in a manner that his patients can more readily grasp. It seems to me that Bion's recent work – apart from its direct contributions to basic theory – provides just this kind of shift in perspective.

No doubt different analysts will abstract different elements from his work, and develop them on different lines. What I have abstracted here, and will try to develop, is a theory of the growth or misgrowth, from the apex of an entity which I shall call the 'conceptual pyramid'.

Bion speaks of innate preconceptions mating with realizations to form conceptions – better terms, I think, and conveying more truth, than the term 'innate idea', whether imageless or not, which I had used before. But I transfer to the new concept of innate preconceptions the same origin and development as I used to attribute to 'innate ideas'; that is to say, I believe them to be the result not of a Lamarckian racial memory, but of the Darwinian selection of chance cerebral mutations; and I think of them as coming into being successively with cerebral maturation, probably during the period from a little before to about six months after birth.

Psycho-analytic experience – for example, of the way the notion of a penis in relation to a vagina seems to bud off from the notion of a nipple in relation to the mouth – suggests that the underlying preconceptions come into being by a process of budding or fission. Phylogenetically considered, the conceptual pyramid is the end result of such innate preconceptions budding off from each other and mating with realizations to form a kind of bunch or pyramid of separate conceptions.

Since innate preconceptions must mate with realizations to form conceptions (concepts, classes or categories as I shall also call them) they cannot form unless realizations are available. The basic compartments of the pyramid are what normally form in a normal or adequate environment. (I will come back to factors, other than environmental ones which can interfere with its formation.)

But if the main compartments of the pyramid are innately predetermined, the rôle of experience is not merely to cause their emergence, one from another, as soon as they are ready to divide. Since each realization (abstracted from a total experience) is more concrete or specific than the innate (imageless) preconception with which it mates, the resulting (imageful) conception is also more specific, and itself functions in turn as a more specific preconception. For example when the innate, imageless preconception of a breast mates with the realization of a particular breast or bottle, certain elements in this experience (depending on the nature of the child as well as on the nature of the sensory part of the experience) are abstracted and stored as a memory image which then acts as a more specific preconception for further realizations of a breast – a process presumably equivalent to what ethologists call 'imprinting'. Moreover, the occurrence of slight *differences* between the now imageful preconception and these further realizations leads to further differentiations within it. In other words, we can distinguish between a primary proliferation, perhaps only into a few compartments, predetermined by innate maturation, and a secondary proliferation which never ceases to expand under the influence of each new experience.

If this were all, such a continuous process of division and particularization would soon overwhelm our memories. But it is counterbalanced by an equally continuous process of generalization brought about by the occurrence of similarities between the realizations of different preconceptions. Categories or classes are not only split to form sub-classes; they are also integrated to form super-classes. So for example, what may have been classed at the beginning as different breasts soon become classed as different aspects of the same one.

The function of the pyramid so proliferating – becoming at once more complex and more simple under the influence of splitting and integration – is to protect us from confusion, or being at a loss, by providing a system of categories, both specific and general, into one of which each new object, or situation encountered can be *recognized*[1] as fitting. By its means, for example, the analyst who is equipped with an adequate number of psycho-analytic theories expects to be able to recognize his patient's associations as a realization of one or more of them. He has only to remember the anxiety which threatens to arise if ever he does feel completely at a loss, to realize how much we depend upon our pyramids of concepts and to get some inkling of the terrifying chaos which easily confronts the new-born infant in the early stages of his pyramid's development.

The system so far propounded has the character of an academic Theory of Knowledge. Such theories are by no means to be despised; but they lack the dimension of depth-psychology. We must therefore equip our pyramid with this other dimension. We can do so by picturing, not one pyramid, but a kind of Russian doll collection of them, each new one fitting outside its predecessor. It now represents the results, not only of development by budding or fission, and recombination, but also of the development of each single concept through what Bion calls different stages of sophistication.

As to these stages, Bion starts with β- and α-elements, and

[1] *Recognition* is one of the key-concepts in Moritz Schlick's *Theory of Knowledge* (1925), a work which has greatly influenced my own thought on the subject.

goes on to dream-thoughts and higher levels. Apart from these, analytic experience seems to suggest three special stages in the development of representational thought, that is, the use of 'concepts' to represent absent or separate objects. In the first, what later may become a representation of an absent or separate object is experienced in a concrete way as an identification, introjective or projective, with the object. Much of Melanie Klein's work was concerned with this kind of 'concrete representation by identification'. Presumably it operates by the same primitive mechanism by which an emotional or kinaesthetic state spreads through a group of any social animal. The second stage is that of 'ideographic representation' in terms of predominantly 'visual metaphors'. Dream thinking, as explored by Freud, is largely of this kind, and some of the difficulty in understanding dreams would seem to stem, not only from resistance, but from the fact that it has become unfamiliar because replaced by the third stage. This is the stage of verbal thought which dominates our conscious activities.

Conceptual progress, whether spontaneous or assisted by analysis, would seem to consist largely in 'translations' from the first two languages into the third. For example, in analysis, the concept of 'father's penis' may sometimes be observed to go through the stages of a sense of concrete identification of the patient's whole body with this organ, to that of ideographic representation, say in dreams of snakes, before the final sophisticated concept, and with it the full Oedipus complex is achieved.

There is still one more characteristic of the pyramid to be stressed: there would normally appear to be good and bad versions of every basic concept it contains (and later, of course, intermediate ones too). That this should be so results from the projection of both aspects of our ambivalence. If we take, as I do, a Darwinian view of instinct, we shall have no difficulty in attributing this ambivalence to the survival value, to almost every species, of a capacity to hate and be aggressive as well as of a capacity to love and be protective. And this for two reasons: not only because aggression is useful in attack and defence, but also because in its projected form it provides a basis for the capacity to fear. An animal without hate to project, and therefore with only good categories in its conceptual pyramid, would be incapable of recognizing real danger situations, and would be too trusting to survive on its own without protection.

This brings me from the construction of the pyramid of concepts to the factors, both in ourselves and in our environment, which may cause it to be misconstructed or misused. The supreme analytic importance of envy is that, if excessive, the attacks it makes on good objects may disrupt the formation of the corresponding good categories. The result is a pyramid that is misformed in this respect, that some, occasionally almost all, of the good categories are missing.

Since the concept of a breast is the first to emerge, a failure to conceive a good one would undermine, at its very source, the capacity to conceive of anything endowed with the quality of love. An approximation of this state produces a world, inside and outside, from which the only escape is by death, either of the body or of the mind as in some psychoses.

The same failure also strikes at the very roots of the capacity to learn. For, as Bion has pointed out, the infant needs the breast, not only to feed from, but for projective identification, the products of which the breast, as it were, returns in a detoxicated state. In other words, the infant who starts with no notion of the nature of his manifold distresses, normally experiences the breast as something that relieves him of them. Only so far as it is felt to tolerate these, and by behaving appropriately (feeding, de-winding, cleaning as required) give back an awareness of them in an intelligible, and so tolerable form, can he learn their nature. The baby cannot think for itself; the breast has to do the thinking for him. But if it does, he soon internalizes it as a part of the core of his ego that goes on thinking (*recognizing* what is the matter) inside himself. If he fails to conceive, and internalize, a good object to do this, he will never be able to contain experience long enough to master it by thought.

Failure to conceive and internalize a breast that converts chaos into sense (β-elements into α-elements and higher forms of thought) may in part result from a defect in the environment. The mother may be too anxious, or too narcissistic, to be receptive of distress; or she may be intolerant of certain kinds of it, and, for example, repudiate the projection of guilt (analysts who have had the experience of being on the receiving end of such projections may feel some sympathy with her in this). In other words, the baby may find no adequate realization to mate with his innate preconception. And since the preconception is of an object that relieves *all* distress, there must always be some environmental failure from the baby's point of view. But there is always some envy too, which is in particular directed against the mother's apparent freedom from distress ('Why should you be happy when I am miserable' our patients say or think). Therefore, it is most likely to be aroused by a mother who is in fact resistant to the introjection of the infant's painful states of mind. In this way, the two factors – the infant's envy and the mother's resistance – can reinforce each other to prevent the formation of the concept of a good mother felt to be capable of providing both love and the basis of a capacity to master difficulties with the aid of thought.

In practice, of course, a failure to form such a concept can never be absolute in any infant who manages to stay alive. But even in relatively normal people, positions approximating to such a disaster may temporarily occur. A patient, before an analytic holiday, dreams 'that her washing machine, which had previously worked so well, suddenly reverses its activity, so that instead of washing her clothes, it messes her with dirty water'. As this was associated with some sense of confusion, I felt the most relevant meaning to be abstracted was that she experienced me as a breast which, instead of absorbing distress, and making it intelligible and so bearable by interpretation, had gone into reverse and (as described by Bion) was felt to be greedily absorbing what was meaningful or good in her associations and filling her with what was unintelligible, or bad. Moreover, I think I had become this sort of bad breast not so much from actual defects in understanding, though these must always play a part, as by the projection into me of excessive, pre-holiday, quantities of greed and envy in her infant self.

I have spent much time in this first step in conceptual development because failure to surmount it stops all subsequent development, while success enormously facilitates all the other steps. But a success which is only partial may be followed by more conspicuous failure later on.

SUCCESS AND FAILURE IN MENTAL MATURATIONS

If in spite of considerable envy (and other difficulties) the concept of a good breast does emerge, envy of the parents' relation to each other may prevent the emergence of the concept of a good penis. The concept of a penis will exist, but it will be of a bad one, and with it only a model of a bad sexuality which the ego either repudiates to remain frigid or identifies with to become sado-masochistic.

Or, if this difficulty is more or less successfully surmounted, the failure may come in the formation of the concept of good siblings. If a good intercourse can be thought of as having taken place, siblings will be felt to exist, but they may be thought of as bad without exception. In this case all colleagues will be experienced as persecutory.

Basic lacunae of this kind in the conceptual pyramid may be thought of as psychotic defects, even when they occur in an otherwise well functioning personality. But there is another and far commoner type of failure: a concept or category may exist, but there may be an emotionally determined failure to *recognize* certain objects as belonging to it. By this means, in the affected field, the accumulation of knowledge is prevented. Indeed, if the failure in recognition is accompanied by an active misrecognition which puts the object in the wrong category, static ignorance is concealed by accumulating error.

Although misconception and misrecognition deserve to be distinguished, because one is much more serious than the other, they would seem to have a common source. For the formation of a basic concept also involves an act of 'recognition' – one in which something in experience is recognized as corresponding to an innate preconception. Failure here can be called a primary failure, while failure to recognize some other object as belonging to a basic category already formed is only a secondary failure in recognition. As distinct from primary failures associated with such mechanisms as massive projective-identification which, if dominated by envy, destroys the category, and in any case blurs its outline, secondary failures seem associated more with repression; and their results are neurotic, rather than psychotic, disturbances of thought. But these can be serious enough – especially if the failure occurs at an early stage either in the proliferation of categories, or in their level of sophistication.

Thus, for example, at the first stage of proliferation, there may as the result of good experiences be a concept of a good breast, but a denial that the actual breast is more than mediocre. And when this is coupled with a claim by the baby to be itself the perfect object, one can be sure that the 'misrecognition' is a defence against the pain of envy. For the same situation is reproduced and studied in analysis with patients whose overriding aim is to accumulate evidence in support of the belief that they are brilliant while the analyst is only mediocre. The envy appears only if he says something which they cannot fail to recognize as 'brilliant', in the sense that it is something they would not have thought of. Then steps are taken, perhaps by depriving him of material, to ensure that he does not repeat his brilliance; and so the danger of intolerable envy is once more removed. There need be no fear of recognizing 'brilliance', since brilliance is prevented from appearing.

As to the level of sophistication at which the failure occurs, some patients give the impression that the process of recognizing, say the parents' relation to each other, has been nipped in the bud from the start. In others it seems to have reached a fairly high degree of sophistication in the unconscious, but the unconscious 'ideogram' has not broken through into preconscious or conscious verbal thought. The Oedipus Complex is precariously kept at bay; and only a slight weakening of repression is needed to precipitate it in full force. To take an example of its sudden emergence (though not for the first time) in a woman whose difficulty seemed to be that she had refused consciously to recognize her mother as a normal wife, asserting that she was frigid or, as she expressed it, 'warped in mind'. Then one night she dreamed 'that she was upstairs with her mother and in a happy frame of mind, till she discovered that the woman in the flat below (the lower as opposed to the upper half of her mother) who was 'warped in body' (from illness) had been receiving visits from an attractive lover. From that moment everything went wrong': murders (of an old woman and a little girl) were committed or impending, for which the attractive lover was blamed – though a cat, masquerading as a baby, seemed in some way to be responsible. In other words, it was the belated recognition of the phantasy mother (whatever the real one may have been) as a loved and loving wife, and not frigid after all, that precipitated the murderous impulses of the Oedipus situation.

The last of the major difficulties to be surmounted, if mental maturation is to be achieved, is the recognition of one's own ambivalence – a recognition which inevitably precipitates depression. For this purpose, new categories for ambivalent objects, both good and bad, have to exist, and there has to be the painful recognition of the self as belonging to one of them. Thus, for example, in order to achieve a full and depressing awareness of psychic reality, the dreamer just quoted had to recognize herself as both the affectionate little girl, who had been so happy at the breast (upstairs), and the murderous cat she became when she recognized the sexual nature of what was going on downstairs.

If the above argument is right, it would seem helpful to distinguish three main hurdles to the construction of the conceptual pyramid and its use in forming a true and comprehensive propositional one.[1] The first is erected by the envy which prevents certain good concepts from being formed at all. The second, which may be erected by envy or jealousy, impedes the use of a category when formed as that to which certain objects can be recognized as belonging. Only if these two hurdles are overcome is the individual exposed to the full force of the pain and murderous phantasies which exposure to envy and jealousy arouses in certain binary, triangular and quadrilateral relationships – that is, in recognizing, as a sucking, his complete dependence for life on the generosity of another object; and a little later, two further relationships, one between his parents, the other between both parents and a sibling, from which he is excluded. The third hurdle – that against the construction of categories of good-bad objects, and the recognition of the self as belonging to one of them – is erected as a defence against the depression aroused by the recognition that, in the inner world, it is the good objects as well as the bad against which the destructive impulses of a good-bad self are felt to have been all too effectively directed.

It is too soon to say how useful in practice this model of conceptual and propositional pyramids with their three levels,

---

[1] That is, a system of assertions allocating members to classes.

and of the three hurdles to their construction and use, will prove itself to be. In the first place, I like it because it stresses what I take to be an important fact: that however much mental illness may be symptomatically an emotional disturbance, it is basically an emotionally determined intellectual disturbance. At the beginning of his life, the patient may have suffered from a deficiency of love and understanding; but by treating him analytically – that is, by injections of truth, and continuing to offer this unpalatable diet almost to the limit of his capacity to stand it – we assume, whether tacitly or not, that the deficiency from which he now suffers is a deficiency of truth. The model of the pyramids, to my mind, helps to make all this explicit.

In practice, it has helped me to keep my eye on the ball as it were, that is, to orient my attention specifically at changes in a patient's capacity to tolerate unpleasant facts. So, for example, it led me to think of the last dream quoted, less as a pre-holiday regression, which in part it was, than as an important advance in a patient's capacity to recognize her mother (for which I stood in the transference) as belonging to the category of wives. Similarly, when new concepts begin to appear in dreams, I have regarded their appearances as an important advance whatever the rest of the context may suggest. And I believe this has enabled me to formulate more comprehensive interpretations which have also been more intelligible to patients.

To conclude: my model of the pyramids is a development, I hope legitimate, from one of the many fruitful ideas recently introduced by Bion – that of innate preconception. I have found the model so developed to be useful in clinical practice. But the extent to which it fully fits the facts, and could be promoted to the status of a theory, remains to be determined by more trial. In any case, it seems to be the fate of all theories, no less than of models, that they eventually become obsolete and are replaced. All one can hope is that they may have an evanescent use.

29
A Note on 'The Three Caskets'

In his paper on this theme, Freud argues that the three caskets of folklore are three women and, more surprisingly, that the leaden one which Bassanio had to choose in order to win Portia is the Goddess of Death. On a recent re-reading of his fascinating essay, it occurred to me that the following postscript might have been acceptable to him: The three caskets can represent, not only three women, as Freud showed from parallels with the Three Graces, the Three Fates, the Three Seasons (the fourth was a later addition) etc., but also – particularly in association with the Seasons – three phases in the life of one woman. Then Bassanio shows by his choice that he will most cherish Portia, not when she is young and golden headed, nor middle-aged and silver haired, but in extreme old age and leaden death. In other words, he will not, like the others, seek to evade the 'depressive position' inevitably repeated in the end phase of their marriage by infidelities with younger women, but will be faithful beyond death. So he alone deserves the bride.

30
British Schools of Psycho-analysis
Melanie Klein and Her Contribution to Psycho-analysis

Melanie Klein was born in Vienna in 1882 and died in London in 1960. She had originally intended to study medicine at the Vienna University and would have done so, had not an early marriage intervened. However, years later during World War I, she had a second opportunity to recapture her old interest in a new form. She came in contact with Freud's work, recognized what she felt she had been looking for and, from then on, dedicated herself to it. She started her training with Sándor Ferenczi during the war and, after the armistice, continued it with Karl Abraham. Both encouraged her to specialize in the analysis of children, at that time almost a new field. (Later she also analysed adults and, at the end of her life, was largely engaged in training analyses.)

One of her early patients was a very silent child. She tried giving him toys, discovered she could interpret his play as if it had been verbal associations, and so found herself in possession of a new implement of psycho-analytic research. The results of her research with this implement, which she began to publish in a long series of papers and a few books, were regarded by some as departures from Freud and are still often criticized as such. Others, including her own teacher Abraham, till his death in 1926, welcomed them as important contributions to analytic insight and therapeutic power. She herself always saw her work as rooted in Freud's and a development of it, which inevitably also involved some modifications.

Since most of the ideas she introduced had their source in her early papers and were gradually developed and clarified by her in later writings, it is not easy to pinpoint them by single references; but a short bibliography of her main publications is given at the conclusion of this chapter. What follows here is an attempted summary of her contributions to theory, although no summary of the work of such an original thinker can do justice to her thought.

To begin with, a word about two distinctive qualities of Melanie Klein's views on technique. First, it is probably true that she developed Freud's conception of transference analysis into 'pure transference analysis', a movement which, in particular, involved the discarding of all forms of reassurance, on the one hand, and educational pressure, on the other, with both children and adults. She felt these could only blur what should be analysed, namely, the transference picture of the analyst as it emerges and changes in the patient's mind. Second, she always tried to direct her interpretations at whatever seemed to be the patient's main anxieties at any given time. Once, at the beginning of her practice, she was herself alarmed by the amount of anxiety she seemed to be arousing in a child patient by this means. But Abraham advised her to persist, and she found that by so doing she was best able to relieve the anxiety the analysis was evoking. After this experience, she never had further doubts about the correctness of her approach.

Coming now to Melanie Klein's contributions to theory, these can be listed under the following heads: early stages of the Oedipus complex and superego formation, early operation of introjective and projective mechanisms in building up the child's inner world of fantasy, the concepts of paranoid-schizoid and depressive positions, a clarification of the difference between two sorts of identification, introjective and projective, and, lastly, the importance of a very early form of envy.

Perhaps the most far-reaching of these, in its effects on theory and practice, is her concept of a paranoid–schizoid position in early infancy, followed a little later by a depressive one. Both presuppose her acceptance of Freud's basic concept of ambivalence, of conflict between love and hate – ultimately of the life and death instincts. In the first position, this ambivalence expresses itself mainly in mental acts of splitting and projection. Thus, in her view, the infant's ambivalence toward the breast, loving when satisfied, hating when frustrated, causes him to divide the object into two: a 'good' breast containing projected love that is felt to love the child, and a 'bad' one containing projected hate that is felt to hate him. Both become internalized, making it possible for him to feel alternately supported and attacked from within himself. Moreover, the reprojection of these inner objects onto the external breast, and their further reintrojection, set up benign or vicious spirals leading to increasing well-being on the one hand, or an increasing sense of persecution on the other.

In particular, the persecutory feelings aroused by splitting and projection of hate are often dealt with by further splitting as a defence, and this can develop into a terrifying sense of mental disintegration.

Although such states of mind are, in her view, characteristic of earliest infancy, she spoke of them as belonging to a 'position' rather than a phase – a word which, on the one hand, avoids the implication that the infant is always split and persecuted, and on the other, by its spatial analogy, suggests an attitude that can be abandoned and again adopted at any time.

As distinct from this position, Melanie Klein held that a very different one begins to be at least temporarily adopted in the second quarter of the first year, when the infant is integrated enough to relate himself to his mother as a whole person. Whereas in the earlier position the anxiety is centred on his own survival, in the later one it centres more on the survival of his good objects, both inside and outside himself. And what, in the last analysis, he fears is that his own destructive and greedy impulses will destroy, or have destroyed, the good breast – an anxiety that may be consciously expressed in later childhood as the fear that his mother, or father, or both may die. Thus, in Kleinian terminology, depression connotes a state of sadness allied to mourning and should be distinguished from such other feelings as the sense of worthlessness or of hopeless confusion that is often mixed with it. In Melanie Klein's view, because some persecutory feelings are always involved, depression is never observed in isolation.

In Kleinian theory, the depressive position is the main hurdle in development. Surmounting it involves the acceptance of responsibility for the damage in the inner world (sometimes also in the outer), followed by mental acts of reparation. But if this acceptance is too painful to be borne, various defences come into operation. Of these the most usual are a regression to the paranoid–schizoid position, or a swing into a manic state, in which either the extent of the inner damage or its importance is denied.

If correct, this theory of early positions of development must be expected to throw light on the psychoses of adults. And it has been applied with an encouraging degree of success to the treatment of some of these disorders by several members of her school, as well as by others influenced by it. Among the pioneers in this field, three of their pupils should be mentioned – Bion, Rosenfeld and Segal – whose example has since been followed by several others.

Although Melanie Klein's ideas about the origin of the superego and early stages of the Oedipus complex began to develop before she had formulated her concept of paranoid–schizoid and depressive positions, the former may be retrospectively regarded as elaborations of the latter. Thus, in her view, the good and bad breasts internalized in the paranoid–schizoid position are forerunners of the superego. In the depressive position, they become more integrated; and, in the developed superego, they contribute to its dual character as friendly mentor and implacable judge.

Meanwhile, of course, the fact that the child has two parents related to each other exerts its influence on his internal objects. Almost from the beginning of her work, Klein believed she had found evidence of the presence of an Oedipus complex at a far earlier age than had previously been thought possible. The child's rivalry in a triangular situation seemed to begin as early as the oral stage, so that his father could be internalized as an object denying him the breast. At the same time, there would also be a 'good' father, split off from the bad one, to be internalized as the donor of, or fused with, the good breast.

Moreover, the two parents could be felt as a combination that either supports the child or frustrates him. Indeed, both the paranoid–schizoid and depressive positions with regard to the breast reappear with regard to this concept of 'combined parents'. In the first position, both a friendly and a hostile combination are felt to exist, and become internalized. In the second position, when these two opposite aspects of the combined parents are more integrated, the child is depressed because his phantasy attacks on the bad ones are felt to have damaged the good ones too.

It will be seen that, in Melanie Klein's view, the developed Oedipus complex and superego formation discovered by Freud have a long and complex prehistory. This configuration Freud conceived of, in the first instance, as a kind of jealous internal father–god, who maintained in his sons the taboos on incest and parricide and tended generally to inhibit sexuality. But Freud seems to have been well aware that much more remained to be discovered about it – for instance, about what form it took in women, whether and how a mother imago entered into its composition, and about its kindly aspects, which he considered a source of consolation through humour. Melanie Klein did not discard Freud's concept; she accepted it, worked backwards from it, and believed she had contributed to tracing it to its source. No Kleinian would claim that this task is even yet fully accomplished.

Another of Freud's concepts, which she also worked on, was that of identification. Its use in his *Totem and Taboo* does seem to imply that he had two kinds of identification in mind. But the distinction was not very clear; and because identification resulting from introjection was already well recognized, the possibility of identification by projection tended to be lost sight of, till Melanie Klein gave it a name, 'projective identification'.

This concept, as used by her school, appears in two main contexts. In the first place, it helps to explain a number of pathological conditions. There are, for example, certain megalomanic states (observable in smaller degree in otherwise normal people) in which a projection of part of the self into someone (often the analyst) standing for an admired parent is followed by an elated sense of identification with him. Or, a similar state of elation seems to result from an intrapsychic projective identification of the ego into the superego. But such forceful penetration is usually felt either to injure its object or turn it into an enemy, and then the outcome is a claustrophobic sense of being imprisoned in a depressed or persecutory interior. But this is not all; for, as Rosenfeld has pointed out, the reinternalization of an object felt to have been injured or made hostile by projective identification can result in depressive or persecutory hypochondria. He has also traced confusional states to the same basic cause: The patient does not know who or where he is because in phantasy he is inside someone else.

In the second place, the concept of projective identification is used to explain the emotional affect some patients may produce in an analyst. When this affect appears to exceed what can be explained in terms of countertransference, Kleinians believe it to be a manifestation of the most primitive means by which a baby can communicate emotions to its mother and, if they are disagreeable emotions, can experience relief by so doing. If the initial motive is to 'evacuate' distress – and distressed patients in need of their next session often dream of needing a lavatory – the angry infant can soon use the same mechanism as an attack designed to distress the mother.

As to the means by which the projection is brought about, I would suppose the baby – or the patient in analysis – to be equipped with a phylogenetically prehuman, and ontogenetically preverbal, capacity to express feeling through behaviour. If so, it must also be supposed that mothers are phylogenetically equipped to understand it. Indeed, in Bion's view, one of the important characteristics of a good mother is an uninhibited capacity to do just this. And, of course, the same applies to analysts. But, as a rule, personal difficulties must be overcome before an analyst can expose himself, without too much anxiety, to the peculiar stresses that sensitivity to a very ill patient's projections seem to involve.

It was through her interest in aggressive forms of projective identification occurring in analysis that Melanie Klein reached her concept of a very early form of envy. For some patients behave toward an analyst as if they wished to destroy any sense of superior equanimity they may suppose him to possess. Moreover, since their dreams often seem to indicate that they feel they do so by projecting their own faecal product into an otherwise admired object to render it worthless, and they do this on occasions when other patients might have felt love and gratitude, she inferred that it expressed a very primitive form of envy directed toward the good breast felt to contain every desired quality that the baby feels he lacks. In this, envy, which aims at the destruction of goodness, is to be sharply distinguished from greed, which aims at appropriating it. Everyone knows, of course, that envy is universal in the human species, and appears to be constitutionally stronger in some people than in others. Freud has also familiarized us with the concept of penis envy in women – a term that includes both the greedy desire to steal the penis and the envious desire to belittle it. That the purely envious component in this could have a forerunner in envy of the breast has seemed unacceptable to some; but many analysts have since found the concept indispensable in overcoming certain hitherto intractable difficulties with patients – in particular, with patients who display a marked negative therapeutic response. Here the aim is to make the patient aware that he is envious, and also to expose the many delusions about the supposedly carefree happiness of other people that his envy causes him to form and that, in turn, increase it. For, although the amount of constitutional envy possessed by any individual seems to be unalterable, much can be done to expose and correct the way it distorts his beliefs.

Enough has been said, perhaps, to give some idea of Melanie Klein's theoretical contributions to psycho-analysis. Of these, the central rôle must be allotted to her concept of a depressive position arising when the infant is sufficiently integrated both to mourn and to feel responsible for the destruction of his good objects in his own inner world of phantasy. The therapeutic aim of those who agree with her is first to analyse the defences against the re-experience of this position in analysis, and, by so doing, also to reintegrate the split-off parts of the self, including the destructive elements responsible for the depression in order that they can be brought under the control of the rest of the personality and used ego-syntonically. So far as this is achieved, it also brings about a better integration of those internal objects that have remained, as it were, unaltered forerunners of the superego, removing much of the superego's bizarre severity and giving it more the character of a friendly mentor. (These views on the central rôle of the depressive position, in fact, largely determined her technique of pure transference analysis. For she believed that any departure involving reassurance prevented, or at least delayed, the working through of this position, and could, therefore, actually be dangerous.)

Of course, the extent to which the depressive position can be worked through in the way described is always limited. But it is the aim of Kleinian analysis and as such has sometimes been criticized as moralistic. That well-integrated people tend to be more 'moral', if this means having a greater sense of mature responsibility, seems to be a fact. But I do not think this result was anticipated, nor is any moral pressure put on patients to develop in any particular direction. That, in a successful analysis, a patient does develop in the described direction seems to be purely the result of the analytic process.

If a reason is sought, I would suppose it to lie in the conditions of our racial past which, if it favoured the development of aggressive impulses, also favoured the development of a co-operative type of man who could harness them for social ends. It would seem that, if freed from psychotic and neurotic disabilities, he tends automatically to develop in this way.

BIBLIOGRAPHY

Klein, Melanie. *The Psycho-Analysis of Children*. London: Hogarth, 1932.
Klein, Melanie. *Contributions to Psycho-Analysis, 1921–1945*. London: Hogarth, 1948.
Klein, Melanie, et al. *Developments in Psycho-Analysis*. London: Hogarth, 1952.
Klein, Melanie, ed. *New Directions in Psycho-Analysis*. London: Tavistock, 1955.
Klein, Melanie. *Envy and Gratitude*. London: Tavistock, 1957.
Klein, Melanie. *Our Adult World and Other Essays*. London: Heinemann, 1963.

31

Cognitive Development*¹

INTRODUCTION: THREE STAGES IN THE APPROACH TO MENTAL ILLNESS

As perhaps often happens, I became preoccupied with a problem – in this case the problem of cognitive development – without knowing why it was of such interest to me. I subsequently discovered some of the reasons, and by way of introduction will outline what seems to me the most rational one.

Briefly then, and with a good deal of over-simplification, I think I became preoccupied with cognitive development as the result of reaching the third of three stages in my approach to mental illness – stages which very roughly reflect successive attitudes which were fairly common in the psycho-analytic movement as a whole.

In the first stage, forty or fifty years ago, my dominant assumption would have been that *mental illness is the result of sexual inhibitions*. This may be profoundly true; but naively understood can lead to very superficial analysis. Moreover, in a subtle way, it can encourage a patient to adhere to the unconscious belief that, instead of giving up his Oedipus complex, he can realize it with the analyst's help and so be master of the world.

In the second stage, twenty to twenty-five years ago, my dominant assumption would have been that *mental illness is the result of unconscious moral conflict*. This supplements, rather than contradicts, the earlier view, and implies a better understanding of Freud's concept of the superego with Kleinian additions about the complexity of the early ego-superego relationship. In particular, a harsh superego is thought of as the result, less of a harsh upbringing, than of an 'intra-psychic

---

* *Int. J. Psycho-analysis*, vol. 49, 1968.
¹ This paper was read before the British Psycho-Analytical Society at a meeting on 6 December 1967.

paranoia' (if I may coin the word). The recipe, therefore, is to try to get the patient to reintegrate the projections which distorted his superego – a process which precipitates what Klein called the depressive position, and provides a motive in depressive guilt for curbing attacks on improved internal figures.

In the third and recent stage, my dominant assumption is that *the patient, whether clinically ill or not, suffers from unconscious misconceptions and delusions.* As before, this assumption supplements rather than supersedes the other two: the patient's inhibitions are a product of his misconceptions, and his harsh superego is itself a misconception. But it is not the only one. I now often get the impression that the deep unconscious, even of apparently normal analysands, is simply riddled with misconceptions, particularly in the sexual sphere. Where, for example, I would formerly have interpreted a dream as a representation of the parents' intercourse, I would now more often interpret it as a *misrepresentation* of this event. Indeed, every conceivable representation of it seems to proliferate in the unconscious *except the right one.*

Such misconceptions of the primal scene used to be attributed to the external impediments put in the way of the child's sexual curiosity. But I am now convinced that, like other animals, he is innately predisposed to discover the truth, and that the impediments are mainly emotional. Indeed, these impediments are by now much better understood. I think, too, we are on the edge of understanding the innate process of cognitive development against which they operate – often with fantastic strength. (See, for instance, what Bion (1962) has written on the conflict between K and —K.)

My aim has been to outline a theory of this interaction (between our perception of truth and the will to distort it). In doing so, I found I could widen its scope to include unconscious (non-psychotic) delusions – in particular, disorientations – as well as misconceptions. But all I have really done is to suggest two new 'hooks' to hang a lot of existing theory on, and even this work is very incomplete. The two hooks relate to the two mental tasks any newborn animal has to perform if it is to survive: the acquisition of a few, I believe innately predetermined, concepts (or class notions), and, what is not innately predetermined, the location of their members in a space-time system. I will now try to explain what I mean by this.

CONCEPT BUILDING

As my starting point, I take from Bion (1962, 1963) the notion of an 'innate preconception mating with a realization to form a conception'; and from Schlick (1925) the view that acquiring knowledge consists, not in being aware of sensory-emotional experience but in *recognizing* what it is. If this means recognizing something as a member of a class, or subordinating it to a concept, Schlick's and Bion's approaches seem to be similar – except that Bion starts with concepts (or preconceptions) which are in some sense innate.[1]

Of course there are enormous difficulties. The 2,000-year-old problem of universals, that is, general notions, is involved. On the one side are the nominalists to whom a class is no more than the common name we give to a number of similar objects or events, or perhaps a convenient logical fiction. On the other, are the realists, descendants as it were of Plato, to whom a class is an ideal laid up in heaven, which we are reminded of whenever we see an imperfect copy. Plato's Ideas, then, would seem to be the mythical forerunners of Bion's 'Innate Preconceptions'.

The difficulty in accepting their existence springs, I think, from the impossibility of imagining them. We can imagine a particular dog, we can imagine a mongrel having qualities taken from many particular dogs; but this is no more than a kind of visual symbol, or name, for the concept 'dog in general' which we cannot imagine.

An innate preconception, then, if it exists, is something we use without being able to imagine it. I think of it as having some of the qualities of a forgotten word. Various words suggest themselves to us, which we have no hesitation in rejecting, till the right word occurs which we recognize immediately I think this is what Bion means by an 'empty thought'. It is also something which, though it cannot be imagined, can be described as analogous, say, to a form waiting for a content. We may

[1] Whether these are thought of as the product of some kind of racial memory or of cerebral variation and selection is perhaps psycho-analytically irrelevant. Personally, I think of them as products of variation and selection.

COGNITIVE DEVELOPMENT

assume its hypothetical existence, develop a theory from this assumption, and see whether the theory so developed fits, and helps to clarify phenomena observed in psycho-analysis.

So far as our present knowledge goes, the first innate preconception to operate in a new-born baby is presumably one of a breast or nipple. Or rather, since the opposite emotions of love and hate may be supposed to colour the preconception from the beginning, of a good breast and a bad one. The two classes, defined negatively as excluding what does not frustrate on the one hand, and what does not satisfy on the other, cover a wide range: a number of objects could be *recognized* as members (or in Bion's terms, could mate with them). But whatever is first recognized as such – a particular breast or bottle given in a particular way – would seem to have the effect of narrowing the class. A memory image of the first member to be recognized acts as a kind of name for the class; but being analogous to an onomatopoeic name, it limits what can be recognized as members to objects that resemble it fairly closely. At any rate, the baby can now be satisfied only by the good breast it has had before, and not by an alternative which would have satisfied it if this had been offered in the first place. A class represented by a memory image functioning as a name is a concept. It differs from an innate preconception in that it results from the mating of an innate preconception with a realization (Bion), or what is the same thing, from the primary act of recognizing a member of an innate class. The process would appear to be the same as that observed behaviouristically by ethologists and called 'imprinting' by them.

Side by side with the development of a concept of a breast, or more specifically, of a nipple, we may suppose the development of a concept of something which receives, or contains, the nipple, that is, a mouth – though the 'psychic flow' can be felt to be in either direction. From these two concepts, it would seem that all, or almost all, of the vast number of concepts we employ are ultimately derived by processes of division and combination (splitting and integration).[1] Moreover, I have the

---

[1] In taking 'nipple' and 'mouth' as the two most primitive concepts I do not wish to exclude the possibility that they may themselves be derived from still more primitive ones, or that we may eventually be able to reconstruct the psychology of the developing foetus.

strong impression that the next step in the construction of a set of basic concepts does not depend solely on external experience, but is itself innately predetermined. The original innate preconception of the good and bad breast or nipple seems itself to undergo a spontaneous differentiation and to bud-off, as it were, other innate preconceptions – in particular, those of a good and a bad penis. If so, the mouth concept is correspondingly differentiated into mouth and vagina. Or it may be that a mouth preconception differentiates into preconceptions of mouth and vagina, and precipitates a corresponding differentiation in the nipple concept. The exact procedure must be extraordinarily complex; but the experience of seeing a patient, who has failed to achieve such differentiations in infancy, begin to make them in dreams occurring in analysis – penis differentiating from nipple, vagina from mouth and anus, and so on – has convinced me that what I am trying to describe does, in some form, normally take place in the first few months of postnatal life.

Assuming as I do that further innately determined differentiations within the two basic innate preconceptions occur in the first few months of postnatal life, and that even a civilized environment provides objects to be recognized as members of the several classes so formed, a baby must be assumed capable of quickly learning to understand the basic structure of all the essential facts of life. In particular, he should be capable of understanding – though not of course in a fully adult way – the relation between his parents, and the way in which other rival babies may be made. Indeed, I believe that, if he does not preconsciously begin to understand this by the time he is about six months old, he never will, nor will his adult sexual life be normal – at least not without the help of prolonged analysis.[1]

Bion has described psychotic mechanisms which attack concept building at its source, so that the 'thought' of an absent object – originally, the breast – is not formed and thinking is impossible. I am concerned here with the lesser disturbances

---

[1] The exact dating of early stages reconstructed in analysis is made more difficult because parts of the self, e.g. an oral part, which are split off and do not undergo emotional development seem to be yet capable of acquiring knowledge belonging to later periods, e.g. the oedipal one. This may retrospectively intensify the oedipal element in the oral stage.

COGNITIVE DEVELOPMENT

which distort concepts rather than prevent their formation altogether and which distort them mainly for the purpose of evading the Oedipus complex. What actually seems to happen is that, while part of the developing personality does learn to understand the facts of life, suffers the pains of an Oedipus complex, discards it from guilt, becomes reconciled to the parental relation, internalizes it and achieves maturity, other parts remain ignorant and retarded. Quite often, no part achieves this kind of cognitive maturity. An individual in whom all parts have achieved it exists only as a standard of cognitive normality which no one quite achieves.

The reasons for the partial failure are to be found in Freud's 'Two Principles of Mental Functioning' (1911). The infant, or some part of the infant, fails to *recognize* what is intolerable to him. There may be a primary failure to recognize a member of an innate class, in which case the corresponding concept does not form. A vital term in the vocabulary of thought is missing. In this way, primal envy of the kind described by Klein (1957) may prevent the formation of the concept of a good breast. (The concept of a bad one always seems to form.) Or if the concept is formed, envy may prevent the subsequent recognition of its members. So a patient may feel that good analysts (breasts) exist, but the analyst (breast) he has is almost never it. The recognition, or re-recognition, of a good penis seems to be a commoner failure, presumably because of the pain of jealousy as well as envy which the recognition would arouse. This, however, can be evaded if the child deludes himself into the belief that this object is given to him and not to his rivals. A similar difficulty seems to impede the formation of the concept of a good vagina; though there is always a concept of a bad one endowed with cannibalistic aims and/or 'sphincter sadism'.

Psycho-analytic observation of the way a patient, who is 'cognitively retarded', begins to develop missing concepts in dreams – penis and vagina separating themselves from nipple and mouth, further developing into a concept of parental intercourse etc. – can be recognized as fitting the theory fairly well. But the theory has to be extended to fit another observation. Such patients do not suddenly become aware of these concepts in a form available for use in catching up on their own retarded sexual development. This may come later. In my experience, the new concepts are likely to be noticed first in what may be called 'dream ideographs'. But these ideographs themselves often seem to have forerunners in physical manifestations, which are sometimes hypochondriacal. For example, a transient series of slight jaundice attacks occurred in a patient each heralded by a physical sensation suggesting a psychosomatic constriction of the bile duct, and seemed to alternate with, or be replaced by dreams which suggested oedipal attacks, by constriction, on an early part-object representation of parental intercourse. The evidence was at first more convincing to the patient than to myself; but it certainly looked as if the jaundice had represented, in a concrete way, the same oedipal fantasy as was later represented ideographically in the dreams. The whole episode seemed to me to be a physiological expression of the rule, discovered by Segal (1957), that 'symbolic equation' precedes the use of symbols, especially in dreams, as a primitive form of representational thought – that is, in the use of images to represent objects and situations which are not at the moment present to the senses.

To fit such observations, the theory of conceptual development has to be extended to include, not only growth in the number and scope of concepts, but also the growth of each single concept through at least three stages: a stage of concrete representation, which strictly speaking is not representational at all, since no distinction is made between the representation and the object or situation represented; a stage of ideographic representation as in dreams; and a final stage of conscious, and predominantly verbal, thought. (I think these stages have some affinity with Bion's (1962) much fuller list of stages in sophistication. But the shorter list is meant to stress stages, not so much in sophistication, as in degrees of consciousness.)

Going back to my primary assumption that *recognition* is the basic act in cognitive development, successful development would now seem to depend on two types of uninhibited recognition: first, the recognition of members of innate preconceptions, and second, the recognition of emotional experiences at one level of consciousness as members of concepts already formed at a lower level. In other words, given an object, say father's penis, of which a thought has to be formed if conceptual maturity (and normal sexuality) is to be achieved, I am suggesting that the development of this thought normally goes through three stages: concrete identification, unconscious ideographic representation, conscious, predominantly verbal representation. If the last stage is reached as it were theoretically, without going through the other two, the resulting concept would seem to be unserviceable for emotional development.

But the same sort of emotional impediments which operate against the formation of a concept in the first place also operate against its development from one mental layer to another. When a concept is not available to complete an act of recognition, its place is usually taken by a misconception.

I will try to illustrate some of these points from an example already quoted in a previous paper (in the *British Psycho-Analytical Society's Scientific Bulletin*). A woman who had always maintained that her mother was 'warped in mind', by which she meant 'frigid', dreamed that 'she was upstairs with her mother and in a happy frame of mind till she suddenly realized that the woman in the flat below, who was "warped in body" (through illness), was receiving an attractive lover. From that moment everything went wrong. Murders of an old woman and a little girl were committed or impending. The attractive lover was suspected of these; but a cat masquerading as a baby was felt somehow to be responsible'. If scanned in terms of conceptual theory, the following conclusions seem to follow: the dreamer's baby self had, at the ideographic level, a concept of a good breast and was capable of *recognizing* herself as enjoying it (upstairs with mother and in a happy frame of mind). She had never had, or had lost, a concept, at the same level, of a good parental intercourse, or if she had, she had refused to *recognize* her own parents' intercourse as an example of it (the woman in the flat below, that is, the lower part of her mother, was 'warped' or frigid). But, in the dream, this devastating *recognition* momentarily occurs (to her astonishment the woman in the flat below receives an attractive lover). She has a concept of murderous jealousy, but is unable to *recognize* herself as in this state. Instead, she projects it into her father (the attractive lover who is thought to be murdering the old woman and little girl, her mother and herself). In this way, a misconception of the parents' intercourse as a murderous assault takes the place of the correct conception.

It is very clear that it is this projection of murderous jealousy, much more than the evidence of any actual quarrels between her parents, that had prevented her from either forming a concept of a good parental intercourse, or of recognizing her own parents as enjoying one. In fact her parents appear to have been happily married, so the misconception is formed in the teeth both of an innate preconception and of experience. Yet there is a part of her that does recognize the murderer correctly as her baby self, the cat. But this is immediately split off and projected – as a defence against the depressive position.

SYSTEM BUILDING

Coming now to the second of the two new hooks to hang old theory on, the baby has not only to form a number of basic concepts in terms of which he can recognize the 'facts of life', but also to arrange their members in a space-time system. Now a system is itself a complex concept but it seems reasonable to treat the two tasks separately since there appears to be a fundamental difference in the rôle instinct plays in each of them: if basic concepts emerge from innate preconceptions, only experience stimulated by innate curiosity can locate their members in a space-time system.

There are two main systems to consider, one to represent the outer world in which we have to orient ourselves, the other, originally an internalization of this, develops into an unconscious system of religion and morality.

Again Bion (1965) has described psychotic mechanisms which attack the sense of time, so that a space-time system cannot begin to form. I am concerned with lesser disturbances which give rise to various kinds of 'disorientation' – a term I use to cover a fairly wide range of phenomena. Essential to the sense of orientation in either system is that it has a base, the O of co-ordinate geometry. This appears not to be normally the body-ego, but something to which the body-ego orients itself as its 'home'. The first base, from which all others would seem to be derived, is the first object to emerge from the new-born infant's sensory confusion, namely the breast or perhaps specifically the nipple. The first space-time divisions to develop are three-fold: a period of enjoyment (being fed), a period of remembrance (having been fed) and a period of expectation (going to be fed). For this can be inferred from the way so many patients orient themselves in exactly this three-fold manner to their daily session.

From the beginning, the capacity to retain a latent memory of the external world system seems to depend on a capacity to internalize the base, at first in a very concrete way. A patient who wished to forget the analytic breast, dreamed that 'she was going to have an operation to remove a small nipple-shaped lump on her head'. That is, to forget it, she had to have the internal nipple concretely removed. I suppose the sense of concretely containing the lost object to be a necessary forerunner of its unconscious ideographic, and finally its conscious verbal representation. In the dream, the concrete stage is itself represented ideographically. Though much is still very obscure and the exact dividing-line is difficult to mark, the division between the inner- and the outer-world systems must be related to the division between concrete pre-representational thought in terms of 'internal objects' and some stage of representational thought.

What is easier to follow is the development of the base, both internally and externally, from breast or nipple to mother as a whole person, to the combined parents, to the idea of a home, a country one belongs to, and so on. So long as the inner and outer relation to these is preserved, we are never disoriented, and to this extent are preserved from acute anxiety attacks. But orientation to the base is easily lost in several ways. I am not concerned at the moment with the ways in which the good base can turn 'bad' by the infant projecting his own aggression into it so that it is misrecognized as bad. Apart from this, the orientation to the good base can be lost in at least three ways: the baby can get into it by total projective identification, either out of envy or as an escape from a persecuting outer world; he can get oriented to the wrong base, in the sense that it is not the one he really needs; or he can become confused in his orientation because his base is confused with a part of his own body.

I will try to give examples of each of these in turn. As to the first – the delusion that one is the base – Rosenfeld (1965) and others have explored its extreme forms in psychosis where the patient becomes totally confused with the analyst. In less extreme forms, the same mechanism is recognizable in those 'egocentric' or 'geocentric' states which result from a partial failure to outgrow the delusion of primary narcissism. The normal, or sane solution involves a humiliating recognition of one's littleness, followed by a grateful dependence which ends after weaning, in the internalization of the lost good object.

Some people, however, especially if their actual abilities and real success enable them to give substance to their delusion, retain it all their lives. These are the narcissistic men or women who live in projective identification with father's idealized penis or mother's idealized breast. Far commoner, in patients (and to some degree in all analysands) is the sense of having lost, through actual failure, this blissful state. Their unconscious analytic aim is, not to outgrow, but to restore it. For example, a woman dreamed 'that she was lying on a couch (as if in analysis); but that (instead of having an analyst) she had a patient, lying at right angles to her with his head close to hers. Then he annoyed her by trying to snatch the pillow'. Assuming, as I think we may, that her 'patient' in the dream was really her analyst, the position of the dreamer's head and mouth, close to the head of the analyst-patient lying at right angles, strongly suggests that the experience of being analysed revived a memory of her infant self feeding at the breast. But the experience is painfully humiliating, and is reversed. It is she who is feeding (analysing) the analyst. In other words, the dream is an attempt, under the dominance of the pleasure principle to deny the reality which, nevertheless, threatens to break through the unconscious delusion; for the analyst claims the pillow – that is, claims to be the breast. Similarly, another patient dreamed 'of an Indian woman exhibiting herself in a very sexy way on the top of a hill'. There seemed little doubt that the Indian woman represented the seductive brown nipple. But the patient recognized her as a repudiated aspect of herself, that is, it is she who is the nipple. Or again, yet another patient dreamed that 'she is holding forth and paying no attention to the little Professor who should be giving the lecture'. She has taken the place of the nipple, and relegated it to an inferior position. (I know this interpretation without evidence must seem unconvincing. But my assumption that I was the 'Little Professor' ultimately standing for the nipple was based on my general impression of the patient built up over a long period. For example, we were already both convinced that she had been very well fed as a baby, but had resented what she felt to be her mother's dominating way of feeding her. In most relationships, she resented not being the 'senior partner', and had, I felt sure, resented it in her first relationship to the breast.)

Closely related to the delusional projective identification with the mother's breast or nipple, is the delusional projective identification with the father's penis. A man dreams, for example, that 'an admired senior is performing a difficult feat on a stage which consists in standing at an angle of 45 degrees and producing fire from his head. To his embarrassment, the dreamer notices the tip of a child's penis showing through the performer's trousers. Fire is produced with an immense effort, but it is felt to be inadequate'. In other words, the baby boy has projected his baby penis into father's to perform the feat of intercourse. But in fact the projection degrades the performance into an inadequate urination.

Elsewhere (1965), I have argued that the whole human race has suffered, in varying degrees, from delusions of being projectively identified with their mothers or fathers, as whole- or part-objects, ever since they began to wear clothes, not for warmth or modesty, but to ape their animal gods by putting on their skins. Robes of office, uniforms, clothes expressing status, and status itself as an invisible garment, still serve the same purpose of maintaining the fiction that we are identified with what we unconsciously feel to be our betters, that is, parents (at part- or whole-object level) who are so much admired and therefore envied.

But it is clinically important to distinguish other motives for projective identification. For example, a patient who used to do it from envy, began to do it from fear as soon as she had accepted her littleness. She had become frightened of a senior colleague whom previously she might have treated with contempt, and then dreamed 'she was crawling into a sleeping bag (associated with myself) to protect her from the fall-out in an atomic war (associated with the caustic criticisms expected from this senior colleague)'.

Coming to the sense of being oriented to the wrong base, since this can be 'wrong' in the epistemological as opposed to the 'moral' sense only if the choice results from a confusion between what is needed and what is sought, 'wrong orientations' are not easy to distinguish from confused ones. But the patient quoted earlier, whose dream of apparently wanting to have an operation to cut out a nipple-shaped lump on her head was interpreted as a wish to have her memory of the nipple taken away, did seem at that time to be predominantly oriented to her father's penis. This was shown for example, in her claim that what she wanted was a husband and not an analyst who stood for a breast – although her dreams and symptoms constantly betrayed her deeper longing for this first object. In other words, she was predominantly oriented to the wrong object.

Orientation to a confused object is the main theme of Meltzer's paper, 'The Relation of Anal Masturbation to Projective Identification' (1966) in which he describes the state of mind of the baby left on the pot after a feed, feeling resentful with his mother and becoming confused with her in the following manner: in trying to find a substitute for the breast, with which he is angry, he unconsciously identifies his own buttocks with it, and himself with his mother, so that he unconsciously does not know which is breast and which is bottom and whether it is his or hers. Preoccupation with the contents of his own rectum (whether faeces or finger) may lead to the sense of getting inside, as in envious projective identification with the breast, but this time it is inside a confused bottom-breast. Then the final outcome is likely to be a claustrophobic feeling often expressed in dreams of being lost in a hostile town or building menaced by enemies, and desperately trying to find a way out, and back to some refuge (the lost breast). An example, in which, however, a misunderstanding of the mother's wishes is blamed for the confusion, appears in another patient's dream that 'she sees a woman on a balcony (sees the breast) and asks her how to get there. The woman makes a gesture which she thinks means that she will find a door behind her. She does, but gets lost in this back building'. In other words, she misunderstands her mother's invitation to reach up to the balcony-breast, and gets lost in her own bottom, also confused with her mother's.

In discussing the spatio-temporal system, I have so far only referred to the relation to the base. But of course it is also something into which all other orientations to secondary figures, whether as parts of the self or siblings, have to be fitted. Confusion with such secondary objects are also common. Moreover, the system, though primarily a space-time one, also gives the mechanical and psychological qualities of the objects in it. But errors here belong to the theme of misrecognitions allocating the wrong objects to the wrong categories which I have already outlined.

Before leaving the subject, however, I would like to say a word about the inner-world system of religion and morality. The base here, of course, is the superego, or more often a number of not very well integrated superegos, themselves in different stages of development from very primitive to fully sophisticated figures. Now the same mechanisms which produce misconceptions and delusions in the outer world also operate in the inner. In particular, aggression can be projected intrapsychically from the ego into the superego, to create the archaic figures. That is, they are the product of an 'intrapsychic paranoia'. And the ego can project itself totally into an admired and envied internal figure to produce an 'intrapsychic megalomania'. Alternatively, there can be the sense of grateful dependence on a good and wise internal mentor. Each of these, and others, are associated with a characteristic morality. Ethical relativists seem to me to have overlooked one reason, other than prejudice, to prefer the last alternative: it is much less under the influence of mechanisms which distort the truth.

In conclusion, I would like to give you my own assessment of the theory I have tried to outline. As I said at the beginning of this paper, it is not in itself a new psycho-analytic theory, but a couple of theoretical hooks to hang a lot of existing theories on, and so to co-ordinate these and make them more accessible to memory. I know it is very incomplete. Parts of it are muddled and perhaps self-contradictory. But already it is of some help to me in sessions in recognizing what is analytically important: first, a patient's orientation to myself as base in his inner and outer world, and secondly, the degree of truth with which he is able to recognize, or misrecognize, all the objects in *his* space-time system. I therefore envisage the possible development of a kind of psycho-analytic geometry and physics with which to represent a patient's changing true and false beliefs about his relation to objects and their nature, in *his* inner and outer worlds. Analysts, as Bion rightly reminds us, should learn to tolerate the anxiety of contact with the unknown. But the better their theory, the easier it is for them to come out of confusion by recognizing, and helping the patient to recognize, his departures from truth.

The development of such a theory to the limit of its usefulness, is obviously a long-term project. I do not know how much further I can get with it at present; but I would like to persuade others to work on it.

REFERENCES

Bion, W. R. (1962). *Learning from Experience*. London: Heinemann.
Bion, W. R. (1963). *Elements of Psycho-Analysis*. London: Heinemann.
Bion, W. R. (1965). *Transformations*. London: Heinemann.
Freud, S. (1911). 'Formulations on the two principles of mental functioning', *S.E.* 12.
Klein, M. (1957). *Envy and Gratitude*. London: Tavistock.
Meltzer, D. (1966). The relation of anal masturbation to projective identification, *Int. J. Psycho-Anal.*, 47.
Money-Kyrle, R. E. (1965). Megalomania, *Amer. Imago*, 22.
Rosenfeld, H. (1965). *Psychotic States*. London: Hogarth.
Schlick, M. (1925). *Erkenntnislehre*. Berlin: Springer.
Segal, H. (1957). Notes on Symbol Formation, *Int. J. Psycho-Anal.*, 38.

Postscript (1977)*

The above paper, published in 1968, was in the main clearly inspired by Bion's theory of Innate Preconceptions. In this postscript, I would like to add something about his theory of the rôle of a mother's capacity for 'reverie' in aiding her child to overcome some of the first impediments to normal cognitive development.

To start with what Bion would call a 'myth', that is, a Theory in Narrative Form: Suppose a very young baby is becoming increasingly aware of the absence of something unknown but necessary to its peace of mind (or the presence of something unknown and intolerable,

* From: *Festschrift for W. R. Bion*, J. Grotstein, ed., Aronson, New York, 1978.

or both, if e.g. the need is to be given the breast and have the hunger taken away) and that his awareness reaches the level of acute anxiety. His mother may have one of three possible responses: she may fail to become aware of her baby's panic (even if she is near), she may become panic-stricken herself, or in her reverie she may respond with the feeling that the poor baby is unnecessarily terrified in a perfectly safe situation. In the last case, her sympathetic lack of anxiety is almost certain to communicate itself to the baby who may then get back the sense of a need to be given or relieved of something, without the panic, and the mother's subsequent behaviour in feeding, dewinding or potting may help her baby to discover what his panic had been about. One may suppose further that a few repetitions of this kind of sequence will help him to perceive what he needs to be given, or to have taken away, instead of projecting panic.

What is more, I think the baby will soon begin to internalize a containing 'breast mother' to contain and think about any crises, so that he may learn to think about and deal with them rationally instead of 'flat-spinning' in them as some of us are in danger of doing all our lives.

It may be worth mentioning, too, that apart from what other character traits may play a part in enabling a mother to aid her baby's first steps in thinking, a major rôle may be allocated to the degree of her own mother's past capacity to help her in this when she was a baby – and so on *ad infinitum*.

Although Bion does not want his α- and β-element concepts to be saturated with meaning, it may be worth enquiring how far they can be fitted into the above 'myth'. To begin with, the panic which is projected is a β-element fit only for projection, while the α-element awareness of a need is the same element tinged with security instead of panic so that it can be stored and remembered. The final knowledge of what is needed may, or may not, be aided by an innate preconception. If it is the need to be fed, there is almost certainly an innate pre-conception of a breast and nipple to mate with the realization of an actual one. But if the need is to be potted or dewinded it is doubtful whether there is any more specific preconception than a general one of a being a breast-mother, to satisfy all needs.

Now to test the theory against a clinical experience: A patient of mine (who may have heard of Bion's theory though not from me) dreamed that she was trying to sweep up prickly pine or fir needles, and put them in a box. But the box leaked and the needles would not stay in. Then an older woman (a mother figure who had recommended her to come to me for analysis) gave her a bag to put in the box after which the needles stayed in. The mother figure then said: 'now you can feed with the others.' In interpreting, I thought the pine or fir needles stood for painful prickly tears fit only for projection. The box which I thought was her baby self could not hold them; but the motherly lady had given her a bag (me as a psycho-analytic breast) which did. I may in some sense have been felt to convert β-element persecuting tears about the bad breast into α-element depressive tears about the absent or injured 'no-breast'. For it was after this that she could feed from it like the others which probably meant from a breast 'remembered' as having satisfied her before and not only momentarily experienced.

It will be noted that the dream also seems to give an account of primal introjective identification; for the breast bag which could hold the painful tears is internalized and put in the leaky box-self. And if I am right, this is what happens in normal development: The infant finds a breast to cry into, and in turn gets back from it his distress in a detoxicated form which is capable of being stored and recalled, if necessary, as an element in thought. Moreover, the container, originally the breast which returned the β-elements as α-elements, is internalized too.

It may be, in the case just described, that the leaky box in which the bag was put represented the real mother's breast which in Melanie Klein's view is the first introject as the core of the ego. For there is some evidence that the real mother was depressed when my patient was an infant and may have been internalized as a breast which could not contain sadness or any painful emotion very well. In any case, I think the bag in the box given by the motherly lady was myself as analyst who, of course, works under much easier conditions.

If for any reason – the baby's envy of a good breast or his greed or the mother's incapacity for 'reverie' – the early projections are not received into a container that can contain them, and return them together with its containing self, all the effects which Bion has described come into being. The projections become more bizarre, and surround the psychotic like a prison.

But if the first step is successfully accomplished, I would suppose that the baby internalizes a breast with a double function: The feeding-breast which Melanie Klein has made us familiar with, and a kind of lavatory-breast which contains what is projected. When internalized, this may later develop into what Freud called the preconscious which contains what is not needed at the moment, but which remains accessible. The difficulty we sometimes experience in finding it is a neurotic problem.

It will be observed that the above argument is mainly influenced by Bion's work. I am by no means sure that what I say is consistent with what Bion means or even whether it is consistent with itself. Indeed it is pretty certain that it is not; for I have discovered that the attempt to be too precise does soon land one in contradictions. But I am quite sure that the attempt to build a theory about the precursors of what one can perceive about thinking is as justified as it was in physics to build a theory about the invisible and intangible molecules, atoms and electric particles of which the tangible universe is thought to be composed.

In conclusion, it may be worth pointing out that work such as Bion's may incidentally help to solve such problems as whether psychosis, or intelligence, is inherited. As to psychosis, if Bion is right, the innate factor is greed and/or envy, and not any specific defect in the construction of the mental apparatus as such. And as to intelligence, no one brought up under the influence of *The Origin of Species* and *The Descent of Man* can have any serious doubt that in some degree intelligence is innate. But again, if Bion is right, the child's mother plays a fundamental rôle in his learning to think and the good or bad effects of this are probably well nigh unalterable, and so could be easily thought to be innate.

32
On the Fear of Insanity

Most people fear contact with the insane – a fact which influenced the past, and sometimes present, wish to shut them away where they can be if possible forgotten. But some primitive cultures have felt them to be especially wise or holy, and even civilized nations have sometimes chosen them as leaders.

This ambivalent attitude can be analytically explained on the assumption that there is always a mad part of the self – though in different degrees in different individuals – for which actually insane persons can easily come to stand. Moreover, the mad part is often felt to be more powerful than the sane part. It can be got rid of by projection, as its external representative can be banished to a mental home; and perhaps it can sometimes be succumbed to out of a mixture of fear and a desire to share its power.

With these general considerations in mind it may be of interest to examine the dream of a patient who had just been disturbed by actual contact with a friend who was having a psychotic episode:

'The dreamer became aware, to his dismay, that a pair of cockatrices or salamanders were nesting nearby. Their offspring would be vipers which would spread everywhere and threaten everything. At first the nest could be seen high up in a tree through the right window. A friend was preparing to shoot the breeding couple – it being vital that they should be destroyed in one shot; as, if only wounded, they would disperse into many unknown places and fatally increase the danger. But much to the friend's annoyance, the dreamer stops him shooting, and asks another friend who is a doctor to do so. And by this time the nest could be dimly seen low down through the left window. Then there was a close-up view of the nest. The cockatrices or salamanders were like two great rounded slugs slightly curved in towards each other. They were just moving, or quivering in a terrifying manner which was hard to describe. And the horror

ON THE FEAR OF INSANITY

was increased by their being a preternaturally vivid blue and purple – though the colour faded so quickly from the dreamer's memory that he could no longer recall it clearly. As the doctor was making his preparations, the dreamer retreated into a room where there were children and shut the door – ostensibly to protect the children, but really because he was himself terrified. Meanwhile, the doctor put paper and powder on the monsters and set fire to it. They quickly shrivelled up a little, became still and looked quite harmless. But for a moment a little tin dog appeared in the flames and quivered before disappearing, and this looked pathetic.'

The dreamer woke, no longer in dread, but sad.

His associations led in several divergent directions which were at first extremely confusing. In summarizing them, I will also arrange them a little to give them greater coherence with respect to the dominant themes implied – without I hope much distorting their meaning. (Some elements, such as the two friends, their different ways of dealing with the situation, and my own transference rôle in them, I omit as not immediately relevant to my main theme.)

The monsters, or rather the horrible way they moved, as if barely able to move, reminded the patient of once being shown an insect (leather-jacket) which lives just under the surface of cornfields and eats the corn; and in so doing is killed by the arsenic sprayed on the corn for the purpose. So are the mice or voles which eat the leather-jackets, the hawks which eat the mice or voles, and sometimes even the foxes which eat the dying hawks. In other words, they were linked with a destructive process of progressive extermination.

A second association was to a science-fiction account of enormous stationary brains half-buried in the sand of a distant dying planet, which were making a 'take-over bid' to control the earth – though whether for the earth's benefit or their own was terrifyingly uncertain. And this led to an association to the secondary pelvic brains of certain dinosaurs.

Now the notion of a brain, with its two hemispheres, in the bottom which is making a take-over bid to dominate the whole, is certainly suggestive of a split-off, insane part of the self which is seeking to dominate the sane part. Moreover, the purpose is fantastically malignant. These hemispheres, copulating as they are to produce a horde of vipers, have an aim which is

435

the exact reverse of a normal parental couple: their purpose is to create, not life, but universal death. No wonder the sane ego was afraid.

But other associations introduced a depressive, rather than a persecutory element. The blue and purple colour – the most terrifying feature in the dream – suggested bruises and more extreme injuries, perhaps to breasts, perhaps to buttocks, perhaps to copulating parents. In other words, the monsters were in some sense also injured objects. At this point, the patient recovered a forgotten memory of new-born puppies he had first seen when he was about four, and which looked and moved quite like the monsters in the dream. He believed he had also seen, with curiosity rather than distress, unwanted puppies or kittens being drowned. Hence the appearance of the dog – a big one which had been a kind of nurse to him – presumably to mourn her puppies.

If, therefore, the monsters represent the hemispheres of a mad, malignant, bottom-brain copulating (like evil parents) to produce destruction, it is also the brain of a baby which as such deserves compassion – an aspect of the dreamer's baby self (and secondarily of sibling).

It should be mentioned that the madness of the friend with the psychotic episode had no detailed resemblance with the 'badness' of the dream monsters. He did, indeed, want his delusions to be believed and in this sense was felt to threaten the sanity of those who came in contact with him; and there was a common element between him and the dreamer in that his delusions included the paranoid fear of secret powerful enemies. But although the sense of the threat and unconscious perception of these similarities almost certainly precipitated the dream there can be little doubt that the mad, malignant baby-brain was a split-off part of the dreamer himself. And this existed in an otherwise comparatively normal person.

Now, if as I suggested at the beginning, such an insane part exists, though in varying degrees, in everyone, the problem arises as to why this should be so. We know a good deal more than we did about the intolerance of reality which conditions the flight into psychosis, and about the mechanisms, such as excessive projective-identification, which operate in it. And here I would particularly refer to the works of Bion, Rosenfeld,

ON THE FEAR OF INSANITY

Segal and others who have followed up suggestions first made by Melanie Klein. But perhaps something can be also learned by putting the question the other way round and asking instead how it is that any part of the mind ever becomes sane.

Eder is reported to have said: 'We are born mad, develop a conscience and become unhappy; then we die.' If this is a despondent view of life, the first part of it seems to me to be indubitably true. Whether the infant mind is wholly unintegrated at birth, or disintegrates at the shock of birth, no one can doubt that the new born infant is in a state of chaos. And the chaos easily becomes a persecution. Sanity, then, is not something we are born with, but, in varying degrees, painfully acquire. The process begins, I think, with the first contact with the breast or nipple, of which there is surely an innate preconception. The resulting concept, developed from the concrete experience of internalizing the first good object, is of something real (not fantastic); and by a process of division and integration of this first concept (a process in its early stages also innately predetermined) a conceptual system to represent the real world, together with its internal counterpart, is gradually built up. The myth of God creating the world out of chaos may be taken as a fanciful description of this process, which I have tried to describe in less vivid, but rather more scientific terms in a former paper ('On Cognitive Development').

But the sane world never wholly absorbs the chaotic one. Perhaps it is never more than a firm island of sanity in a sea of chaos which continues to exist unconsciously. Meanwhile, the chaotic part, which has not been tamed by contact with reality (and in particular a real perception of the breast) appears to undergo its own macabre development. I suppose it to consist, in the first instance, of innate preconceptions together with the potential affective and conative responses to these; and here terrifying preconceptions and destructive impulses seem to predominate. They do not, however, mate in a normal way with real perceptions to form realistic concepts. But this does not imply that they undergo no development. Perhaps they are capable of producing primitive hallucinations with which they can mate to form various kinds of misconception. At any rate, concurrently with the development of a sane self in a sane world, I think there is always, in varying degrees, the development of a mad self in a mad world of its own creation.

Moreover, the insane part is experienced as a terrifying enemy, whose aim it is to rob the sane part of its sanity and take its place.

Now if, indeed, the major aim of the insane part of the self is to take over and dominate the sane part, the structure of relations between the two is similar to the internal structure described by Meltzer ('Terror, Persecution, Dread': *International Journal of Psycho-Analysis*, Tyranny: Scientific Bulletin No. 24, 1968) as operating in addictions and perversions – except that the addictive or perverted parts are not consciously dreaded but succumbed to because they seem to offer protection against a particular form of persecutory anxiety.

Taking first the similarities, I would suppose that the 'take over bid', which I assume with Meltzer to be common to all of them, is a defensive response to a threat arising in infancy from the development of a sane or normal part of the self. For the suspicion must then begin to disturb the insane, perverted or addictive parts, which have hitherto ruled unchallenged, that common sense, however limited in scope and restricted in application, is superior to omnipotent, and usually destructive, fantasy; that healthy food and drink (originally mother's milk) is superior to drugs (originally, perhaps, the baby's own destructive faeces and urine); and that normal sexuality is superior to perversions which cannot achieve the innately given aim of reproduction. But the one emotion which these most primitive, arrogant and envious parts of the self can least stand is a sense of inferiority. So enormous forces are brought into being to convert, pervert or override the sane or normal parts from which the threat proceeds. Moreover, the aim is not fulfilled by the conquest of other parts of the self alone, but attempts the conquest of other people too. The psychotic, the addict and the pervert all display, in varying degrees, a proseletizing zeal.

As to the difference between the three conditions, they seem to me to represent different arrangements of the same elements; and for this reason, psychoses, addictions and perversions are sometimes interchangeable. And one of the difficulties in getting a clear picture of the internal structure in any one of them seems to reside in the capacity of the split-off part of the self to undergo a metamorphosis while it is being analysed. For example, the same patient, a little later (when his psychotic friend had become sane but slightly manic), in the course of a long dream 'accepted a lift offered by a tall man in hunting clothes who was driving a sort of chariot drawn by two plump white horses – horses which at one time seemed to have faint purple marks on them'. These marks reminded him of the blue and purple of the monsters in the earlier dream. Clearly then the dreamer was now a sort of Patroclus to an Achilles father (or elder brother) who slew his enemies, and from the marks on the horses presumably beat his wife (the dreamer's mother). Comparing this with the earlier dream, in the first, persecutor and persecuted seem combined in the figure of the blue and purple monsters, whereas in the second, they are separated into sadistic huntsman, or chariot driver, and the horses with the purple marks.

Furthermore, if the second dream has the structure of a sadistic perversion (phallic father and son combining against mother and probably her other children), the first, I suspect, has latent in it the seeds of a masochistic one. For consider the rôle of the first helper who was going to shoot the monsters when they were 'high up on the right side'. The monsters themselves, it will be remembered, were the insane part of the self represented as a copulating couple begetting vipers, and they were 'pelvic brains', that is they were situated in the rectum – in fact, recognizable as persecutory faeces. And when they were 'high up'[1] they were inaccessible to external forces. How then were they to be dealt with? I suggest by a compulsive and masochistic passive homosexuality, the primary aim of which was not erotic satisfaction, but the destruction by a sadistic intercourse of the internal persecutors – a desperate short-term cure for psychosis which would have become compulsively repetitive. (In fact the patient concerned had never been overtly homosexual either in an active or passive way, but there was evidence of both being latent in him.) In the dream, however, this solution was rejected, much to the fury of the friend – ultimately a sadistic homosexual part of the

[1] Possibly also a reference to the 'full moon' when insanity is popularly supposed to be at its height.

self – because some inkling of the real faecal nature of the persecutors brought them 'low down' and accessible to the more appropriate treatment with 'paper and powder'.

It is worth noting there that, since the monsters were also associated with a baby part of the self, and with dead rival siblings (the drowned puppies), the persecutors which the first helper wanted to kill included the ghosts of these, which, in Meltzer's view, are the most ultimate object of terror.

To complete the survey, we can imagine the effect of other slight changes in the elements. For example, a regression from the anal to the oral position could have turned the homosexual perversion into a drug addiction – to destroy the inner persecutors, this time by poison. Or again, in the second dream, if the sadistic huntsman had not been allied with the dreamer against his mother (and her children, since the war-chariot implies a host of enemies), but had protected her, and them, from him, he would have been metamorphosized into a familiar kind of paternal superego.

It would seem, then, that by a separation and recombination of the elements which compose a split-off internal object, it can appear at one time as a mad omnipotently destructive part of the self, at another as a war leader with sadistic propensities, and at yet another as an archaic superego suppressing the ego's sadism by means of its own – which it acquires directly from the Id.

The practical differences are, however, considerable. The insane tyrant offers nothing but universal destruction; and (failing analysis) can be dealt with only by desperate remedies – self-destructive perversion or addiction. The sadistic tyrant offers the glories of war, or hunting, to those who accept its leadership. And this can be maintained so long as the accumulating guilt can be denied. The archaic superego may be acceptable because, by punishing the ego for its destructiveness, it protects it from depressive guilt. But throughout a bewildering series of patterns, the elements in the kaleidoscope remain the same.

Postscript, 1977 – On re-reading this paper, I now feel that what I described as the insane person's wish to make others insane could sometimes – perhaps often – be the wish to make others understand the agony and terror of being insane. From the observer's point of view, these two could be difficult to distinguish. But if the observer is an analyst and the insane person is his patient, it is of the utmost importance that the correct distinction should be made.

Another point is that the dream of the cockatrices or salamanders could be more simply described as a 'misrepresentation' or 'misconception' of the primal scene if the movement of these creatures – so terrifying to the dreamer – in fact represents the movement of the labia or buttocks (or, at the whole object level, the couple) in intercourse, felt not to be creating normal babies but viper faeces, not to replenish but to destroy the world. In other words, the dream could represent the transformation (misrepresentation or misconception), under the influence of hate and envy, of a good parental intercourse into its destructive opposite. And this too is the kind of hate that torments madmen.

33
The Aim of Psycho-analysis

Although I have tried to write this short paper in such a way that it can be understood without specific reference to any previous work of mine, it is in fact a supplement to my paper on 'Cognitive Development' (1968).

The aim of an analysis may be defined in various ways. One of these is that it is to help the patient understand, and so overcome, emotional impediments to his discovering what he innately already knows. My aim in this paper is to elaborate this statement.

It should be obvious from my reference to innate knowledge that it is with the cognitive aspect of instinct (instinctive knowledge) that I am most concerned; and that, since I am devoting a paper to it, I consider it to have been insufficiently stressed in psycho-analytic theory before. But, at this point, I am arrested by that inner voice which those who have been analysed acquire and which strives to continue the analysis long after it is over and those who did it are dead. 'You claim', so it seems to say, 'a creativity which you deny to us: the child we misconceived or misbegot is now to be correctly conceived or begotten by yourself. Remember that, in the inner world, parthenogenetic creativity is a megalomanic delusion. All you can do, and surely this is enough, is to allow your internal parents to come together and they will beget and conceive the child'. I believe this to be profoundly true. Freud, under the influence of his electrostatic model of the mind, with its cathexes and counter-cathexes, may have insufficiently stressed the cognitive element in instinct about which so little was known at the time. But the notion of innate knowledge, always latent in idealistic philosophy and recently systematically studied by ethologists, is not mine. All I have to do is to allow theories, taken from different fields, to fertilize each other.

In my previous paper (1968) I tried to make a start by

allowing one of Bion's notions (that innate preconceptions mate with realizations to form concepts) to mate both with Schlick's theory (that knowledge consists in recognizing something as a member of a class) and with Plato's theory of ideas (that a particular object is recognized as an imperfect copy of an ideal or general object laid up in heaven). For if, by heaven, we mean our own phylogenetic inheritance, it seems to me that Plato was here very near the mark. The difficulty of course is that we cannot imagine a general object, only a particular example of it, or the name of the class. Yet we have no difficulty in recognizing a new member. Our 'phylogenetic inheritance', then, contains class notions which we cannot imagine, though we can recognize their members. This is the cognitive part of the innate response which precedes the affective and conative.

Variation and selection may be expected to have laid down an immense amount of potential information in this way, which probably comes into being in stages mainly during the first few weeks or months of post-natal life (not counting what develops before). Experience, through the mating of innate preconceptions with realizations to form concepts, both fixes and refines it in our preconscious and conscious thought.

It remains, as my major task, to allow these notions to fertilize the immense body of psycho-analytic experience. This is again a task of recognition, though immensely more difficult, not because it is so hard to recognize what is significant, but because it is impossible to be sure that one has recognized all that is significant for the purpose. Moreover, all adult thinking, all later acts of recognition, are hampered by the difficulties which beset the first ones, and we have all had some difficulties with these.

Among these first ones, and without being sure that I have selected all that are significant, I will select three: the recognition of the breast as a supremely good object, the recognition of the parents' intercourse as a supremely creative act, and the recognition of the inevitability of time and ultimately death. The third seems of a different order from the other two, and I am not sure in what sense it is to be regarded as innately predetermined. Certainly, the fear of death is paranoidal and results from the recognition of a murderously competitive split-off part of the self which threatens the self (persecutory anxiety) or its loved objects (depressive anxiety). But when the entity into which this part of the self is put is really as dangerous as it seems, there is no distortion; and one must suppose this to be the mechanism evolved to provide us with rational fear. But to fear death is not the same as to recognize its inevitability, which is a fact forced on us much against our will by the repeated experience that no good (or bad) experience can ever last for ever – a fact perhaps never fully accepted.

This brings me back to the first of the three acts of recognition I selected; for probably the main impediment to the recognition of the breast as a supremely good object is the fact that it cannot be enjoyed for ever. If, as I suppose, there is an innate preconception of such an object, and if no mothering that keeps a child alive is so bad that it fails to provide some realization of it, the concept of a good breast must always at least begin to form. But the breast itself is first periodically, and then permanently, lost. If the development is to be favourable, the thought, the 'no-thing' in Bion's terms (1962), or memory of the lost breast as signs or 'names' of the concept which has begun to form, survive and are most painfully mourned – a process which ends in what Melanie Klein called the internalization of the first good object. To what extent the internalization of the first good object is the same as establishing a concept, or the most primitive and concrete form of this process, it may be hard to say, but at any rate the capacity to mourn, or pine for a loss, and the capacity to remember the lost object are inseparably linked. Without the memory there can be no mourning, and without the mourning there can be no memory. And if the development is to be unfavourable, this is what seems to happen: there is no concept and no capacity to mourn. The baby in whom this concept – the good internal breast – has been lost can have no memory or expectation, and cannot recognize it even if it is again put in his mouth. Thus, for example, a patient dreamed that a friendly man helps him up to a platform to meet a very important lady, a duchess or queen. But the lady has no face, her head being a kind of fleshy knob, which he finds most unattractive. But it is clearly the nipple itself which he has seen and cannot remember.

The more usual case, of course, is somewhere between these two extremes. Some concept of the first good object, some memory and some expectation exists in the deep unconscious, but it is much impaired – and I would suppose the patient whose dream I have just quoted was of this type. This is I think indeed the general case which explains why the earliest memories are always consciously lost, and possibly explains why no one's capacity to think is wholly undisturbed. At any rate, as analysts, we are all familiar with the way patients tend to forget us and our work over holidays and weekends, and sometimes seem to have little hope of ever seeing us again from one session to another.

Particularly after a holiday two things seem to happen which are not, perhaps, as closely related as they seem. On the one hand, it is not only that the memory of us as a good object has disappeared, we have turned into a bad one. And although we are blamed for many real and imaginary offences, the main one seems to be that we were not there when wanted. On the other, we no longer seem to be what the patient is really looking for; and this I think is not merely because we have become bad, but because the patient has found a spuriously satisfying substitute.

The discovery of the spuriously satisfying substitute comes about I think in this way. The baby who has been kept waiting too long in relation to his own capacity to wait and whose memory and expectation of the good breast begins to be destroyed will begin to be lured by an even earlier memory which seems never to be entirely lost – that of the interuterine condition. Quite often, as Meltzer has pointed out (1966), this is linked with the discovery and exploration of his own bottom, which both resembles the breast in shape and also seems to provide an entry into the kind of place from which he dimly remembers that he came. The result is a most confused and complicated state in which in fact he is in touch with a substitute for the breast and in projective identification with it inside it.

We may also suppose that, in getting in this condition, he is also influenced by another innate preconception which is perhaps just beginning to develop, namely that of intercourse. But if he 'recognizes' his own fantasy of getting totally inside his mother as an example of intercourse, the recognition is really a misconception likely to be used to counteract the true conception, which is beginning to form, of his parents' creative relation to each other.

The point I am making here is that the more firmly a child's first good object is established inside him, and his unconscious and even to some extent his conscious memory of his first good relationship is preserved, the easier it will be for him to conceptualize his parents' intercourse as a supremely creative act; and this is so, not only because the memory of his first good object mitigates his jealousy, but also because he will have had much less incentive to construct a misconception of intercourse as a by-product of fantasies of projective identification.

Where there has been a favourable development, and the concept of the first good object is well established, together with the capacity to remember it with love, there is far less difficulty in being able to recognize the parental relation as an example of the innate preconception of coitus as a supremely creative act – especially as this is reinforced by a memory of a good relation between the nipple and the mouth. Of course, this discovery or recognition arouses jealousy and ushers in all the conflicts of the Oedipus complex. But it will be easier to overcome them, and after a renewed period of mourning for the child-parent marriage that can never be, to internalize and establish a good concept of parental intercourse as the basis of a subsequent marriage which may in fact take place. But where the development has been unfavourable, the misconception of intercourse as a by-product of fantasies of total projective identification will remain as a nodal point for the development of every form of perversion and insanity. The commonest – indeed perhaps the universal case – involves a mixture of the two extremes, one part of the personality developing normally or sanely, while other parts stay still or develop in a perverted or insane way.

The perversions are so varied, and perhaps still so imperfectly understood, that I will only attempt to deal with one which also puzzled Freud in his paper 'A Child is being Beaten' (1919). It seems to me that perversions of this kind can be correctly, but incompletely, interpreted by any of a large number of statements, which collectively disclose the many steps of its development. 'A sadistic father is having intercourse

THE AIM OF PSYCHO-ANALYSIS

with the child' takes us a little way, but is unlikely to do much to remove the perversion. 'A good father is beating the devil out of the child's inside' may also be appropriate and takes us a little further with its implication that the child suffers from the fantasy of having a devil penis inside his gut. But this contrasts with 'A bad part of the child in the father is killing the babies inside the mother with whom the child is in projective identification'. Then there are other statements which may take us deeper still: 'The child's oral sadistic impulses are in the beater while he himself, or rather his bottom, is in identification with the breasts.' If this is indeed the pattern there will probably be some notion that the beating is to go on forever (in the next world as in the Rodiad), so that the concept of mortality, which I think is the initial difficulty, is itself denied. Moreover, the whole perversion begins with the misrecognition of the baby's own bottom as the spurious substitute for the breasts which have been forgotten.

To sum up, in a few points, what I have been trying to say:

(1) Our innate inheritance includes certain general ideas, which we cannot imagine, but which enable us to recognize examples of them, and so to form corresponding concepts. I think the essential difference between a preconception and a concept is that the concept has something corresponding to a name – originally the image of the first example of the preconception to be recognized – and so can become an object of thought.

(2) Among the many innate preconceptions we may be endowed with, two are of particular analytic importance: the good breast, and the good creative intercourse. And I think they are of such particular importance because there is so much difficulty in establishing the corresponding concepts.

(3) Whether, and in what sense, the idea of death is an innate preconception I cannot say. But apart from the paranoid fear of being killed by one's own projected aggression, the baby has the experience forced upon him that no good experience can last for ever. In the short run, it may be easier to forget a lost good object, or to forget its goodness, than to mourn for it – especially if its loss is attributed to hating it for being absent. To a variable degree, the memory always seems to be impaired.

(4) At the same time, an object falsely recognized as the lost good object comes into being as the apparent object of desire. When this is the baby's own bottom, confused with its mother's breasts, it becomes the nodal point for a great variety of perverse formations. These act as a substitute, not only for the lost breast-relation, but also for the good creative intercourse, which therefore fails to be recognized as such. But I do not wish to imply that this is the sole type of misconception that can arise.

(5) Only so far as the good breast is mourned and remembered without a substitute can the developing child recognize the creativity of his parents' intercourse, pass through the turmoil of the Oedipus complex, and eventually internalize them as the model for his later marriage.

At the end of this short paper, I ask myself again if there is anything in it to justify my rather pretentious opening paragraphs in which I seemed to promise something new, which, by implication, would be useful to the practice of analysis. From a personal point of view, all I can find, perhaps all one can ever expect to find, is the sort of cross-fertilization I spoke of, in which, to quote another example, Bion's notion of innate preconceptions are linked with Meltzer's on anal masturbation and projective identification to produce the notion of a 'spurious substitute' for the real object which is no longer remembered. But in what sense is this notion and others like it of value either in the theory or the practice of analysis? Perhaps I can claim some theoretical advantage if they help to bridge the gap between psycho-analysis and ethology. But to justify this paper to this Society I would have to show that they are of use to the practising analyst; and here I can only say that I think they have been useful to myself, and could be useful to others who think in the same way.

As to the main differences between this and my previous paper on cognitive development, I have here much more stressed the fear of its death as a major factor in the loss of the memory of the first good object, and linked this directly with the discovery of the 'spurious substitute', which I had previously discussed under the heading of 'Disorientations'.

ACKNOWLEDGEMENT

I am indebted to Dr H. Segal, who read the manuscript and made suggestions which I have gratefully incorporated.

REFERENCES

Bion, W. R. (1962). *Learning from Experience*. London: Heinemann.
Freud, S. (1919). A child is being beaten: a contribution to the study of the origin of sexual perversions, *S.E.* 17.
Meltzer, D. (1966). The relation of anal masturbation to projective identification, *Int. J. Psycho-Anal.* 47, 335-342.
Money-Kyrle, R. E. (1968). Cognitive development, *Int. J. Psycho-Anal.* 49, 691-698.

34
Reviews

Explorations in Autism. By Donald Meltzer, John Bremner, Shirley Hoxter, Doreen Weddell and Isca Wittenberg. Scotland: Clunie Press. 1975. Pp. 250.

The authors of this book are modest in their claim, stressing that they have located problems rather than solved them (p. 5). But if their main theory can be substantiated – and a prima facie case for it has been made – I think the book will deserve to be called a breakthrough. For, as far as I know, it gives the first coherent theory of autism, which, till now, has been a very baffling as well as a heart-rending illness.

Their overall theory rests on (and incidentally gives further support to) several recent theories about early failures in development, such as Bion's on mothers with an insufficient capacity to tolerate their infants' projective identifications of distress and rage; Meltzer's on 'dismantling' as an earlier defence against pain than splitting, by which multisensual concepts of things that can be seen, felt, heard, tasted and smelt are dismantled into their unisensual elements; Esther Bick's on children who in early contact with their mother fail to internalize her holding function so that they do not form a 'psychic skin' to hold them together; and also on children who fail to form three-dimensional concepts of objects which can contain spaces, and are therefore unable to identify either projectively or introjectively. The alternative identification by a skin-to-skin contact she calls 'adhesive identification'.

It is clear, I think, that children who suffer from these defects in order to escape pain will fail in the very first steps in concept-building which must precede their construction of a world-model. And because of these initial failures what Melanie Klein called the 'primal splitting' between good and bad objects will fail too, and this, of course, will cause other failures, including a failure of the Oedipus Complex to develop in a recognizable form. In particular, such a child will fail to learn to speak or think in words and so will be without an essential element in his equipment for dealing with all these later hurdles in development, which indeed can only crop up after the autistic state has been dealt with – and then, because of the loss of time, perhaps never adequately. For example, the lalling period in which a normal child expands his vocabulary is likely to be over before he begins to have a vocabulary to expand.

Not much of this theory was, I think, in the authors' minds at the beginning of their research. They selected work which had been done by Kleinian psychotherapists with four autistic children, who, although frighteningly obscure at the outset, subsequently seemed to arrange themselves as representatives of four stages of autism: Autism Proper, Primal Depression in Autism, Disturbed Geography of the Life-Space in Autism and The Residual Autistic Condition and its effect upon Learning.

These four case histories form the centre of the book, and analysts who read them will surely admire the courage and tenacity of those who devoted so many years to what at the outset might well have seemed quite hopeless cases. A Preface and Conclusion by Meltzer summarizes the theory which distilled itself out of the cases and, as I said before, may well prove to be a breakthrough. My own outline above of this theory is far too short and sketchy to be any substitute for a detailed study of this well-written and extremely interesting book.

Introduction to the Work of Bion. By Leon Grinberg, Dario Sor, Elizabeth Tabak de Bianchedi. Translated from the Spanish by Alberto Hahn. Scotland: Clunie Press, publishers to the Roland Harris Educational Trust. 1975. Pp. 82.

There is a fairly widespread belief among analysts, which I share, that Bion's works are both very important and very difficult to understand. Moreover, the difficulty is felt to reside in the novelty of the notions introduced rather than in any obscurity of expression, which is expected to become clear as soon as the novel notions are recognized for what they are.

The book to be reviewed is a summary of Bion's works arranged in such a way that an understanding of one notion is likely to help the reader to understand the next one to be introduced. And I think this aim has been very well achieved and that, by this linking of one new concept with another and by the general discussion of them, Bion's works are made a good deal easier to understand. And if the reader, as I did, still finds some notions difficult, perhaps this is a salutary experience. For it makes one realize that however much analysis one thinks one knows, there is always an infinite amount which remains unknown to one – in other words, that psycho-analysis is an endless quest.

Whether this review of a review, or 'transformation of a transformation' to use one of Bion's terms, will make it any easier, I do not know. But as a start it occurs to me that some of his notions become easier if one remembers that much of what he is writing about is that mysterious thing called instinct, particularly the cognitive aspect of it which is now, for the first time, being psycho-analytically explored. For instance, although he expressly calls them instinctive, it is easy to forget that the 'basic assumptions' which can, be believes, be observed in a group, are in his view instinctive. In fact, I think they are the same sort of things that he calls 'innate preconceptions' in individual psychology. In other words, I think that just as there is an innate preconception of a breast which mates with the realization of being fed by a real breast or bottle to form a conception of one, so in a group there are basic assumptions that the 'dependent group' is there to be nurtured by someone, the 'fight-flight group' to fight or flee and the 'pairing group' eugenically to create the next generation – that is, to breed a hero. Presumably, something in the actual setting determines which 'basic assumption' will be recognized as active.

There is nothing in the least improbable in this, and there may well be other analogous forms of basic assumptions, or innate preconceptions appropriate to groups, which remain to be discovered.

Some of Bion's 'new' concepts are introduced from another science, e.g., mathematics, where they are already familiar, to aid thinking in psycho-analysis. Thus, for example, a mathematician may project a triangle in space in such a way that its shape is entirely 'transformed' except that its three-sidedness or triangularity remains 'invariant'. So, too, a manifest dream is a 'transformation' of latent dream thoughts in which again certain elements remain 'invariant'. Bion stresses the important differences in types, or groups, of transformation, which he names 'rigid motion transformation', 'projective transformation' and 'transformation in hallucinosis' – the latter two being characteristic of psychosis.

Many, strictly speaking perhaps all, of Bion's new concepts are the result of his noticing 'constant conjunctions' (Hume) or 'selected facts' (Poincaré). This is so, for instance, of the relation 'container–contained' ($♀♂$). The more one thinks of it, the more one sees what a very basic relation this is, as it crops up again and again in so many situations: the individual mystic in the group, the emotion in the mind, as well as the form suggested by the $♀♂$ signs of a penis in a vagina. And to use this last example, the three forms commensal, symbiotic and parasitic, of the relation which Bion distinguishes are surely invaluable in the study of frigidity and impotence as well as in psychotic conditions in which the patient appears to have no psychic container for his emotional explosions which are felt to expand into limitless space.

The notion of 'catastrophic change' which, according to Bion, is brought about in some degree by every effective interpretation, and which does alter the mind that receives it into itself, applies both to the effect of the mystic on the group and to that of the analyst's interpretation on the patient. In both cases, efforts will be made to neutralize it and to maintain the *status quo*, but if the mystic or the interpretation is accepted, the group or the patient will develop.

What I have just written links up with the most significant application of the relation container–contained ($♀♂$), namely to the distinction between the psychotic and the neurotic or normal parts of the personality. If the initial relationship between the psychic baby as the contained and the psychic Mother as the container is too parasitic, the result will be a predominantly psychotic individual. That is to say, if the projections of the baby are too much dominated by greed and envy and the mother's capacity to 'contain' this by means of 'reverie' is too low in proportion to what should be contained, there will be no normal reintrojection of a 'detoxicated' version of what was projected, and no introjection of a maternal container, so that no normal development of thoughts or of an apparatus to 'think them' can occur. Bion represents this by ♀♂. The β-elements projected by the baby are not returned as α-elements, so that more and more are projected with results which we will come back to.

Bion is careful not to say too much about what β and α-elements are or the α-function that converts the one into the other, partly because they are too primitive for anyone to apprehend and partly because by leaving them 'unsaturated', or not fully defined, research about them remains open and is not closed. But to make them a little clearer to myself, I sometimes think of β-elements (or things in themselves) as the most elementary bits of sensation and feeling not yet developed into elementary percepts (α-elements). Or perhaps, as the book under review suggests, β-elements include some very elementary percepts, and α-elements the same elementary, sensual, perceptual and emotional experiences 'transformed into visual, auditory and olfactory images, or other kinds of image, which can be stored and used in the production of dream thoughts, unconscious thinking during wakefulness, dreams and memories. And if either of these alternatives is so, the α-function may be originally the mother's reverie, and later as this is internalized, the attention of the child; for it seems to be this which converts the most elementary sense impressions into the kind of percepts that can be stored by a process perhaps analogous to, but more primitive than, the mating of an innate preconception with a realization. If so, the 'elements of perception', colours, shapes, etc. used in thinking may well be innately predetermined.

Once this process has started between baby and mother, there is no reason why it should not develop smoothly and produce more and more complicated thoughts and an increasingly efficient apparatus to think them. And this does happen in the non-psychotic part of the personality. But the psychotic part also exists, in varying degrees, in everyone and Bion also traces its development: the failure of the β-elements to find a container to convert them into α-elements ensures that more and more complicated 'bizarre' elements containing unwanted bits of the self and bits of the object they are projected into are formed and imprison the psychotic. And what makes the situation worse for him is that any attempt by the non-psychotic part of his personality to escape from this situation by means of the development of rational thought must make him aware of his illness and so of his inferiority to saner people. But this knowledge is so painful to a man whose innate envy may well make him unusually anxious to be superior that it is attacked by every means at his disposal. For this reason Bion says that if the psychotic is once brought to become aware of his illness, he must never be allowed by his analyst to forget it, and that if he reaches this point, he has become a 'sane psychotic'. I am not sure that I know what this means – perhaps that, if he knows and admits that he is subject to delusions and hallucinations, he need no longer automatically believe them. At any rate, it seems likely that some brilliant thinkers have approximated to this.

Although the psychotic approximates to the paranoid–schizoid extreme, and the normal individual more to the depressive half of the same scale, Bion assumes that everyone oscillates to some extent between the two, a process which he designates by the sign PS ↔ D. And this has a particular relation to his ♀♂ signs – presumably because the contained's relation to the container, or the container's to the contained, can oscillate in this way from symbiotic to commensal to parasitic and back, that is, between the depressive and the paranoid–schizoid parts of the scale.

Another notion of Bion's which I think is of the utmost importance is that of a fourth type of transformation other than rigid motion, projective and in hallucinosis. This is transformation in O, where O is the unknowable ultimate psychic reality. It cannot be known, it can only be 'become'. And what this means can perhaps be conveyed by an illustration or model – though not, I fear, a very good one. Suppose the analyst with the aid of the patient has been painting a picture of the patient. So far as it is correct, it will represent the analytic knowledge of the patient and analyst 'about' the patient. But if all goes well there comes a point – in reality many successive points – at which the patient steps into his picture and 'becomes' it. This, I think, is the 'catastrophic change' without which the patient can only know about and not be some hitherto unacknowledged part of himself – so far as this has been revealed in the analytic painting. I have the impression that this final step may often partially fail without either the patient or the analyst being aware of it – particularly, perhaps, in some so-called 'interminable analyses'.

At the end of this discussion, it may be worth mentioning a statement of Bion's which has perhaps given his friends more trouble than any other. It is that a true thought may exist without a thinker. But if it is thought by a thinker it cannot be true. Possibly this means that a true thought, which is true because it mirrors some piece of external or internal reality, may come into being in a dissociated way. But as soon as claimed by the ego, and owned by a thinker, it is restricted by a container, the ego, and can no longer be wholly true. But this is a very tentative guess at what Bion means, and may be wholly wrong.

Many other notions of Bion's are discussed in this book, which also discusses the notions I have mentioned much more fully than I have. Indeed, the reading of this review is no more a substitute for reading the book under review than reading the book under review is a substitute for reading Bion in the original. But I at least have found that to read both, the original and the commentary, is extremely helpful and to many of us perhaps essential if we are to grasp Bion's difficult but important work.

35

On Being a Psycho-analyst

It is probably true that the average layman has only a rudimentary and fallacious idea of what a psycho-analyst is and does. If so, the fault is possibly partly the analyst's for using esoteric language, and partly the layman's for believing the language to conceal supremely important knowledge economically available only to the few and so envied and disparaged. As this idea, if really held, must be damaging to analysis, my aim in this paper is to correct it – and incidentally to clarify my own mind, or rather the part of it which is still a layman. It is true of course that the analyst does know more than the layman about what is generally unconscious. But a moment's reflection will convince him that, since he knows more than the previous generation of analysts, the next generation is likely to know as much more again. In other words, the knowledge any one generation has is only relatively impressive – or even adequate.

Suppose an analyst in his chair behind a patient on his couch. This is the best position, because if they were facing each other, the purely sensual impression each had of the other could distract them from the 'psychic impression'. As it is, the analyst can see the clothed patient or imagine, as a medical doctor might, what he looks like unclothed, or inside his body. But as Bion has so often pointed out, what is important to the analyst is his patient's thoughts and feelings, and these cannot be sensed – in fact, they do not belong to the physical world at all but to the psychic one. Nor strictly speaking do the patients' perceptions of objects, though loosely speaking, they are often treated as if they belonged to the physical world.

How then does the analyst perceive them? By 'projective-identification', one of those esoteric words supposedly invented to confuse the layman, which in this context, means that he 'perceives' something in his patient because he has put it there from his own psyche. But this is not a confession that the analyst is paranoid and simply interprets what he projects into his patient. Of course it is not always easy to differentiate a normal projection from a paranoid one in which something hated or guilt-provoking in the self is put into someone else, as in the parable of the Mote and the Beam. In the normal one, the observer consciously knows he would feel such and such in such and such a situation and assumes that the observed person, who is seen to be in this situation, would have these feelings. In the case of the analyst and patient, the analyst, in virtue of his own previous analysis, is conscious of much in himself which he was not conscious of before and, on appropriate occasions, can 'see' or 'intuit' that they are unconscious in his patient. It is worth noting that what is interpreted in the patient, say anxiety, is 'transcendental' (non-sensible) to the analyst but that its concomitants – paleness, trembling, an alteration in the pitch of the voice, etc. – are 'immanent' (sensible).

As to what the analyst knows and the patient does not, this can be listed under a number of theories: Transference, Oedipus Complex, Repetition–Compulsion, Introjection and Projection (Freud), Paranoid–Schizoid and Depressive Positions, Envy, envious form of Projective-Identification (Melanie Klein) and Origin of Thoughts and Thinking (Bion), as well as some others not used in this paper, such as Confusional States (Rosenfeld), Symbolic Equation (Segal), absence of Psychic Skin (Bick), Dismantling as opposed to Splitting (Meltzer).

Of these, Transference, discovered very early by Freud, is perhaps the most mysterious. But it is that without which analysis would be impossible. In order to allow it to develop, the analyst must be careful not to obtrude his own personality, in particular his likes and dislikes and whether he likes or dislikes the patient. Of the three emotional links Bion stresses, L (Love), H (Hate) and K (Desire to know), only the last is relevant and should be strongly felt. This piece of reality I think the patient usually becomes aware of, and whatever other feelings he 'transfers' onto his analyst from his mother, father or siblings, one part of him does believe that the analyst has a benevolent interest in his personality and for this reason tends to trust him. I said that Transference was mysterious and I think the analyst feels this as soon as it has become apparent that his patient is unconsciously treating gaps between sessions, weekend breaks and holidays, as if he (the patient) were a baby about to lose the breast or bottle. So the analyst's most basic transference rôle is that of part-object nipple or breast, whole-object mother, part and whole object father, sister, brother and so on.

With ordinary patients, who are not iller than the average, or who are not more unconscious of aspects of themselves than ordinary people, a transference soon develops in which negative and positive feelings from the past are transferred onto the analyst in the present and can be recognized and interpreted. (Its intensity being partly curbed by the reality feeling that he is concerned only to get to know them in order to help them to get to know themselves.) But sometimes there are difficulties: for example, the patient may chatter in an apparently friendly way which the analyst can understand only at its conscious level. There appears to be no deeper, no symbolic, meaning, or if the analyst thinks he sees one and tries to interpret, the patient fails to understand him and makes him doubt whether his interpretation was correct.

Leaving aside such cases, I will try to describe the course of the more ordinary analyses, in which the analyst seldom feels so baffled. That he does not feel baffled because he is becoming complacent is, of course, a possibility. But this, too, may be left aside for the present. In an ordinary analysis, then, examples of jealousy, envy and so on (which are unconsciously murderous) can soon be recognized as transference phenomena and interpreted. For instance, strong dislike of someone else suspected, or known, to be in analysis with the same analyst may be interpreted as envy or jealousy of a sibling whom the patient may consciously imagine he has always loved; and if the interpretation is eventually recognized as right, progress will have been made. But a more fundamental pattern, now recognizable in many forms, thanks to the work of Freud, extended by Melanie Klein, Bion and others, concerns the many 'defences' which any patient will use against the discovery that, in unconscious fantasy, he has destroyed the thing he loves.

This I think is the most basic issue in the whole of analysis, and, for a start, links two separate discoveries of Freud, Transference and the Compulsion to Repeat. As to the Compulsion, Freud's Theory was that a 'traumatic event' was either remembered *or* endlessly repeated. But this again links with Freud's Theory of the Oedipus Complex, for the murder of a father (or mother) in unconscious fantasy is a traumatic event. And once a patient is in analysis the 'endless repetition' is almost certain to be played out, in a disguised form, in the transference, and may indeed be one of the reasons for the very formation of a transference.

We come now to the next questions: Why does the crime have to be endlessly repeated? And why is the recovery of a memory, or at least a conscious certainty that the crime is still being repeated symbolically in the transference, a necessary condition for the release from the compulsion and all the misery of mental illness? I do not know a certain answer, but I suppose it to be that, until the patient has become conscious of his envious or jealous wish to kill something or someone who stands for a part or the whole of his analyst or of someone the analyst is felt to love, there is nothing to counteract his destructive wishes. But as soon as the patient becomes fully aware of them and also of his love for whomever it is that his analyst stands in the transference, the crime is deeply mourned, never again repeated and eventually felt to have been forgiven. However, the depressive agony of this process is so great that the patient would rather resort to almost any defence against it – including the defence of destroying his own capacity to think.

This, I repeat, is the most vital theory in analysis, but it is a theory which has developed in stages from a specific theory related to the Oedipus Complex to a very general one in which the first murdered 'thing' was not a person but a 'part object', such as a nipple, breast or penis. That innate 'preconceptions' of such part-objects are of enormous importance in the human unconscious is difficult to believe without a great deal of evidence, for example, from their symbolic appearance in dreams (and dream-analysis still plays an important rôle in analysis); but the aesthetic importance of the dome (St Peter's or St Paul's) and the column (Cleopatra's Needle, Nelson's Column and earlier megaliths) may be acceptable as some evidence of this. Jung's 'archetypes' are probably much the same as innate preconceptions in theory. But there may be many differences in practice.

The 'thing' that has been loved and destroyed may be felt to be outside or inside the self. At its 'whole object' level it may be mother, father or sibling (a loved and hated baby). But as I have already said the fact that it is unconsciously felt to have been destroyed by the patient's own self is so painful that enormous defences are erected against this knowledge, the most basic being the destruction of the capacity to remember or to think at all (Bion). This of course, is the psychotic solution, never wholly absent even in so-called normal people whose memory at least has been attacked.

Ordinary repression which Freud discovered many years ago is perhaps the latest and most sophisticated form of this defence, in which no memory is permanently destroyed, only forgotten. However, when the memory or conviction is extremely difficult to recover in analysis, one may wonder whether it is not linked with the more serious defence, I think, depicted in a dream in which the patient had to have a nipple-shaped lump on her head cut out. This probably stood for the 'concrete memory'. And the reason why the memory of it had to be cut out was probably because it was the concrete memory of the thing the patient most loved and believed she had destroyed.

In general, defences seem to divide into two main types: either that part of the self which believed it had destroyed what it most loved is split-off and put into someone else who is blamed and hated for this murder (scapegoat type of defence), or the capacity to think is attacked and sometimes totally destroyed. As to the former, I think it a good technical device, whenever a patient (or the analyst) hates anyone with a particular virulence, to enquire whether the hated person is not a split-off part of the self.

A similar device may also help with some obstinate masochistic perversions. But in this case the masochist probably projects his sadistic self into his sadistic partner, while he himself identifies, projectively or introjectively, with his original victim. The original murder is not remembered or mourned, but endlessly repeated with this difference that either no one is slain, or if there is, it is the self and not the loved object. It is difficult to estimate how many actual deaths of all kinds may not be brought about in this sort of way. In such cases, it may be assumed that the original fantasy murder was a sex-murder.

As to the defence of destroying ones own capacity to think, this is probably much more common to some degree than used to be supposed, and is by no means confined to psychotics. Indeed the better understanding we now have of it – thanks largely to Bion's theory of the origin of thoughts and thinking, has probably helped to bring about a reclassification of 'normal' and 'psychotic' people, into 'normal' and 'psychotic' parts of one person. Bion's theory of thought starts with the notion that a thought is not a thing, but a 'no-thing'; and as the first thing that is not there when wanted is the breast (which may in fantasy have been murdered for not being there) the first thought is of a 'no-breast' inseparable from the (possibly guilty) mourning or pining which has to be accepted if thought is to be tolerated at all. In fact, the first proto-thought (α-element in Bion's theory) is fit only for projection. The next step depends on whether there is a real Breast, capable of *reverie* and so of accepting projective-identification – instead of adopting a defensive attitude against it, which I think is very common – and also on whether the baby can accept the breast as such. For some babies are thought to be so envious by nature, especially of an untroubled breast, that they put their painful feelings into it to destroy its calmness and not into something felt to be willing to contain them to relieve and help the baby. But, if a breast capable of containing the painful projected feelings is there, and if the baby can use it for this purpose, the first steps in the development of normal thinking take place. This Breast-Mother who can act as container (through reverie) is gradually internalized as a kind of memory-holder which can contain proto-feelings and thoughts (β-elements) and turn them into something that can be stored till wanted (α-elements).

But how do these theories help the ordinary analyst? I think he has already learnt from Melanie Klein's work to recognize when his patient is projecting into him. And Bion's work has made it easier for us to distinguish between a desperate projective-identification and a destructive one, or, as possibly both forms were there, to see which was the predominant one.

I say this because I believe (though not with certainty) it both easy and terrible to mistake a desperate projection for a destructive one. For by this means, I think, the beginnings of a constructive link between patient and analyst may be destroyed. Of course, it is also a mistake to fail to interpret a destructive projection; but, if it is missed, the chance to see it again is sure to recur.

At this point, I think it worth trying to consider the relation between first thoughts in Bion's theory and first internal objects in Melanie Klein's. From the dream I quoted of the woman who was to have a nipple-shaped lump in her head cut out because, as I interpreted, she wanted to forget the nipple, it would seem as if these two, i.e., the first 'thought' of the nipple and the first 'concrete internalization' of it, were the same. And if this is true, early projective-identification must be experienced as a very concrete process. That is to say the baby who cannot stand the thought that he has, in fantasy, killed the nipple by biting it off, must have projected a concrete nipple into a receptive breast and then re-internalized the breast with the concrete nipple inside – and in the case of the dream, presumably into the dreamer's head.

Alternatively, the murdered nipple may appear from dreams to be buried in the patient's faeces. Here it is again concrete, but also concealed so that it cannot be remembered and mourned. But only if this last step can be achieved can the patient recover from his nameless depression.

Here we may be reapproaching, by a roundabout route, the Oedipus Complex mentioned near the beginning. For can it be that the notion of the murdered nipple buried and forgotten in the faeces is a kind of proto-version of the fantasy – possibly, in some sense, an innate preconception, of father's penis, later the whole father, having been castrated or murdered and then concealed in the same sort of way?

What is common to all these patterns is the existence of two objects, one intensely desired, necessary to life and loved, the other frustrating and hated. The hated one is felt to have been killed by hate; but as in another aspect, it too is necessary and loved, it is now mourned and if the mourning and the guilt is too great to stand, the very memory of it, or at least the memory of its value is lost and many other defences can be adopted.

In a fairly easily recognizable form of the Oedipus Complex, the father is felt to be responsible for any delay in the baby getting to its mother either for love, warmth or milk and, if the baby cannot stand frustration, his anger is murderous. And this can be re-experienced and verified by anyone, in particular older people, who cannot stand being kept waiting. It is visibly depicted, for example, by Masefield in *The Hawbucks* where the Squire's rage at being kept waiting seven minutes for his luncheon by his favourite daughter and her friends makes him throw away (murder) the longed-for food. The whole pattern here can be recognized as Oedipean if one interprets the favourite daughter as the mother and her boy friend, who is wrongly blamed for the lateness, as originally the father, and the meat as the breast. I know these sort of substitutions must seem artificial, but they are of the very essence of symbol formation as it has to be interpreted in analysis.

It seems likely then that these earlier patterns of loves and murder in fantasy are precursors – recognized as such by Melanie Klein – of the later Oedipus Complex discovered by Freud in which the hatred of the father was based on sexual jealousy. And presumably, envy too, for the father and his penis has that earliest form of superiority based on size alone. He is enviously hated because he is bigger and has a bigger penis preferred by mother to the baby's little one, and for this reason it is attacked in fantasy by every conceivable form of sadism and believed to have been destroyed. Thereafter, the main effort is to cover up the crime. The whole fantasy forms an oscillating pattern which, without analysis, and sometimes in spite of it, is endlessly repeated.

It would seem, from what I have written, that the analyst who has become convinced of the truth of a number of theories as applied to himself in his own analysis ought to be able to recognize them in most of his patients, and convince them too. And I think it probably true that an analysis of three to five years with a reasonably good analyst and a reasonably normal patient is reasonably successful. But the end product is seldom as 'normal' at the end as he had hoped to become at the beginning. This is usually explained, quite truly, by saying that analysis is an endless process and that the ex-patient should be his own analyst till the end of his life. Yet there is something not wholly satisfactory about this apologia. It is as though one were to say, rather complacently, that the ex-seminary has become a priest. But this does not guarantee that he has also become a saint. I suspect that something similar (though less fanatical) to becoming a saint – in the sense of becoming fundamentally more concerned for and about other people than about himself (that is, more grateful and more generous) does happen on occasions in analysis and perhaps if we were to be really satisfied with ourselves, it ought to happen almost always. Indeed the steps to this condition are very similar in psycho-analysis and Christianity. The well analysed individual has discovered that he bit off the nipple in fantasy, or something similar, has repented and mourned this crime, and the good objects, which had been destroyed, are felt to have come alive inside him, to have forgiven him, and to remain as an internal mentor. And presumably, something rather similar has happened to the Christian Saint. He has discovered a Judas-part of him which has betrayed his Lord and having bitterly repented of and mourned this crime, his all-forgiving Lord is felt to have risen from the dead inside him. The parallel is very close, the main difference that I can see being that, in the analyst, the crime has been committed in his inner world of fantasy and, in the Christian, in his external world of history. But we are assured that, in our unconscious, the inner world is just as real as the external one. I do not know whether it is easier or more difficult to become an analytic saint than it is to become a Christian one. But if analysis is allowed to continue to develop, I think it will become easier to become an analytic one. The psychic difficulties are perhaps equal, but the analytic technique for dealing with them is still developing. Meanwhile, perhaps each side should be more charitable to the other.

It should be clear from what I have said that although I think analysts know a great deal about the unconscious, much of what they know is 'as through a glass darkly'. In other words we are always on the expanding frontier of a dark continent, which like physics, perhaps may have no end. If so, their Faustian *'Schön weiss ich viel, doch möcht ich alles wissen'* is robbed of any tincture of complacency.

Chronological List of the Published Writings of Roger Money-Kyrle

1927 Belief and Representation, *Symposion*, Heft 4
1928 The Psycho-physical Apparatus, *B. J. Med. Psych.* vol. 8
1928 Morals and Supermen, *B. J. Med. Psych.* vol. 8
1929 Critical abstract: Roheim's 'After the Death of the Primal Father', *B. J. Med. Psych.* vol. 9
1930 *The Meaning of Sacrifice*. London, Hogarth
1931 The Remote Consequences of Psycho-analysis on Individual, Social and Instinctive Behaviour, *B. J. Med. Psych.* vol. 11
1931 A Psychologist's Utopia, *Psyche*. London, Kegan Paul
1932 *The Development of the Sexual Impulses*. London, Kegan Paul
1932 *Aspasia*. London, Kegan Paul
1933 Psychology and Ethics, *Science Forum*, vol. 1
1933 A Psycho-analytic Study of the Voices of Joan of Arc, *B. J. Med. Psych.* vol. 13
1934 *Homo Insipiens*. Nineteenth Century, London
1934 A Psychological Analysis of the Causes of War, *The Listener*, 7 Nov. 1934
1934 Discussion: Sexual Regulations and Cultural Behaviour, *B. J. Med. Psych.* vol. 15
1936 Psychology of Superstition, *Science & Society*, vol. 1
1937 The Development of War, *B. J. Med. Psych.* vol. 16
1939 *Superstition and Society*. London, Hogarth/Institute of P.A.
1941 The Psychology of Propaganda, *B. J. Med. Psych.* vol. 19
1944 Towards a Common Aim: A Psycho-analytic Contribution to Ethics, *B. J. Med. Psych.* vol. 20
1944 Some Aspects of Political Ethics from the Psycho-Analytic Point of View, *I.J.P.A.* vol. 25
1948 Social Conflict and the Challenge to Psychology, *B. J. Med. Psych.* vol. 21
1948 Religion in a Changing World, *Rationalist Annual*, Watts
1950 Varieties of Group Formation, *Psa. & Soc. Sc.* N.Y., I.U.P.
1951 Some Aspects of State and Character in Germany, *Psa. & Culture* N.Y., I.U.P.
1951 *Psychoanalysis and Politics*, London, Duckworth/N.Y., Norton
1953 *Towards a Rational Attitude to Crime* (Pamphlet). London, Howard League
1955 The Anthropological and Psycho-analytic Concept of the Norm, *Psa. & Soc. Sc.* vol. 4
1955 Psychoanalysis and Ethics. An Inconclusive Contribution to the Theory of the Death Instinct. *New Directions in Psycho-analysis*

CHRONOLOGICAL LIST

1956   The World of the Unconscious and the World of Common Sense, *B. J. Phil. Sc.* vol. 7
1956   Normal Countertransference and some of its Deviations, *I.J.P.A.* vol. 37
1958   Psychoanalysis and Philosophy, *Psa. & Contemporary Thought*
1958   On the Process of Psycho-analytic Inference, *I.J.P.A.* vol. 39
1960   On Prejudice – A Psycho-analytic Approach, *B. J. Med. Psych.* vol. 33
1961   *Man's Picture of His World.* London, Duckworth
1963   A Note on Migraine, *I.J.P.A.* vol. 44
1963   Melanie Klein and her Contribution to Psycho-analysis, *Bull. Assn. Psychotherapists*, No. 4
1965   Megalomania, *American Imago*, vol. 22
1965   Review: W. R. Bion – *Elements of Psycho-analysis. I.J.P.A.* vol. 46
1965   Success and Failure in Mental Maturation, *Sc. Bull., Brit. Psa. Soc.*
1966   A Note on the Three Caskets, *Sc. Bull. Brit. Psa. Soc.*
1966   British Schools of Psycho-analysis, *Am. Handbook. Psychiatry. III*
1968   Cognitive Development, *I.J.P.A.* vol. 49
1969   On the Fear of Insanity, *Sc. Bull. Brit. Psa. Soc.*
1971   The Aim of Psycho-analysis, *I.J.P.A.* vol. 52
1976   Review: Meltzer *et al.* – *Explorations in Autism. I.J.P.A.* vol. 57
1978   Addendum to 'Cognitive Development', *Festschrift for W. R. Bion.* (Ed. Grotstein), N.Y., Aronson

Reviews

Aklen, A. H. B. *Pleasure and Instinct. Ant. J. Psa.* **11**, 108 (1930)
Barton, R. F. *Philippine Pagans. Int. J. Psa.* **19**, 514 (1938)
Bateson, R. F. *Naven. Int. J. Psa.* **18**, 341 (1937)
Benedek, T. *Insight and Personality Adjustment. Int. J. Psa. Int. J. Psa.* **28**, 53 (1947)
Bews, J. W. *Human Ecology. Int. J. Psa.* **17**, 257 (1936)
Bicudo, V. L. *Sublimation, Splitting and Obsessional Symptoms. Rev. Braz. Psicanal.* **1**, 80 (1967)
Bion, W. R. *Elements of Psychoanalysis. Int. J. Psa.*
Brend, W. A. *Sacrifice to Attis. Int. J. Psa.* **17**, 383 (1936)
Buschke, A. *An Introduction to Sexual Hygiene. B. J. Med. Psych.* **13**, 82 (1933)
Ellis, H. *Sex in Relation to Society. B. J. Med. Psych.* **17**, 380 (1938)
Exner, M. J. *The Sexual Side of Marriage. B. J. Med. Psych.* **13**, 82 (1933)
Flugel, J. C. *Men and their Motives. B. J. Med. Psych.* **14**, 295 (1934)
Flugel, J. C. *Population, Psychology and Peace. Int. J. Psa.* **27**, 158 (1946)
Flugel, J. C. *The Psychology of Clothes. Int. J. Psa.* **18**, 122 (1932)
Forbes, M. *Oedipus and Job in West African Religion. Int. J. Psa.* **41**, 645 (1960)
Fox, C. *The Mind and Its Body. B. J. Med. Psych.* **14**, 300 (1934)
Glover, E. *The Dangers of Being Human. B. J. Med. Psych.* **16**, 295 (1937)
Glover, E. *War, Sadism and Pacifism. B. J. Med. Psych.* **14**, 394 (1934)
Griffith, P. *A Synthetic Psychology. Int. J. Psa.* **9**, 129 (1928)
Hayley, T. T. S. *The Anatomy of Lango Religion and Groups. Int. J. Psa.* **28**, 120 (1947)
Hollitscher W. *Sigmund Freud, An Introduction. Int. J. Psa.* **28**, 201 (1947)
Hunter, M. *Reaction to Conquest. Int. J. Psa.* **18**, 69 (1937)
Jaques, E. *Equitable Payment. Int. J. Psa.* **42**, 526 (1961)
Kohler, W. *Gestalt Psychology. Int. J. Psa.* **11**, 511 (1930)
Layard, J. *Stone Men of Malekula. Int. J. Psa.* **25**, 172 (1944)
Lippmann, W. *A Preface to Morals. Int. J. Psa.* **10**, 487 (1929)
Man, 1932, 32: Diskussion über die Urkenntnis des Zeugungsvorganges bei dem Primitiven *Imago*, **19**, 283 (1933)
Marañon, G. *The Evolution of Sex and Intersexual Conditions. B. J. Med. Psych.* **13**, 82 (1933)
May, G. *Social Control and Sexual Expression. B. J. Med. Psych.* **14**, 200 (1934)
Meltzer, D. et al. *Explorations in Autism. Int. J. Psa.*
Moxon, C. *Freudian Essays on Religion and Science. Int. J. Psa.* **8**, 286 (1927)
Popenoe, P. *The Conservation of the Family. Int. J. Psa.* **8**, 108 (1927)
Rhine, J. B. *New Frontiers of the Mind. Int. J. Psa.* **19**, 262 (1938)
Ringdom, L. *The Renewal of Culture. Int. J. Psa.* **10**, 486 (1929)
Roheim, G. *Animism, Magic and the Divine King. Int. J. Psa.* **11**, 234 (1930)
Roheim, G. *The Origin and Function of Culture. Int. J. Psa.* **26**, 79 (1946)
Roheim, G. *Psycho-analysis and the Social Sciences. Int. J. Psa.* **29**, 68 (1948)

Ruffkin, J. N. *Great Logicians. Int. J. Psa.* **6,** 520 (1925)
Streeter, B. H. *Reality: a New Correlation of Science and Religion. Int. J. Psa.* **8,** 43 (1927)
Suttie, I. D. *The Origin of Love and Hate. Int. J. Psa.* **17,** 137 (1936)
Unwin, J. D. *Sexual Regulations and Human Behaviour. Int. J. Psa.* **15,** 354 (1934)
Walker, E. M. and K. M. *On Being a Father. Int. J. Psa.* **11,** 350 (1936)
Yellowlees, D. *Psychology's Defence of the Faith. Int. J. Psa.* **11,** 349 (1930)
Young, E. L. *A Philosophy of Reality. Int. J. Psa.* **12,** 246 (1931)
Zuckerman, S. *Functional Affinities of Man, Monkeys and Apes. Int. J. Psa.* **15,** 361 (1934)

Index

abortion 103
Abraham, Karl 50, 249n, 408, 409
acting out 384
addictions 438, 440
Adler, Alfred 116-17
adultery 98-101
advertising, commercial 169
aggression 82, 158
   and anxiety 304
   and death instinct 296
   first objects of 145 & n
   greed and envy as 306
   against loved objects 197 & n
   and masculine sex impulse 82, 147
   oral 189, 196
   origins of 83, 106, 136, 142, 145-7
   projection of 144, 212, 218, 236
   and restitution 173
agnostic 69
ambition 139
ambivalence 150, 153, 210, 221, 305, 370, 371, 400, 405
anal: masturbation 448
   phase/stage 32, 34n, 52
   position 440
   -sadistic impulses, and medicine man 49-50
analysis, *see* psycho-analysis
analyst, *see* psycho-analyst
Angell, Sir Norman 135
animal(s): gods 427
   as parent symbols 377, 388
   phobias 54
animatism 142, 143
animism 143, 294-5
anthropology 118, 354
   and concept of the norm 231-2, 262
   and cultural relativity 254, 282
   psycho-analytical 88, 91, 230, 243
anthropomorphic: reasoning 344-5
   world conception 10
anthropophagy 44
anxiety: in analysis 333
   and death instinct 287
   defence(s) against 205, 373
   depressive 194, 197n
   and despair 196
   persecutory 197n, 209, 290, 373
   psychotic 372
   relief from 173
   unconscious 183
anxiety hysteria 38, 53-5
apathy 201

aphanisis 65, 71n, 288
Aphrodite 214
appeasement viii, 180 & n, 181, 192, 214, 218
armament firms 159
arrogance 380, 381, 383, 386, 388
Astarte 214
atheism 64
Atkinson, H. G. 41, 149
atrocity(-ies) 214
Augustine, St 120
Australia, primitives in, *see* primitive peoples
Austria 101, 226
authoritarian societies 249
authoritarians 208-9, 234-42, 262, 280
   see also conscience, authoritarian
authority: attitudes to 161-2
   fear of 270-1
autism 450-1
autocracy 222
Avenarius, Richard 13, 309
avoidance reaction 17, 18, 26, 27, 37-8
   and repression 23-7

baboons 148
baby, *see* infancy/infant
Babylonia 222
basic assumptions 452
behaviourism 16 & n, 57 & n, 286, 293, 325n
Belgium, 'rape' of (1914) 214
belief 265
   and representation, confusion 1-16
   system of 358-9
   theory of 1-2
Benedict, Ruth 230
Berkeley, George 307-8
beta-elements (Bion) 309n
Bick, Esther 450
biology 311, 323
Bion, Wilfred 250n, 309n, 337, 342n, 350n, 352, 362, 364, 367, 374, 387, 397-406, 411, 413, 417, 418, 419, 420, 422, 430, 433, 436, 443, 444, 448, 449, 450, 457, 458, 461
   review of his *Elements of Psycho-analysis* 389-96
   review of *Introduction to the Work of Bion* 451-6
birth: ceremonies 38, 52-3
   shock of 311

INDEX

Bishop, Adrian xiii
black magician 48–9, 51
Blacker, C. P. 58n
blood feud 154, 156
blood letting 52
body-ego 313, 424
body image 295n, 324n
body scheme 295n, 324n
Boers/Boer War 170, 214
Brangham, Lt. Col. 233
breast 312, 320, 323–4, 327
  and bottom, confusion 428–9, 445, 447, 448
  as 'container' 390–1, 401, 431–2, 462

  'good' and 'bad' 409–11, 419–21
  identification with 377
  incorporation of 349–50
  infant at 88–9
  infant's concept of 401
  innate preconception of 398, 431, 437, 444, 447
  opposing impulses to 204n
  projection into 381–2
  recognition of 443–4
  two concepts of 276
  two functions of 432
Brierley, Marjorie 283n
Brill, A. A. 49
Britain, and patriotism 190–1
British Institute of Psycho-Analysis 210
British Psychological Society 57n, 198n, 353n
brother(s) 196
  elder 172
Buddha 223
Byron, Lord 214

callousness 208–9
cannibalism 51, 151, 152, 154
capitalism 94, 107, 159, 164
CASES (in order of appearance in the text):
  59-year-old obsessional neurotic (Brill) 59
  young girl with bolster ceremonial (Freud) 60
  young woman with obsessional fear of leaving tap running (Reik) 60n
  stockbroker 70
  'Wolf-man' who dreamed of wolves as a child (Freud) 54, 126–9
  patient who projected his uselessness into analyst 336–9
  patient who feared the analyst would 'blow first' 350–1
  woman patient with migrane 361–5
  patient with jaundice attacks 422
  see also dreams

castration: fear of 274, 275, 288
  psychical 124
  threat of 25
  wish in analysis 335
catabolism 293, 296
catastrophic change 453, 455
categorical imperative (Kant) 306
censor 4, 24, 26, 112
ceremonials 64
character: analysis 208
  authoritarian, *see* authoritarians
  and defence mechanisms 260
  development 175
  German, *see* Germany
  humanist, *see* humanism (-ists)
  independence of 163
  and infantile experience 229–30
  national 241
  neurotic 226
  transmission 238n
child(ren): analysis of 36, 408
  introjection and projection in 185
  and morality 187
  observations of 182
  see also infants
Christ 88, 121, 123, 223
Christianity 92, 120, 465
Churchill, Winston 137n
Cinema 160
civil service, German 236
civilization, and repression 139
class/classification 392–3, 398–9, 405n, 417, 418, 419, 421, 443
clothes: and delusion of divinity 377–9, 388
  and status 427
cognitive development 416–33
collective security 157
Collingwood, E. F. xiii
committees, functioning of 386–8
common sense 309, 315, 320, 324
  world of 9–10, 324–5, 327, 328 & *n*
communists 170, 213
complex: Oedipus, *see* Oedipus complex
  parental, 149, 151
compulsion(s) 60
  case illustration 60n
  to control analysis 351
  and medicine man 50
  repetition 460
concepts/conceptions 392, 395–6, 418, 420–4, 444
conceptual pyramid 397–401, 403, 405
concern 314
conflict: inner 173, 226, 287
  political 371
confusional state 359, 374, 412–13
conscience 69, 303
  authoritarian 279
  defences against 367

471

conscience—(*contd.*)
  dissociated 251
  group 134
  humanist 280, 281, 283
  leader as 173
  projection of 305
  structures of 233
  two types of 272, 276–7
  variety of 197
consciousness 8
  and neural processes 19–21
conservatism 192, 193
constipation 59
'contained' and 'container' (Bion) 390, 453–5
contemplation, philosophic 329
contempt 355, 380–1
continuity, principle of 295 & *n*
contraception 103
contrectation 77–8
conversion, religious 120, 121
copulation, killing as 153; *see also* intercourse
counter-transference 330–42
  positive and negative 337–9
creativeness 206, 301, 442
  see also work, creative
credulity 163–5
crime: irrational attitudes to 246
  public attitude to 250
  rational attitudes to 251
criminal(s) 33, 36
  relatives of 248
  as scapegoat 250, 367
  as sub-group 251
crowd behaviour 165
cruelty 59
cure, analysis and 58
curiosity 299–300, 368
  scientific, analyst's 331, 339, 341*n*
cynicism 182–3, 193, 205
Czechoslovakia 170, 214, 216

dancing, ritual 377
Darwin, Charles 149, 293*n*, 376
death: fear of 23, 288, 289 & *n*, 295 & *n*, 296, 304, 443–4
  of good object 448
  innate idea of 447
  and pain 78
death instinct 146 & *n*, 287, 289–90, 292, 296 & *n*, 304, 333
decapitation 124
defence mechanisms 259
  and politics 368–71
  and prejudice 358
  two types of 461
  see also manic defence
delinquency, and Nazis 240

delusions: infantile 136
  of persecution, *see* persecution unconscious 417
democracy 174, 205, 370
democratic character 233
denial, mechanism of 180–1, 206–7, 217, 220, 373
depersonalization 325
depression 121, 132, 143, 153, 156, 250, 410
  capacity for 250
  defences against 183, 205, 206, 405
  first onset of 276
  nameless 463
depression, economic 167, 173
depressive anxiety 444
  and morals 29*n*
depressive position 314–15, 328, 338, 407, 410, 414
  and morality 68*n*
  and reparation 116*n*
despair 196
destructive impulses 90, 304, 437
  inversion of 42, 43
  and war 131–2, 134–6
  see also aggression
determinism 326*n*
deterrence 251, 252
devil(s)/demons 171, 173, 175, 188, 211, 220
  possession by 164, 187*n*, 218
Dicks, Henry 206, 231, 233
discipline, regard for 235
discontent 108
  and Oedipus complex 84–5, 95, 105–7
disintegration, terror of 288 & *n*
dismantling, defence of 450
disorientation 424
Disraeli 141
divinity: delusion of 377–9
  of kings, *see* kings
divorce 103
dogmatism 359, 374
Dostojewski, Fyodr 30
doubt, and philosophy 302, 307 & *n*
dream(s) 213, 393, 453, 460
  claustrophobic 428
  of lavatory 413
  thoughts 392–3, 395, 400, 454
  INSTANCES OF (*in order of appearance in the text*):
  of two straws 350–1
  of patient with migraine 361–3
  of 'dogs' to be given to two women 380–1
  of 'Regency Buck' 381–2
  young man insults an official 385
  of baby shark 385
  of washing machine 402

dream(s)—(contd.)
  of woman 'warped in body' 404-6, 423-4
  of nipple-shaped lump on the head 425, 428, 461, 463
  of another patient trying to snatch the pillow 426
  of Indian woman exhibiting herself 426
  of little Professor 426-7
  of performer producing fire from his head 427
  of crawling into a sleeping-bag 427-8
  of woman on a balcony 428-9
  of sweeping up prickly pine needles 431-2
  of breeding cocatrices or salamanders 434-6, 441
  a chariot driver with two plump white horses 439-40
  a very important lady with no face 444
dualism 13-14, 310-11, 315
Duau Islanders 156
duel(s) 83
Dumas, A. 86n, 87

economics 177 & n, 200
Eder, David 223, 437
education: and analysis 194, 203
  and production of normality 35
Edward IV 226
ego: and object 328
  part- 314
  and super-ego, tension 195-7, 304
  two enemies of 384
egocentric states 426
ego-ideal 43, 44, 53, 55, 357
egoists, political 208-9
Egyptian king(s) 89, 222
Einstein, Albert 253-4
ejection 185 & n
election(s) 371
  (of 1931) 169
  (Germany, 1933), 371
'elements' of psycho-analysis (Bion), 390-4, 399, 401, 431, 432, 454, 462
Elizabeth I, Queen 212
Ellis, Havelock 84n, 100, 102, 124n
emotion 368n
empathy 332, 340
Empire, British 191
empirical method: and ethics 178-9, 266-7
  and morality 187
  and psycho-analysis 199
employment, control of 200
end(s): choice of 177-8, 183
  and justification of means 177n

endoctony 149
endogamy 149, 150, 157
engrams 55
enlightenment 35-7
entrepreneur 193n
entropy principle 79n, 293 & n 295-6
environment 401
  and character 242
  effect of 201, 326 & n
  modification of 98
envy 75, 93, 108, 306, 355-6
  and conceptual pyramid 401-3, 405
  and crime 252
  early form of 409, 413, 421
  and jealousy, distinction 108
  and Oedipus complex 95
  of parental gods 301
  primary 349
  see also penis envy
Epicureans 304
Eros 146
ethical absolutism 190
ethical relativism/relativity 182, 190, 199, 253-4, 306, 429
ethical revolution 106
ethics 265
  doubt and certainty in 303-6
  and morality 178, 189n
  psycho-analytical theory of 184-97
  science and 176-7, 198-9
ethology 398, 419, 442, 448
eugenics 76, 90, 96
evolution 78, 90, 294
  and psychology 76
existential propositions 5-8
exogamy 149
experience, role of 398
eyes: and insight 368
  and migraine 362-3

face-saving 386
family 211-12
  ideal 168
  tradition 72
  and war 86, 242
fanatic(s) 215, 216
fascism 240
Fascist character 206, 231, 233, 240, 242-3
fatalism 326n
father: child's relation to 162 & n, 195-6
  figure, internal 181
  figure, and Nazis 191
  identification of, with mother 52, 55
  image, splitting of 141, 171-2
  (and) Imago 48, 71 & n
  introjection of 53, 55
  as model 225

473

father:—(contd.)
  as mother substitute 66
  and Oedipus complex 66, 86, 195
  repressed hatred of 270–1
  and sacrifice 91–2
  symbol, group leader as 221, 223
  see also parent(s)
Fatherland 213, 235, 371
female genitality 291n
Ferenczi, Sándor 50, 408
fetishism 128–9
fixations 32, 33, 84
  anal 50, 52, 55
  oral 51, 52, 55
flag, importance of 156n
Flügel, J. C. xiv, 82n, 202 & n, 220
food refusal 44
fornication 101–3
France 98, 102, 119, 213
France, Anatole 110, 111n, 112, 123n
Frazer, Sir James 151
Frederick the Great 239, 241
freedom 174, 214, 220
  fight for 191
free-thinkers 29
Freud, Sigmund 16, 50, 60, 82, 139, 211, 229, 286–7, 305, 317, 331, 366, 376, 377, 442
  on aggression 83, 91, 96, 146
  on conscience 303–4
  on counter-charge 24
  on counter-transference 330
  on death instinct 287, 289, 293, 296, 304
  on destructive impulses 90
  on dreams 400
  on guilt 276
  on humour 412 (see also below WORKS)
  on identification 412
  on melancholia 249
  on morals 195
  on morality 256, 283
  and over-optimism 37n
  on paranoia 179
  on penis envy 116
  on pleasure principle and reality principle 22, 369
  on primal horde 148–9
  on religion 63
  on social motives 202
  on superego 113, 120, 273–5, 304, 372
  on three caskets 407
  on transference 459–60
  (see also Oedipus complex)
  WORKS: 'A Child is being Beaten' 446, 449
  'Anxiety and Instinctual Life' 305n
  Civilization and its Discontents/Das Unbehagen in der Kultur 65n, 82n, 96, 202n
  The Ego and the Id 195
  'From the History of an Infantile Neurosis' 126n
  Group Psychology and the Analysis of the Ego 92n, 202n, 210, 341n, 350n
  'Humour' 113n, 120, 274n
  Mourning and Melancholia 180n
  'Thoughts for the times on War and Death' 140n
  Totem and Taboo 10, 40, 91, 151, 159
  'Two Principles of Mental Functioning' 421
frigidity 124, 403, 405, 423, 453
frustration 146
funeral rites 38, 40–2

Garibaldi 214
genital stage 32
German Personnel Research Branch 231, 240
Germany: authoritarian/humanist/fascist characters in 234–43
  character development in 231
  and Great War 86, 157, 164, 213, 217, 226, 230
  and Nazism/Second World War 163–70, 172, 174, 180, 190–1, 206n, 207, 208, 230, 281
  after Second World War 204, 207, 229, 230
  see also Hitler; Nazism
Gestalten 311–13, 323, 327, 328n, 329 & n
Gladstone 141, 170, 214
Glover, Edward 131, 134n, 142n, 156
God 308
  avenging 171
  and conscience 69
  and ethics 178
  fear of 64
  seeking of 66
  and super-ego 120, 122
  as symbol of father 64, 67, 69
  as symbol of mother 67, 89
  see also Jahveh
god(s): father and 222
  leader as 173
  war 174
Goebbels, Dr 165–6
grandeur, delusion of 383
greed 75, 304, 306, 372, 413
  jealousy and 99
Greek: culture 378
  democracies 222
  philosophers 299
grief 206

INDEX

group(s): Bion's theory of 452–3
  enemies 216, 221, 227
  formation of 211, 216, 227
  hypochondria 218, 219
  ideal 225, 226
  leader 221, 226
  prejudices 357
  primary 210
  sub- 226, 369
guilt: in analysis 338
  arousal of 276–7
  capacity for 273, 278
  collective 207, 243–4
  and criminals 248
  defences against 372
  denial of 279, 305
  depressive 206, 209, 235, 249, 261–2, 276, 278
  inherited sense of 42
  and morality 184, 187, 189
  persecutory 219–20 & n, 235, 249, 261–2, 275–7, 279
  and politics 181, 370
  and superego 195–7, 273, 372
  two elements of 272, 275–6
  unconscious 159
  of victim 247

Haddon, — 154n, 155nn
Haldane, J. B. S. 8n
hallucinations 21–3, 125–6, 130, 259, 437
Hargreaves, Dr 160n
head hunters 46, 152, 154
heaven 93
  as derivative of womb 89
hedonism, positive and negative 77n, 79n
Hegel, G. W. F. 241, 301
Heimann, Paula 296, 330, 331, 341n
heredity 326 & n
  see also inheritance
heretics, burning of 218, 220
  see also Inquisition
hero: imitation of 30–1
  saviour 172–3, 175
Hesse-Doflein 147n
Hicklin, Margot 233
Hindenburg, Paul von 172
historians, social 241
Hitler, Adolf 137n, 141, 165–6, 168–9, 172, 191, 204–5, 206, 218 & n, 219, 224, 239, 241, 242, 371
Hobbes, Thomas 316
Hohenzollerns 239, 240, 242
holidays, patients' reaction to 445
homicidal mania 132
homosexuality 54, 55, 90, 117, 148, 158, 339, 439–40
  passive 381

honesty in marriage 99–100
Honiteaux, — 128n
Hopkins, P. 74 & n, 87n, 202n
humanism(-ists) 199, 200, 208–9, 234–42, 262, 278–80, 306
  and insight 278
  and political behaviour 281
Hume, David 8, 307–9, 313, 327, 329, 453
humour 412
  see also Freud WORKS: 'Humour'
hypnotism 350n
hypochondria 143, 153, 169, 218, 412, 422
  group 218, 219
hypocrisy 108
hypomania 279
hypoparanoids 279
hysteria, mass 170
hysterical symptoms 61

id, envious 383, 384
ideal(s): imitation of 175
  psychology and 215–16
idealism(-ist) 5, 14, 442
  political 72–3
idealization 204, 205
  over- 355
identification 143, 144, 150–1, 154, 162, 310, 314, 350n
  adhesive 450
  capacity for 315
  and concrete representation 400
  with dead father 42
  introjective 432
  with parents 377
  two forms of 331, 339, 409, 412
  (see also projective identification)
  with victim 46–7
ideogram/ideograph 404, 422–3, 425
ideographic representation 400
ideology(-ies) 177
  conflict of 190, 192, 193, 198
Iliad 152n
illness, concept of 256
Imago 69, 70, 71, 150–1, 158
  paternal/father 210, 236
Imago Group 376n
immortality 288
  craze for x
imperialism 86
impotence 70, 453
  mental 336–7
  see also potency
imprinting 398, 419
impulses, ingestive and excretive 78n
incest 150, 195, 274, 412
incompetent character 33

475

incorporation 151, 162, 179
  loving/destructive 186
  see also internalization; introjection
India, caste in 380
Indians, North American 225
individualism 192, 193
individuality, loss of 134
infancy/infants 312–14
  and death instinct 292
  first concepts 276
  and *Gestalten* 312
  hallucinatory gratification of 22–3
  and mother, *see* mother
  and parents, *see* parents
  picture of the world in 259, 297, 308, 309, 310, 327, 329, 348, 358
  and state of chaos 437
inferiority: delusional 380–2
  projection of 382
  sense of 161, 438, 455
Inge, W. R. 134
inheritance: of mental experience 41, 45, 55–6
  and normality 35
  phylogenetic 443, 447
  see also innate; racial memory
inhibition 18, 25, 97
  freedom from 28, 30, 183
  of the Imago 70
  normal 34
  removal of 36
  and society 98
  types of 30–1
initiation: of medicine man 48
  rites 52
injustice 388
innate: ideas 397, 447
  knowledge 442
  modes of thought 322
  preconceptions 258n, 395, 397–9, 402–3, 406, 417, 419–20, 422, 424, 437, 443, 447, 452, 460
  (*see also* breast; intercourse; nipple; penis)
  releasing mechanisms 323
  responses 322–4
Innes, Keith xiv
Inquisition 188
  see also heretics
insanity 439n
  fear of 434–41
  see also psychosis; psychotic/insane part of self
insight 236n, 270, 280, 339
  diffusion of 194, 203
  and health 282
  and politics 280–3
instinct(s) 285–6
  cognitive aspect of 442, 452
  Darwinian conception of 289, 400

death, *see* death instinct
  definition of 294n
  and innate phantasy patterns 287, 327
  life 289, 304
  nature of 320–4
  psycho-analytic theory of 323
  satisfaction of 176
  and self-knowledge 79
  of self-preservation, *see* self-preservation
institutions, status of 385–9
insult: concept of 382–5
  response to 383–4, 386
integration 283 & n
intellectuals 191
intelligence, inheritance of 433
intercourse: innate preconception of 445, 447
  and morality 187n
  parental 441, 443, 446, 448
  (*see also* primal scene)
internalization 444
  see also incorporation; introjection
interpretations 333, 341n
  of anxiety 409
  and change 270, 453
  choice of 272, 394
  confirmation of 344n, 345
  denial of 343
  resistance to 318–20
introjection 142, 179, 313
  aggressive 260
  aims of 314
  in analysis 332, 334
  definition 97
  of father 42, 48
  and incorporation, distinction 185n
  role of 185–6
introspection 367
intuition 316, 340, 344n
invasion 156
inversion 132, 140, 150, 181, 206, 291
  political 192
Iris 214
Irish, the 214
irritability 100
Isaacs, Susan 344n
Islam 92
Italy/Italians 214

Jahveh 174, 182, 188
James, William 2, 311
James-Lange theory 368n
Jaques, Elliott 347n, 374
jealousy 98–9, 145, 196
  unconscious 103
Jerusalem, Prof. 264n

INDEX

Jews: ancient 157, 299
  Hitler and 166–7, 170, 219
Joan of Arc 109–30
Johnson, Dr Samuel 309
Jones, Ernest xiii, xiv, 104, 130n, 140n, 202 & n, 223, 287, 288, 316, 317
Jung, C. G. 115, 460

Kant, Immanuel 304, 306
Keith, Sir Arthur 366
Keynes, Maynard 177n
king(s): divine/deification of x, 151, 222, 223, 379
  divine right of 222
Kitchener, Lord 172
Klein, Melanie xiv, 28, 136, 137n, 142, 182, 195, 203, 211, 219, 249, 273, 275, 311, 331, 334, 335, 360, 370, 377, 400, 407–15, 437, 444
  on anxiety 234, 290, 410
  on death instinct 287, 304, 409
  and depressive position 68n, 260, 314, 328, 338, 410–11, 414
  early career of 408
  on envy 252, 355, 409, 413–14, 421
  on guilt 184, 261, 372
  and over-optimism 37n
  on paranoia 179, 181
  on paranoid/persecutory position 260, 275, 356, 374, 409, 411
  on projective identification 347, 412, 413
  on splitting 210, 410, 450
  on super-ego 237, 409, 411–12
  see also Oedipus complex, early stages of
  WORKS:
    'A Contribution to the Theory of Anxiety and Guilt' 263
    Contributions to Psycho-analysis 317, 319n
    Envy and Gratitude 108, 317, 349n
    'Notes on some Schizoid Mechanisms' 341n, 349n
    The Psycho-analysis of Children 317, 319n
    Contribution to *Science and Ethics* 190n
knowledge 403
  equation of, with breast 348
  instinctive/innate 442
  primitive 258
  theory of 399
  two types of 35
Kobéua 48

Lamarck, Ch. de 321
  see also inheritance of mental experience; racial memory

Lang, Andrew 118, 125n
language: construction of 309–11, 313, 315
  and verbal thought 315–16
latency 104–5
Le Bon, Gustave 89n
leaders 221–4
leadership 174
  craving for 241
League of Nations 136
learning, capacity for 401
legislation 200
Leibnitz, G. W. 294
Lenin 224
life span 291
life task 116
lion, imaginary 144
Little, Margaret 341n
Locke, John 307
logic 178, 256, 309
logical positivism, *see* positivism
loneliness 77–8
Lorenz, Konrad 311, 317
love: and hate, conflict 204
  projective identification and falling in love 350n
  rediscovery of 189
luxury, demand for 75

Mach, Ernst 11, 309, 327
magic 153, 155, 327
Mahoun, Francis xii
Malinowski, Bronislaw 102, 104
mana 142, 150, 223
mania 45, 153
manic defence 144, 370, 373
manic-depressive 47
manic disposition 151
manic process 143
Marett, J. R. 142, 149n, 155n
Marias, — 104n
marriage 99–102, 108, 150, 152
martyrdom 121, 125, 129
Mary 214
masculine protest 116–17
Masefield, John 464
Masoch, — 128
masochism 291 & n, 350n
  and religion 63, 69, 92, 120–1
  and war 134
masochistic character 226, 249n
mass: depression 174
  hysteria 170
  movements, social 63
  psychosis 174
  suggestion 160
masturbation 77
materialism, monistic 313
maturation 328, 397–406

477

maturity 175, 283
  cognitive 421
Mead, Margaret 225, 230
mechanistic world conception 10-11
medical science, origin of 49, 50, 52
medicine: patent 171-2
  primitive 219
medicine man 38, 48-50, 143, 153
mediumistic phenomena 126
meekness 384
megalomania 168, 376 ff., 412
  intrapsychic 429
melancholia 43-5, 55, 132, 153, 168, 180n, 224, 249
  see also depression
melancholy 92
Meltzer, D. viii-ix, x, 62n, 376n, 428, 438, 440, 445, 449, 450
  review of *Explorations in Autism* 450-1
memory 310, 315, 328, 447
  attacks on 461, 463
  -holder, mother as 462
  images 5, 325n, 419
  inherited, see racial memory
  and mourning 444
mental health 200, 232, 243
mental illness: causes of 416-17
  nature of 406
Merejskowski 33
Messe-Doflain 82n
metaphysics 178, 187, 264
metapsychology 287 & n, 293
migraine 361-5
militarism 183
miscarriage 363
missionaries 255
Mohammed 223
  see also Islam
Moll, — 77
Money-Kyrle, R. E.
  Aspasia 140n
  The Development of Sexual Impulses 57n
  The Meaning of Sacrifice 86n, 91
monism 15, 313
Moore, George 31
moral: attitude 272
  character 260
  disease 251, 252
  feeling, criminals and 248
moralism, and Kleinian analysis 415
moralists 177
morality 68-72
  aggressive 185
  ethics and 178, 184
  in inner-world system 429
  militant 189
  negative 185
  and obedience 234
  and Oedipus complex 195
  origin of 184-5, 274

political 187n
primary 186-90, 197
and repression 105
sexual 187n, 280
sources of 68 & n, 274-5
and super-ego, see super-ego
unconscious infantile 29
morals: definition of 29
  freedom from 28
  and inhibitions 28-9
  two types of 29n
mother: capacity for reverie 430-2, 453-4
  as 'container' 390-1, 453-4
  figure, good 212
  goddesses 214
  infant's relation to 142
  longing for 66, 77-8, 96
  receptiveness of 401-2, 413, 450
  see also breast; parent(s)
Mother Church 214
Motherland 156, 212-13, 227
mourning 272n, 444
  and perversion 62n
mouth: and aggression 186
  as primitive concept 419 & n
Munich settlement (1938) 170, 174, 180n
murder, political 177n
Murray, Margaret 109
Mussolini 141, 224
mythology/myths 85
  (Bion) 367, 392, 395, 430
  of creation of world 437

nakedness 377-8
Namier, Sir Lewis xiii
Napoleon I 141, 172
Napoleon III 224
Napoleonic Wars 173
narcissicm 376, 426
narcissistic stage 34n
national paranoia 133, 135
nationalism, French 224
natural selection 76, 147n
Nazism/Nazis 166, 168-71, 174, 180, 188, 191, 206, 219, 234, 235, 240-1, 274
'necessary adjuncts' 343, 346, 347
negative therapeutic response 414
negativism, moral 182-4
nervous apparatus, and Freudian concepts 20-1
neurosis: and inhibitions 32
  in peace and war 91, 134
neurotics 273
neutrality, ethical and political 202
newspapers 160
  see also Press, the

INDEX

Nietzsche, Friedrich 33
nightmares 164
nipple, innate preconception of 419 &
  n, 420, 431, 437
Nirvana Principle 146*n*
nominalists 418
normality: analyst's concept of 255,
    257
  analyst's own 349
  anthropologist's concept of 255
  concept of viii, 179-80, 248, 255-7
  in criminals 248, 250 & *n*
  definition of 283
  description of 33-4
  in politics 193
  positive characteristics of 183-4
  relativist definition of 282
  and removal of inhibitions 32
  in societies 232

objects: good/bad 186, 196, 203, 278 &
    n, 312-13, 358, 405, 463
  internal 180 & *n*, 183, 196, 203,
    220
  part 142, 196
  percept- 326-7
  projection of internal 186
  and subject, division 325
observation in analysis 390, 395
obsessional neurosis 38, 49-50
obsessionals 273
Oedipus complex xi, 65, 85, 97, 145,
    446, 448, 460, 464
  achievement of 400, 404
  and aggression 83
  early stages of 409, 411-12, 464
  evasion of/failure to achieve 421,
    451
  inverted 66
  and Joan of Arc 114, 117-18
  and latency period 104-5
  persistence of 65, 96-7
  and politics 74
  regression to 100-1
  and religion 63, 91
  and revolution 87-8
  and war 140
Oedipus myth 53, 367, 368
oligarchy 222
omnipotence 10, 168, 384
  and anal urge 50
oral: aggression 146
  phase/stage 32, 34*n*, 50, 52, 420*n*
  position 440
  sadism 142
O'Shaughnessy, Edna vii, x
Osiris 39-40
Oxford University Anthropological
    Society 138*n*

pacifism 131, 155, 159, 181-4, 188,
    221, 384
paranoia 38, 54-5, 132, 144, 164, 168,
    179, 184, 187, 217
  national/group 133, 135, 170
  political 192
  treatment of 275
paranoid anxiety 156
paranoid defence 145
paranoid/persecutory position 260, 275
paranoid-schizoid position 356, 409,
    411
paranoid-schizoid state 374
parental complex 149, 151
parents: 'bad' 179, 224
  baby's concept of their relationship
    403-5, 420, 421, 434,4, 446
  composite/combined figure of 145*n*,
    172, 213, 218, 411, 436
  and counter-transference 331, 333,
    339-40, 341*n*
  'good' 224-5
  ideal 76, 175, 179
  imagos 181
parricide 56, 91-2, 150, 157, 195, 274,
    412
  and Osiris myth 38-40
  and primal horde 42
patient: analyst's relation to,
  see psycho-analyst
  compulsive control of analysis by
    351
patriarchal homes 236
patriotism 190
Paul, St 160
Peleus 53
penis: envy 116-17, 128-9, 414
  'good' and 'bad' 420, 421
  innate preconception of 463
Penrose, Lionel xiii
percept(s) 19-20
perception 310, 315
perceptual field 8-9
perceptual situations 286 & *n*
periodicity: of neurosis 47
  of seasons 47, 53
persecution: delusions of 132, 144, 164,
    179, 181, 217
  sense of 164
persecutor, internal 175, 180, 200, 270*n*
persecutory anxiety 438, 443-4
  and morals 29*n*
persecutory position, *see* paranoid
    position
perversions 146, 438, 439
  anal-sadistic 49
  and analysis 36
  and inhibition 32
  later definition 62*n*
  masochistic 461

479

perversions—(contd.)
　nodal point of development of 446, 448
　and sublimation 59
　and symptom, distinction 61–2
　war as 140
phallic: symbolism 129, 140, 152
　worship, sadistic 188, 191
phantasy: and instinct 287
　and perception 310
philosophy 264 & n
　classical 297–8, 301, 305
　of infant 313
　motives for 299–303
　mystical 314
　and psycho-analysis 297, 309, 311
　systems of 7
　see also individual entries, e.g. positivism
phobia(s) 60, 127
phylogenetic studies 146
physics/physicists 295
　world of 15
Piaget, Jean 311
Plato, Jean 311
Plato, 29, 266, 267, 306, 418, 443
play, interpretation of 408
pleasure, capacity for 183
pleasure principle 259, 369, 371
poets 316
Poincaré 453
Poland 173
political: callousness 207–8
　conscience 208
　idealism 72–3, 76
　motives 203–4
　parties 371
　propaganda 169
politics 72, 198–9, 215
　and guilt 206–7
　and insight 280–3
　and Oedipus complex 74
　and paranoia 180–1
　and party system 205, 372
　psycho-analysis and 370–4
　and psychology 203, 366
　and self-deception 368
Pope, election of 222
population, over- 138, 373
positivism 177, 265
　logical 298, 299n
possession: by devil, see devil
　by evil spirits 219
potency: intellectual 335
　see also impotence
prayer 327
precocity 103, 149
preconceptions: in development of thought 393
　innate, see innate
preferences, moral and political 265–8
pre-genital characters 33

prejudice 353–60
　dogmatic 359
pre-natal experience 322n
Press, the 133, 135
　see also newspapers
Preuss 41–2
primal: brothers 41–7, 51–5
　Feast 377
　horde 40–2, 148–9, 196
　Man 149, 151, 152
　see also primeval man
　scene 129n, 417, 441
　see also intercourse
Prime Minister 223
primeval man 85, 86, 92
　see also Primal Man
primitive peoples 41, 102, 120, 138–9, 141, 151, 153–5, 167, 182, 219, 225, 355, 377
　and mourning 45–6
　Australia 44, 45, 230
　Central Australia 221–2
　South Australia 40
　Australian shaman 48
　Duau Islanders 156
　Kobéua 48
　Malays 155n
　Maori 41, 44
　Melanesia 44
　Septchacs 155
　Torres Straits 155
　Trobrianders 102–4, 274
　Warramunga 46
prison 252
prohibitions, and precepts 68
projection 132, 136, 143, 164, 175n, 185 & n
　of affects and objects 180n
　aims of 314
　altruistic 73
　in analysis 332, 334–5
　defensive/paranoid 259, 260, 347
　function of 346
　of guilt 207, 279
　in infancy 179
　in politics 206
　and prejudice 356
projective identification 107, 114n, 335, 340, 341n, 347, 350–2, 383, 403, 409, 412–13, 425, 445, 457
　and capacity to think 390, 462
　and falling in love 350n
　with nipple or penis 426–7
　and notion of permanent world 15
promiscuity 34n, 99–101
propaganda 86, 134
　manic phase of 171–4
　psychology of 160–75
　religious 169
　terrorist 171

480

propitiation 220, 277
Prussians 239–40
psycho-analysis: aim of 58, 137, 268–9, 442–8
  basic procedure of 318
  and character changes 260
  collective 209
  different schools of 272n
  and education 35
  end product of 464–5
  framework of 342n
  and guilt 277–8
  interminable 456
  its mode of operation 271
  and normality 194, 232
  political 370
  a research method 267
  a science 343 & n
  social benefits of 137n, 208
  and sociology 201–2
  understanding in 332, 333, 335
psycho-analyst(s): and absolute standards 255
  anxiety in 399, 430
  and experience of chaos 351 & n
  as father Imago 71n
  inferences of 347
  and insane patient 441
  own analysis of 349n, 458
  and patient 330–42, 457–9
  patient's envy of 404
  and patient's projective identification 413, 426
  and psa. theories 389
  sense of responsibility of 269
  super-ego of 333–4
  technique of 345
  his tolerance 331
  see also counter-transference
psychologist, dilemma of 198–9
psychology, academic 297
psycho-physical parallels 21
psychosis 89, 168, 438–9
  analysis of 411
  flight into 436
  inheritance of 433
psychotic/insane parts of personality/self 403, 436–8, 453–4
  nodal point for development of 446
psychotic phase of childhood 145
puberty 111, 115
puberty ceremonies 102
punishment: effects of 252
  irrational attitudes to 246
  need for/seeking of 249n, 251
  talion 273
purification ceremony 368

Quicherat, Jules 111n
quisling 192

racial: altruism 80 & n
  character 230
  improvement 76
  memory 321, 398, 418n
  (see also inheritance of mental experience)
  prejudice 353–5
racialism 230n
radicalism 192, 193
Ramsay, Frank xiii, 16n
Rank, Otto 87n
rape 152n, 156
rational: age(s) 59, 63
  attitudes 245, 251
  thought 257, 260–1
rationality 262
realists 5, 14, 418
reality: intolerance of 436
  nature of 320
  principle 259, 369
  sense of 174
  testing 189
  theory of 307–9
rearmament 135n
reassurance 340
rebirth rites 52–3, 55
recognition 399 & n, 403–5, 418, 419, 421, 422, 443
regression 84
  of libido 43–4
Reich, Annie 341n
Reik, Th. 60n, 91, 149
Reinach, Solomon 28n, 68 & n, 69
relativism/relativity: ethical, see ethical relativism
  and normality 282
  psychotherapist and 262
  of values 268
relativity, Einstein's theory of 253
religion 63–8
  and aggression 90–2
  as consolation 88–9
  decline of 202
  founders of 223
  and idealization 204
  in inner-world system 429
  negative 63–4, 69
  origins of 91
  positive 65–6, 72, 76
  and super-ego 120
removal reactions 58, 78
reparation 68n, 116n, 185, 189, 193n, 206, 220n, 244, 277
  analyst and 331, 333, 337, 339
  criminal and 252n
repentance 251
repetition compulsion 460
representations, analogous/literal/multiple 3–4
repression 97, 403, 461

repression—(contd.)
 and avoidance 23-7
 primary, secondary, tertiary 105n
 return of the repressed 27
restitution 115, 118, 119, 158, 159, 173-4
reversal 358
revolution 84-5, 87, 92, 95
 bloodless 223
 ethical 106
 primal 55
 and war 141
Revolution, French 88, 95, 169
Revolution, Russian 169
Rickman, John xiv, 221
rites: funeral 38, 40-2
 initiation 52
 rebirth 52-3, 55
 secret 51
Roheim, Geza 82n, 114, 141, 144, 147n, 149 & n, 153, 156, 221n, 225, 230, 243
 abstract of 'After the Death of the Primal Father' 38-56
Roman Emperors 222
Rosenfeld, Herbert 335, 342n, 348n, 350n, 374, 411, 412, 426, 436
Rousseau, Jean-Jacques 88, 305-6
Russell, Bertrand 99n, 107, 288n, 297, 310, 317
Russia 96, 157
Russo–German pact 173
rutting period 47, 53, 55, 147

sacrifice 91-2
sadism 121n, 175n, 196, 271
 and hatred of cruelty 90
 oral, *see* oral
 and punishment 250
 and religion 92, 121
 and sex impulse 291 & n
 and war 134
sadistic impulses, infantile 179
saints, analytic/Christian 465
salvation 171-2
Satan 171, 219, 220
 see also devil(s)
scapegoat(s) 306, 347 & n, 367, 368, 375, 461
 criminal as 250, 367
scepticism 304
Schilder, Paul 295n, 324n
Schiller, Friedrich 87
schizophrenia 335, 348n
Schlick, M. xiii, 1n, 14, 258, 263, 298, 326n, 399n, 418, 443
Schopenhauer, A. 79n
science: and ethics 176-7
 and philosophy 300

scientific picture of the world 12
scotomization 180, 181, 183-4
Scott, W. Clifford M. 276n, 295n, 324n, 341n
Searl, Miss 79n
security, international 243
seeking reaction 18, 24 & n, 25, 58, 146n
Segal, H. 317, 411, 422, 437, 449
Segal, Paul 299n
self, and object, distinction 291
self-confidence, manic/delusional 376-7
self-consciousness 202
self-deception 368
self-interest 368
 and ideals 193
self-knowledge 59, 72, 76, 274, 280, 283, 306, 368
 biological consequences of 76-9
 individual consequences of 59-62
 social consequences of 62-3
self-preservation, instinct of 78, 79, 288-9, 296n
self-reproaches 43, 55
self-righteousness 207, 279
self-sacrifice 134
sensations and ideas 325
sentimentality towards criminals 246 & n
sexual play in childhood 104-5
sexuality, pre-genital 32
Shakespeare, William 316
shaman, Australian 48
shame 357
shell shock 134
siblings 403, 440
silence, in melancholia and mourning 44
Simons, Professor 79n
sin 121, 219
 sense of 92
skin, psychic 450
slave raiding 155
slump, the 167, 177n
Smuts, General 295
social change, psychological consequences of 201
socialism 87-90, 107, 192, 193
 delusion of 93-4
 pseudo- 193
society 204
 'bad' 242
 and the criminal 252
 normal 189, 255
 psycho-analysis and 178
 sexual conventions of 98
Society of Friends 221
sociology 201
 and relativity 253-4
Socrates 118, 126

INDEX

solipsism 314, 325, 328
Somali tribes 152
Sophists 29
soul 13
Spartans 225
sphincter sadism 421
spirits, possession by 162
splitting mechanism 205, 210, 274, 302, 304, 348, 370, 410
  of part of self 43
  in politics 372
  primal 450
  of self and object 367
spurious substitute 445–8
spy mania 164
State, personification of 157
status 379–82
  of institutions 385–8
  jockeying for 382, 384
  symbols 378
Stendhal 84
Stephen, Adrian 160n
stimuli: and innate responses 311, 322–3
  primary and secondary 57–8
  removal of 17–18, 176n
  sign- 323
Strachey, James 269n
subjective monism 313
subjectivism 309–11, 324, 327, 329
sublimation 106n, 176
  analyst's 341n
  collective 63
  inhibition of 70
  negative 60
  positive 61
  and symptom, distinction 59
suggestibility 161–5, 175
suicide 155, 219
superego 143, 150
  and analysis 71n
  of analyst 333–4
  changing concept of 196, 275
  and criminality 249
  early stages of 409, 411–12
  ego's projection into 412, 429
  and ego-ideal 357
  and ethics 178
  formation of 97
  functions and qualities of 112–13
  and God 69
  identification with 383, 387
  innate 105n
  and Joan of Arc 113–29
  and morality 31, 188, 274, 416–17
  and parent imagos 182
  paternal 234–7
  penetration of, by ego 377
  projection of envy into 383, 384
  and sadism 122, 124

  and society 274
  and war chief 157
super-man 33, 36–7
superstition 167, 171, 182, 219
symbol(s): of internal objects 190
  over-determination of 172
  primary 323 & n, 324, 327, 328n
symbolic equation 422
symbolism 312
  linguistic 309, 312
sympathy 236n
system building 424

taboos 64, 98, 105–7, 149–50, 157, 195, 274, 412
  endogamic 86
  and mourning 44
technique, analytic 409
teleological conception of the world 10–11
telepathy 327
Thanatos 146
theism 10
theocracies 222
theologian 178
thermodynamics, second law of 79
thinking: Bion's theories of 390–6, 462–3
  destruction of capacity for 460–2
thought: development of 400, 432–3
  disturbances 390, 403, 420
  empty 418
  innate modes of 322
  libidinal cathexis of 50
  pre-representational 425
  pre-verbal 310, 313
  processes, early 203
  and thinker 456
  verbal 315–16
thumb sucking 58
time, sense of 424
Timor 45
Tinbergen, N. 294n, 311, 317, 321
Torres Straits 155
totalitarianism 199, 204, 283, 305
totem(s) 86, 221
  phylogenetic 54, 55
trade unions 108, 218n
transference 458–60
  analysis of 409, 414
  positive 71n
transformations in groups 453, 455
transvaluation 206
trinity 172
trophy hunting 152, 154, 156
truth: perception and distortion of 417
  pursuit of 269, 272 & n, 369

483

unconscious, the: concept of 26
  contents of 269
  influence on political behaviour 208
  restitutive urge in 173–4
unconscious fantasy(-ies) 212, 219
  and propaganda 175
  understanding in analysis 332, 333, 335
unemployment 240, 241
universals 418
University College Psychological Society 82n
utopia 93, 96
  and aggression 88
  definition of 82
  socialist 94
Utopists 221

vagina, 'good' and 'bad' 421
value(s): relativity of 268
  reversal of 188
vengeance, acts of 45–7, 55
vice 219, 220
vicious spiral 260, 270, 333, 410
Victoria, Queen 212
vindictiveness 207, 246
virginity 103, 115
visions of Joan of Arc 110–12, 122, 127

war 84–8
  Boer 170
  causes of 131–7, 158, 190–1, 217, 386
  civil 141
  in civilized communities 155–7
  dances 153
  and fear 134, 139
  First World War/Great War 86, 91, 156, 157, 164, 230, 240, 373
  god 174
  morality of 279
  motives of 138–45
  origin of 147–51
  'paranoiac' theory of 145
  of primal brothers 42–4, 55
  in primitive communities 151–3
  and psychotic process 153
  religious 157
  Second World War 180, 190, 195, 198, 229, 231, 373
  sexual fantasies in 87
  trials 205
watch committees 220
Weimar Republic 240
Wells, H. G. 34
Westermarck, E. A. 253, 263
Western culture 244
White Man's Burden 157
Whitehead, A. N. 1
wife raiding 150, 152
will to live 294
William II 239
Winnicott, D. 342n, 360
wireless 160, 209
wisdom: and conscience 278, 280
  and insight 267, 306
Wisdom, J. O. 308, 317, 343n, 345n
wish-fulfilment 328
witch(es) 143, 220
  hunting 164, 170, 218
Wittgenstein, L. 264n, 298, 310, 317
'Wolf-man' 54, 126–9
womb 89
work: capacity for 183
  creative 185, 189, 194
world: common-sense 324–5, 327, 329
  creation of 348
  inner picture of 189 & n, 258–9, 300–2, 309
  real/permanent 7, 15
  our representation of 8–15
  thought-model of 315
worthlessness, sense of 351, 382, 383
  see also inferiority

Yahweh, see Jahveh
Yenchen, Arthur 134n, 137n

Zuckermann, S. 104n, 140n, 147 & n, 148n